MORE PRAISE FOR

COMPETITOR TARGETING

Winning the Battle for Market and Customer Share

"Gordon provides an essential framework for understanding the nature of competition and competitors. It will equip you to make your company more profitable."

—*Selwyn Rabins, President, Alpha Software Inc.*

"In this rapidly changing world, it is imperative to not only make your critical customers the key of your focus, but you also need to target intense competitors, old and new, as perceived by those very critical customers, in order to win in the marketplace and thereby raise shareholders' value. Ian Gordon gives you a no-fail step-by-step approach to succeed in this endeavor."

—*Ed Newman, Chairman, CEO & President, Xybernaut Corporation*

"Why should you read this book? For CRM, it offers not only strategically relevant models but also practical solutions. And it reinforces that you share your customers with your competitors, so that it is imperative that you focus on both."

—*Peter Bergmann, Market and Trend Research, BMW Group*

"*Competitor Targeting* takes CRM to a new level. This is the first book on CRM and competition and a worthy successor to *Relationship Marketing*, Gordon's previous ground-breaking book. *Competitor Targeting* encourages companies focused on individual customer relationships to also manage competitors. Gordon shows, step-by-step, how to do this strategically, tactically, and in real-time, with practical road maps and instructive comments."

—*Peter Jones, President and CEO, Personus*

Also by Ian Gordon

Relationship Marketing: New Strategies, Techniques and Technologies to Win the Customers You Want and Keep Them Forever
(0-471-64173-1, John Wiley & Sons)

COMPETITOR TARGETING

WINNING THE BATTLE FOR MARKET AND CUSTOMER SHARE

IAN H. GORDON

JOHN WILEY & SONS

Author's Note
Implementation of some of the concepts described in this book can create significant opportunity but may also lead to competitive retaliation and legal, antitrust prosecution or other negative consequence. Before assessing and adopting the ideas presented here, discuss and evaluate the options and implications with your legal counsel and other advisors. Consider the various risks (as well as the opportunities) that your organization might face if it proceeds with any of the suggestions mentioned in this book. As noted, involve your lawyers at the outset of your consideration and certainly long before conducting any competitive intelligence, communicating with outsiders and implementing your strategies. The author and publisher expressly disclaim any liability or loss, or risk, personal or otherwise which is incurred as a consequence, direct or indirect of the use or application of the contents of this book.

John Wiley & Sons Canada Limited
22 Worcester Road
Etobicoke, Ontario
M9W 1L1

National Library of Canada Cataloguing in Publication Data

Gordon, Ian, 1952 June 19-
Competitor targeting : winning the battle for market and customer share

Includes index.
ISBN 0-471-64410-2

1. Competition. 2. Business intelligence. 3. Market share.
I. Title.

HD38.7.G673 2002 658.8'35 C2002-903304-4

Production Credits
Cover design: Interrobang Graphic Design Inc.
Printer: Tri-Graphic Printing

Printed in Canada
10 9 8 7 6 5 4 3 2 1

319515

To Joanne, Lauren and Evan

Contents

Preface

"The key to investing is not assessing how much an industry is going to affect society, or how much it will grow, but rather determining the competitive advantage of any given company and, above all, the durability of that advantage."[1]
—Warren Buffett

Competitor Targeting

This book is about targeting competitors to win selected, valued customers and make your firm more competitive. The main focus here is on the specific competitors that represent a business threat or opportunity and the *individual* customers you and competitors serve. This book discusses how to target competitors and increase your share of the customers you value most by combining customer relationship management and competitive intelligence principles with sound business judgment and planning.[2] Beating competitors requires that a company develop competitively superior capabilities,

[1] "Mr. Buffett on the Stock Market," *Fortune*, November 22, 1999, p. 220.
[2] A company's share of the customer is the proportion of an individual customer's total expenditure on goods and services with all vendors, including those of the company.

so this book considers how to target competitors strategically to create the capabilities needed to gain customer and market share.[3] Methods such as acquisition, joint venture, collaboration, competitor analysis and even weakening the other company are considered in an attempt to create new shareholder value. Additionally, the book reviews how to beat competitors tactically, customer by customer and, in the real-time battle to win access to the customers your company cherishes, to interact, collaborate and create new value with them.

Of course, revenues can come only from customers. Competitor targeting does not diminish the importance of customers but suggests that the company, while looking at demand in a market, should also consider supply-side issues to improve its success. An examination of specific competitors can help the company to develop new business opportunities and additional revenues and improve its performance.

Yesterday's competitors tended to be large and slow-moving so that analyzing them and predicting their next moves could be done without very much difficulty. Today's challenge is that competitors are often smaller, fast and flexible, and even large companies are often highly mobile, competing in new ways and on new battlefields. New competitors emerge, and old ones disappear. Customers and suppliers become competitors, while competitors become customers and suppliers. In short, the battlefield is complex, making it hard to identify, understand and assess the enemy quickly enough to make a competitive difference. This book addresses these issues and discusses how to choose the right competitors to beat, how to plan to beat or collaborate with them, and how to succeed strategically, tactically and in real time.

Competitiveness is not just a state of mind, helpful though such an orientation is. Rather, competitiveness requires that the company recognize that a customer focus is important but may not be enough to secure increased shareholder value. For this, competitors merit attention and these competitors may not be the same as those with which the company has historically competed. The company should consider incorporating a competitive context into what it does, including targeting competitors—the right competitors—to create

[3] Market share is the annual revenues a firm derives from a market comprising all customers within a defined geography and industry, divided by the total expenditure by all these customers with all vendors, in aggregate, on like goods and services. Instead of a currency ratio, market share may also be measured in units or according to weight, length, volume or size, for example.

new shareholder value. This means that the company needs to understand the competition, especially as perceived by the customers it values most and use this and other competitive knowledge to change aspects of its technology, processes and human resource skills to win in the marketplace.

A Customer Focus Is Not Enough

Many companies are investing heavily in CRM and related technology. They are creating customer contact centers and setting up and integrating multiple channels for customers to access their companies. More generally, their plans call for putting the customer at the center of their organizations. While this strategic intent and these initiatives are valuable, many companies are not yet obtaining a material financial return from their investments. Part of the reason is that CRM is often seen as equivalent to technology, a view communicated by many software companies seeking to provide their solution to the CRM issue. As such, many companies have yet to advance customer relationships because they have not dealt with issues other than technology. In particular, few companies have incorporated a competitive context for their CRM or broader business strategies, which makes it less likely that their strategies will succeed and CRM investments will pay out. Even where companies are doing an excellent job and customers are delighted, a competitive context is important because competitors can have higher levels of customer satisfaction and may be planning to improve even more. Just as a rising tide raises all ships, so does strong marketplace demand mask a company's competitive weaknesses. But when demand weakens, the absence of a meaningful competitive strategy can become all too apparent when competitors try to grow at your expense.

Although understanding and beating competitors is now more challenging than ever because of the sheer numbers involved and the speed with which they move, it remains possible—in fact, essential—to identify who to beat and how. This is not to say that companies should pay less attention to CRM or whatever else they are doing to deepen bonds with valuable customers, but paying exclusive attention to customers as a basis for a company's future may not be sufficient to build profits and may even be perilous. As Warren Buffett, Michael Porter and others have suggested, competition affects *industry* profitability, and competitive advantage is the main factor that drives *company* profitability.

In some ways, customers and competitors are two sides of the same coin. The challenge for business has always been to identify, attract and retain valuable customers and to do so more effectively, collaboratively and efficiently than competitors. This book asks and seeks to answer the question: should your company spend more to beat, collaborate with or learn from competitors or can it succeed by focusing on customers alone?

One might answer that the best way to beat competitors is to be close to customers. Perhaps. But what if other companies, maybe even ones that are stronger than yours, want your most valuable customers? Would they get them? More generally, how does a company gain and sustain advantage in these times of a rapidly changing competitive landscape? If a company is to beat the competition, which specific competitors are to be beaten?

This book takes the view that there are three types of competitors:

1. those that represent a potential threat to your organization
2. those that offer much opportunity to profit
3. those that can help your company to learn and improve

These companies *can* be identified, and individual companies *can* be targeted. This targeting can achieve your company's business objectives without losing any customer focus. Indeed, attention to customers, especially the right ones, will intensify as you choose where, when and how to fight the business war strategically, tactically and in real time.

Competitive intelligence (CI) is an important tool in competitor targeting and is now being practiced to some extent by most companies.[4] While many companies use CI to keep themselves abreast of developments in their main competitors and to provide selected information for tactical advantage such as pricing, fewer use CI to make their firms more competitive strategically or in the routine resolution of their most pressing business issues. Fewer still have linked CI with CRM. This presents an important opportunity for companies to win one customer at a time.

---

[4] There is much evidence for the growth of corporate interest in CI. In 1986, a few hundred people met to form The Society of Competitor Intelligence Professionals (SCIP) in Washington. SCIP now has about 7,000 members. Since 1982, I have led open-market and in-house CI training sessions for over half the Fortune 500 companies and hundreds of others in North America, Europe, Asia and Africa.

Different Competitors Merit Attention

Just a decade ago, it was possible to know and understand each major competitor quite completely. This was true not only for large companies but for smaller firms with local and regional markets. The competitive set—those companies that perennially challenged one another for marketplace position—were typically the same companies. To know what they would do in the future, one simply needed to understand what they had done in the past and, given recent changes inside and outside the company, what they might do next. In short, although competition was tough, the enemy was known and understood, and planning to win in this more static environment was relatively straightforward.

Today, so much is changing, and rapidly. Whether it be the accelerated pace of company formation, organizational mobility, industry restructuring such as mergers, acquisitions and bankruptcies, new market entrants, regulatory change or technology proliferation, the competition is fierce, fast-moving and cutthroat. Now, to talk of intense competition is to understate the challenge severely. Today, companies face threats on many fronts and from many quarters. Sometimes these challenges come from unexpected quarters, such as from companies with which the company has collaborated. Whatever the source of the competitive issues, as in all business practice, the matters are best managed by facing up to them. Companies can understand their competitors, even fast-moving ones. They can obtain intelligence in sufficient time to influence decision making and they can balance their customer orientation by deciding how best to manage competitors.

Incorporate a Competitive Context into Organizational Capabilities

It is not enough to simply pay more attention to competitors or to view beating them as an important cultural shift. Most companies need new capabilities to win. For example, while many companies have implemented aspects of CRM and sales force automation (SFA), few have incorporated competitive intelligence (CI) into either system. Using CI in a CRM system, companies can understand which competitors are also seeking to serve their most valuable customers and what customers think about them. They can develop a real-time (or near-real-time) ability to respond to competitors' moves. In short, they can shift the share of customers from competitors to their own company, one customer at a time. Other examples include attention to the resources and capabilities the company has relative to its most important competitors, with a view to making the necessary changes to ensure superiority. If all companies are using the same vendor to supply similar enterprise resource planning (ERP) systems, for example, what will make your firm's technology infrastructure better? If all employees have similar skills to a targeted competitor, how will your performance be better in the future? If your processes for customer engagement, retention and collaboration are similar to those of specific competitors, how will you create more value with customers than competitors are able to?

In this book, we discuss the capabilities that are needed to target competitors, including enhancements to business processes, people and organization, technology and customer and competitor knowledge, insight and predictive abilities. You may recognize some of these capabilities in the context of a customer focus. Here we discuss how to apply these considerations to beat competitors.

Target the Right Competitors

Capabilities are important. So is focusing them in the right way at the right time against the right enemy. By definition, to compete means trying to win, but companies need to be clear about what winning means. Which race are they running? Each firm must have the foresight to run the right race—one it *can* win. And the firm must know against which *specific* competitors it is running. To be clear, it is not enough to talk in general terms of customer satisfaction, beating the competition or even of beating companies that have been identified. A company needs to satisfy its chosen customers better than specific competitors. Doing this allows the company to win customers over, one at a time. Doing this repeatedly and for many customers helps a company not only gain customer share but market share. Just as CRM focuses on individual customers, competitor targeting looks at specific competitors to help the company beat those that want the same valuable customers.

Picking the right strategy means having a vision of the future and understanding the barriers, especially those represented by your competition, preventing you from achieving your objective. What is holding you back? Why do you not have twice the market share that you do now? Why do you not have twice the share of customer from the purchasers you want? Why does your company not control substantially the market for the goods or services you supply? The answer to questions such as these comes down to supply-side as well as demand-side considerations. For example, in most industries, there are now more suppliers selling more variations of products and services through more distribution channels than just a few years ago. Even though companies may want to limit the inroads of these new competitors by getting closer to their customers, this is sometimes hard to do.

Some companies try to bond with customers by creating new and mutual value, which has the effect of increasing a company's share of its customer's future spending. It can limit encroachment by competitors within preferred accounts or force competitors to compete for yesterday's business—customers rebuying previously contracted orders, which can be less attractive than entirely new business. In an effort to limit customers' switching behavior, some companies offer a broader and deeper range of products and services. This is called competing on scope. Other barriers to switching include the use of communications, e-business and other technology and approaches, such as by locating a company's own employees on-site to bond with the design teams of a customer.

Few companies have sufficiently looked at their opponents' customers to assess opportunities to win them over. Some companies do have limited plans in this regard, but often these plans are either not supported by sufficient facts or do not plan to change enough to ensure competitive superiority. Sometimes, tomorrow's most formidable competitors have not been identified nor have plans been made to win in respect of the key success factors that will define the nature of tomorrow's industry. While specific events in the future are obviously not known in detail, a range of alternative outcomes to a number of important issues can be anticipated.

Companies can choose to manage uncertainty by planning for all conceivable events, or they can build capabilities that can adapt to a range of possible outcomes. Many companies are embracing the second approach, believing that the strategic capabilities they need to win are reasonably clear, even if individual events in the future are not. Increasingly, beating competitors is less about developing winning competitive strategies than about conceiving and implementing competitively superior capabilities that can, for example, do the following:

- arm a company with the customer and competitor knowledge, insight and predictive abilities it needs to win

- provide more efficient and effective business processes than the competitor
- deploy more relevant and timely technology, which allows customers to engage and interact with the company as they wish and which provides real-time information and management reporting
- attract, retain and develop human resources who have the abilities needed to win in the future

Know the Foe

In the sometimes counterintuitive[5] world of both clicks and bricks, competitors may come from nontraditional sources. Perhaps your company finds itself competing with an Internet-enabled new entrant or with customers or suppliers that are beginning to do what you do. Perhaps formerly stagnant companies are now exploiting a new technology or process. Perhaps the competitor is a newly energized old foe that has found its way. Or perhaps your biggest competitor is the environment in your own company—for example, the culture that holds you back and the absence of new ideas to really make a difference. Ask yourself what you are competing for. Which customers do you want? What do you want of them? Why do you not have them? A few more repetitive "whys" and behold, you know how to become the main competitive force in the market.

Some may see the main competition as the company's own success because nothing hinders new highs as much as positive reinforcement from prior good achievement. For example, a company may become wedded to its business model after obtaining good results, only to have competitors adopt new models that make the old way less tenable. The business model is subject to challenge particularly with the advent of the Internet. The Internet has had the effect of reducing some aspects of differentiation, commoditizing

[5] I say counterintuitive because, when companies deal with individual customers, much of what they thought they knew has been turned upside down. For example, companies used to target markets. Today, using the Internet, customers are as likely to target suppliers. Before, companies set prices. Today, customers assemble the features for which they are prepared to pay. Before, companies knew their products better than customers, but today, many customers of automobiles, for example, have learned about the products before entering the showroom and can know more than the salespeople who sell the cars.

many products and services and allowing customers to shop for and compare goods and services. Some companies operating according to traditional business models have been slow to appreciate the potential competitive opportunity and threat of the Internet. Enter Stelios Haji-Ioannou, who has founded a number of companies that start with the name "easy" and which appear to have a common interest in benefiting from service commoditization. Using the Internet and product and service standardization to reduce costs in a number of industries, he has launched companies such as the following:

- easyJet: a low-cost airline taking advantage of the deregulation of the European airline industry. It transported over 6 million passengers in the past year using a standard fleet of Boeing 737 aircraft. Over 80 percent of customers buy their tickets on the Internet.
- easyEverything: a chain of over twenty large Internet cafés in Europe and North America, which use industry standard computers (HP) and flat screens.
- easyRentacar.com: an Internet-only car rental service in Europe that has standardized small cars (Mercedes-Benz A Class and Smart cars) and offers extremely low prices.

The success of the easyJet venture has led other airlines to target it and launch business units to compete. Airlines are trying to displace this new entrant, an unfamiliar position for some among these large, less flexible companies.

Priceline.com also saw the potential for commodization. Unlike easyJet, their business model was not to own and operate an airline, but rather to function as an information intermediary and market maker, matching customers and airlines. They established a process by which customers set prices that vendors (such as airlines, hotels and rental cars) either accept or reject. More than novel, this was revolutionary when first introduced for the airline industry and changed the rules by which many seats are bought. Delta liked the idea so much—or feared the emergence of a nontraditional competitor to such an extent—that they bought an ownership interest in the company. This now achieves similar benefits to the easyJet model, in that clicks (Priceline) and bricks (Delta's aircraft and operations) are somewhat aligned.

In many ways, a company is as much defined by its competitors as by its customers, products and services. The company's strategies, customers and competitors establish the boundaries for a product-market space within which a company operates more or less profitably. While companies have examined many issues associated with their strategies and customers, typically, less attention has been paid to defining the competitors that are a source of revenue and shareholder value or which may limit the company's ability to attain its objectives. An imprecise or inaccurate definition of the company's competition may be as injurious as lapses of strategic judgment with respect to markets, customers, products, services or technology, for example. Some companies that fail to achieve their potential do the equivalent of crossing a highway looking out for oncoming cars, only to be hit by a truck. Chapters, a major Canadian chain of retail superstore booksellers, successfully navigated a complex competitive array of cars on their competitive highway. They dealt with smaller bookstores, managed publishers and handled government, but they overexpanded their physical stores and overcommitted to a reduced-margin Internet storefront. With weakening results and a depressed share price, a truck driven by another chain of booksellers, Indigo, rolled over them in a hostile takeover.

Overcome Internal Barriers

As in the classic Pogo cartoon, Walt Kelly noted, "we have seen the enemy and he is us." Some companies are like that. Perhaps they first need to shed the notion that focusing only on customers will help them win in the long term. There are four main competitive strategy alternatives: pioneers, fast emulators, slow emulators or opposers.[6] The pioneering company—like 3M, Sony or Dell—has learned to consistently develop innovative products, services or processes. The fast emulator copies competitive success rapidly. Some among Matsushita's[7] Japanese competitors have referred to it in this light. Slow emulators

[6] This categorization differs from, but builds on, breakthrough ways of thinking about competition in:

- William T. Robinson, "Market Pioneering and Sustainable Market Share Advantages in Industrial Goods Manufacturing Companies," Purdue University, 1984. This paper considers pioneers, fast followers and late entrants.
- R.E. Miles and C.C. Snow, *Organizational Strategy, Structure and Process*, McGraw Hill, New York, 1978. This book presents four competitive business strategies as Prospector, Defender, Analyzer and Reactor. Each category varies according to definition of the product-market domain and the company's position in it.

[7] Matsushita is well known for its Technics and Panasonic brands.

look for areas of opportunity unexploited by the pioneers and try to do better than the fast emulators after they have done sufficient analysis and preparation. Some governments have looked at pioneering innovation in the USA, EU and New Zealand, for example, and then replicated aspects after due consideration. Finally, opposers of innovation may have much to lose from change. In days gone by, ice makers resisted electrical refrigeration, carriage manufacturers resisted the inroads of the automobile and mail services did not embrace electronic mail. Laggards in many industries often have not been very successful in growing their companies.

Smaller companies can grow by emulating products, services, business processes or other innovations that others have demonstrated as feasible. For example, small manufacturers of tape can profit by copying aspects of 3M's success. A number of companies competing with 3M in any of its three areas of competency—coatings, abrasives and adhesives—have found lucrative opportunities to coexist or compete, often in the same distribution channel. But first they needed to overcome their own innate desire to focus all their spending on the development of their brand equity. One way is by making products such as masking tape or sticky notes for the big-box warehouse stores that sell private-branded products beside 3M's. Next time you visit companies such as Staples, take a look at the store brand, and you will often find a competitor without strong brand equity or meaningful product differentiation living profitably under the innovation and pricing umbrella established by 3M.

Companies trying to run a business race should note that a race is, by its very nature, relative to others. No business operates as a completely unique enterprise, absolute in all respects. Businesses succeed or fail according to their performance relative to others. Any firm spending money or allocating people, time or knowledge without asking "How will this make us better than a specific competitor?" is throwing resources at an unknown enemy as they pass, hoping to hit someone in the process. Luckily for some, most companies are doing just this. Consider the last time your company hired or promoted a vice president. Did anyone say, get us someone who is better than the VP at a Competitor X? If you cannot find someone better than hire the person from the competitor.

Few business plans pay much attention to competition. Plans often refer to improvements such as becoming better by being faster; making a product heavier or lighter or less expensive; obtaining ISO or other quality accreditation or certification; or bonding more tightly with chosen customers. These are all good things to do, to be sure. But in all of this, the implicit competition is your company as it now exists. And that, quite simply, might be the wrong competitor on which to focus. This is a recipe for running a race without end, without progress that customers will value, possibly running in the wrong direction and ultimately having no assurance that you will be first to cross the finish line.

Conclusion

Today, many companies are thoroughly invested in improving the customer bond and deepening the relationship one customer at a time. This relationship marketing, by whatever name—including CRM, electronic CRM (eCRM), and one-to-one marketing [8]—focuses on choosing and keeping individual customers. However, focusing exclusively on customers—even individual customers—may not be enough to build the business because competitors may be doing precisely the same thing and may have the potential to do it better. On the other hand, trying to manage fast-moving competitors can be challenging and expensive. The good news is that there are processes and technologies that can help you to do just that, while at the same time, making it harder for competitors to win the business you want. This book discusses how to determine which individual competitors represent the greatest threat (or opportunity) to your firm and how to compete against them. Most companies can identify such a competitor (or group of competitors), but they do not often use this insight to build profits either one customer at a time or more comprehensively. This book is intended to help companies integrate strategies for bonding with customers and beating competitors. As Mr. Buffett suggests, it is competition that is the major constraint on a company and its profitability.

[8] We defer discussion of the terminology to later in the book. These terms are not the same, although many companies use them interchangeably. For the moment, we do, too.

Organization of this Book

This book has been organized as follows:

In Chapter 1, we discuss the new marketplace in which companies compete to win. A marketplace that is quite different than it once was. Now, companies face nontraditional competitors in crowded marketplaces, in which everyone seems to want loyalty from the same customers. In this environment, being focused on customers may not be enough to help the company succeed.

In Chapter 2, we take the position that a company should look two ways: at the important, individual customers it has chosen and the specific competitors it intends to beat. We note that focusing only on customers through CRM will help ensure that customers are well taken care of and their value recognized, but paying attention to competitors will take care of the company and its employees, shareholders and others who depend on the organization's success. We discuss the preparations a company should consider to become more competitive and beat selected competitors.

In Chapter 3, we confirm that a competitor focus has the potential to increase a company's revenues and shareholder value by discussing the link between a competitive initiative and shareholder value. It is important that the marketer be in a position to articulate the linkage and potential for a competitive focus to create new business value for the company. The chapter goes on to discuss the changing nature of competition and the benefits of being among the first to focus on individual customers and specific competitors as a source of shareholder value.

Chapter 4 addresses competitor targeting more fully and provides a framework for planning to beat specific competitors. This chapter shows, step-by-step, how to do research and develop a plan that will deal with many of the important competitive barriers a company faces in the marketplace.

Chapter 5 considers competitive intelligence, which is an essential ingredient in ensuring that the company makes the right competitive decisions. We provide an overview of the conduct of competitive intelligence, ranging from a competitive intelligence system to actually gathering the intelligence.

In Chapter 6, we review strategies and tactics for targeting selected competitors. We build on the principles of CRM and offer new suggestions for strategies to gain customer share.

Chapter 7 notes that focusing on customer satisfaction is not enough to succeed if competitors satisfy your customers even better. In some cases, working harder to succeed may not be enough to win. There can be times when you need to make a loser out of a competitor you have targeted. This chapter raises a number of provocative considerations.

In Chapter 8, we discuss an alternative to beating competitors or making them into losers. We review why and when to collaborate with competitors. We note that some competitors can help you succeed with your most important customers. We call these complementary competitors complementors and discuss selected strategies for working with them to mutual advantage.

Chapter 9 concludes the book by bringing together a number of new and previously presented ideas and considering issues associated with competing for tomorrow's customers and transitioning to a more competitive enterprise.

Competitor Targeting has been written to add new value to your business. By its very nature, this is a mass product, made more relevant if it is customized to your requirements. When you read this, you may want to keep notes in three lists: items that you will implement, things to think about and areas to discuss with others.

If you would like to discuss any aspect of this book with me or inquire about public speaking engagements or consulting assignments, I can be reached at:

Ian Gordon
Convergence Management Consultants Ltd.
1054 Centre Street, Suite 289
Thornhill, Ontario, Canada L4J 8E5
Telephone: 905-881-7463
FAX: 905-881-8545
Private e-mail: gordonih@aol.com
Internet: www.converge.on.ca

Acknowledgements

My special thanks to clients over the years. It has been a privilege to work with you. I would like to recognize here great companies such as Alcan, Ameritech, Apple Computer, Armada Bates, Bell Canada, Canada Post Corporation, Canadian Broadcasting Corporation, Cargolux, Chrysler, CFM Majestic, CGI, Compaq Computer Corp., Delano Technology, Ernst & Young, Ethyl Corporation, Experian, Fastforms, Ford, G-Comm Marketing, General Electric, Goodyear, Hewlett-Packard, IBM, Kodak, KPMG, MDS, Microsoft, Mitel, NAFA, NCR, Nortel Networks, Ontario Power Generation, Parker Hannifin, Sprint, Toshiba, Wolters-Kluwer and Xerox. I would also like to thank the governments of Canada, Ontario, Newfoundland and Iowa; consortia of many companies and associations in the automotive manufacturing, automotive retailing and heavy equipment and resource industries; and the many other companies of varying sizes in different countries and industries with which it has been a privilege to work.

Great clients and colleagues make consulting a rewarding journey. It has been a pleasure to work with talented, ethical and imaginative consultants at Convergence. My thanks to the very capable practice leaders, Jeremy Fox, Bob Love, Leon Rucker, Bob Stacey and Ed Starr. My appreciation also to the exceptional professionals with whom we have associated and whose friendship, guidance and collaboration has helped to show the way. In particular, I would like to thank Bill Band, Alex Binko, Alex Bruner, Chris Green, Peter Held, Vijay Jog, David Little, Mike McClew, Mark Nesbitt, Steve Rosenberg, Jag Sheth and Charles-Antoine St. Jean.

To my wonderful family Joanne, Lauren and Evan, thanks for bearing with me on this journey. You make everything possible.

Thanks to the professionals at John Wiley and Sons, and particularly to Karen Milner, Elizabeth McCurdy and Ron Edwards who have patiently, kindly and with great intelligence guided this project to completion.

CHAPTER 1

The New Marketplace

"A summer's day; and with the setting sun
Dropped from the zenith like a falling star."[1]
—John Milton

The marketing world as we knew it is over. Technology has transformed it by enabling entirely new ways of conceiving a relationship with customers, allowing economical access, communications and transactions with individual customers. The broader competitive context is sometimes lost in the race to implement better and better technologies in pursuit of customer relationship management. But technology is also changing the rules for strategic competition and turning them upside down, especially in industries that are information intensive. There are many other changes under way that are further transforming industry structure, stakeholder relationships and the pursuit of profit. This chapter examines important industry and marketplace directions that are changing traditional marketing and creating an opportunity for companies to target specific competitors one customer at a time and in aggregate. We start with a consideration of competitor targeting and then review selected marketplace changes overall and in this context.

---

[1] John Milton, *Paradise Lost*, 1667.

Competitor Targeting

Why Target Competitors?

It is clear why companies want to get closer to their customers, but why target a competitor? Reasons will vary from company to company, but they might include the following:

- Learn from the competitor, so that you can improve.
- Develop a differentiated position with the competitor's most important customers, with a view to increasing your share of individual customers' expenditures, whereby these customers buy from both companies.
- Develop a differentiated position with the competitor's customers you have selected, causing these customers to buy from you instead.
- Gain advantage relative to targeted competitors in order to strengthen your business directly at their expense, especially with respect to the limited resources you both need. For example, you may want to do the following:
  - Benefit from the favoritism of common suppliers.
  - Hire the best staff (including their employees).
  - Accelerate commercial processes—the time it takes from conceiving an idea to market introduction to reaping the rewards.
  - Gain better access to financial resources, such as equity markets.
  - Develop distribution channel alignment and loyalty.
- Achieve competitively superior results for shareholders.
- Identify competitors that are relatively benign and/or who represent potential partners in specific situations, perhaps in battle with other competitors.
- Establish how and where the company can best collaborate with competitors.
- Identify whether or not to acquire a competitor.
- Win specific bids or contracts.

Companies must win with the customers they consider most important—those that offer the most potential for profit and growth. Winning implies prizes and a process. The prizes are the customers the company values most highly, and the process is bonding with customers while beating defined competitors. Most companies have worked to develop customer relationships but not hard enough to manage competitors and to benefit at their expense. By controlling aspects of a competitor's destiny, a company can improve financially, operationally and strategically. A company can win in the future by planning a process for competitor engagement that is thoughtfully planned and relentlessly executed.

Competing is a state of mind to be sure, but it is also much more. It is a strategy and a process. The strategy involves the company's decision to select certain customers and its choices regarding the development of a competitively superior customer bond. The plan the firm uses to develop individual customer bonds may lead it to beat specific competitors overall. By planning to win, the company will stop thinking about competing in the context of organizational culture or being tougher or even working harder. Instead, the company will emphasize who to beat and how to win. Competitor targeting is a cornerstone for competing and is thus a central component of a company's business strategy.

What does it mean to win, and how will you know when you have won? Starting in the minds (corporate and/or individual) of the company's most important customers, *winning means making it easy for customers to choose you and hard for them to choose your defined enemy*. Start with the customer's key purchase criteria. How are competitors positioned in respect of these criteria? What are the trends or changes in this positioning? What capabilities should you put in place now that will improve your positioning relative to competitors strategically, tactically and in real time.

Competitor Targeting: A Definition

Let us start this process with a definition of competitor targeting that focuses more on the process than the destination.

Competitor targeting is the process of selecting a competitor that represents an important opportunity or threat to your company, especially in respect of the individual customers your firm wants, and then planning and implementing strategic, tactical and real-time initiatives to help the company achieve its business objectives.

There are a number of implications that flow from this definition:

- As mentioned, competitor targeting is a process, not a project, benefit or outcome.
- Competitor targeting requires that a competitor be selected so that your company can achieve its competitive aims, such as:

  - learning from competitors that are not in your core markets or customer accounts
  - transferring market or customer share to your company from those competitors that are
  - protecting markets or customers from competitor inroads
  - collaborating with selected competitors to provide the value customers want
  - more generally, ensuring that your company has a strategic, tactical and real-time competitive edge
- Competitor targeting is complementary with CRM. Indeed, it recommends that the customers most important to the future of the company be chosen first, before implementing a competitor targeting initiative.
- Competitor targeting requires that your company win those customers most important to your company's future. If you win or lose with other customers, treat that as experience, but you *must* win with the customers on whom your future depends.
- Competitor targeting is about competing for the future. This requires that a plan be developed to ensure that competitors contribute to the value of your company by accelerating your growth or improving your efficiency or both. This can be done by:
  - beating specific competitors so that you can win, either overall or especially in the customers you value most
  - collaborating with specific companies as partners, where so doing is in your mutual interests

Competitor targeting is a new discipline that knits the company's strategic and tactical initiatives together to focus on a specific competitor so that your company can develop new shareholder value. Because competitor targeting considers supply from the industry to the market, it is a supply-side perspective and quite different than demand-side considerations typically associated with marketing. Competitor targeting uses some of the same tools as marketing, especially by starting with an understanding of customers and their purchasing behavior. Competitor targeting also has its own unique set of principles, whether to beat the enemy or to collaborate with them. Most often, this means finding the best ways to win either now, later or much later.

Collaboration and Competition

Collaborating with competitors can provide customers with the value they want. (We have devoted Chapter 8 to a discussion of this.) Recently there has been a trend for companies to cooperate with competitors in selected areas, such as research and development and making products for one another. Collaboration is an important opportunity to improve returns to shareholders. However, even when collaborating, there remains the underlying potential for the situation to give way to battle. If now is not the time nor place to beat some competitors, perhaps there will be a day of reckoning. New competitors will seek their fortunes in the same markets or with similar customers as yours. Over time, even in those areas where growth seems endless, markets and customers do mature. When demand consolidates, there are fewer buyers and opportunities for new value creation. Taken together, factors such as these suggest that eventually there is less potential for companies to live and let live. Survival of the fittest continues to apply on the corporate landscape, although this may be less evident in times of prosperity. Those fleeter of foot, sharper of mind, better armed and better supported earn the right to live and fight another day and to evolve to a higher state. Those content with the status quo eventually wish they had moved faster and earlier to improve their competitive position or reduce competition.

Customer Collaboration

Winning starts and ends in the minds of customers. To win requires that the company do many things well, including:

- becoming sufficiently entrenched to serve each customer repeatedly
- collaborating with customers in new areas they are considering
- joint planning and helping customers to accomplish their strategic and other goals
- blurring the lines between where the company ends and the customer begins so that a true collaboration can take place
- becoming proactive in proposing how to help customers most

The first hurdle a company needs to overcome is customer access—being given an opportunity to listen and learn—without which the firm will always be an arm's length supplier. Suppliers of this type are less informed, less able to predict and ultimately less relevant, and as a result they emphasize price more than they do strategic value creation.

Collaboration with your most important customers can and should be the starting point for winning. Collaboration helps you to know what it will take to secure a larger share of the business of your most important customers. Then you can move to ensure that specific competitors either are locked out of the value-creating process, or they collaborate with you to help you deliver the value your customers want and that you choose not to do yourself.

The Changing Nature of Competition

Targeting competitors requires prioritizing the main competitive challenges the company faces and a clear understanding as to the nature of competition. A company's competition is what customers consider to be substitutes for the products or services the firm sells. Substitutes can be similar products in form, function or benefit. They can also be alternative uses for funds or time, both of which can also limit the sales of a company.

More typically, it is useful to think of competition as the group of companies that the customer sees as more or less similar. This can be called a strategic set and is changing as a result of:

- declining product, service and company differentiation and the willingness of customers to switch for a lower price
- digital convergence, which enables product and service proliferation, especially in technology industries
- changing regulations, which has allowed competitors to enter industry sectors from which they were previously excluded by law
- globalization, which has created new competitors in domestic markets
- the Internet and electronic marketplaces, which has allowed smaller, often local and regional companies to extend their market and customer reach

In the following, we review the changing nature of competition.

Today's Competitors

Today's competitors include those that companies have traditionally faced in the marketplace, but now there are also a number of new entrants. For example, some supply customers with other products, some exploit new technologies or business models, and some enter from overseas. Whether old enemies or new ones, competitors can be managed but only if companies have prepared to do so.

Emergence of Non-Traditional Competitors

New opportunities are often at the boundaries of traditional industries, such as communications, computing, content and carriers. Boundary-area opportunities have offered potential for some time, although they have not always been seen for what they are. A case in point: in 1975, Nortel Networks (then Northern Telecom) introduced computerized switches for the formerly analog environment of the telcos' central offices. This was an early instance of computing and communications convergence, and it vaulted Nortel—then a small player in the switching industry—into contention in the first tier of competitors. A number of other telecom equipment firms, such as AT&T and GTE, then rushed to introduce their own computerized switches.

Competition in this fast-changing world is for the customer's expenditures, not simply for the products and services the company has historically produced. Industry convergence and competition on scope has also created nontraditional competitive sets. For example, you can buy telephone services from a bank and communications services from a cable television company. More generally, it is likely that the major area of convergence in the future will be between financial and telecommunications services.

Convergence creates nontraditional competitors, as companies begin to compete on one another's turf. Before Nortel, RCA had the same opportunity, the one that Nortel exploited, but it thought of itself as a computer company rather than a telecom equipment firm, and it failed to make the transition into the new arena. Nortel, with preexisting relationships, proved more adept at innovating product than RCA's attempts at market and customer development.

More recently, the expansion of bandwidth afforded by the introduction of fiber-optic cabling and radio-frequency technology is creating an explosion of opportunity, much as the Internet did before. Now companies can ask themselves "What would we do differently if bandwidth were much cheaper?" The last time companies asked similar questions occurred when the prices of computer memory, storage and processing were falling sharply. That allowed new companies and industries, such as the minicomputer and personal computer industries, to spring up. Companies in a wide variety of industries began to computerize their own equipment, from lathes to televisions. The reduction in bandwidth costs could have similar implications, with opportunities emerging for universal video telephony, access to remote television stations, wireless Internet access and video-on-demand being among the major areas of potential.

Convergence is discussed in Chapter 6 for its strategic implications when targeting competitors.

Global Competition Not Just for Markets

Distance is increasingly an irrelevant consideration in the business model of many industries. Companies used to locate near markets, labor, raw materials or suppliers to help ensure access to the resource they adjudged particularly important. The Internet has changed this. New economy companies pay special attention to competing for human resources, often locating where skills and attitudes are best and/or costs are lowest so that they can have the edge in technology and be faster in developing and implementing strategic capabilities.

An executive of a company in Alberta, Canada providing document imaging services to New York lawyers, among others, worried that her firm was too distant from its market and that local competitors were better able to serve customers. As well, her firm lacked a Web strategy and the alliances needed to assure lawyers that their documents were secure. With this in place, her firm could well prosper from a remote location because, in the era of the Internet, physical distance is less important.

Companies are now used to doing business with suppliers in remote locations. In fact, they often do not know or care where their suppliers are located. Markets are now global and companies, small and large, compete globally for business. The lines between small and large firms are changing as customers are quite willing to buy from the supplier they judge to be best, regardless of size or location.

Major, old economy companies have long been found in most countries around the world, applying the mantra "think global and act local," tailoring their offer in each country as local preferences require. The Internet has meant that all companies are now in effect global—from IBM and General Electric to Percy's Vintage Magazine Advertisements and Bernie's Collectibles.

As markets and companies become global, so too have resources of all kinds become global commodities. Labor flows with more or less ease from country to country. Capital scoots around the world at the speed of greed. Knowledge proliferates, and secrets are few. The five key resources, the building blocks for which all companies compete, are:

1. people
2. time
3. money
4. technology
5. knowledge

All are in global supply, subject to the vagaries of global markets, and accessible by all companies. Where resources are particularly scarce, it can be helpful to identify your competitors' resources so that these can be transferred to your company from theirs. For example, can you hire their best people, lock up their sources of raw material, create or cement relationships with their suppliers or sign leases with landlords where you know they want to open new stores. When Future Shop, a major Canadian retailer of consumer electronics, became aware that Best Buy planned to enter the Canadian market, Future Shop acquired exclusive leases in many locations. Without an opportunity to locate in the best areas, Best Buy decided to acquire Future Shop rather than compete with it, which appears to have been Future Shop's intent.

Competitive Advantage on the Back Burner

Given the complexity in managing competitive advantage and delivering near-term results, marketers are paying less attention to competitors and more to customers and market segments. Their rationale is straightforward enough: customers buy products and services—competitors do not. Customers pay the bills—competitors do not. If you want to *sell* products and services, pay most attention to customers, they say. More than this, companies note the difficulty of predicting what their competitors might do and even who they might be. In the world of clicks and bricks, a competitor is as likely to be virtual as real. The competition could be one large killer company or many smaller ones, each siphoning off sales like death by a thousand pin pricks. Competition could be a new entrant without the shackles to legacy investments, ready to focus on the weak points of a company that is less flexible, or it may be a nontraditional competitor or a revitalized old-style company.

In this there is little to dispute. But the difficulty of the competitive challenge does not negate it. If you want to make money, competitors and competitive advantage merit attention. And they require at least as much focus as that which is accorded customers—more, if you take the view of Mr. Buffett and recognize the challenge of competing amid rapid change. Focusing on customers alone, whether using the traditional rules of marketing or even the individualized one-to-one approaches of customer relationship management (CRM), is not enough to win in these supercharged times.

As a consultant, I have had the opportunity to review marketing and strategic plans from several companies in a single industry. In these situations, I am often struck by their similarity. Plans, if found on the sidewalk minus their cover pages and company name, should still be identifiable by their contents. The trouble is that they rarely are. Many companies see the future the same way, plan to capture the same obvious opportunities, and set about doing that in much the same manner. With similar views on the future of an industry, common customer and market segment choices and similar visions for their companies—often even using the same words[2]—it is hardly surprising that customers see so little difference among the suppliers in a marketplace. If customers say that vendors and their products or services are not highly differentiated, much of the reason stems from similar management thinking and a lack of real competitiveness built into plans.

The opportunity exists for companies to adopt initiatives to improve competitiveness, particularly if attention to competitors has been neglected recently. Invest for competitive advantage before competitors begin to do likewise and pay attention to your company as a source for their future prosperity.

New Competitors Challenging Old Business Models

Traditional go-to-market channels can also encumber a business. Computer companies with dealer networks found significant resistance in developing direct sales, creating an opportunity for OEMs selling directly to customers, especially for Dell, the main such firm. An encyclopedia company's sales force refused to sell a CD-ROM version because this would have reduced their commission on bound volumes. Game over. People who are right for one era in a company's growth can be dead wrong in another. For example, the CEO of a technology company personified the command and control authority of a military-style, 1950s corporate leader. In a tough market, when jobs were scarce and competitors could be bought, this company prospered. In a better economy, the company lagged, and the board replaced the CEO.

[2] For example, many financial services companies have vision statements using the words "trusted financial advisor" of their customers.

Companies have within them the seeds of their own destruction, none more so than the investments they have made. Unless fairly evaluated and depreciated or written down, these investments shackle the company to an untenable strategy by limiting its options. For example, copper wire laid in the ground decades ago limited telcos from adopting new business models while these assets were carried on the books and needed to be earned out. In the e-economy, companies unburdened by such investments, have forced competitors to challenge their own vision, business models and even accounting. As mentioned, in the case of copper in the ground, it is interesting that few of the traditional telephone operating companies have been the ones laying glass fiber. A focus on trailing earnings and earn outs from book assets, rather than changing the business model so the company can win, can lead to the telescope being pointed the wrong way—at the past, at the wrong sources of profit and at the wrong competitors.

Investments made in people and process are as important as investments in physical assets including plant, equipment and technology, and these legacy commitments can mire the company in the past even more than financial investments. Consider how slow some companies have been to move to change their vision from bricks and mortar to include the Internet, to arrive at a so-called clicks and bricks vision and business model. Car dealers, for example, have long said that the Internet is not a material consideration for their business model, even though many customers now enter the dealership armed with as much or more information than the salesperson. The car manufacturers were left to develop a business model that included the dealership and the Internet. While the impact has yet to be fully felt by dealers, the difficulty some have had in developing a new business model—one based on customer access, interactivity, information and relationships—will result in the dealerships role being redefined by the manufacturer. Auto dealers have lost control of their destiny and most don't even know it.

The challenge for new economy companies is as profound as that facing more traditional, long-established organizations. While the newcomers may be unfettered by the rules of the past, not having a sense of history may condemn some to repeat the mistakes of old economy companies earlier in the industry life cycle. For example, some new economy companies, so focused on technology, have poor logistics and fulfillment processes. Outbound logistics may be bad enough, but the returns process—inbound logistics—for most dot.com e-tailers, has been horrid. As old economy companies accelerate their integration of the Internet, they will become even stronger competitors for some new economy companies. For example, companies such as Saks and Toys "R" Us have powerful brand equity, but they have had such a small Web presence that e-tailers are not concerned. All this is changing as the old guard moves forward with new concepts and techniques and focus on the things that matter most in the eyes of the customer. For example, established retailers know that shoppers do not want the latest technology on the Web site, if it means complicating and slowing the purchase experience. The dot.coms, sometimes lacking needed research, may go for special effects and complicated three-dimensional visuals that are shunned by many shoppers.

Both new and old economy companies increasingly are breaking apart their value chains, focusing on their core competencies and outsourcing nonstrategic requirements. This, in turn, is creating large outsourcing businesses for companies such as Xerox, which provides mail room, print on demand and receptionist services to companies not wanting to allocate efforts and resources here. Old and new economy companies are starting to appear alike, as both seek to provide customers with the services they expect.

Acquiring or developing expertise in the ways of the new economy is challenging enough, but the bigger issue is how to integrate the new with the old. Companies that have done it well, such as Charles Schwab & Co., have the potential to foster deeper relationships with customers and, in the process, build their businesses in the face of intense competition from newer players such as E*Trade Securities Inc. and Ameritrade Inc.

Given the sweeping changes suggested here, companies guiding themselves in terms of marketing strategies that depend on the 4 Ps of marketing—product, price, promotion and placement—may have the wrong map to the pot of gold at the end of the rainbow. The traditional rules of marketing are now obsolete, rendered so by changing technology and industry structure. The 4 Ps of marketing have little meaning in an era in which technology can allow for each of these to be unique and customer-initiated rather than vendor-packaged. Simply put, the old rules of marketing do not work very well anymore. The era of traditional marketing is over.

Ten Factors that Killed Traditional Marketing

Marketing as we knew it is over. By managing the selection of a target market, assessing their needs and delivering profitably to these requirements, traditional marketing was supposed to create revenues and profits for the company. And for many years, it did—for the most part. The success of the so-called packaged goods companies, such as Nabisco Brands, Unilever and Procter and Gamble, is testimony to the success of traditional mass marketing of mass products through mass channels to mass audiences. But today, the old rules of "mass anything" are simply not enough to help ensure marketplace dominance. Ten factors have killed traditional marketing:

1. Insufficient Near-Term Financial Results
2. Fragmentation of Markets into the Smallest Segment: The Individual Customer
3. Proliferation of Competition
4. Margins Collapse
5. Time Shrinks
6. Technology Advances and Costs Decline
7. Customers Innovate
8. Customers Target Companies
9. Collaboration Increases
10. Battleground Includes Customer Access

Insufficient Near-Term Financial Results

Do you remember the Wendy's commercial where the tiny, white-haired lady scrutinized a competitor's hamburger and asked "Where's the beef?" Today, many chief financial officers seem to be asking the same question of marketing. Simply put, nonmarketers do not often see results from mass marketing or even segment-based marketing. Ask many CFOs, investors and venture capitalists, and they will say that marketing simply has not achieved its promise of differentiating and developing enduring, competitively superior, value. That is, they do not often see the margin and volume gains that marketing departments are expected to deliver. Marketers wanting to subsegment into ever-smaller segments, including the individual business or consumer, are challenged by financial managers who have not seen the long-term payouts marketing promised before, and they may be loath to commit yet more funds in search of longer-term benefits. This not only limits the funds available to marketing, but it forces marketing to be more and more tactical, measuring results and demonstrating success.

This creates a catch-22. Spending to develop a company's positioning in the mind of customers is often needed to spur demand ("pull") in the marketplace and help make distribution channel discounts and other initiatives ("push") more successful. Spending on long-term strategic capabilities is also needed to define and deliver entirely new value for and with customers, such as Web-enabled initiatives. Without these strategic marketing investments, marketers concentrate on tactical programs, the effectiveness of which can diminish over time without strategic spending, which further challenges the credibility of marketing. In the days before "Internet time," long term to a marketer meant three to five years. To financial managers and investors, it has always been dinnertime. Now, the preference financial management has for short-term results is further supported by the organizational power they have achieved in many companies. Marketers are now challenged to operate on the timetable of financial managers and produce and demonstrate meaningful results, ideally between now and dinner!

Competitor targeting can help marketers find new sources of short- and long-term revenue and profits. If your company is driven by near-term financial results, consider whether competitors can yield some of their revenues to your company. As will be discussed, this can be achieved quite quickly, and the revenues, once obtained, can be retained over the long term.

Fragmentation of Markets into the Smallest Segment: The Individual Customer

Segments in many markets are growing smaller and smaller, with competitors seemingly prepared to address even the very smallest. This is the reverse of mass marketing, whereby customers were aggregated into fairly large segments. This new phenomenon may be termed disaggregation, whereby markets dissolve into their component parts. Increasingly, companies are marketing to segments that are unique—segments of one. Now each individual customer is the focus of marketing attention.

According to the traditional rules, marketing sought to create extra value for customers by combining those with similar needs into groups marketers called segments. Customers within these segments would have their needs addressed by companies targeting the segment as a whole. This worked well for a while. For example, in the heavy equipment industry, specialized companies emerged to cater to segment-specific needs for forest products, such as logging equipment, and for the mining industry, in which high-capacity earth-moving equipment was needed. Neither of these applications had been well addressed by the full-line equipment manufacturers.

Over time, though, the segments grew crowded. Specialized companies competed with full-line suppliers now willing to specialize and with new entrants from other segments and countries. This left little or no respite from competition for the smaller companies trying to survive by catering to smaller and smaller niches. At the end of the day, no niche was small enough to provide shelter from competition because many companies were looking for incremental volume from their customers and were quite prepared to produce small numbers of specific goods or services in search of more sales. The specialized companies were either acquired by full-line vendors or they failed. Few have been able to soldier on to prosperity.

With competitors catering to individual customers, companies must understand whether customer-specific marketing will create value the customer wants. If not, there may be opportunities to aggregate demand and market to segments. More typically, unique customer value can be created, making it necessary for many companies to master the creation and profitable management of individual customer relationships. This has usually been done without a competitor orientation, mostly because management of the individual customer has been hard enough without complicating it even further. Now the opportunity is there for the company employing competitor targeting principles to think of competition in each of their customer accounts and plan to increase their share of customers. That is, by treating each customer as a market, companies can both create unique customer value and do this better than competitors. This principle applies equally to businesses marketing to other business customers (B2B) and to those catering to consumers (B2C). The difference is in the planning and execution of relationship marketing and competitor targeting. B2C companies usually need different deployment of technology than companies serving other businesses, although not necessarily more.

Proliferation of Competition

In most marketplaces, competition has proliferated, both from new companies and from new products and services from existing firms. The drivers of this increased competition have included:

- more readily available funding for new ventures and expansion of existing companies

- market fragmentation, already referenced
- regulatory change—often associated with industry restructuring
- convergence of industries and technology
- globalization of companies
- reductions in trade restrictions
- new production, customer management and communications technologies
- new media vehicles, including many uses of the Internet, customer-specific mail, and e-mail
- new distribution channels, often associated with increased scale, such as the so-called big-box retailers that offer an expanded array of products and services

The old rules of marketing benefited from stability in industry structure. If you knew your current competition and could assess their strengths and weaknesses, according to the old rules, it would be easier to differentiate and plan marketing initiatives. Now, new competitors often emerge, sometimes without fanfare, to snare your customers and divert your sales. Existing competitors introduce new products and services with increased frequency. This proliferation of companies and products makes it increasingly difficult to stay on top of the information needed to make a competitive difference, further challenging marketing personnel. By adopting competitor targeting, it is possible to manage more competitive intelligence and put it to more direct use than ever before. But first, companies need to buy into the concept of competitor targeting. Those that do, and do it before their competitors, can create change from which some competitors may never recover.

Margins Collapse

In many industries, the compression of margins is a fact of life and a phenomenon without end. Computer manufacturers plan their business with the recognition that margins are in decline, constantly innovating processes, cutting costs, predicting the impact of Moore's Law and O'Dell's Law[3] and changing their business models to avoid

[3] According to Gordon Moore, one of the founders of Intel Corporation, the processing power of computer chips doubles and the costs halve every eighteen months. Michael O'Dell, an Internet visionary with experience at ARPAnet, Bellcore and a Worldcom ISP, said famously that Internet bandwidth demand doubles every three months. (He also made a number of other interesting Internet-related observations, including: "If you're not scared, you don't understand.")

"flying the company plane into the ground," as the president of one computer company said. Margin collapse is not just for manufacturers. In retailing, the concept called the "wheel of retailing" notes that companies with more efficient processes enter and gain market position at the expense of companies that have grown fat or unfocused over time. The demise of Canada's famed T. Eaton Company, a venerable mass merchandiser, is a case in point. Eatons, Canada's combination of Marks and Spencer and Bloomingdale's, was unable to defend against the entry of Wal-Mart. With more efficient logistics, a sharper market focus and better consumer value, Wal-Mart expanded and Eaton's went into receivership, now emerging under new ownership as more Bloomingdale's than Marks and Spencer. The Internet, by turning many goods and services into commodities, has driven yet more margin out of some business models, even in cases in which companies thought they were protected. One company developed extensive relationships with a major account only to have the customer place all its procurement on the Internet in a public auction. What business the company was able to retain was at substantially reduced margin.

The decline in margins has three major impacts:

1. The existing business model may not sustain the company. On the one hand, companies cannot rely on narrow niches for their profitability because the margins even there are often insufficient for sustaining it, let alone growing the company. On the other hand, firms find it difficult to broaden their market appeal because of the many competitors in most arenas and the costs of entering new markets. Business forms companies, for example, need to broaden their product and service range to make up for declining sales of traditional business forms. While the market for electronic forms, workflow and document management is large few business forms companies have the resources, people, technology and culture to do well in the new areas.
2. New, profitable business models are hard to define and even harder to make operational. If companies are increasingly finding their products and services commoditized, they might choose to recognize this and build their business models to cater to the buyer interested in comparing value. The transition may have profound impacts on existing customer relationships if not handled well. Additionally, some companies may not be able to balance their focus on customer relationships with similar attention to commoditization. Some firms might do better to create

new lines of business to pursue commoditized business than attempting to transition their company to this business model. British Airways did this in its pursuit of the budget traveler and in response to the market success of easyJet in Europe.

3. Reduced margins make it hard for the company to reinvest in the business and in the customer relationship. But more than making it hard to fund a transition to a new business model, just sustaining what the company has done historically is increasingly difficult. Reduced margins make it difficult to afford new products, such as technologies that advance the customer relationship and strategic spending to create consumer pull. To reinforce a previous point, the attention of financial managers may cause the company to invest in short-term, more assured areas of return. However, these tend to be associated with operational efficiency rather than effectiveness. The cumulative result of many such investments is that the company becomes the sum of its short-term commitments and is ill-prepared to fight a strategic war with a firm that has a more coherent vision with spending aligned in support of the company's direction. Many dot.com and other technology companies can surely appreciate this challenge.

Declining margins can be a way of life while companies descend into a chaotic fight for survival. Alternatively, firms can find ways to enhance margins while making their companies more strategic, relevant and competitive. There are a number of roads to this destination, and competitor targeting can either add value to most of them or become a key focus of the company in its own right.

Time Shrinks

Traditional marketing cannot function well in an environment in which time has been taken out of management processes. Technology companies in Silicon Valley talk (and operate) in terms of Internet time and warp speed. They contrast "their" time with that of companies in other industries, much as one would talk of dog years in relation to those of humans. This was all quite quaint when the phenomenon was confined to one industry and region. Now, the time between concept and execution is lightning fast in most industries. With less time available to plan, companies depend more and more on the marketer's experience and judgment to make the right, often reactive, decisions. The company that competes in time does a number of things quite differently. For example:

- Research: There is no time for this, at least not for extensive mass research.
- Competitor Analysis: Make it quick. Keep it focused.
- Planning: If the internal management view is that plans are outdated as soon as they are written, the plans need to be brief. Marketers make the plans into living documents, with frequent updates rather than developing sterile tomes.
- Organization: Multifunctional task forces allow companies to move quicker to develop and implement key initiatives. Companies structure around their core strategic value, outsourcing the balance. One of the world's major banks sees this as an iterative process. Once strategic value is created and the organization adapts, aspects of a repetitive or administrative nature can be outsourced.
- Processes: More automation is used for processes that incorporate business rules for internal operations and customer communication. To the extent possible, the customer interface becomes one that is self serve and the company automates many of the processes that touch the customer, allowing the firm to handle more inquiries and transactions without increasing all costs in proportion. This is one of the reasons companies encourage customers to use the Internet rather than call centers to obtain information and transact business.
- Knowledge: Product, process, technology and employee knowledge is managed and reused. Customer and channel intermediary knowledge form the basis for CRM, including an ability to predict customer and channel member requirements, sometimes before they themselves know.

There is potential for the company that competes in time to incorporate more competitive context into their management decisions. It is not enough to be fast if the competitor is just as fast and, more importantly, right. By monitoring specific competitors, the company has an opportunity to incorporate competitive intelligence in their decision making, helping them to be better than defined competitors decision by decision, leading to dominance over a period of time. It is curious how many management decisions are taken rapidly without this competitive intelligence. The intelligence is available quickly. Some companies even use designated employees to shadow the competitors. These shadows participate in key meetings to advise how competitors might respond to specific courses of action the company is considering or to provide other useful competitive perspective.

Technology Advances and Costs Decline

Technology advances and improvements in price and performance underlie many of the changes now facing the traditional marketer. For example, dramatic declines in the costs of memory, storage, bandwidth, processing, engineered materials and components and software have given companies the power to identify and assess individual customer relationships. Improvements in bandwidth and compression have changed the economics of mass communications and enabled the marketer to interact with individual customers in pursuit of better relationships. Figure 1-1 describes selected technology drivers and their enablers as well as other factors that have changed traditional marketing, including deregulation and regulation of industries, especially telecommunications,[4] and customer and industry issues, such as those discussed next.

In the new, technology-enabled marketplace, not only has traditional marketing become less relevant, but the new technologies also facilitate the targeting of competitors and their more effective management, both customer by customer and in aggregate.

Customers Innovate

Marketers operating according to the historical rules of marketing have been trained to balance technology innovation with customers' needs. Consumer products marketers have been particularly adept at developing products that meet needs they first identify in the marketplace. Marketers would not build new products or create new services without first assessing whether customers will buy from them. The new marketplace has challenged the marketer's traditional approach because the dramatic proliferation of new products and services has been met with an equal customer appetite to buy and use innovations. Consumers have been buying new computers every few years and trash the old ones quite willingly. Businesses have implemented new enterprise resource planning (ERP) systems, new call center technology, new networks and much else in the belief they must spend on technology (invest, they say) or they will fall behind. The pace of innovation on the supply side could never have continued were it not for a similar expansion in demand. As investors and lenders shy away, slowing

[4] Telecommunications is singled out here because regulatory changes, such as those referenced for the USA and EU have changed industry structure, enabled digital convergence and other innovations and have ultimately made one to one communications an economical consideration for many companies.

Figure 1-1: Enablers and Drivers of the New Marketplace

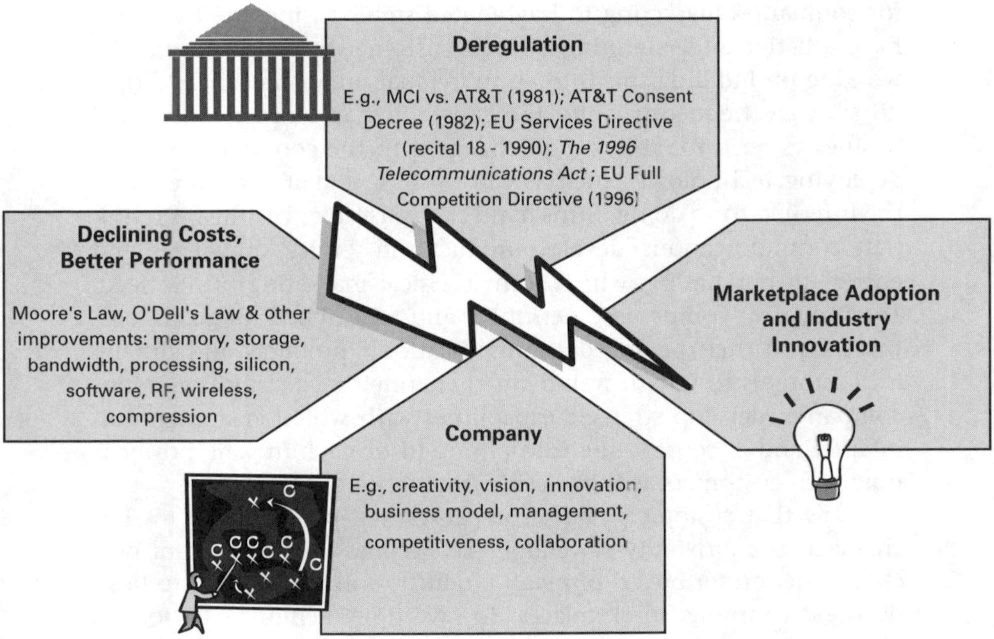

demand is having more profound impact on the supply of innovation than an absence of ideas or shortages of key inputs, such as human resources. In this new marketplace, competitor targeting can take a number of interesting forms, many quite different from the approaches historically used by marketers. For example, some companies already target the shareholder value of competitors, seeking to transfer some of this to their firms.

Customers Target Companies

It used to be that the vendor targeted the customer. In the new marketplace, the customer is just as likely to target the vendor. For example, consumers find out about companies, products and services on-line. Word of mouth has become less important in decision making as customers find new virtual constituencies to interact with and to learn from. Search engines further help customers target the companies that have the best products or services.

In business-to-business situations, particularly for large enterprises, companies know their targets well. In consumer marketplaces and for companies marketing to fragmented small businesses, they may have a better understanding of their customer by type and may be working on building this into an individual understanding. As they do so, they frequently build the capabilities consumers and small businesses need to interact and engage with the company, often by deploying technologies such as call centers, e-mail, e-business and the Internet. In so doing, firms hand each customer the means to initiate communications, develop product and service knowledge and engage in purchasing, which turns classical marketing on its head. Traditionally, companies identified and researched targeted customers and then packaged communications, products and pricing for customers to buy in well-defined channels of distribution. Now, companies develop strategic capabilities with which customers can interact and encourage them to phone in or click in. The power is now with customers as they decide from whom to buy.

Now that customers target companies, the purchase process has changed. The proximity of vendors has become a less important purchase criterion for buyers of many products, both in business to business and consumer marketplaces. To save time or money, customers sometimes let the vendor initiate their own sale, rather than formally repurchasing from the company. This is the case for customers agreeing to have their accounts debited for magazines or telecommunications services, for example, and often occurs for companies that maintain inventories at their customers' premises. Other process changes in the new marketplace include companies that establish auctions to buy a broader range of goods and services from the lowest bidder than they might previously have purchased using a tendering process.

The vendor alone used to make the pricing decision. In the new marketplace, the customer often decides the value they want more or less independently of the seller and takes charge of the pricing decision. Go on-line to buy a car, choose the features you want and then find out the sale price. Unhappy with the result? Choose the features again and reprice until you are happy with the value bundle. You might prefer to delete certain options, such as a CD player or security system, and pick them up in the aftermarket when you need them. The responsive vendor will unbundle pricing and offer you the selection and choice you desire. Increasingly, the car industry is doing this by going to a make-to-order mass customization process rather than selling vehicles that already have option packages.

When customers that are very much desired by the company target their suppliers, the nature of competition changes. In the new marketplace, superiority must be achieved in dimensions such as brand equity and other relationship bonds, both tangible and otherwise. Competitor targeting provides an opportunity to create real and perceived differentiation, making it more likely that a customer will select your company over another.

Collaboration Increases

Technology and associated process changes enable products to be cooperatively designed, developed, tested, piloted, provided, installed and refined. Products are less often pre-defined, researched in the laboratory and with customers and packaged. Previously, products were bundles of tangible and intangible benefits the company assembled because it thought that these were what customers wanted to buy. Today, products are an aggregation of individual benefits customers have helped to select or design. The "product" resulting from this collaboration may be unique and highly tailored to the requirements of the customer. Much more customer-specific knowledge goes into the product than was previously the case. To some extent this applies also to services. Check into a hotel, and if you have not already specified your preferences when you booked on the Internet, the hotel will want to build a profile on you to ensure that your preferences are met without fail. And each time you stay with the chain, your personal files will be updated so that the hotel can anticipate your needs.

Customers want to participate in decisions regarding the value they receive and the prices they pay. They expect to pay a single price for a standard offer but are willing to pay more for options, often far more than the actual value of the option. Car manufacturers have long understood that options have a much higher margin than the base vehicle. Give customers a chance to have an even more tailored solution, and they might pay more again. Alternatively, they will expect options they do not want to be removed from the bundle and deleted from the price. If the clothes don't fit, don't charge for alterations!

Business-to-business companies such as General Electric have long known that collaboration early in the design process leads to sales throughout the life of the product. The concepts developed by these companies, such as involvement and interaction, tracking the purchase decision and understanding the purchase process, are now being applied to consumer marketing using technology to automate the business rules and communications methods.

Collaboration opens a new front for competing. Companies have an opportunity to create deeper customer relationships through innovation, and those finding the path first to collaborative innovation will be better positioned to win. Competitor targeting can help a company define what winning means. With this knowledge, the company can run the business race against a visible foe.

Battleground Includes Customer Access

In the new marketplace, where durable customer relationships are highly prized, companies try to offer as broad an array of products and services as customers want from them. More than creating new competitors out of other suppliers, the challenge is now to secure more favorable access to customers, a particular challenge for business-to-business firms. Additionally, the competitive set from which the customer selects is narrowing. As companies begin to resell some products in addition to those they make, there are fewer reasons for the customer to entertain as many suppliers. The battleground thus is shifting to one of customer access.

This can apply also to the distribution channel. Here, companies with long product lists compete with others having long lists, too. There is potential for companies to be crowded out by competitors selling broader or deeper lines. In some industries, this is creating tiers of companies. First-tier companies have customer access and the primary customer relationship. Second-tier firms supply the first-level companies but are often cut off from the end customer. This is happening in many industries in which companies are choosing to be either broadly based suppliers that manage the customer relationship or narrow specialists that supply all comers, often including tier-one vendors. The auto assembly and aerospace and defense industries have long been organized in this manner, but now others, such as printing and even consulting services, are moving this way. However, specialists have difficulty retaining their differentiation and competitive position and many are being acquired by vendors with broader lines. As technical knowledge proliferates, product and service specialists find that competing on product or service excellence does not provide shelter from competition and that they also need to compete on relationships.

Companies consider distribution channels to be theirs, as the mechanism to transfer a product or its title to the customer. Technology shifts the power of distribution from the supplier to the customer, changing the supply chain into a demand chain, one that is initiated by the customer rather than by the vendor. When companies such as Compaq consider manufacturing or configuring computers to order, they are, in effect, saying that the era of the product, as we knew it, is over. Now the company not only listens to the customer, but it interacts with each one in real time. The production or assembly processes begin only when the order is placed, whether by the customer or an intermediary.

Technical skill and even operational performance is not sufficient to win customer access. If the customer's open door is a sought-after prize, not only must the company keep the door open, but the competitor must be prevented from walking through.

The new marketplace requires new rules for marketing. Companies have done well to prioritize customers and seek more durable customer relationships. The opportunity now is to go a few steps further and compete for the business of individual customers.

All Marketing Becomes Relationship Marketing

If marketing has reached the end of the road, as several of the above changes suggest, what is to replace it? Many companies believe that the future of marketing is relationship marketing and have invested in a number of changes in support of this belief.

First, a comment regarding relationship marketing and customer relationship management (CRM). Many people use the two terms interchangeably, and so, in the discussion that follows, we do as well. However, I view relationship marketing as more general than CRM. Relationship marketing explores the principles for creating new and mutual value for and with individual customers. CRM, by definition, is about management of the customer relationship, which seems to suggest less attention to new value and innovation, and relationships with other than customers, such as channel intermediaries, employees and suppliers. More than this, because the term CRM is used by so many technology vendors selling boxed software solutions, many companies equate CRM with a technology implementation. Technology alone is not enough to create, develop and maintain customer relationships, although it can obviously help. Companies are now finding out the hard way that relying on an expensive technology solution to improve customer relationships may not create new shareholder value.

While many companies are embracing relationship marketing, most are focused almost exclusively on one stakeholder—the individual customer. For them, relationship marketing can create mutual value for each employee, supplier (supplying collaborator might be a better term for the CRM-driven company) and others, including specific investors.[5] We raise relationship marketing and CRM here for an important reason. Relationship marketing, in its end state, is not a competitive strategy but a customer- and stakeholder-centric one. As relationship marketing strategy is not relative to another company, the adoption of relationship marketing or a CRM technology solution may or may not achieve competitive advantage or help the company defend against competitors. Many companies that have invested heavily in CRM are now finding that they are not much ahead of competitors, especially those that have done likewise.

CRM and Competition

Business can be seen as a strategic triangle, with the company, the customer and the competitor at each corner. Figure 1-2 illustrates this, with the company wanting to bond with chosen customers and doing so better than competitors.

Figure 1-2: Competing for Customers

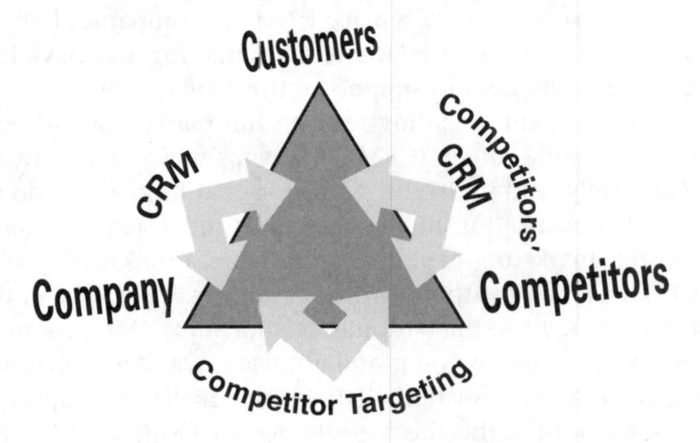

Let us consider the first side of the triangle: the linkages between the company and its customers. This was formerly segment-based marketing. Today, with the ability for companies to interact and engage with individual customers, this edge of the triangle becomes CRM.

Most marketers say that, their CRM efforts notwithstanding, customers' are more fickle than ever. Many of the same desirable customers are courted by competitors, each promising what the customer

[5] For a more detailed consideration of relationship marketing than is possible here, the reader is invited to review my previous book: *Relationship Marketing: New Strategies, Techniques and Technologies to Win the Customers You Want and Keep Them Forever*. Toronto: John Wiley and Sons, 1998. ISBN 0-471-64173-1.

wants, which reduces differentiation companies are able to communicate about their products and services. The advent of on-line purchasing has accelerated switching. Now, with a click, a customer can dart effortlessly from vendor to vendor and be as likely to buy from companies around the corner as around the world. If the company only competed with weak competitors, the firm would get the desired results from its CRM initiative. But most companies compete with some strong competitors and it is the strength of competition that determines whether the CRM initiative will create new customer and shareholder value. CRM and competitive advantage are thus two sides of the coin that helps determine how much shareholder value is attained.

While some companies pay attention to competitors, this attention is often an informal part of the job for many employees and managers. When companies have formalized their competitive assessment, it is sometimes left outside the context and content of CRM. In short, it is the rare company that has fully integrated a competitive context into its vision and strategies, including CRM. More than this, few companies have developed the competitive context and content they need to manage individual customers profitably. Companies compete for share of market, share of customer and share of customers' future spending. Since share is a measure of *competitive* success, competition should feature prominently in any CRM initiative. Yet, with new technologies, changing buyer behaviors, emerging alliances, nontraditional competitors, industry restructuring and organizational efficiency, sometimes there is not enough time to do everything, and attention to competition can receive insufficient investment and management attention.

CRM is headed in yet more capital-intensive directions as technology vendors and consultants encourage companies to invest heavily in electronic CRM (eCRM), which is CRM that is technologically enabled. With eCRM, companies seek to develop strategic capabilities for customer engagement and automate key processes within the company and between the company and its stakeholders to deliver rapidly the value customers want. As such, eCRM has important potential benefits for companies. But the question, often unasked, is what are competitors doing with eCRM, and will adoption of a particular approach be better than the road down which the competitor is headed? Moreover, could the company achieve better results by investing in other areas, such as recruiting people with different profiles, training existing staff and managers, process improvements and customer collaboration?

Competitor Targeting

The second side of the triangle is the area overlooked in much of the attention to CRM. This is the line between the company and its competitors and represents the opportunity the company has to manage competitors or collaborate with them for business advantage. As mentioned, the process for singling out specific competitors and planning to beat them or benefit with them strategically, tactically and in real time is called competitor targeting.

Competitors and Their CRM Initiatives

Finally, the third side of the triangle is CRM, with which competitors seek to bond with their customers, some of whom may be the same ones you value. The competitors' state of CRM and the relationships they have with customers is an important basis for learning from them and determining how best to beat them.

Let us envision the end state of relationship marketing. A company will have developed processes and deployed technologies to integrate with customers and create the value each valuable and chosen customers wants. The company will have developed their people as collaborators with customers, as farmers rather than as hunters of accounts. Internal capabilities will have been materially improved, including interfaces for anytime anywhere customer access, real-time customer knowledge and insight that lets a company know when a customer is ready to buy and in what they will be most interested. Let us suspend judgment and belief for a moment and imagine that this has occurred. Will the company have satisfied shareholders? Will the company be the most significant factor in its industry? Will the best employees flock to work with the company? Perhaps.

But the answer is more rooted in answers to other questions—questions that deal with competition—than it is in CRM. For example, if the company is indeed doing the right thing with CRM, will it reach its destination faster than competitors? Does it have better processes, technologies, people and customer knowledge and insight than its competitors? The fact that many companies are committing large sums of money to CRM and other initiatives and still succeeding without a competitive context is testimony to the fact that many of their competitors also lack the required competitive context. All this is about to change. Technology makes a renewed competitive focus possible and strategy makes it desirable.

Today's Customer

Customers' needs never change, although their wants might vary according to economic and other circumstances. Today's customer has more choice and more opportunity to choose. These two changes are the result of company and product proliferation and new technologies but are not associated with consumers per se. Today customers can choose from among more products, services, companies, locations and ways of buying. And customers have more technology to help learn, compare, communicate and buy. Here we discuss two important issues:

1. Age of the Individual Customer
2. Customers Flit

Age of the Individual Customer

Marketers have long talked about the age of the customer and now it has arrived—and then some. Technology has put customers in charge of the information they seek, their information processing, their vendor connections and their buyer behavior.

In the era Before Digital (perhaps we should call this almost prehistoric time BD), the company focused on specific strategies. In the After Digital era, much has changed in the way companies cater to customers. Businesses create capabilities, such as the ability to produce a wide variety of products and services, and put these alternatives in front of the customer like a smorgasbord. With less or no pressure, customers avail themselves of the features and benefits they seek, at a price they wish to pay, collaborating with the supplier's personnel or interacting with technology to obtain a custom solution. If they like what they see and the value they receive, they will be back. If too much is asked of them (such as time investment, information or price) or too little is given them (such as information, value, variety, novelty or service), they are gone in a mouse click, perhaps never to return. This would seem to suggest that business is only about the Internet. Of course, this is not the case, but increased volume and profit are always made where change is occurring. The most significant recent area of change has been the Internet's enablement of other opportunities. So, the Internet has reasonably merited considerable attention by management, just as cash flow and customer profitability are receiving focus today.

Figure 1-3: Five Considera"tions" in the Internet Era

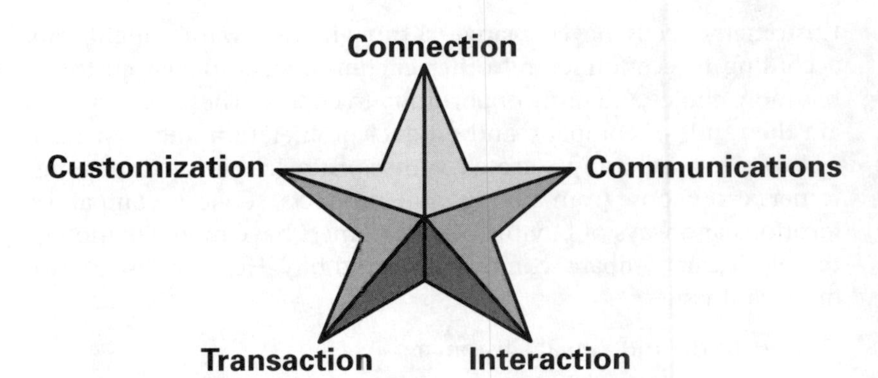

As described in Figure 1-3, the main customer opportunities enabled by the Internet are five considera"tions": connection, communications, interaction, transaction and customization. They determine how best to:

- connect with the customers they want
- communicate with each customer using their media preference
- interact with individuals in a manner they find satisfying, which may also require integration of the Internet channel with others, such as customer contact centers
- engage in a secure transaction
- meet the customer's individual expectations in terms of product, service, price, reverse distribution (returns) and logistics, among other areas of customization

In this age of the customer, the word "custom" is put back in "customer." Now companies bring to consumers the same approaches with which they have long served businesses. Technology lets them do this, so each customer is able to obtain a tailored offering. Of course, this looks a lot like "back to the future" as companies try to replicate in technology what the independent merchant did in our parents' generation. The better ones knew their customers well and were able to predict what they needed, when they would buy and what would keep them coming back. Their tools were memory, insight and personality. Today, companies are working hard at the first two of these, putting into technology the business rules and capabilities that provide purchase tracking, customer profitability and predictive modeling, for example. Some, like DaimlerChrysler with its spectacularly successful P/T Cruiser, are trying to develop products that combine benefits that cross multiple market segments and develop personality in their brand equity.

Competition in the age of the individual customer remains that of substitution, but the nature of substitution has changed. In previous eras, customers selected or substituted products, in the process choosing among vendors. Today, it is common for customers to first select or substitute among companies, then choose the product. In many industries, products have insufficient differentiation to command unique positioning by virtue of their functional attributes. For example, does your company really care which brand of paper they use in photocopiers? When customers select companies, they are often communicating that the firm or its brands resonate with them. Typical dimensions of resonance include personal and social benefits. Consumers who choose Nike or BMW do so because they think the brand positions them favorably in social settings, not necessarily because the shoes or cars are much better than those of competitors. Other than brand equity, there are a number of other dimensions of bonding that customers consider when selecting among alternative suppliers. Examples include structural, value, attitudinal, personal and information and control, which we discuss in Chapter 6. Differentiating in respect of these dimensions raises the issue of competitive superiority. This, in turn, offers an opportunity for competitor targeting.

Customers Flit[6]

It used to be that companies could count on recurring and growing revenues from loyal customers. This remains the holy grail. But, when companies do not give customers meaningful reasons to continue to do business with them, buyers flit, picking and choosing from an almost infinite assortment of products and services from an expanded array of suppliers. Customers want value and sometimes variety. For example, the number one reason customers choose the car they buy is that they want a change from what they now have. The Internet enables comparison and feeds the want for novelty. Of course, companies themselves are part of the reason why consumers

[6] For additional discussion on this subject, the reader is referred to S.M. O'Dell and J.A. Pajunen, *The Butterfly Customer: Capturing the Loyalty of Today's Elusive Customer*, Toronto: John Wiley and Sons Canada, 1998.

click their way to competitors. Without a compelling reason to stay, many will flit to another vendor and alight there for a while. Charles Schwab, a brokerage leader with 3 million individual investors and over $850 million in on-line revenues, has learned how to keep customers in the cutthroat world of e-trading and flitting customers.

The era of sell, sell, sell is over. Today, customers are less interested than ever in buying what the company wants to sell. This does not seem to stop so many companies from simply wanting to sell harder—and yell louder. This simple truth is behind many failed marketing programs. Customers want sellers to solve their problems. Vendors must provide what customers want, not just what the company makes. Alternatively, with so much choice so readily available, the customer could flit away in a mouse click. The responsibility of the vendor is to give chosen customers no reason to do so.

The New Technology

Consumer choice is more the result of industry and competitive factors and the proliferation and increased performance of technology at the supplier, in the network and on consumers' desktops. New technologies have given the consumer more power to choose and the supplier more opportunities to manage that choice. In this section, we discuss how the new marketplace has been changed forever by new technologies.

Technology Killed Mass Everything

Broadcasting is out, just as mass anything is out. Now, technology lets the marketer communicate with individual customers according to the medium each prefers, with the message most relevant to the individual and in a time and manner most likely to have influence.

From the service history of your car, the dealer can confirm that you are ready to buy another vehicle. From your household profile, it may be established that your family has grown since you bought your previous car. From your interactions with the company's Web site, completion of questionnaires and perhaps a review of the cookies on your computer, it may be established not only that you are beginning to look at a new vehicle, but also the kinds of things that appeal to you. The potential is there to tailor a message to you that will be much more relevant than standardized communications. GM has recently assessed which prospects may be interested in specific vehicles and has sent them the kinds of communications most likely to help influence their purchase decision. Doubleclick and an Internet-related advertising company assembles data from a network of companies, including Alta Vista, to communicate with individual prospects on the Internet in the most effective way, giving each prospect a message most likely to influence his or her behavior.

Increasingly, one-way communications typically employed by marketers with their customers—such as mass advertising, promotional offers, manuals, price lists, product literature and warranty response cards—is being replaced with two-way communications to involve the customer much earlier in all matters that affect their future purchase behaviors. The challenge for the marketer is to design processes and incorporate technologies to engage the customer without driving costs through the roof.

Technology has killed mass everything—mass marketing, mass production and mass communications. Mass marketing was destroyed when technology transformed each customer into a distinct market. Mass production ended with the application of technology for the customization of production, allowing every company to build a single unit for you alone. Mass communications, first transformed by technology to allow marketing to specific segments, now lets companies interact as never before with individuals. In short order, the world of communications has moved from broadcasting, to narrowcasting (focusing on specific segments), to pointcasting (targeting the individual) to conversing (engaging each individual company and consumer in a dialogue).

Figure 1-4: Changing Communications

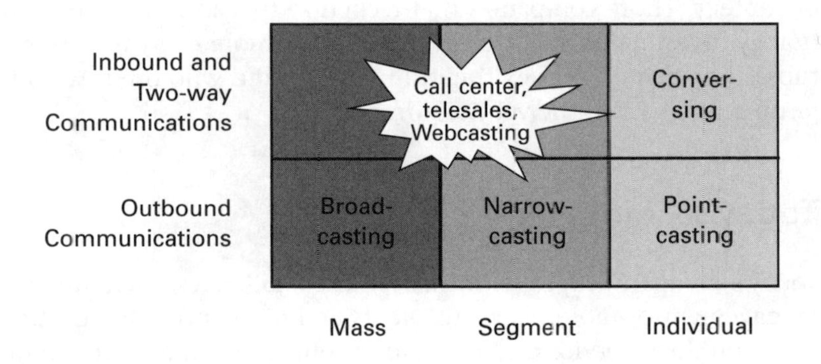

As discussed in Chapter 6, the digitization of analog media—such as voice, video, sound and data—has created entirely new industries, with many of the opportunities coming at the boundaries of computing, communications, content (such as applications software and databases) and carriers (including cable television, telecommunications services and broadcasting). Thus, America Online (AOL) benefited initially from the convergence of computing and communications to become the world's largest provider of e-mail and information. More recently, through its acquisitions, it has new interests in the printing, publishing, cable TV and music industries, and it is looking to create and lead new businesses where new media has the potential to change the rules of business. Thus, although on the surface AOL may have overpaid for Time Warner—possibly enough to have secured the next three largest content companies—AOL obtained venerable brand names and content to use in new ways, as well as a cable system. It has, in effect, become the world's largest convergence company. With the laying of fiber-optic cable and the potential for communications equipment companies to make light switches, bandwidth may no longer be a limiting factor for communications, and many more convergence-related applications will be founded to create new customer value and wealth.

The adoption of technology at the customer interface presents one of the greatest challenges and one of the most important opportunities for a company to win in this age of the individual customer. As technology becomes this huge funnel cloud into which so much capital and so many people seem to be swept, those without knowledge of technology and what it can do will become the subordinates of the technologically literate. This applies equally to companies, with the proviso that technology will always remain a tool in support of strategy. Those companies that recognize this and integrate technology investments in a strategic manner are more likely to win over those in search of the next big thing (NBT[7]) and who often seem to jump at the beat of the vendor's drum.

Today's Company

Today's company copes with many more challenges, including the management of more fickle customers and differentiation at a time when product, service and company proliferation makes this more

[7] NBT—Next Big Thing, yet another TLA (Three Letter Acronym).

difficult. Although technology has enabled customers to select among vendors, it also lets companies be more active in managing the customer throughout the purchase process. Here are ten of the areas in which today's company is different from yesterday's:

1. Companies Choose Customers
2. Companies Morph
3. Marketplaces Have Fewer Levels and Different Intermediaries
4. Products and Services Are Becoming Commodities
5. Companies Compete on Scope
6. Companies Redefine the Word Focus
7. Companies Go Virtual
8. Customization Is Free and for Everyone
9. Customer Relationships Can Lock Competitors Out
10. Cash Is King Again

Companies Choose Customers

If the customer is targeting the company, so too is the company becoming much more selective about the customers with whom it chooses to have a relationship. Before, any customer with money to spend was coveted. Retailers and companies in most other industries threw their doors open in the morning and wondered who would walk in. Big buyer or small, purchaser of high margin products or low, all were served. After all, the revenues and profits were seen to be incremental. Today, much of this thinking has changed. Retailers and other commercial enterprises still serve customers who want to buy something, but they are more proactive in the customers they seek. A customer is no longer simply a customer. Companies have awoken to the notion that customers come in several forms, which they usually categorize according to their profitability and growth potential, ranking them best, average and worst. In a way such as this, companies differentiate their customers and determine how and even whether to serve each type of customer. Some send their worst customers packing—ideally to competitors—to have the dual benefit of improving their own profit and weakening that of their competitors as the bad customers eat away at their earnings.

Consider the banking industry, in which customers wishing to invest or borrow money are still coveted. Customers are channeled according to the type of client (small business, corporate, high net worth individual, etc.). Consumers are encouraged to move from face-to-face banking to the ATM, telephone and on-line banking, each of which has progressively lower transaction costs. Building on this observation and by analyzing customer data and allocating costs appropriately, a Swedish bank found that the top 20 percent of its customers generated all the profit, while the remainder lost the bank money. The bank then invested nearly all its new capital in improvements for profitable customers. Although it lost some patrons, high-value customers increased overall profitability by making more use of the bank. Many financial services firms are triaging their customers into best, average and worst and managing each according to their strategic value (including profitability and growth potential). One bank, when restructuring branches, invited only its best customers to go to new locations. The others were asked to close out their accounts.

Getting rid of customers may prove easier than obtaining new ones of the type you covet. The chairman of a major US on-line brokerage has noted that deep pockets may be the ultimate difference here, with the winners being prepared to pay more for a customer than their competitors are.

Companies Morph

With technology changing so much about the nature of business—including strategy, velocity and logistics—the battleground for competition has shifted dramatically. No longer are competitors sitting ducks, with their strategies staying stagnant while you aim your weapons. Now companies are highly mobile. They compete in time. They compete for the future. They morph before your eyes, changing their nature, style and even business model as they respond to threats and conceive opportunities. The faster they morph, the more they are likely to survive if they can afford the cost of change and if their best customers like where they are headed.

Northern Telecom first changed the world by digitizing the central office switch. Then it bought Bay Networks to position itself as an Internet company, Nortel Networks. At the old Nortel, it used to be said that the company did not need to be the first to market, even though it often was, so long as it was not last to learn. The crash and burn of its stock price in 2001 has made the new Nortel impatient as it tries to survive and grow. Not surprisingly, the company sees its main competition as time and its main barrier as complacency. It has also seen Cisco as a more important competitor than its historical foes, such as Alcatel, Lucent, Siemens and Ericsson. In competing with Cisco not only in the marketplace but to acquire emerging technology companies, Nortel remade itself completely and, for a time, very successfully. Its focus propelled the company to new highs as the Internet infrastructure was built but weakened the company when this spending slowed.

Egghead is another, more extreme, case of morphing. This discount retailer of computers failed in the bricks and mortar arena in 1998 and closed all its retail outlets. The company recognized the strength of its brand and returned, phoenix like, as Egghead.com to become a major on-line e-tailer. While this example of morphing is an extreme one, most companies are adding and discontinuing products and services so fast that although each action is closely linked to the immediate past, the company changes completely over a period of time.

Many or most of the products winning companies sell today did not exist two or three years ago. Staff is younger, more energetic, less connected with the past, more focused and more willing to take risks. As companies morph, they invest heavily in technology, looking for new ways to win and keep customers; improve products, services, communications and processes; and make their businesses more efficient.

Companies change as they respond to market, technology and financial opportunities, sometimes transforming so quickly that it is very difficult for competitors to understand them and predict what they will do next. When GE started its corporate transformation, the senior analysts at Westinghouse should have had the time and ability to make sense of the changes under way in their arch rival (although they appear not to have used the information available to them). Within a few short years, GE had shed businesses where it thought it could not win and emphasized new arenas and existing businesses where it thought it could.

GE after Jack Welch was a very different company than before him. Now GE is again challenged to change, this time even more quickly than was possible in the time of "Neutron Jack."[8] Now Web-enabled competitors with little need to worry about historical investments can win over GE's customers with a mouse click, creating the

[8] Some attribute this nickmame to a time shortly after Welch's appointment as GE's president, when buildings would remain standing but, like the effects of the neutron bomb, the people inside were gone. This nickname is now rarely used, as most people respect the changes Welch made and his profound vision for the company.

prospect that competitors without investments in plant, equipment, patents or buildings could do more to damage GE than Westinghouse ever did. Once GE has transformed, this time to become a clicks and bricks company, it will be very different compared to the Welch years and even more vastly changed from the preceding era.

Marketplaces Have Fewer Levels and Different Intermediaries

The Internet is having a number of major effects on the nature of business. One of the significant changes is the reduction in total markup as products move from production to consumption. Some people refer to this change as less "friction," and the fewer levels between producer and consumer as "disintermediation." Disintermediation creates new challenges for companies wanting to access, communicate and transact with individual consumers. Chief among these challenges is developing awareness among consumers that your company exists and then getting them interested in trying your offer. Another challenge stemming from disintermediation is that of dealing with new, nontraditional companies that may emerge as "reintermediaries" or "infomediaries." These companies may step into the information void experienced by some consumers or take advantage of the excess of supply over demand in many industries to create new business models and value propositions for consumers. In short, they may make it easier for buyers to compare and purchase.

Companies such as Auto-By-Tel have inserted themselves into the value chain by making it easy for customers to compare vehicles and prices while, at the same time, making it easier for dealers to sell cars. This has created new challenges for automakers as the infomediaries have significant economic power, the potential to change buyer behavior, direct sales traffic and, in the process, reshape entire industries. No wonder the likes of GM and Ford have developed Internet strategies that appear to take into account the emerging power of infomediaries, whereby consumers can find out more about car prices and costs than was ever available publicly.

Products and Services Are Becoming Commodities

The Internet has placed an infinite store shelf at the purchaser's desktop. Now the world's products literally are available for purchase by buyers hunched over keyboards whether they are next door or tens of thousands of miles away. Proliferation of suppliers and products has reduced perceived differentiation in many industries and made price competition more important for the successful vendor. Call this "commoditization" of products and services, whereby there is less differentiation, and price has become key. In the age of the customer, companies charging higher prices than the average in the marketplace for like goods must find credible and sustainable value to support the high prices or risk losing all their business overnight. Whether vendors of candy or construction equipment, watches or washing machines, wood chips, potato chips or computer chips, companies recognize that their markets are becoming commoditized. Three main factors are causing this:

1. widespread availability to the buyer of pricing, product and cost information
2. the elimination of distance as a factor limiting economic market access
3. the proliferation of suppliers and products to which the customer has access, including used products that can be substituted for new

In commodity markets such as wheat and oil, companies selling at the going rate secure sales, those selling below the going rate sell all they can make, and those above the market price may sell very little or nothing. If the customer can change most goods and services for those of competitors, what then will make customers loyal?

Commoditization has two main impacts: companies must either drive for a parity or lower cost position so they can be price-competitive; or they must try to create value for and with customers that will maintain loyalty. Charles Schwab does this through providing timely and customized information. Amazon does this through product variety, customized alerts about the availability of new books and real-time intelligence. For example, the company's information that "Others who have bought this book also bought books by so and so," helps encourage additional purchases.

The effect of reintermediation and commoditization has been at once to change the nature of competition for those companies unable to create demonstrably differentiated customer value and to change one of the locations at which the battle is fought—at the level of the infomediary.

Companies Compete on Scope

In previous eras, companies wanted to be bigger so that they could have scale economies. Today, rather than competing on scale, companies compete on scope, offering a broader and deeper assortment of products, services and solutions. Competing on scope is more challenging than competing on scale. Anyone can acquire their way to scale, but while many companies try to buy others to create a one-stop shop for their customers, only good management can build profitable businesses on this strategy of scope. When the company owns the various components of the increased scope of products and services on offer, it will face challenges associated with this increased complexity such as lower levels of equipment utilization, finding specialized people and keeping them busy and training staff to have a broader range of knowledge. When the company associates with allies to provide the full range of scope, it still can face daunting challenges integrating the value the customer expects. So, a printing company may decide to job out certain types of printing for which it is not well suited, but it still must satisfy the customer with the printed products from its suppliers.

Companies Redefine the Word Focus

Management wants focus, by which many financially trained CEOs will talk of narrowing lines of business, products and service ranges. This approach worked well in previous eras but can be disastrous today if companies cut products and services that are important to their most profitable customers. Focus should not just mean identifying and concentrating on the most profitable and strategic lines of business while reducing or eliminating the others. Focus, seen this way, while providing a simpler business operation and potentially a more profitable one in the near (perhaps only the very near) term, ignores two things: the customer and competitors. If providing unprofitable products keeps profitable customers, why would one not continue to find a way to provide the products these customers want?

Many years ago, I marketed cat food. One of the flavors, tuna, came from the same production line used for tuna destined for humans.[9] This cat food flavor was unprofitable for the company, and the accountants wanted to charge more for it or discontinue it. The trouble was that customers bought several flavors of the brand at the

[9] Which is why the plant manager would take home cat food for tuna casserole. I watched him closely for an impact on his appearance or demeanor, but he never did become a good mouser!

same time and did not expect price differences. The potential was there to lose profitable customers by taking an apparently logical pricing action. Worse still would have been the discontinuation of the flavor. Consumers—the cats—loved the tuna. Other flavors seemed to bring out their finicky side, but they could not get enough of the tuna. Without tuna, the company would have had a lineup of products that cats would have found of marginal interest, leading owners, in due course, to try to appeal to the cat's appetite with new brands.

Today, focus means choosing customers on whom to concentrate and then competing on scope, giving each one they value a broader and deeper range of products and services. But this has the potential to be messy since the broader the range of goods and services offered, the more complex the operating and billing processes become. Having a broader scope requires that companies either use technology to make the scope more manageable, narrow the customer base so that scope complexity is not as challenging or both. If customers are not differentiated and everyone is offered a broader range of products and services without using technology to simplify this task, "competing on scope" would rapidly resemble "losing on chaos." Choosing customers gives the company an opportunity to align its scope with customers having something in common, such as needs, processes, technologies, access requirements, relationship and service expectations.

Companies Go Virtual

What you can see and touch is rapidly becoming worth much less than what you cannot. Just as Nike changed the footwear industry by controlling the process for the production of shoes while its competitors insisted that only they could make shoes worthy of their brands, so, too, are many companies today identifying the core of their future competitiveness and outsourcing the rest. They outsource repetitively until they do not exist physically, but they have control over the touch points of strategic value such as brand equity, product quality processes and customer satisfaction. They exist virtually. Dell and Cisco have shown how this can be done, and companies such as Lucent and Nortel are shedding physical operations as they proceed down a similar path. This makes much sense, especially for shareholders, for the following reasons:

- There is a much higher return on assets employed in a company that has few physical assets. However, high levels of goodwill for acquired companies can offset this benefit.

- There is less product obsolescence as product ownership can be externalized either to the outsourcer or the channel intermediary, reducing liabilities associated with discontinuing product.
- There is an ability to redeploy rapidly in an uncertain world, with few anchors constraining the redeployment.

Competing on scope encourages value chain specialization. It also causes the company to think hard about those aspects of the value chain it should outsource and those areas in which it should seek to compete with itself. Yes, compete with itself. Thus, when Bata Shoes began to market brand-name shoes such as Nike and Adidas in their stores in addition to the shoes it made itself, they shifted their strategy of end-to-end value chain control to one of process management in the interest of their customers. While it may well be true that customers of businesses focus first on the company then on its products, in this era of lesser differentiation, consumers often want their brands.

A retailer has three options: develop differentiated brands, offer the advertised brands of others or both. Insisting that customers buy only store brands can make salespeople as busy as the Maytag repairman. Bata was quick to understand this. It now offers the brands that kids want, knowing that although their own brand is strong, they cannot match the cumulative media expenditure of companies such as Nike, Adidas, Reebok and others in the development of brand equity. They don't have to. All they need to do is to offer consumers variety, including their excellent shoes and those of brand-name manufacturers. This is a lesson other retailers are applying in other industries, such as Tandy in consumer electronics (Radio Shack) and many mass merchandisers in their various departments.

It is interesting to note that few shoe companies themselves own the means of production, as Bata does. Nike, for example, is content to own the processes by which shoes come to market. Its focus is mostly on design, branding and market development. It leaves manufacturing to third parties. Bata continues to control more of their value chain than they might need, and there may be opportunities for it to further sharpen their value chain specialization.

Virtual competitors can be targeted in new ways. For example, the competitor's best suppliers might now deal with your firm exclusively or might provide your company with preferential terms or other benefits. In general, the greater the complexity, the more there is potential for something to go wrong. Competitor targeting can aid Murphy's Law by creating new challenges for the competitor.

Customization Is Free and for Everyone

Twenty years ago, it was observed that quality—formerly only applicable to high-end products and services and hence only within reach of the rich—was now becoming available for everyone, thanks to advances such as automation, reengineering, statistical process control and total quality management. Taken together, these advances effectively made improved quality free to the company providing it. Yet, the wealthy still had their suits individually tailored, their financial advice dispensed personally and their cars assembled to their own specifications, for which they were prepared to pay a premium. No longer. Today, the cost of customization is nil, or it may actually have a negative cost, as in the computer industry.

There, building a computer for a customer instead of for inventory can help the company stop costly end-of-life price reductions while providing the customer with the most powerful computer at the lowest price. Dell learned early that production for inventory inevitably resulted in prices being slashed to move unsold product prior to discontinuation of a line or item. The acceleration of new product introductions meant that there would be more and more price write-downs on products that had not moved out of the warehouse or through channel intermediaries. So Dell built to order, which meant that there was no inventory accumulation and no accounting surprises. Compaq and others are now doing likewise while trying to integrate the dealer into the customization process, such as by having the dealer configure subassemblies to customer order. Within a very short time, most cars will also be configured by the customer and built individually by the factory, eliminating costly finished goods inventory and making sure the customer gets what he or she wants. So each customer is getting custom products and services. Finally, the word "custom" within the word "customer" is having some real meaning again.

It is hard to target a profitable competitor that has developed meaningful value for individual customers. Although many companies position themselves as customizers, few have developed impregnable customer relationships, which leaves room for companies to target competitors by winning over their best customers.

Customer Relationships Can Lock Competitors Out

As companies compete on scope, they face existing competitors that want the same customers and nontraditional competitors that are expanding into their product-service turf. Product-market boundaries no longer define companies, but their customers do. In this world, all that separates one company from another is the favorability with which customers view them in the context of the next purchase. More generally, the willingness of customers—business or consumer—to collaborate with companies to create the value they want gives (or denies) companies competitive advantage. Generally, customers will collaborate only with a few companies.

Companies employ the principles of customer relationship management (CRM) to manage each customer for increased profitability. The main premise is that the relationship with each individual customer is the main asset of a business and that the value of this asset can be managed to increase shareholder value. CRM is enabled by new technologies and process changes such as those associated with the customer database, data mining tools and processes by which the customer is engaged and developed. Customer databases give vendors an opportunity to interact with the customer over the customer's purchasing lifetime as never before.

Mass customization of products, services and communications puts teeth in the concept of CRM, helping each customer to receive a unique, tailored solution—sometimes literally. Levis offers expanding baby boomers and others who depart from standard measurements the opportunity to have jeans made to their sizes. Actually, although each customer perceives a unique product, the jeans are assembled from a range of components, which makes mass customization feasible. Given this, companies are increasingly paying attention to the management of the customer relationship. Still relatively early in its development, CRM has for many companies focused on identifying profitable customers and providing them with the value they merit. This has been a good start. But for most companies, competitors are not yet locked out of their accounts. If this is the case in your situation, the relationship with the customer has yet to be more fully developed.

A relationship in business, as in personal life, requires participants to create new and mutual value. Anything else, and the relationship is a depreciating asset, relying on some event or circumstance in the past that led to the current situation. A vibrant relationship, one that locks competitors out, is one that is always creating new and mutual value. Here is the acid test. Do you routinely work with the customers you value most to achieve what you both want, in a way that you both clearly understand? The answer to this for many companies is no and the opportunity for improvement is clear. Innovation processes in many companies remain mired in the typical and traditional research-design-develop-produce-sell paradigm and have yet to fully invite the customer into the processes of planning for new value creation.

Cash Is King Again

When interest rates are high or money is in short supply, financing of initiatives depends much more on the availability of investment capital. In the past, companies needed to manage cash and grow the company from low-cost and self-generated funds. Firms used strategic assessment methods that required growth from internally generated funds. The BCG matrix,[10] which employed the now-famous terminology of cash cows, stars, dogs and question marks, was one such method.

For a while, companies operated without cash restrictions. First, they used junk bonds, which helped businesses large and small to contend with capital shortfalls. In the old economy, access to meaningful capital was a clubby affair, with established companies having an edge over new entrants. Then equity markets opened up to help smaller companies and start-ups in the new economy, although the volatility of equity markets has made this funding uncertain. Venture capitalists and others provide funding, too. It used to be that they complained that they could not find the right combination of good ideas and quality management more than that they lacked capital.

With reduced stock market valuation for technology stocks, cash and internally funded growth is once again becoming important. In this era, cash is once again king. Good ideas are important, as are the people who can actualize them, but now investors are much less eager to leave management alone with its ideas. They are less willing to forego near-term returns for the prospect of a longer-term payoff. Once investors could justify huge commitments of capital to companies such as Amazon.com. Founded in 1995, by 2001, Amazon had market capitalization of over $5 billion and 29 million customers, a remarkable rate of growth. In 1999, when Amazon had revenues of $1.6 billion, investors supplied $1 billion to help the firm to grow further, even though it lost $720 million. In 2000, Amazon had revenues of $2.8 billion but still lost $1.4 billion. In 2001, Amazon will likely achieve revenues of over $3 billion, but now investors want short-term profits. CEO Jeff Bezos is now focusing less on the benefits of

[10] And its derivatives, including the G.E. matrix and the A.D. Little lifecycle matrix

building brand, business and market share and more on profits. Most other dot.com companies that have survived the sharply lower stock market prices are following a similar path. They are no longer seeking to balance survival and growth. Their attention has been on prudence and the short term and less on brand development and capabilities needed to grow their businesses. Their risk is finding the balance and avoiding the dual perils of underinvestment and overexpansion.

In the go-go years of the dot.com market expansion, it was axiomatic that to be a capitalist, one needed capital, preferably someone else's! Now that sources of equity and debt funding are in shorter supply, companies need to grow from internally generated funds. Once out of vogue, these methods can again help a company to survive and prosper. Competitors can also be assessed using these tools, and the sources of their cash can be identified and managed to your advantage.

In Chapter 2, we discuss preparing to compete, including the competitive imperative and focusing on specific competitors to win.

CHAPTER 2

The Competitive Imperative

"Let him who desires peace prepare for war."[1]

—Falvius Vegetius Renatus

As noted in Chapter 1, having a customer-focused strategy, important though it obviously is, misses the larger context of the company in its industry. It is the absence of competitor considerations and a narrow and exclusive focus on the customer relationship that has led many companies to implement a plethora of programs without creating longer-term advantage. Individually, each program may seem to be worthwhile, but taken together, they may well miss the fundamental objective: to increase the company's share of each customer's expenditures. Improving customer relationships can be measured in absolute terms, but customer share is a relative measure and requires a competitive context.

Businesses have historically considered markets and market segments. More recently organizations are operating with more granular data, disaggregating segments and considering how to establish and build enduring relationships with individual customers. By also thinking about competitors as individuals, the opportunity exists for companies not to consider the competition in general, but to identify and plan to beat specific competitors. Moreover, companies can consider

---

[1] Original in Latin: *Qui desiderat pacem, praeparet bellum* (Falvius Vegetius Renatus, *De re militari*, c. 375)

these competitors in the context of individual customer relationships. This implies knowledge of the company that will lose so that you may win, customer by customer.

This chapter takes the position that a company should look two ways—at the individual customers it has chosen and the specific competitors it intends to beat. Seen another way, focusing only on customers through CRM will help ensure that they are well taken care of and their value recognized. But paying attention to competitors will help ensure that the company itself, its employees, shareholders and others who depend on the organization are also well looked after.

If certain competitors must be overcome for you to win the customers you want, it may well be appropriate for you to plan to weaken those rivals first and then in tandem with a relationship marketing initiative. This is what competitor targeting is all about. As there are no existing rule books for targeting competitors, here we present the core concepts.

Competing Is a Process

Competing is more than a state of mind or a desire to win, important as these factors may be. It is a process. It starts with knowing which customers are vital for the company, identifying and prioritizing the competition and then developing a plan to beat or collaborate with priority competitors, using all the tools available to the company to win.

Technology Enables Competing

Traditional marketing, including the principles of competitive engagement used by many managers, has been killed by technology and its enabling capabilities. These include:

1. Mass Storage
2. Automation of Business Rules
3. Processing Speed
4. Convergence

Mass Storage

The emergence of huge data stores has made possible the development of databases on all customers. For retail clients, for instance, this includes household information, their transactions, payment history, credit and contacts with the company, and much else. Technology has permitted a granularity never previously seen in traditional marketing, whereby customers were aggregated into segments and products were marketed to a virtual customer—someone with specific attributes, perceptions, attitudes, purchase behaviors and timing. In reality, few among us ever fully resembled this idealized customer.

Automation of Business Rules

Business rules are the quantified methods by which decisions are made. By automating these rules—putting into computer code the decisions made—companies have unparalleled potential to use data to treat each customer as an individual. In areas such as communications and mass customization, each customer can receive the value he or she wants and interact with the organization as he or she prefers. Behind the scenes, the company has developed the business rules that allow the customer to specify which mode of communications they prefer, how certain behaviors are to be rewarded or discouraged and how the company and the customer can achieve their separate and mutual ends.

To illustrate, both retailers and banks watch customers' credit scores. If your score drops below a certain number, your credit dries up, or worse. Credit scores are in essence a series of automated rules derived from a detailed review of customers, transactions and payment histories. Want to know when and what a customer might buy next? In this case, the business rules established by predictive modeling software can let you know. More generally, traditional marketing could never treat each customer as an individual, nor could it effectively create opportunities for a company to up-sell, repeat-sell, cross-sell, profit-sell or otherwise assist customer profit management. But automated business rules can accomplish this.

Processing Speed

The emergence of affordable computers processing vast amounts of data at lightning speed gives companies an important additional capability: the opportunity to engage the customer in real time. Marketing, according to the traditional rules, involved much preplanning and thinking about the 4Ps: product, price, promotion and placement. But it never provided a process view of customer access, engagement and retention. It never offered an opportunity to create new business and customer value when it really counts, in real time, when the customer is interacting with the company. Fast and affordable computers, databases, software and bandwidth have created an opportunity to combine granular marketing with real-time interaction in the mutual interests of customer and vendor.

Convergence

As discussed, the convergence of computing, communications, carriers and content has created entirely new marketing opportunities and, in the process, enabled the company to manage the customer relationship. Computing and communications technologies let companies deploy the insight they have gained from customer databases to interact with customers and do so economically. The Internet, as the most important manifestation of convergence, revolutionizes one-to-one contact, information dissemination and commercial interaction. The old marketing rules simply do not work very well in the context of the Internet and the individual customer.

In the era before pervasive technology, the marketer's traditional approaches to competitive engagement employed the selection of a target market and allocation of available resources to the so-called 4 Ps of marketing: product, price, promotion and placement (distribution). Technology has changed the basis for competition by breaking down the target market into the customers who individually comprise it and by fundamentally changing the 4 Ps of marketing. Now that most companies in most marketplaces are adopting this approach to marketing, how is a company to gain competitive advantage? The same capabilities that caused the demise of conventional marketing and enabled CRM also let a company target specific competitors and beat them.

The Discrete Customer

Technology has killed marketing because it destroyed the fundamental concepts used by marketers: target market selection, positioning and the 4Ps and it destroyed these concepts largely because every aspect of marketing can be made discrete by technology. Importantly, each customer can now emerge from the group to have his or her unique needs individually met. In so doing, competing has changed because the company must now win at the individual customer level, not by outselling the competitor, but by outenabling and outcollaborating with the customer. That is, the company must work with chosen customers and give them more capabilities than they have ever had, allowing them to achieve their objectives as they wish.

Traditional marketing broke down markets into groups in which customers had needs that were common, in the so-called market segments. But even within these segments, while customers had selected needs and some of their attitudes and perceptions in common, they tended to differ from one another in a number of material ways, many of them behavioral. Technology liberates the individual from the group and lets the company communicate with and serve each according to his or her uniqueness. Now technology lets the marketer distinguish among customers according to their importance and their behaviors and not just by what they say or how the marketer thinks they should be grouped with others. In business-to-business markets, customers that were relatively more important to the company always merited different treatment. Now technology makes it possible for all companies and the individual consumer to receive special attention as well.

In the process, the behavioral perspective on customers becomes more important than their attitudes and perceptions, the underpinning of traditional marketing. Technology lets marketers operate according to a stimulus-response model, focusing on the returns for the marketing programs. In the era of segment-based marketing, returns on expenditures were much harder to assess, and marketers resorted to complicated research methodologies to "prove" the efficacy of their advertising and promotional efforts. Now, technology lets the relationship marketer track fairly accurately the returns on spending.

In the era of the discrete customer, CRM involves not target markets and the 4 Ps of marketing, but customer selection and the 11 Cs, described in Figure 2-1.

Figure 2-1: The 4 Ps of Marketing Become the 11 Cs of CRM

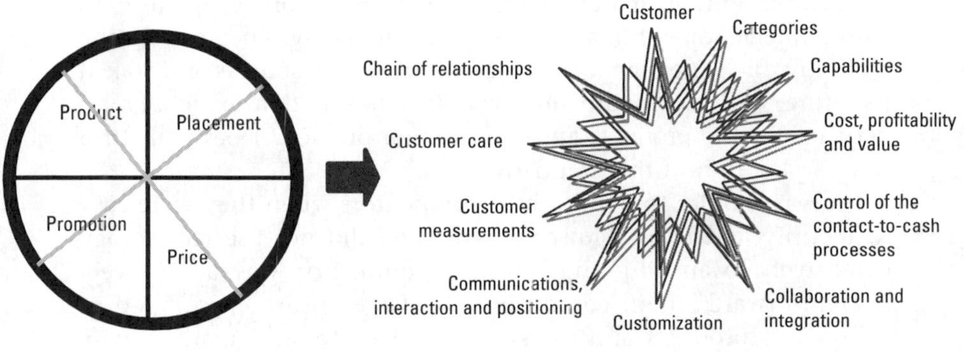

Product
Placement
Promotion
Price

Customer
Categories
Capabilities
Cost, profitability and value
Control of the contact-to-cash processes
Collaboration and integration
Customization
Communications, interaction and positioning
Customer measurements
Customer care
Chain of relationships

CRM strategies expanding on the 11 Cs outlined in Figure 2-1 help companies bond with the customers they have chosen to serve. But if all companies are beginning to operate according to these same rules, how is one to stand out? Relationship marketers need to pay attention to another, vitally important C, the management of which will create yet more challenge and higher rewards: Competition.

To manage competitors in this new era, companies must develop strategies for each of the 11 Cs in the context of the competitors they need to beat or those with which they wish to collaborate. But which competitors are the most important?

Focusing on Competitors

At the same time as companies seek to bond with individual customers, they must understand competitive threats in securing and retaining the customers they choose as the basis for their future. These threats might come from established, traditional competitors, new entrants or nontraditional competitors that begin to compete on scope, giving the customer more of what they want. In some cases, what customers want might be what you now provide, which could make an instant competitor out of another company that also supplies the needs of your customers. The challenge for the company is to recognize the potential for a threat before it emerges and to plan to win before the battle is engaged. Every war has been preceded by great planning. Wars are most typically won before they are ever fought, with the superiority of the plans and the focus of resources dictating who wins. Business wars are no different. Just as countries develop competitive scenarios, appoint people to shadow the enemy, profile leaders and get inside their heads, so do many companies.

The conduct of competitive intelligence in support of operations and, to a lesser extent, competitive strategy is well established. What is not well done in many companies is focusing on competitors to gain strategic, operational and real-time advantage in precisely the areas in which the company has committed its resources and staked its future. Which company must your firm beat to dominate the marketplace for the products and services you provide? Does your firm have a plan to beat this company?

It was simpler to plan to beat competitors when they were easy to identify and know, slower moving and did not use technology extensively. Managing the old-style competitor was a relatively straightforward affair comprising, in large measure, competitor analysis of products and markets and plans to shift market share from them to you. Today, when markets are individual consumers or businesses rather than whole segments, the old ways of managing competitors do not work. Now companies battle for each customer they choose to depend on for their future success. The methods for keeping specific customers and capturing competitors' customers are important considerations in the development of competitive strategy that works in today's environment of technology and CRM.

To return to the earlier question of which competitor needs to be beaten, one needs to ask what a competitor is. The answer is that it is a company that the customer sees as being able to supply goods and services that are substitutes for yours. Thus, your chosen customers can tell you who your competitors are. To think that you can define your competition by yourself is no more appropriate than defining customer needs in the absence of objective research.

Competitor Proliferation

If you open your wallet now, you will see another problem for the development and maintenance of customer relationships and of an effective, focused competitive strategy. How many credit cards do you have? How many other pieces of plastic are there? If your wallet is like mine, it is bursting at the seams with credit and loyalty cards for airlines, bookstores, gas stations, mass merchandisers, mass transit, phone companies, photography and video stores and library cards. It is a wonder that these overflowing wallets do not cause purse snatchers to stumble or men's pants to fall down.

Many companies use loyalty cards to track customer transactions. Some relationships are rewarded, but sometimes the rewards are pitiful or absent, even for important customers.[2] Generally, the customer has time and attention for only a small number of relationships. And remember that the plastic in your wallet is only one manifestation of the multitude of companies wanting your time, attention and business. Increasingly, the competition for this time and attention is making the video store a competitor of the gas station and the gas station a competitor of the bank.

Some firms limit this competition by joining networks of companies in different industry sectors, all with similar interest in developing

---

[2] One gas company invites customers to continually swipe their cards at the pump without providing any reinforcement for their behaviors. Customers cannot be too impressed with their feeble attempts to reward and reinforce behavior. Does the name Pavlov ring a bell?

customer loyalty. Examples include the Air Miles Reward Program and airlines' frequent flier points programs, such as Air Canada's Aeroplan. One consideration here is whether the company that is building the most brand equity is the network operator or the vendors.[3] Nevertheless, the formation of these networks creates new dimensions for competing and lowers the costs for managing individual customers in industries in which lifetime value may not justify independent initiatives.

Prioritizing Competitive Initiatives

We have discussed the fact that there are many competitors and many ways to engage them in battle, but it is essential to set priorities if the company is to use a competitor orientation to advance its business interests. Often, a way to understand competitive threats and opportunities for improvement is to examine the customers the company has just lost.

Companies lose as many as half their customers every five years on average, but many have been able to mask the churn of their existing customer base by emphasizing their sales growth. Just keeping the customers you have can save a significant amount because securing new accounts is extremely expensive. One vertical market software and solutions company has noted that it is focused on existing customers and will no longer court new accounts. This may be a little extreme for some companies, but the logic can be powerful. Simply increasing the retention rate can lead to dramatically improved profits. Research shows that a 5 percent improvement in customer retention can lead to a profitability improvement of 25 percent or more in industries such as software, industrial products distribution, insurance brokerage, business banking and auto service. In the case of credit card companies, the profits can more than double from this simple improvement in retention.[4] Additionally, it can cost six times more to secure a new customer than to serve an existing one.[5]

The battleground for winning the competitive war is in the mind of each *individual* customer you have chosen to serve for your mutual future. When that customer is a business, the battleground is a sort of "virtual mind" representing all the decision makers in the

---

[3] In preparation for an initial public offering for Aeroplan, the market valuation of this entity was estimated at around $1 billion, possibly more than the airline itself.

[4] Data from Bain Consulting.

[5] American Marketing Association.

account. The virtual mind to be won by your company includes the decision-making unit and its criteria for selecting a supplier in respect of issues such as collaboration, alignment and purchases.

Relating to Competitors

The main ways to improve share of customer, once core strategic capabilities are in place, are:

- beating competitors
- coexisting
- collaborating

General Motors, in developing its Internet strategy, also considered how best to beat competitors—whether to collaborate or concede to them.[6] GM considered five types of companies in addition to its most direct competitors, such as manufacturers like Ford and DaimlerChrysler. These additional competitors included portals, information providers, transactional companies, dealers and services companies. Portals are companies like AOL that provide a gateway to Web sites on the Internet. Information providers are one type of portal (also called an infomediary) that give consumers information about cars and prices, for example. Transaction companies may include infomediaries that can sell consumers a vehicle. Auto-By-Tel is one such company.

In addition to beating or collaborating with competitors, some companies may choose to acquire competitors or to coexist and accept them as they are. In the following, we briefly review selected issues for their implications on the competitor-driven company. Acquiring competitors need not be a lengthy discussion here, so we consider the other three areas, paying most attention to collaboration.

Beating Competitors

Many companies pay attention to beating competitors, and it is one of the main focuses of this book. See Chapter 7 for more on how companies can consider how to beat competitors in real time, outperform them, block them out and shut them down. Having reviewed this, though, we caution that a competitor focus in itself

[6] Marianne Kolbusak McGee, "Wake-Up Call." *CMP Media*, September 15, 2000.

should not limit a company by establishing boundaries on what it could be. Companies that define themselves by only their competitors may not be able to rise any higher than they. On the other hand, businesses that pay no attention to competitors may not last long enough to achieve their potential.

Companies traditionally have included a competitive strategy in their business plans, and most would agree that good plans should have some competitor considerations. However, if a competitive strategy becomes a serious focus for the business, the potential exists for a company to be defined and ultimately limited by its perspective of the competition. For example, if Bic defined itself as a pen company competing with the likes of Scripto, the firm might not have become a leader in disposable razors and lighters. Rather, Bic saw itself as a company in the business of making high volume consumer products with its plastics technologies, which enabled it to see opportunities and competitors more broadly.

New value creation is an important area for companies and especially those pursuing CRM strategies whereby the purpose of the company is to identify and create new value with individual customers. The competitor orientation adopted by most companies limits customer-specific innovation because it concentrates on markets and products rather than individual customers; it also measures success by market share rather than customer share.

You are probably familiar with the five forces of industry profitability, described in 1979 by Harvard's Michael Porter.[7] He noted that competition concerned:

1. management of competitive rivalry
2. threat of substitutes
3. threat of new entrants
4. bargaining power of customers
5. bargaining power of suppliers

Porter's views on these issues served companies well in an era when industry capacity could be managed. Today, that is very hard or even impossible to do, especially in the technology and service businesses that comprise so much of the global economy. In the era of CRM and customer-centric business models, Porter's five forces do not serve the company sufficiently because they do not talk to the issue of competitive advantage that comes from one-to-one relationships

[7] Michael Porter, *Competitive Strategy: Techniques for Analyzing Industries and Competitors*. New York: The Free Press, 1980.

and the creation of new value. In the era of CRM, companies beat specific competitors by creating new value, customer by customer and transaction by transaction. This has been much of the focus of the book to this point.

Coexisting

The second approach to competing is to peacefully coexist with competitors. This policy of laissez-faire can succeed under the following conditions:

- Industries are stable and profitable.
- There are significant barriers to entry.
- Companies share a common view of the future.
- Each company knows and accepts its role.

When these conditions exist—and there are not many arenas where they do—industry profitability can continue, and all companies can be rewarded. With little reason to disrupt the status quo, companies can live together more or less in harmony. Funeral services and some types of pharmaceuticals and resource industries can relate in this way. Here, when companies compete, it may be more for scarce resources than for customers. Oil companies, for example, compete aggressively for oil rights in specific territories but less so in getting customers to their gas pumps. When companies coexist passively, a firm has to consider whether or not a breakthrough strategy would reward shareholders more than pursuing the status quo. Generally, most already operating by these principles prefer to continue within the parameters of their historical role, leaving real innovation to newcomers.

There have been many occasions when companies did not appreciate an emerging competitor for what it was and chose to coexist with them when a more assertive position would have rewarded shareholders. In 1945, the Haloid Company, funded by a small grant from Battelle Memorial Institute, was researching photoconductivity innovation in Rochester, New York. Nearby Eastman Kodak was also in the business of imaging, albeit with photography. Kodak ignored its neighbor and under its very nose emerged a major corporation, which Haloid renamed as Xerox. Not only did Kodak miss out but IBM made a similar mistake. In the late 1950s, a consulting firm helped IBM to decide whether or not to acquire Xerox. It said that the world market for copiers would never exceed 5,000 units.

Sometimes companies, ignoring history, are condemning themselves to repeat it. Kodak could have led in digital imaging but is now just one of many companies in the arena. Xerox moved quicker to become digital but may be overlooking emerging companies that can create new value for its customers. For example, DeCopier[8] uses chemicals to remove copier toner and printing inks, including toner from copies made by Xerox. Companies wanting security do not need to shred their documents (which can be reassembled in any event) and they can benefit the environment by reusing paper.

Collaborating

Companies applying the principles of CRM know that they must bond with customers by collaborating to create new and mutual value. Many companies are applying these principles not only with customers, but also with other selected stakeholders such as employees, suppliers and distribution channel intermediaries. Few companies apply these concepts to competitors because they do not see a role for their rivals in serving their customers. Fearful of losing customers, companies try to control all aspects of value-creating processes. In some cases, it might be quicker, less expensive and to the advantage of individual customers to cooperate with competitors to do this together.

The term "co-opetition" has been coined[9] to describe the apparently paradoxical relationship of simultaneously competing and cooperating with competitors. However, there are few industries within which genuine co-opetition pertains today. One is the aerospace and defense industry, in which today's collaborators on one project may compete on another tomorrow. More typically, where co-opetition is cited as a business rationale for cooperation, it can be a veiled attempt by one company to prosper at the expense of another. For example, companies can cooperate and use the intelligence to compete at a different place or time, as has often happened in joint technology developments since the earliest days of computing. Some companies also gain advantage strategically, lever the relationships of their competitors and avert and delay a skirmish or battle that could do them harm today. A major US telephone operating company (telco) used the word "co-opetition" when it worked with Internet Service Providers (ISPs) while providing its own similar capability. In

[8] www.decopier.com

[9] Ascribed to Raymond Noorda, who founded Novell (in 1973), by Adam M. Brandenburger and Barry J. Nalebuff in their book *Co-opetition*. New York: Doubleday, 1996.

reality, the company provided customers with a complete solution that favored their own ISP. The problem with most co-opetition is that it is more about competition than cooperation.

In some corporations, cooperating with an enemy is the equivalent of traitorous conduct. For years, companies have created this image, and in so doing, may have blindfolded themselves to some of their strategic options. Not all competitors are equally bad, just as not all customers are good. If the CRM movement has taught us anything, it is that companies should identify and differentiate among their customers so that different value can be created for and with each. As yet, companies have not differentiated similarly among their competitors, separating the good from the bad. There are a number of reasons why this has not been done:

- *Competitors change.* While customers remain in focus, the competitive set within each customer can vary, and the competitive set between customers is even more likely to differ.
- *Core value is not defined.* Some companies have an excellent appreciation for the core value that is central to the firm's future and is not to be shared. Other companies have yet to fully describe where they will encourage collaboration and where they will not.
- *Complementarity is not determined.* Competitors can be complementary to your company in many areas, as discussed in Chapter 8. In association with a consideration of core value, some companies have not assessed where their customers would benefit from a broader scope of products and services and what the gaps are, whether for each customer or more generally. When companies do arrive at an understanding of where competitors could complement the firm, they sometimes arrive at the same notion and strategy simultaneously. Not long ago, broadcasters decided they needed to own and control some of the content on their network and lever this content on the Internet, leading to a stampede by broadcasters (and others) to acquire content companies, as AOL did with Time Warner.
- *Conditions change.* A company that your firm does not see as a competitor today could become a ferocious one tomorrow. Consider the impact of digital convergence and industry convergence and how companies that formerly were in different areas compete today. Banks compete with brokerage houses, telcos with cable television companies and software companies with broadcasters, to pick a few areas.

- *CRM has not yet achieved its potential.* Most companies want to see more progress with CRM before increasing complexity by introducing the notion of beating specific competitors in the minds of individual customers. This deferral may be precisely the reason some companies are not yet realizing CRM's possibilities and deepening customer relationships. Without a CRM vision and strategy and with no CRM plan and competitive context in their dealings with individual customers, some companies cannot help but underachieve on their CRM investments.
- *Culture remains unchanged.* Although much may change about a company and its environment, its views of competition often remain static. Competition is bad and competitors must be defeated, goes the conventional wisdom. As with so much in the counterintuitive world in which we find ourselves, wisdom is anything but conventional. There is no precedent for wisdom in this era, so decisions based exclusively on history may lead companies to the very opposite of what they want. For example, defeating a benign competitor completely may create new competitive challenges from new directions, a view developed early at Microsoft in its toleration of Apple. Today, companies would do much better if they did not use the word "generally" in front of any other word and certainly not in advance of competition. Few competitors are generally bad. Most have potential value to your customers and even to you. The key is to know when the competitor can add value for your shareholders—whether it is for certain of your individual customers or elsewhere in the value chain such as working together on R&D or cooperating for distribution.

Customers and Competitors: Look Both Ways

This chapter has reviewed selected issues in business that impact on the customer relationship and competition. As we saw, technology has destroyed the traditional approaches to marketing but has also created entirely new opportunities to cater to the needs of individual customers and beat specific competitors, creating new strategic possibilities both ways.

Companies focusing on their best customers stand to benefit significantly from simplification and cost management and the creation of value the customers want and often initiate. But by itself, this may not be sufficient to help a company to win. The principles of CRM are now increasingly well understood by many companies in the same industry. Sometimes they all identify the same customers and develop similar plans to bond with them. If the CRM plans are similar and all the companies have good people and similar financial resources, what then will ensure their relative success?

All business initiatives need competitive context because, without that, there is no assurance that the journey will lead to improved results relative to others in the industry. In the rush to implement CRM and other initiatives, some companies have paid insufficient attention to identifying who they must beat if they are to succeed. At the top of any industry pyramid, there is room for but one winner, and that company will have succeeded by simultaneously creating the value that chosen customers want and doing so in a manner that is competitively superior. Other winners may well have gained the top spot in the pyramid by identifying specific competitors to beat. Looking at customers, companies will be addressing opportunities associated with CRM and eCRM. Looking the other way—at competitors—they will adopt the principles of this book and target competitors for business advantage, increasing their competitive focus strategically, tactically and in real time.

Preparing to Compete

Employing tactics to beat the competition without having a competitive strategy is like looking for Atlantis without a map. You might find it, just as you might beat the competition, but your chances are slim in either case. While competitive strategy development should precede formulation of tactics for competing, there are five other preconditions that would greatly facilitate effective implementation for competitive advantage. These include:

1. Executive Support
2. Leadership for a Competitor Orientation
3. Training
4. People
5. Technology

Executive Support

Have a leading executive, preferably the president, provide visible support for a competitor targeting initiative. This support would ideally include tangible evidence of the person being invested in the outcome of the initiative, such as a white paper or reference in a key speech or communications with employees. The communications should stress that winning is not just a state of mind, important though this may be. The communications could go on to make a number of points, such as those at the commencement of this book and including the following:

- Winning means competing, and competing is a *process*.
- Winning includes CRM (and other key initiatives the company may be undertaking), but it is much more.
- Winners win against defined losers.
- Winning occurs in the minds of selected customers, transaction by transaction, contact by contact, until bonds cement and extend the relationship.

The president should also be careful not to lessen the firm's attention to customers by focusing on competitors—the last thing that is being suggested. To maintain focus on both areas the president should note that the intent is to be customer-focused *and* competitor-driven and that, just as the company is focused on each customer as an individual, so, too, should it now consider each competitor as a specific threat or opportunity. In short, executives should seek some cultural transformation, the most important ingredient of change being their own visible commitment to being competitor-driven.

Leadership for a Competitor Orientation

Cultural change starts at the top of organizations. The president who wants the company to beat a defined enemy can provide leadership to those who report directly to him or her and establish expectations from their departments that have both competitive context and content. For example, he or she can require intelligence on competitors in subordinate's monthly activity reports and for competitive context, from the task forces led by the company's executives. Having identified the main competitor the company is to beat, the president can call for plans to win in each product market and measures that track the company's progress. With this intelligence, the president has the potential to monitor, track, coordinate and manage competitor-focused tactics.

Taking this leadership to create a competitor orientation further still, the president can demand that the company has a clear competitor focus in all its main initiatives and also in the day-to-day activities of most personnel. Hiring a new chief financial officer? Look for one who is better than the one at the targeted competitor. As mentioned before, if you cannot find a better one, hire theirs. Deciding which software to deploy? As part of the evaluation decision, consider what the targeted competitor uses and how the software you are looking at will be better than theirs. If it will not be better or more cost effective, buy the software your competitors has. In short, every position and every activity has the potential for competitor comparison, and the president can ensure that this comparison be made explicitly in internal reporting. If employees know who the enemy is, and have some guidance about how to focus their role for competitive advantage, each staff member will make a contribution to the overall war effort. The introduction of a competitor orientation into everything the company does can be powerful indeed.

Training

Train staff at all levels in the company about what competitiveness means for each person. What actions and behaviors are appropriate for, and expected of, each employee? What should they *not* do? More generally, how can the company profit by targeting specific competitors and the competitor's customers and opportunities? How can the individual make a contribution to the initiative overall, for the company, to their division and to their product or service line?

Competitor targeting training can take a number of forms, but it essentially seeks to inject a competitor orientation into all the main value-added tasks of employees. If they are responsible for R&D, what is the competitor's level of productivity (such as number of patents per employee)? What percentage of the company's sales this year are from products or services that did not exist three years ago, and what is the percentage that applies to the targeted competitor? And so on.

Simply put, everybody in every position has to understand and apply competitor intelligence on the company you wish to outperform, and each person should ensure that relevant data are considered and applied so that the company can align to beat the targeted enemy to win and keep and develop the customers you value most. To facilitate this, each person should be trained in the use of the company's databases for customer and competitor knowledge so that this information can contribute to the individual's assessments and actions.

Training should be provided to ensure that staff report on the competitive context of their internal work and similarly for their other important tasks such as performance appraisals and compensation structure and plans. When employees ask the company for money for an initiative they wish to undertake, they should include competitive considerations with their financial, market, operational and mandate justifications. "How will this initiative make us better than the targeted competitor?" is a good question to ask before approving any investment.

People

Employees make a huge difference in developing strong customer relationships and consistently beating defined competitors, and leaders, with their plans show the way. Technology (discussed next) plays a key role in supporting people, but at the end of the day, people, effectively using the technology and dealing with customers and other stakeholders, remain critical ingredients for business success. Companies focused on CRM and competitor targeting should consider their human resources in a new light, as though they were customers with competitive choices, which of course they do have. Employees, like customers, should be singled out for individual treatment according to the value they want and the value they can and will create. Those employees who matter most merit special care, just as the company's best customers do. Most companies offer their best employees rewards and recognition, with an occasional promotion as part of both. But the company focused on a competitively superior customer relationship does more, such as the following:

- Employee-centric development plans allow employees to have individual, personal plans to help them along their own unique journey in a way that matters to them while creating shareholder value.
- Employee reward and recognition recognizes achievements that contribute to beating specific competitors.
- Employee-centric databases go beyond traditional human resource information system (HRIS) to describe the person, track his or her progress, quantify the value each creates for the firm and project the value of the individual over an extended period.
- Processes, customers and roles are matched to specific people, with the databases playing an important role in the matching and identification of skills-upgrading potential.
- Employees with a broader scope of knowledge are able to function effectively in many areas.

- Technology can be used to make the employee more effective, not just more efficient, such as prompting questions for the bank teller in real-time conversation with the customer.
- The culture and leadership is geared to fostering trust and cohesiveness.

Identify the profile of the personalities the company should ideally recruit. Some companies hire for attitude and train recruits for skill. They know who is an employee of the company when they first meet the person. Yahoo! is such a company. It has a four-point basis for hiring the talent that make opportunities happen: people skills, spheres of influence (sort of like talent magnets, each with an ability to attract good people), "zoom in, zoom out" (having relentless focus, with perspective), and passion (having the drive and will to do something they consider valuable). Perhaps your firm could also have profile elements such as these. In addition, your firm could consider identifying individuals at competitors who could be potential recruits. Profiles developed of people at competitors can also be used to help project what the company might do and should be included in the competitive intelligence initiative, as discussed in Chapter 5.

It is good to have employees who maintain good relationships with customers and it is even better if these employees also have excellent relationships with the company. Without the last-mentioned, companies have difficulty in securing strategic alignment of their personnel and processes. Measure the state of this employee relationship today (think more broadly than simply measuring employee satisfaction), set targets for the quality of these relationships and manage and measure your progress. Understand employee's competitive choices by undertaking compensation surveys of targeted competitors. Know the competitor's working environment, including the culture and the expectations their managers have of employees. Identify the weaknesses of working there relative to your own company. Have a plan to help the employees according to their unique perspectives and needs as individuals.

When a competitor's employee joins your firm, make a big internal communications splash. Allude to the reasons the employee joined your firm, including some direct quotes. With care, you can demonstrate that the competition is a bad place to work. In one instance, a major technology company has long characterized their main competitor as a firm run by Darth Vader and somewhat akin to an evil empire. Employees have bought the story and Darth himself does not help his own cause by promoting family members, firing good people and being somewhat erratic.

Technology

Technology has long provided potential for competitive advantage simply by deploying tools that make the company more efficient and effective compared with competitors. Now technology can do more.

Bonding with Customers, while Shutting Competitors Out

Bonding with customers is an important objective of CRM[10], which, when well executed, has the potential to not only create new value with customers but keep competitors from doing likewise. Customers generally prefer to keep things simple by narrowing down the number of suppliers and the types of technology they use. When considering their next major initiative, they are more likely to work with one company than another based on a variety of factors, including prior experience and vendor capabilities. Over time, the company that assists its customers to achieve their business and personal objectives is more likely to cause the door to be shut on targeted competitors. One company in the intensely competitive digital imaging industry offers customers the opportunity to engage the company and monitor the progress of each order using the Internet. Once familiar and comfortable with this process, customers are less likely to be interested in switching to competitors. Not only does the self-serve capability of the store front appeal to customers who now know how their orders are progressing, but it also reduces the vendor's costs, and allows them to free up customer service personnel.

Monitoring Competitors

Develop a plan to monitor and analyze competitors and to integrate this understanding with your planning processes. Monitor competitors to understand them as a company. Analyze their market, customer, operation and financial position. Track the senior management who work for the competitors. Actions such as these can help you predict their actions. This is the subject of competitive intelligence, covered in detail in Chapter 5.

Targeting Competitors' Consumers

While companies have the ability with or without technology to target the business customers of competitors, technology makes it possible for

[10] For a detailed road map for implementing CRM, see my earlier book *Relationship Marketing: New Strategies, Techniques and Technologies to Win the Customers You Want and Keep Them Forever*, John Wiley & Sons, 1998.

companies to target the individual consumers of the competitor. Perhaps you have visited the local supermarket and received coupons when you paid for your groceries. Some of those coupons were likely selected by a computer after your groceries were scanned, with the value also determined by the products you chose. Do you buy Crest? Perhaps Colgate wants to win you over to its product next time and is prepared to provide you with an extra incentive in the form of a high value coupon. Some car companies buy lists of car owners of specific makes, models and vehicle ages to target the owners of competitors' products and use direct marketing to engage the targeted customer in a dialogue.

Competing tactically and in real time requires considerable technology. For example, technology helps customers to help themselves. It allows salespeople to be up-to-date in their information about the customer, their contact with the firm and the competition. It enables the customer contact center to be able to recognize the importance of each call, know what needs to be communicated and help the customer. Technology should be deployed in the context of customer relationship management and competitor targeting. In short, use technology to develop capabilities that can aid implementation of competitive tactics. These capabilities could include:

- Competitor Databases
- Intranet Access to Competitive Data
- Software
- Data Security

Competitor Databases

Establish competitor databases to track competitors' performance with respect to key success factors for each customer you have chosen for the future of your company. If one customer wants his or her suppliers to provide simple solutions at low prices and to be more focused on transactions than on relationships, track your performance relative to that of competitors. Tracking should assess what the customer thinks or what is going on in the organization's collective mind—the cumulative and balanced perspectives of the people who make up the decision-making unit.

Intranet Access to Competitive Data

Offer Intranet access to staff so they can share common intelligence, third-party and in-house documents, allowing reports to be based on consistent data and giving employees more time to analyze data rather than develop it.

Software

Implement software to track and monitor competitors—such as new product introduction, media communications, positioning and prices—and to communicate price comparisons to sales and other staff who set prices.[11] Track potential customers who have visited competitors' Web sites before they enter the company's own site. By putting cookies[12] on a user's computer, companies can observe the progress of visitors to and through their site. They know who returns and can track and manage the actions of customers in real time, providing content based on learning about the visitor's interests and preferences. Companies try to do this without being too obvious.

The customer who has visited a competitor's site and picked up a cookie there, can also be tracked and managed, in this case, with a view to ensuring that your company wins in the purchase decision. For example, if GM knew you had just looked at a Lincoln on the Ford site, it could entice you to test-drive a Cadillac and offer an incentive it knows will appeal to you by examining other cookies on your computer. Companies can use intelligence from Internet advertising, measurement and research companies such as DoubleClick (www.doubleclick.net) to collect information about prospects and customers of competitors. Some companies collect data such as:

- The Internet address (IP), which can allow you, with a bit of work, to determine the geographic location, company, type and size of the organization. The IP network identification is a 32-bit number, which identifies not only the network but the individual computer.
- Internet communications from which information such as the browser, operating system, browser language and Internet service provider can be determined.
- How visitors move through a company's Web site, including the pages they view.

---

[11] Examples of software that accomplish this purpose are referenced in Chapter 3.

[12] According to Foldoc (The Free On-line Dictionary of Computing), a cookie is a handle, transaction ID, or other token of agreement between cooperating programs. The claim check you get from a dry-cleaning shop is a perfect mundane example of a cookie, the only thing it's useful for is to relate a later transaction to this one (so you get the same clothes back).

Data such as these allow a company to target visitors to competitors' Web sites in addition to their own. Most companies are particularly concerned about increasing the conversion rate of their visitors and the repurchases of their existing customers. Part of the solution is to engage visitors in a competitively differentiated communication, with customized content and positioning based on their demonstrated behaviors, including site visits and page views.

Data Security

Develop levels of data security that have an appropriate balance between keeping secrets confidential and sharing intelligence within the firm. It is obviously important for a company to keep its secrets secret but it is also important for employees to be well-informed and able to use the competitor data. Of course, access control is needed, but do not go overboard. As a rule of thumb, have less security than you are inclined to implement, especially for publicly available and purchased reports. Your own data, reports, plans and other documents that could have significant impact on your or the competitor's business may well merit higher levels of security, with the most critical competitor-oriented documents accessible only on a need-to-know basis.

Databases, Privacy and Security

Here we consider using customer data for competitive advantage, as well as selected concerns for the privacy of the individual and security of the data.

Databases

Databases carry with them the potential for scrutiny in ways you may not have considered. Some countries have laws that allow individuals and companies to review your databases if they have reason to believe that you are maintaining information on them. Consult with your lawyers about the potential for competitors (and customers) to demand a review of your data and reports, and make appropriate allowances in the design and development of your database environment and security processes, policies and procedures. You might also consider asking to review competitors' data on you, which could be very revealing.

Data inducted into a company's intelligence system should be used for what it was intended and could be destroyed if it has no further use. Legal advice should be sought regarding the building of any database, particularly those of a sensitive nature such as those in which law enforcement or other authorities may have interest.

Because the customer typically has a legal right to see the databases you maintain, you might as well let this happen so that errors can be corrected and fears allayed. Companies can help avoid customer concern by using customer data so that it does not provoke a response. For example, sending the customer a newsletter including both standard and customized, but not personalized, content is one way to help avoid the appearance of knowing too much. I stayed at a hotel where I saw a number of advertisements that had my name on a card held by one of the actors, inviting me to buy. I was both in awe at the technology that did this and was concerned about the use of my name in this way. Companies should dumb down their use of data to avoid concerns such as these.

Some companies use software called "spyware" to better understand their customers and those of their competitors.[13] We are not advocating its use here but mention it because others might be using this software to better understand you. Spyware may be resident right now on your machine, placed there when you approved a license agreement, which allowed this software to be installed without you thinking about the purpose or nature of this little application.[14] And if you try to uninstall the software that does this monitoring, the main software application you thought you were buying may not work. This can be the case for so-called ad-bots, which place customized advertisements on your computer. Some software surreptitiously or silently placed on your computer may interfere with other software, may not be removed when the main application with which it was installed is removed and could allow hackers to gain entrance to your machine. Companies and astute personal computer users guard against some of these nefarious possibilities by using firewalls.

The following companies provide user-sourced data to on-line advertisers, agencies and others and some of them may be able to offer interesting opportunities to target competitors' customers.

---

[13] While software that operates without the user's knowledge, including spyware, has the potential to compromise some aspects of privacy, in some cases, this may also be the price that users are quite prepared to pay in order to receive benefits from the software company or their partners.

[14] Software license agreements, which customers approve, have many clauses and terms, so that the existence of surreptitious software is often not highlighted and its purpose not immediately apparent.

Whichever company you work with, consider carefully the implications for the privacy of data, both as used by the on-line agency and within your own firm. Companies that may potentially be helpful for customer data include Radiate (www.radiate.com), which gathers user information in many ways and forms and may work with online media companies such as Adforce, Adsmart, Advertising.com, DoubleClick, Flycast and 24/7 Media to help provide personalization and customization of advertising and other aspects of the experience. Some examples of Radiate's data gathering include the company's own software, which, when installed in association with their advertising technology, establishes a unique identifier. Radiate takes information from software companies and individuals that use its advertising technology in their application. Radiate may ask the user for other information in association with their software, such as name, e-mail address, phone and fax number, address, tax ID or Social Security Number and Web site.

With the user's permission, Radiate gathers demographic and personal data, both of which are aggregated for use by advertisers and may lead to mailings from the company and others. When it processes software registrations, Radiate has information on the credit card, name, company name, address, e-mail address and phone number, which may also result in mailings being sent to the information supplier.

Acxiom Corp. (www.acxiom.com) also collects customer data, creates a single view of the customer across the enterprise, helps companies recognize customers when they interact with the company and communicates as they each prefer. People provide Acxiom with information willingly when they register to receive information, a free trial, subscribe to products and services or participate in a contest, for example. Acxiom gathers information such as the person's name, address, telephone number, e-mail address, type of business, credit card number and other personal information.

Comet Systems (www.cometsystems.com) provides cursors that customize the look of a computer. Sometimes associated with software such as this is a unique identifier. The identifier can facilitate, for example, counting of visits to sites that are part of a software firm's marketing initiative.

Other sources of customer data that can be integrated into a thorough view of the customer include government records on an individual's personal, professional, financial and litigation history. For example, information such as birth, marriage and divorce, professional accreditation, liens and property ownership is available in the public domain. Companies such as Acxiom, DoubleClick, Equifax,

Experian and TransUnion combine records from sources such as these, credit reports, product warranty cards and consumer surveys to develop detailed customer profiles.[15]

Privacy

Privacy is obviously a major concern of customers. Some unscrupulous vendors, while assuring customers that the private information they provide will be treated as such, have allegedly shared that data with third parties.[16] The company that does not address privacy concerns seriously will find itself at odds with the people who provide the data, the media, lawmakers and legislation.[17] Yet the data individuals supply can be vital for the company wishing to develop closer relationships with individual customers and the customers of competitors, especially for companies marketing consumer goods and services. One way of limiting backlash from consumers and others is to be fully open and explicit in all communications and use of data. When asking customers and prospects for data, state how it will be used and make sure that the company has the ability to keep its promises. Highlight the application and purpose of the data request in the end-user license agreement, even when the primary software vendor is another company. Have strict policies to retain users' trust, and communicate these. There is no such thing as overcommunication in respect of the privacy interests of users.

As can be seen, by monitoring customers' behaviors and linking this with other data, a company can know a great deal about clients that can be used to add value to the relationship and defeat targeted competitors. In the right hands, this information can be helpful to the customer, but in the wrong hands or used inappropriately, the customer's interests could be compromised. For example, before issuing life or disability insurance, a smiling representative of the insurance company plunges a needle into your arm to draw blood for analysis. Too much fat in your diet? Cholesterol measures are there for all to scrutinize and for inferences to be made. Telephone companies watch long-distance calling patterns and customize call plans for the particular caller. Say an employee of the phone company recognizes that you call overseas often and phones your home to offer

[15] John Rendleman, "Customer Data Means Money," *Information Week*, August 20, 2001.

[16] A case to this effect is pending in Missouri, according to *eCompany*, with details provided in the November 2000 issue, p. 56.

[17] Such as the U.S. *Gramm-Leach-Bliley Act*, passed in November 1999, which includes privacy provisions.

a deal on calls to a certain country. Your spouse answers and begins to wonder about the calls, which may have been of a private nature.

Sound far-fetched? Consider that your bank account files, credit charges, post office box numbers and contents, social security earnings, safe deposit box contents, phone call logs and IRS records are all available as commodities, from private investigators and others willing to obtain this information for you—or someone else.[18] And much more information can be obtained using perfectly legitimate means, as we have discussed. Companies can and do buy your motor vehicle records to get your address, birth date, height, weight and the model of the car you own. If you have moved, change-of-address information is available from the post office. The record of your creditworthiness is available from credit bureaus. Your shopping habits and the goods you buy are known to retailers from their checkout scanners. Your reading habits can be obtained from the subscription lists of publishers. Loyalty cards can tell the marketer much more about where you fly and stay, and what you buy. Call-detail recorders let the hotel know who you called when you last stayed there. They also track the movies you watched. New technology enables your face's features to be digitized and recorded, then singled out from high-resolution video of crowd scenes. Car rental and other companies are installing devices to track your car's location and your cell phone allows your whereabouts to be established, too. Your computer's new operating system could soon enable tracking of transactions and Web site visits with even more efficiency. Big Brother—or an unscrupulous company, perhaps your competitor—really could be watching. And now wireless communications are creating new dimensions of challenge for people wanting to protect their privacy from those able to monitor their transmissions.

The boundaries of what can be watched are extending, not just with wireless, but also in a number of other dimensions. Biometrics — software that matches facial measurements from a database with camera observations—has the potential to track your every move. E-mail and Internet surveillance software is being widely used to track e-mails between people and monitor visits to chat rooms, page views, uploads and downloads on the Internet. Software from companies such as Omniquad, SoftEyes and SpectorSoft monitors what you have on your computer screen and more.[19] Shareware and inexpensive software is

[18] Jerry Rothfeder, "Invasions of Privacy," *PC World*, November, 1995.

[19] SpectorSoft's software records computer screen displays, incoming and outgoing e-mails, all key-strokes and Web site views, and monitors chats. It automatically takes snapshots of the screen, from once per second to once every few minutes. Omniquad has similar softwarre to this. It also has software to examine system activity and develops a log of past actions for inspection.

available to let you monitor a computer by secretly logging keystrokes and sending a log file to your e-mail address. In short, Big Brother, snoop, supplier, customer or Uncle Sam is or could be watching. For example, the FBI's Carnivore[20] software analyzes e-mail for its content, ostensibly in search of unlawful material. Because of the packet switching nature of Internet Protocol (IP), the software can only separate lawful and unlawful communications after it vacuums and reviews all the e-mails from an Internet Service Provider, including those from perfectly legitimate correspondents. We are assured Carnivore will only be used to learn about those who are breaking the law. Rest assured!

Security

It is hard to place limits on competitive behavior, but boundaries do indeed need to be established. Research has shown that some companies pursue unorthodox or illegal initiatives with the justification that that their competitors must be doing it, so, to be competitive, the company has to do likewise. One executive pronounced himself at war with his competition. Any action, he said, was justified to beat them. When pressed, he affirmed that he would do anything to win, even blackmail, extortion or planting a spy on a competitor's payroll. Company policies need to be established, communicated and enforced, or the legitimacy of the company is at risk.

If you think everyone in your company should know—in the interests of a more open culture—accept the possibility that some of the information sharing may help competitors. The reverse may be equally true. The information base from which employees frame their decisions will be narrow indeed if all the company's secrets are kept closed to them. In the interests of balancing these two perspectives, you should consider rating information according to need to know, such as what levels of security are required for specific types of information. Do not entrust the categorizing of the information to security professionals because, if they have their way, they might stamp top secret on everything.

Consider having information security plans in three areas: physical, electronic and process. Traditional security professionals should be responsible for the plans to secure the physical premises, while IT personnel should develop data and technology security plans.

[20] Recently, Carnivore was renamed DCS1000.

Finally, plans should be developed to ensure that personnel are sensitized to the potential damage they might cause by giving away secrets inadvertently, such as at conferences or over the telephone. The head of the department with competitor analysis and action responsibilities should review the plans from the various areas.

The Business Case

As the company prepares to adopt a greater emphasis on competitors, senior management typically requests a plan for the activity and a business case for any associated investments. The need for a plan is clear and this book provides ways to assist in this planning. The development of a business case is more tricky, particularly if management expects that the investment will be based on additional revenues or a targeted level of customer or market share. While one can quantify this in detail, it has been my experience that it is better to have a competitor targeting expenditure considered an investment in strategic capability and a fundamental requirement of the business. One can demonstrate that it is reasonable that the company will earn out the required investment by exceding a specific level of sales, but it can complicate the business case by making very specific revenues estimates. Once one becomes embroiled in debates regarding revenue, the investment process will be delayed, and an opportunity to engage in a higher-level strategy will be lost. More specifically, resist a temptation to respond to questions such as, "By how much will our market share increase if we fund this initiative with $X?" Questions such as these are usually posed by financially oriented people who want to manage with facts. You might be tempted to ask what the return on investment (ROI) is on financial or business planning—but resist. Instead, seek management consensus that the plan that has been developed will be good for the company for a number of strategic and financial reasons.

When developing the plan and investment requirement, do not focus on the need for more competitive intelligence even if your company has not paid sufficient attention to it. Concentrate more on the opportunities and approaches associated with beating specific, defined competitors, especially to win the customers you cherish most. This is more likely to engage management and secure support than a detailed review of a plan for a competitive intelligence system, for example.

This chapter provided some considerations for the necessary preparations a company could make before it plans to target competitors. In Chapter 3: The New Competition, we confirm that a competitor focus has the potential to increase a company's revenues and shareholder value. The chapter goes on to discuss the changing nature of competition and the benefits of being among the first to focus on individual customers and specific competitors as a source of shareholder value.

CHAPTER 3

The New Competition

"A man cannot be too careful in the choice of his enemies."[1]
—Oscar Wilde

Before we explore specific ways to assess and beat targeted competitors, we first confirm that a competitor focus has the potential to increase revenues and shareholder value. That is, while we know that competition is important, the link between a competitive initiative and shareholder value should be understood if the company is to invest resources on this pursuit. More than this, many executives have stock options as a component of their compensation, so shareholder value is doubly important to them. Therefore, it is important for the marketer to be in a position to articulate the linkage and potential for a competitive focus to create new business value for the company.

This chapter goes on to discuss the changing nature of competition and the benefits of being among the first to focus on individual customers and specific competitors as a source of shareholder value.

Shareholder Valuation

By focusing on competitors, a company can increase profits and accelerate profitable growth, both of which will be readily noticed by

---

[1] Oscar Wilde, *The Picture of Dorian Gray*, 1981.

shareholders as increased value. Although there have been periods in overheated economies when the rationale of stock valuation was sometimes hard to fathom, over the long haul, two issues stand out as meriting attention for business strategy and operations as the key drivers for financial performance:

- Lever the firm's assets and generate operating efficiencies.
- Grow the company profitably.

Firstly, a competitive focus can help the company gain increased efficiency. This can be achieved by understanding why a targeted competitor has secured better financial performance and shareholder valuation. By closely examining the makeup of a targeted competitor's profitability, returns on investment and shareholder perceptions, the company can address opportunities to build its own performance. For example, IBM might notice that Dell uses fewer assets in the generation of revenues, operating as it does as a somewhat virtual company. IBM might then decide to replicate some of the learnings.

Secondly, the company can grow faster and even more profitably by paying attention to selected competitors. Not only can it understand how to improve profitability by carefully analyzing competitors, but it can identify weaknesses in targets that it can exploit, leading to accelerated growth. Thus, Hewlett-Packard may determine that Dell's direct sales business model, while an advantage to some customers, may not appeal to those wanting a more comprehensive solution than computers alone. This might lead HP to focus on account and relationship management benefits when targeting some of Dell's business customers.

Thirdly, the company may be able to weaken targeted competitors and strengthen itself simultaneously. Hiring away key personnel from the competitor might accomplish this, and so will firing unprofitable customers. Not only will you save money by losing them, but some will go to the targeted competitor and become a drain on their profits. Your company will thus achieve improvements in your financial performance while weakening that of the competitor.

Opportunities from a Competitor Orientation

CEO and other executives who are being compensated partly through stock options, in part for creating shareholder value, will be particularly receptive to opportunities to build shareholder value. The following may provide additional ammunition for any business case you might wish to assemble in support of a greater competitor orientation and a focus on specific competitors to complement the customer orientation that is likely already a focus of your company.

It can readily be demonstrated that a company will experience a rise or fall in sales next year according to the aggregate change in customers' purchases less the change in competitors' sales.[2] There are three main ways to improve your sales through ongoing operations,[3] as described in Figure 3-1.

Figure 3-1: Improving Sales

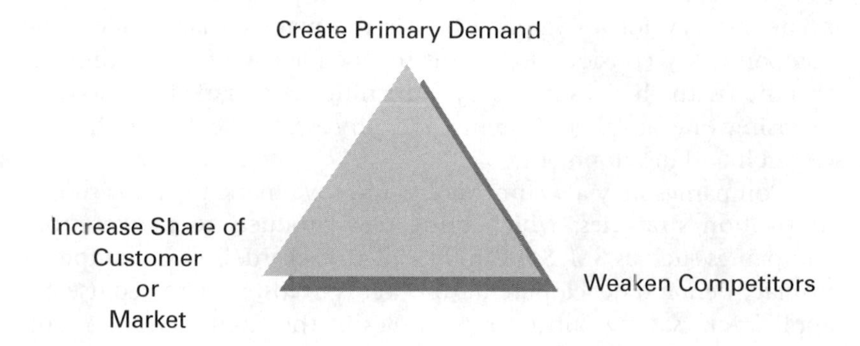

[2] Consider an equation that balances the sales from an industry (inclusive of distribution channel intermediaries) to customers in a marketplace over a lengthy period (i.e., no inventory buildup or depletion effects): Sales made by suppliers in an industry = Purchases made by customers. Let us number the companies in an industry and call the sales made this year by company one S_1, sales by company two S_2, and so on. Similarly, if we number the customers and use a similar convention for purchases, then C_1 denotes purchases by customer one this year, C_2 are purchases by customer two, etc. The above equation may be rewritten as follows, where "n" denotes the sales by the nth company or purchases by the nth customer: $S_1 + S_2 + S_2 + ... + S_n = C_1 + C_2 + C_3 + ... + C_n$. Projecting ahead for next year, we could adopt the same terminology, except this time we use the letter T to denote next year: $S_{1T} + S_{2T} + S_{3T} + ... + S_{nT} = C_{1T} + C_{2T} + C_{3T} + ... + C_{nT}$. Subtracting equation (2) from equation (1) yields, after some rearranging: $(S_{1T} - S_1) = (C_{1T} - C_1) + (C_{2T} - C_2) + (C_{3T} - C_3) + ... + (C_{nT} - C_n) - (S_{2T} - S_2) - (S_{3T} - S_3) - (S_{nT} - S_n)$. The points made in this section can be derived from this equation.

[3] Mergers and acquisitions and other structural changes also increase sales, but not through ongoing operations.

Create Primary Demand

The first approach is to ensure that customers in the marketplace, in aggregate, buy more next year compared to this one. There are a number of ways of doing this:

All Customers

The life cycle of many products and services is shortening. Markets are developed rapidly, and new products are launched to replace the old ones. Once most customers have an opportunity to buy the company's existing products and those of competitors, the firm can consider building the market as a whole by creating primary demand from all customers so that it can benefit. This is an especially appropriate strategy for a company that is the market share leader. The company may consider doing this independently of competitors or together with them, such as by launching an e-marketplace, cross-licensing one another's patents and processes or collaborating on research and development.

Companies may also innovate to improve market share. Product innovation strategies, which bring new products to market from companies such as 3M, Sony and Hewlett-Packard, is one example of primary demand development. Another is to foster increased use per application, say by putting more holes in the Comet cleanser can. Companies can also create additional or alternative applications such as by using baking soda to remove odors in carpets as well as in the refrigerator or by encouraging customers to drink Coke at breakfast, when other beverages are consumed more often.

Chosen Customers

An alternative approach that is appropriate if your company is not presently the market share leader is to create primary demand for or with those customers for which the potential is greatest to secure the largest increase in purchasing demand. In this case, companies choose the customers with which they will innovate and collaborate in this process. In business-to-business markets, this involves paying special attention to the best companies such as the largest ones or those making a significant effort to break through. Thus, in Canada, companies like NCR pay close attention to the individual purchase requirements of the five main financial institutions that dominate the industry because these organizations comprise the majority of demand for NCR's technology.

Companies focusing on consumer markets should also pay attention to their best customers. Identifying best customers and prospects is a central underpinning for the development of a relationship marketing strategy and is now widely practiced, especially in consumer services such as airlines, hospitality, car rental and retail.

Competitors' Customers

A company could also create primary demand for the customers of targeted competitors. This has two main benefits: near-term sales improvement and longer-term market success against weakened competitors. By winning over the best customers of selected competitors, the company challenges the source of the competitor's success—their revenues. A competitor successfully targeted in this manner will not only relinquish customer position but will also be weakened more generally in the market, especially once the change in momentum becomes apparent to all.

Increase Share of Customer and Market

Some customers are much more important to a company's success than others, and it should strive to build its share of customer with them. This means the company needs to displace from its best customers all competitors and particularly those that it has targeted to beat. Many companies try to displace competitors from customers even when customers have little reason to switch. While this can be done, it is often costly. Often, it is better for a company to position itself favorably in respect to future possibilities. That is, among the most important ways for building customer share is the attention a company gives to winning share of the customer's future spending. By positioning the company to win future business from chosen customers, the company can transfer customer share over time.

Before deciding how to increase customer share, a company should ask two main questions: which customers and which competitors? The main customers are those who represent the core of your business, the ones you have identified as important after a financial and strategic assessment. The main competitors from which to shift customer share are the ones your customer considers important, especially for their next purchase. These competitors might be not the traditional ones but perhaps emerging firms and others that offer substitutes for the products or services you sell.

There are, of course, a number of ways for improving customer and market share, and we discuss many of these later in this book.

Weaken Specific Competitors

Ensure that the customers you have chosen to focus on will buy more from you in the future by increasing the perceived and real gap between your company and specific, designated losers that you will create. These losers will be created in the marketplace account by account, customer by customer, and over the longer term, for each of the underlying strategic drivers of the business such as research and development, manufacturing, information technology and other capabilities.

While competition in the market and even within specific customers is important for the company, it is at least as important for the company to compete successfully for the capabilities that will result in marketplace dominance and winning and keeping chosen customers.

Individual Customers, Specific Competitors

Yesterday's competitive battle was to win markets and market segments, to shift share of market or share of market segment from the competition to your company. Competitors sought to outsegment one another, looking to create new relevance for customers while continuing to operate according to the paradigm of productization and packaging for products, pricing and communications. As we have mentioned, technology has changed the rules of marketing and made it possible and even necessary to serve the individual customer as though each were a separate market. This, then, is the ultimate segment—the segment of one. The new challenge here is to understand the mind of each *important* customer, the ones you have selected to serve as the basis for your future. Then the opportunity is to manage the attitudes and behaviors of these chosen customers to the advantage of your company compared with the alternatives the customer has in his or her mind, which represent specific competitors you must overcome to win.

There are a number of challenges implicit in this statement:

- How do you get to know individual *consumers* well enough to influence their attitudes and behaviors?
- How do you understand and manage the complex decision-making processes in many *companies* (as opposed to consumer marketplaces mentioned above)?

First, knowing the individual consumer requires identification of the customers on whom you choose to focus. The competitive war starts in the minds of customers, who may now, in this age of technology, be considered to be individual customers. And the battles continue, likely without end. Now, we must establish in whose minds the battles of this war are to be engaged. A number of books pay close attention to the question of customer selection, so we provide only an overview here, setting the stage for a discussion about competition.

Figure 3-2: Important Customers

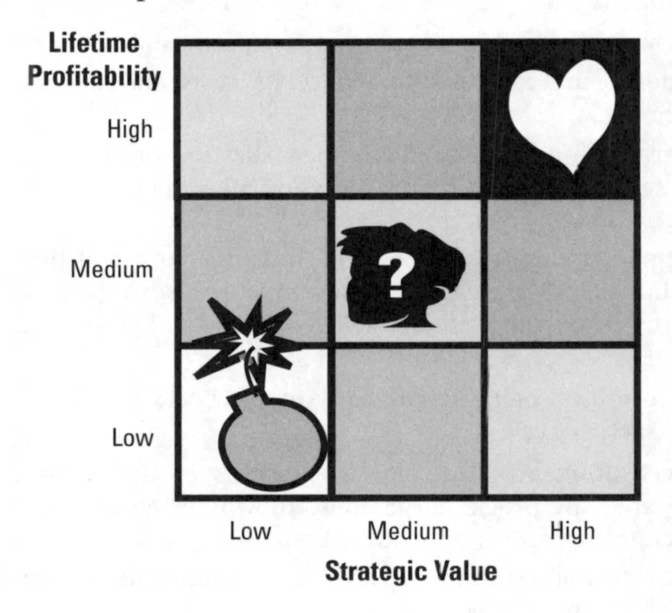

Identifying Important Customers

Some customers merit more attention than others according to their value to the organization. Consider your customers in terms of those that are most profitable to your company today and their strategic value to the future of the company as described in Figure 3-2, which charts customers' lifetime profitability and strategic value.

Lifetime profitability is determined from a consideration of the following, for each customer:

- lifetime revenues, including an assessment of the potential for existing revenues to be grown

- lifetime costs, including assessment of the costs to sell to the customer and to serve the customer once the sale has been made, including all communications and support costs
- share of spending made with the company: past, present and projected future
- business relationship history, including their loyalty and willingness to form progressively deeper relationships with the company

Strategic value is determined by considering issues such as the following:

- how the customer helps the company to improve, for example, by:
  - providing a test bed for new products, services and processes
  - guiding the company to reduce its costs and improve its processes
  - assisting innovation and commercialization of new products or services such as offering ideas and allowing their facility to be used to test concepts
- a company's competitive position in an account, and how the customer helps the company gain competitive advantage such as by providing competitive intelligence and other preferential treatment
- how customers help the company more widely in the marketplace, such as by:
  - accelerating adoption of new products in the market, for instance, by providing referrals, allowing their names to be used for references or in advertisements
  - providing access to third parties such as distribution channels or the customers' customers
  - assisting with marketplace positioning by levering the customers' brand name or reputation, for example
  - partnering for additional value creation with third parties or in other country markets
- financial considerations other than lifetime profitability, such as:
  - the contribution the customer's business makes to overall business viability, such as fixed cost absorption[4]
  - the rate of sales, profit or lifetime value growth

[4] Care should be taken that plant loading and overhead absorption do not become the basis for customer retention and focus. In the long term, all costs are variable. A thoughtful plan should treat them this way.

- opportunities for key customers to help the company afford strategic investments that can be more widely used once implemented

Once this assessment has been conducted for all customers, the company has a number of important decisions to make, including:

- deciding which customers merit priority attention and how to deepen bonding with them such as by rewarding, recognizing and otherwise investing in the relationship
- determining what to do about customers that have intermediate levels of lifetime and strategic value to the company
- deciding whether or not to fire the customers that have low lifetime and strategic value

From consideration of issues such as these, customers can be triaged into best, average and worst. The best customers—those who have a high lifetime and strategic value—should be singled out for important treatment and additional investment planned for those relationships. Average customers can be made more strategic by changing processes for value creation and be made more profitable by considering how to improve the efficiency of value delivery. For example, a company supplying large corporations, small companies and individuals should probably not manage all types of customers the same way. For example, processes to create new value with larger companies would differ very much from the processes to interact with and engage smaller customers. Big customers may require different technology applications, for example, and more or different use of people throughout the purchase process and after-sales service.

In some cases, customers can and should be disciplined to align with processes that better represent their value to your company. Banks do this by encouraging their individual customers to use the automated teller machines, telephone banking or the Internet rather than customer service representatives. If customers insist on being served by humans, some banks impose an additional charge, which is a form of discipline.

Those customers who have low levels of lifetime and strategic value and cannot be made more valuable to the company might be fired. There are numerous instances of companies that have done this, one of the most extreme examples being the case of Nypro, a company that provides plastic injection molding to the automotive industry to manufacture things such as seats. In 1987, the company had 800 customers and sales of $50 million, but ten years later, it had

65 customers and sales of $450 million. At one time, Nypro had just 50 customers after firing the rest. Their approach was to focus on those customers who wanted a relationship that was mutual. (Not a bad idea—ever try marrying someone who wanted nothing to do with you?) Having chosen the customers they valued most and who valued them, too, Nypro simplified their business processes and organized around their most important customers. Other companies have done likewise, firing customers to achieve a more profitable and strategic portfolio of customer relationships. Sometimes, the customers do not know they have been fired. For example, smaller clients of large accounting and consulting firms sometimes are frustrated with large bills and lack of service. They attribute this to many things except the one that is often at work—they are being fired.

Calculating Lifetime Profitability

As mentioned, there are a number of issues to be examined when companies determine the priority of their customers. Two of the main issues when choosing customers are lifetime profitability and the costs of making processes flexible enough to deal with individual customer requirements, as outlined in Table 3-1.

Table 3-1: Customer Profitability

Lifetime Profitability of Customer

- lifetime revenues of customer
- lifetime costs, including measures of cost-to-serve
- share of customer spending—past, present, future/projected share of the customer's business predicted based on trends and the firm's position with regard to the customer's strategic initiatives
- customer history and business retention
- contribution to strategic value in areas such as competitor knowledge, innovation, process improvement, cost reduction, acceleration of adoption of new products in the market—whether by referral, reputation or other factors—and the extent to which the business is required based on current fixed-cost absorption

Cost of Making Processes Flexible

- customer knowledge and insight
- customer access, interaction and engagement process

- production
- inbound and outbound logistics processes, including warehousing and distribution
- order, shipping, billing and financing processes

Preconditions for Catering to Individual Customers

A number of preconditions exist if the company is to single out individual customers for unique attention. Not only must the customers meet the requirements of the company, as suggested previously, but the company should be prepared to adapt somewhat to accommodate a degree of uniqueness that may be entirely new to them. The table below presents a number of considerations for a company making the customer selection and rejection decision.

Table 3-2: Preconditions for Selecting and Catering to Individual Customers

- Each customer must want a solution that is unique, customized or personalized and see that he or she has derived additional value from the company catering to this need.
- The company must derive a value premium for providing unique value, either in reduced costs, a higher price or both.
- The company's capabilities—people, process, technology and knowledge/insight—must be flexible and adaptable enough to accommodate the individual preferences of customers. If they are not, the company must be prepared to make the necessary changes to its capabilities.
- By providing the customer with an individualized solution, the bond between company and customer must deepen, and the customer must want to repeat this experience or engage the company in another opportunity to create value together.
- Individual customers must be economically accessible for the company to interact and communicate with them, which is particularly important for fragmented consumer markets.
- The business model to warrant mass customization of process, production and communications, among other areas, must be economic. For example, while groceries can be bought on-line, the process has not yet been economic for most firms providing these customized shopping services because it is still quite costly to fulfill, transport and deliver individual orders.

Individual Customers, Specific Competitors and Strategies

Having triaged customers into best, average and worst, the key challenge is how to manage competitors in each of these customers. One approach is to consider each customer and the company's position compared to specific competitors. This can be done most readily for business-to-business customers, although technology makes it possible to undertake a similar assessment for individual customers.

Consider Figure 3-3. By charting individual customers and the company's competitive position, the firm has an opportunity to decide upon a course of action in each account. Some alternative strategies are identified for each of the main options suggesting, for example, that companies may wish to plan to breakthrough to win their best customers' business from stronger opponents. If it becomes apparent that the company must beat a few competitors repeatedly to keep the most valuable customers, a broader competitive strategy is indicated. In this case, a company could consider options for weakening a competitor overall such as by targeting the customers upon which they depend, developing preferred relationships with their suppliers or hiring their best people. Approaches for managing competitors are discussed in later chapters.

Figure 3-3: Customers, Competitors and Strategies

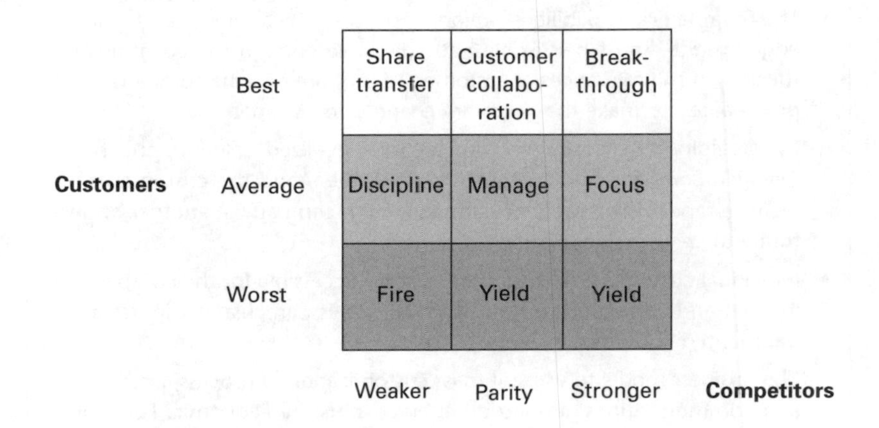

It is usually appropriate to defer a competitive focus until the true nature of the competition is known, and this increasingly must await analysis of decision making, changes in decision makers and detailed consideration of internal company data. For example, if process changes can provide large savings to the customer, internal personnel most affected by reengineering and current suppliers who benefit from the status quo might both be barriers to be overcome by a new vendor wishing to propose alternative processes. To illustrate, a company selling outsourcing services for print management can find that the main obstacle is the manager of the customer's printing facility. This person could feel threatened by any such outsourcing activity so the company may need to approach others such as financial management or the president, to secure the desired change in operations.

Purchase Decision Making and the Individual Customer

It is easier to single out, understand and manage the business customer than the individual consumer for competitive advantage. Nevertheless, consumers can be understood as individuals if the company uses technology well and obtains customer information whenever possible. In companies in which this investment has been made, individual consumers can be profiled according to their purchasing and product return behaviors and their inquiries and other interactions with the company. These data can be supplemented from other sources, such as information supplied when the individual first opened accounts, credit history, data that may be shared with credit reporting agencies or shared or purchased from other organizations and so on. Some companies integrate in the consumer profile those behaviors of the customer that precede and follow the actual purchase. Examples include inquiries and complaints from data logged by the call center, information from sales force automation and logs tracking the customer's Web site visits. This information is supplemented with questionnaires directed to individual consumers.

In addition to understanding the individual consumer's purchasing and other behaviors, a company also needs to examine their purchase decision-making process and the household as a purchase decision-making unit. For example, an automotive service provider intent on catering to an individual could understand what other vehicles there are in the household to see if there are additional opportunities to develop business.

The following questions typically need to be answered before a company can determine how best to influence the consumer's behavior:

1. When is this customer likely to buy (again)?
2. What will be the main criteria for the decision to purchase the product or service? What does this purchase mean to the consumer in terms of risks associated with making the wrong decision?
3. What media do customers prefer?
4. Which companies are potential suppliers for their next purchase? How do consumers view our products or services in relation to those of competitors?

The first question can be established with some degree of accuracy by studying such things as historical behavior (what is this consumer's frequency of replacement purchasing), especially when aided by software support and predictive modeling. Predictive modeling attempts to describe, from the data at hand, the customer's purchase behavior. The triggers for the consumer's purchase can also be established with some assurance, both by asking the consumer in a research exercise and by modeling it, as suggested above. For example, if my car is five years old and needs significant repairs, I may be more eager to buy a new vehicle now than if my car was newer or needed fewer repairs.

The second question can also be assessed with some assurance, based on the selection criteria used by the customer for previous purchases and data they may have provided by answering questionnaires, for example. The risk that the purchase represents to the consumers and their assessment as to the differentiation of brands must be established. Figure 3-4 illustrates this. For example, if the consumer views the purchase of golf clubs as risky for social reasons ("What will my friends think of me if I show up with this set?") and considers brands to be highly differentiated, he or she is likely to go about deciding what to buy quite differently than if the purchase decision is more routine and the products are not highly differentiated.

Some consumers might view the purchase of a broom or toothpaste as a routine purchase. Is Joe Consumer going to spend more time deciding on golf clubs or on toothpaste, and where will he get the information needed to make the purchase decision? Who will Joe ask? What will influence him? Answers to questions such as these can be obtained from Joe himself, or even by inference, by asking a sample of people with a profile similar to his. In the latter case, although each decision influencer cannot be targeted to aid the purchase decision Joe is going through, at least the media that people such as Joe rely on and view as authoritative can be established and used as part of a broader marketing initiative.

Figure 3-4: Nature of the Purchase Decision

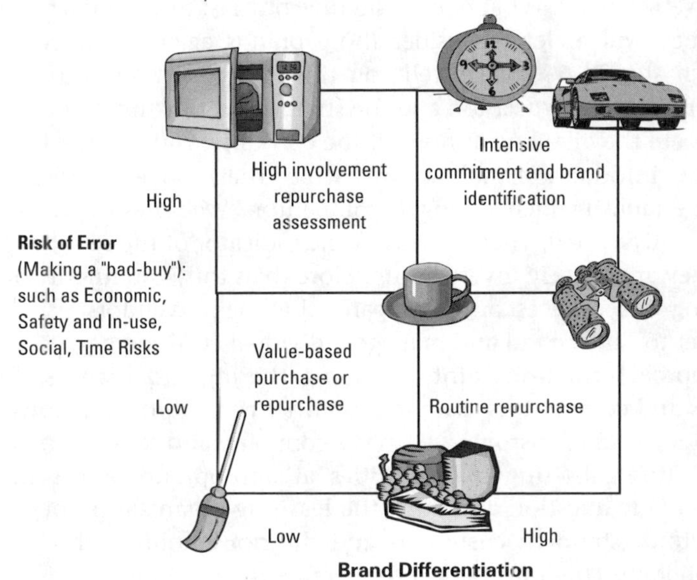

The third question, which deals with the means of communications, may also be established with some assurance by observing communications patterns and by simply asking the question at an appropriate time or venue. Customer-specific catalogs or newsletters can be produced and sent to e-mail or fax addresses, as indicated. Several companies provide customer-specific communications capabilities of this nature. More challenging is to tie in personal and nonpersonal communications while keeping the message consistent. For example, it has happened that a financial institution approached a customer in the search for his investment business just as another department within the same organization sought to tighten his credit. Now, there's a mixed message.

Question four is the crux. Before a customer makes an important purchase, a set of acceptable companies is mentally considered. The company needs to find out the following:

- Which competitors the customer is considering before making a purchase?
- Whether their company is on the list?
- What the customer's view is of the company and its competitors?

Gathering Information from Individual Customers

Answers to questions such as these require that information be gathered, managed and used well. There are a few ways to do this. One is to look at prior purchase behavior with customer-specific research, perhaps Web-enabled. What brands did they buy last time? It is a good bet that they will at least consider those brands again. Your customer research should be able to tell you this and also more information about the purchase decision and the strategic set of competitors. What brands are they looking at now? If the consumer is using the Internet to gather information and has not disabled their cookies, your company can establish which among its competitors' Web sites the consumer has recently visited. That is a reasonable indicator of the set of companies they are actively investigating. More than this, you might consider using the services of a company that helps vendors using the Internet to understand and manage individual customers.[5]

Approach the task of information gathering and analysis of customers and competitors as a process rather than a project. Flowchart the interaction of customers with the company and seek to introduce information-gathering opportunities at appropriate points in the process. One question at a time, the learning organization begins to better understand its customers and the households within which they operate. The information to describe the individual consumers, to understand their strategic set of competitors, to know vendor positioning and to predict their buying behavior can be known in a reasonably economic manner. Of course, the costs of the management and use of the information will depend on their lifetime value and importance to the company.[6]

Decision Making in Organizations

Decision making in organizations is complex and made more so by the need to compare your company to competitors. If your account management process does not already deal with this, describe the

[5] A number of consulting and research companies provide such services. Contact the local chapter of the American Marketing Association for a list. Our own firm (at www.converge.on.ca) provides these services through our division, CRM Surveys Inc.

[6] For a discussion on the calculation of lifetime value, see my book: *Relationship Marketing: New Strategies, Techniques and Technologies to Win the Customers You Want and Keep Them Forever*, Toronto: John Wiley and Sons, 1998, p. 92.

decision-making unit—the titles, people and departments—that makes the purchase decision in each of your business customers. What is the relative importance of the members of the decision-making unit in respect of specific types of purchase decisions such as selecting a new vendor repurchasing routinely or modifying the repurchase to some extent? This is established by asking the right questions at sales calls and closely observing interactions among decision makers. Who tends to defer to whom? Whose names are invoked authoritatively by the customer when talking about the purchase decision? For example, if you hear: "I will refer your suggestion to Jennifer Jones for her comments and will let you know her views when we meet again," you have a pretty good idea who the more important decision maker is.

The relative importance of the decision makers needs to be scored (by you or those with the best knowledge and understanding of the customer) with the people or department of importance in the company adding to 100, as demonstrated in Table 3-3. These data should be captured and introduced into sales force automation programs, allowing a detailed customer profile to be managed and updated. Data such as this can be used together with information on the customer's purchase criteria to decide how best to appeal to customers and beat competitors.

Next to be understood is the process by which the purchase decision is made by the decision-making unit. Who initiates it? Who analyzes the alternatives, recommends, approves and executes the purchase order? As mentioned, how does a repeat purchase differ from a modified rebuy[7] decision and how do both differ from an entirely new purchase decision? The roles of each decision maker can be recorded, as suggested by the following table.

[7] A modified rebuy is one whereby the customer reorders a product or service with only a few changes. For example, perhaps a sofa manufacturer has been ordering upholstery in rolls of a certain width and now wishes to obtain the same fabric on narrower rolls. In this case, the buyer does not need to requalify the supplier or reexamine the product but needs asssurance that the changes they want can be done.

Table 3-3: Relative Importance of Decision-Making Unit for the New Vendor Selection Decision

Decision Maker	Role	Relative Importance in the Vendor-Selection Decision
President	Approves	20
Vice President, Marketing	Initiates	20
Vice President, Finance	Approves	15
Director, Marketing	Recommends	15
Marketing Manager	Analyzes	20
Purchasing Manager	Executes	10
Total		100

It is important that any shifts in relative power within the decision-making unit be understood and examined. Decision-making shifts within a company are common as product and service knowledge becomes more widespread and as the purchase decision moves from a new-buy situation to a straight rebuy[8] or modified rebuy. One of the issues for the company wishing to manage its customers is whether to compete according to the decision making framed by the customer or to shift the basis for that decision such as by targeting more senior or different decision makers.

For example, if your company is a value-added reseller of personal computers and you have found that product margins are insufficient to provide a respectable return on investment, you may have decided to displace competitors from large volume opportunities or provide an expanded array of products, services and solutions. The latter can mean shifting attention away from junior decision makers in purchasing or information technology to the customer's more senior executives who see a broader picture. Making the situation more complex are issues such as whether or not the customer actually knows the total cost of ownership in addition to the initial purchase price, which is usually well understood. Some companies provide assessment and consulting services to help customers appreciate hidden costs for which they may not be accounting.

[8] A straight rebuy occurs when the customer reorders a product or service without any changes.

In addition, computers and equipment are usually funded from a company's or department's capital budget, while a more complete solution set may come from splitting the funding between capital and operating budgets. For example, consulting services, training and ongoing costs such as maintenance and support are operating, not capital, items. Issues such as these require additional skill in arriving at the real opportunities in the account and the decision maker responsible.

Decision-Making Criteria

Earlier it was noted that data on the decision-making unit, when used together with information on purchase criteria, can help the company decide what to do to appeal to customers and beat competitors in specific accounts. These criteria can be determined from the formal lists provided to all suppliers and in some cases, the criteria are even written by incumbent suppliers! But more typically, the formal criteria are supplemented with informal considerations and can vary from person to person in the decision-making unit. For example, the purchasing manager typically focuses on different issues than the user of the product or service. These informal criteria must be established by communicating with the key decision makers in a series of meetings.

The next issue to be addressed is the strategic set of vendors and the positioning of competitors in respect of the key purchase criteria. Customers—each member of the decision-making unit—will usually tell you who they buy from and what they like about them. Sometimes they will also tell you what they do not like, but here, they are generally more guarded. Where they do dwell on the negatives of their suppliers, they may be trying to influence your company by indicating, say, that a lower price might help secure their business. Their views about your firm in respect of their criteria may be a little less honest and may be polarized resulting in a less revealing understanding of the important middle ground. For example, they might respond fairly quickly by saying that your communications with their company is excellent rather than reflecting on the specifics of the communicators and the communications patterns and before providing a balanced perspective that is unlikely to have these extremes.

Four ways to secure a more balanced assessment are as follows:

1. Use a third party to explore these issues.
2. If your company has adopted the principles and processes of CRM, involve the customer relationship team that may be focused on this account presently.
3. If you do not have a customer-focused team, ask sales personnel to do this.
4. If you have a joint company-customer account group working together in your mutual interests, they could undertake this assessment. This group is likely to be multidisciplinary in nature, drawing on people who interact with one another from across both organizations such as purchasing, IT, sales, accounting, R&D, operations etc.

Whatever you decide, complete a chart similar to Table 3-4 on the next page, which assesses the customer with respect to their main selection criteria, and the positioning of your company and your competitors—those companies the customer feels could substitute for you. In other words, who you think your competitor is does not much matter, but which company your customer thinks could replace you is vital. Table 3-4 could be the outcome of the customer's deliberations, which shows ratings of the importance of purchase criteria and the rankings of the performance of your company relative to two competitors. When rankings are multiplied by ratings and the result totaled, the company is able to compare the value it delivers to the customer with that of competitors.

A further refinement would be to identify criteria in the minds of each decision maker and then to weight the scores by the relative importance of the decision makers, as discussed previously. For reasons of simplicity, this multidimensional view is not presented here, but the reader should consider undertaking this deeper analysis to understand better where and how to manage the account and to what purpose. Additionally, while this view describes purchase decision making for businesses, it is possible to complete this analysis for every consumer—either directly, on-line or through inference—based on their buyer behavior.

At this stage, you have the information you require to understand the needs, expectations and preferences of each of the individual customers you choose to serve, whether they are individual consumers or businesses. Through a thoughtful review of behavioral data and research with individuals, you have an ability to separate the strategic perspectives from the tactical. You can know which of your main competitors are in each account and where to focus to beat

Table 3-4: The New Vendor-Selection Decision-Making Criteria

Decision-Making Criteria	Ranking of Importance (adding to 100 total points)	Rating of Performance (1=Very Poor and 10=Excellent)		
		Your Company	Competitor A	Competitor B
First price and cost in use	25	7	6	5
Information systems, reporting	5	5	5	6
Collaboration and joint planning	8	4	5	6
e-Business capability	5	3	6	6
Service quality, responsiveness	15	5	6	5
Customer acceptance	10	8	9	4
Product conformance to specifcations	20	8	8	8
Delivery	5	8	6	5
Returns policy	2	7	5	8
Financing, payment terms	5	5	3	8
Weighted Total	100	641	640	589
Value of your company compared to major competitors		-	+0.2%	+8.1%

them. You can then aggregate the individual account assessments and sort the data to show which competitors represent the most significant overall threats and opportunities. This assessment shows you the strategic and tactical challenges that each competitor represents for your company, whether in specific accounts or in the market at large. In essence, you will have explored two of the information requirements to complete the three main legs of the strategic triangle (Figure 3-5), the third one being the development of competitive intelligence and the integration of that in decision making for strategic, tactical and real-time advantage.

Figure 3-5: The Strategic Triangle and Information Requirements

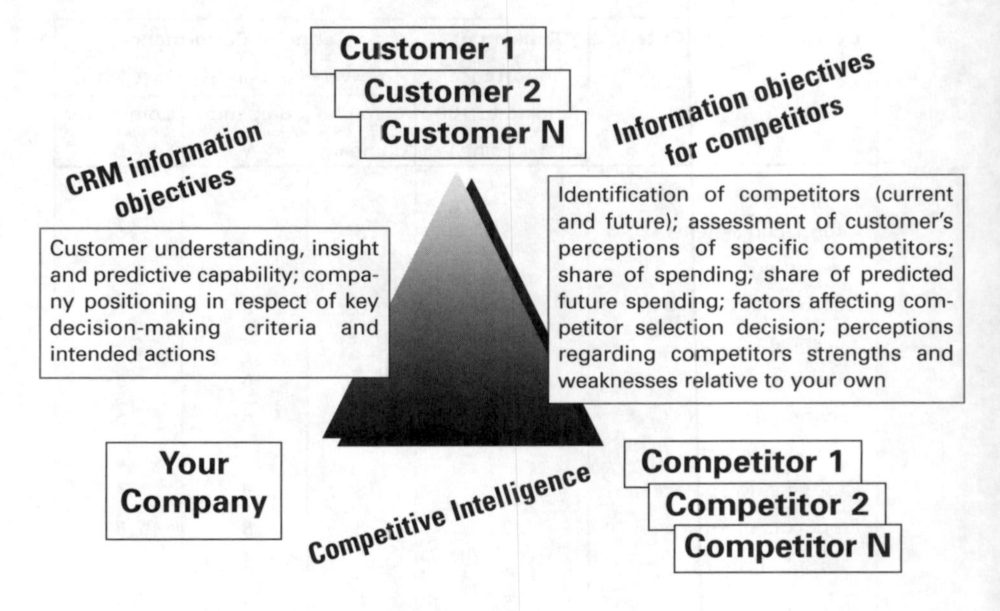

In this chapter, we reviewed the importance of a competitor focus and demonstrated how such an orientation has the potential to increase a company's revenues and shareholder value. This review can help a marketer to advance the concepts of this book by articulating the linkage and potential for a competitive focus to create new business value. The chapter also reviewed the changing nature of competition and the benefits of being among the first to focus on individual customers and specific competitors as a source of shareholder value. In the following chapter, we provide a framework for planning to beat specific competitors and show how to do customer research and develop a plan that will deal with many of the important competitive barriers a company faces in the marketplace.

CHAPTER 4

Planning Competitor Targeting

"Would you tell me, please, which way I ought to go from here?" [said Alice.]
"That depends a good deal on where you want to get to," said the Cat.
"I don't much care where," said Alice.
"Then it doesn't matter which way you go," said the Cat.[1]
—Lewis Carroll

This chapter provides a framework for planning to beat specific competitors. Ask yourself why your company is not twice as big or profitable. What is holding you back? The answer is often that the main constraint on your growth has to do with not being competitively superior in the areas that are most important to your chosen customers. Your competitors affect your success by competing for business that could be yours. By competing for the resources you need, competitors also make it harder for you to succeed in the future. If your company is to unleash its full potential and achieve what it is capable of—its destiny—it will successfully and repeatedly compete for the most important customers in the market. By winning here, it can win more broadly and attract the resources it needs to continue to grow profitably.

---

[1] Lewis Carroll, *Alice's Adventures in Wonderland.* 1865.

Customer Relationships

Beating competitors to achieve your company's goals means competing for customers, and winning that contest will secure the future. Today's battles are being fought for the future because it is there that improved marketplace positions are to be secured and money is to be made. Customer relationships provide a bridge to the future. They do so in a number of ways, including the following:

- Innovation—Strong customer relationships help companies to conceive, test and introduce winning products and services. Close relationships reduce the risks of innovation because they allow new products and services to be tested and improved before rolling them out to others.
- Improvement—Close relationships with demanding customers can be a company's most important asset as these customers help to make the company better. These relationships can make the company better by helping to shorten the product development cycle, accelerate the processes from concept development to cash and improve the company's operational efficiency, among other areas.
- Leverage—Well-known customers provide opportunities to lever their reputation in a marketplace and help secure the business of the customer's competitors. A potential customer would think that if their largest competitor bought it, how bad can it be?

Taking the obverse view to show the importance of having the right customer relationships, if your company has relationships only with the least profitable, least supportive customers in a marketplace, it need not worry about competitors because survival will be its main concern.

While customer relationships provide a bridge to the future, the company needs to carry things across this bridge, from innovative concepts to leading technology and from consistent quality to improving efficiencies and value. The problem is that your competitors also want relationships with the customers you value, and they might have more to offer your valuable customers in certain areas or perhaps all areas. And some competitors might have very good relationships with certain key customers, providing them with a basis for their business and a launching pad into your customer base. The battle for the future requires a thoughtful understanding of the industry's past, present and how the future might unfold. Then a company can take action to achieve its potential.

Industry's Past

How has your industry evolved? Examine industry shipments or revenues since the industry's inception and consider the major factors that have caused the main changes. Some of the factors will be exogenous to the industry. Take, for example, the rise in demand for copper for armaments during the Vietnam War. That had considerable impact on consumer and industrial markets. If your company made copper electrical wiring, perhaps it was less able to compete with alternatives, such as aluminum, that were offered as substitutes for a short period of time as a result of marketplace dislocation.

While some of the factors may be exogenous and others are in response to industry economics, many of the changes that have shaped industries have been made by prime movers. Which companies have been the prime movers, and in what dimensions did they innovate? Historians often say that to forget the past is to be condemned to repeat it. Certainly there are lessons for businesses to learn from the evolution of their industry so they do not make the same mistakes. Importantly, understanding the past and knowing what has changed since can allow a company to do the same things it did before but now be more assured of success.

Perhaps companies such as Atari remembered too much about the past when they thought that the market for consumer electronic games was a fad, and an unprofitable one at that. Atari attempted to change itself into a computing company in order to remove itself from the vagaries and uncertain challenges of the games industry. Other than its brand name and logo, which have shown surprising endurance, Atari is now gone. Companies such as Nintendo, Sega and Sony have demonstrated much more interest in participating in the games industry and have shown that this industry is not only large and profitable, but has an ability to endure.

Business is people. Companies that are prime movers are driven in the early years by an individual with a compelling vision, resources and an ability to follow through. They are the pioneers—the people who conceived, developed and commercialized truly original products or services. Generally, the inventor and commercializer are not the same person but a team working together. Teams can be pairs of people like Chester Carlson, who in 1938 developed the first Xerox, and Joe Wilson who commercialized it. Teams can also be larger, like Gordon Moore and Robert Noyce, inventors of the integrated circuit, who founded Intel Corporation in 1968, and Andy Grove who built the business of the company.

Sometimes the team is just one person who is both inventor and entrepreneur, like Kodak's George Eastman, Polaroid's Edwin Land and inventor Bill Lear.

After the pioneers come the copiers—those who emulate and proliferate products and services with similar attributes or benefits. After this come the nichers—the segment developers, flankers and niche in-fillers with more narrowly defined products with more appeal to specific audiences. Over time, acquirers move in—the money people and professional managers as industry consolidators and organizers. Then come the revitalizers—those who seek to reinvigorate a company and even an industry, like Steve Jobs did famously at Apple. Finally, the vultures swoop in to pick up value as they find it or carve it from companies unable or unwilling to deal with competition and change. This is illustrated in Figure 4-1.

Figure 4-1: Industry Evolution and Prime Movers at Specific Stages

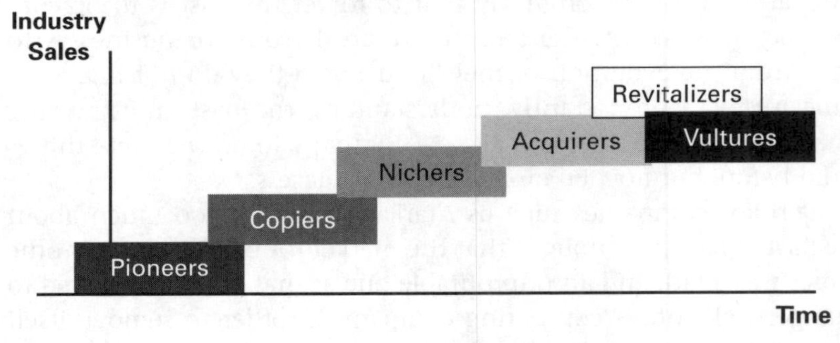

Examples abound of pioneering spirits and visionaries who made an industry from a product or service, only to see others change the industry structure and direction. For example:

- Henry Ford created the automobile industry through mass production, while GM's William Durant consolidated it and Alfred Sloan organized it and created market segment alignment for the organization.
- Thomas Watson might not have created the mainframe computer,[2] but he substantially developed and organized the industry. He

[2] In 1945, John Mauchley developed and built the Electronic Numerical Integrator and Computer (ENIAC), which is widely regarded as the first digital computer, its many drawbacks notwithstanding. In building this computer, he stood on the shoulders of other pioneers, such as Wilhelm Schikard, who invented a primitive device of sprockets and wheels in 1623 that could perform basic calculations. Pascal and Babbage developed more sophisticated computational machines, while Herman Hollerith invented a punched card tabulator that was used for the US census in 1890, heralding a new era in computation and time-saving. His company was a forerunner of IBM.

missed many of the major changes that were impacting it, but mainly the declining prices and increasing performance of computer chips that made possible industry subsectors of smaller computers (such as minicomputers and personal computers), computer networks and companies (such as Novell, Digital Equipment, Compaq, Dell and Apple).

- Sony Corporation's Akio Morita pioneered many consumer electronic innovations, including the Walkman, which his market researchers told him had insufficient potential. Thus far, not one company has emerged as the consumer electronics industry consolidator and organizer principally because of the rate of company failure, the pace of change and innovation in the industry, its fragmented nature and modest profitability.[3]
- Whether or not he created MS-DOS, Microsoft's Bill Gates did create the personal computer operating system and applications software industry, while others have sought to find less contested or specialized opportunities, particularly in association with technology developments in areas such as networking and databases, and digital convergence including content, communications and the Internet.

If you consider how your industry has evolved, it should become evident which companies and which people in those organizations have been the prime movers. Now you can frame hypotheses to examine in the planning process, to be considered shortly. If Company A has been the main factor recently shaping your industry, where will it innovate next? How might one profit from this knowledge or manage the risks inherent in the change? Are this company's weaker competitors more exposed to change than your company, and how might they and their customers be affected by the prime mover?

This consideration will rapidly bring to the surface a new range of issues. While your objective might be to win over the customers of specific competitors, it may become apparent that you first need to outperform the competitor in a variety of crucial dimensions or find new ones that are very relevant to their customers. It may also cause you to wonder if being a pioneer has material advantage over being second or third into a marketplace. Where barriers to entry and exit from an industry are low, companies can sometimes wait to learn from the successes and mistakes of others before choosing how to compete.

[3] Since the inception of consumer electronics, it is reported that the industry's profits are cumulatively negative. That is, when taking into account all the companies that have come and gone over the years and the money they have made and lost, the industry as a whole has not made a profit.

Industry's Present

Why is your company the size it is and not twice as large or half the size, for example? Why are there the number of companies there are in your industry? Why do some companies grow faster and are more profitable than others within your industry? What are the key success factors for participation in your industry today, and how are companies positioned in respect of these success factors? That is, what would it take for any company to succeed in your business today, and how are the incumbents doing now when you review their performance and capabilities for the factors that determine success? For example, if companies in your industry depend on great salespeople, where are the best ones now? If companies need great product or service ideas to move them forward, where are the innovative minds or idea-generating partner relationships today? Among the customers that are most important to you now and in the future, why do you not have all of their business? Why do your competitors even exist?

One of the ways to understand why your industry is the way it is is to use the force field to review what has helped the industry to develop and to explore what is holding it back today. What is the potential of the industry in terms of aggregate sales or shipments or in terms of profits, return on investment or shareholder valuation? Why has the industry not achieved its potential? What is holding it back?

A few years ago, a few pioneering companies such as Everdream and Centerbeam launched the concept of subscription computing. The idea was straightforward enough. Companies, especially small to medium-size businesses, would pay a single monthly charge for their computers, networks, software and support services. This industry has been recognized as having a promising future by many industry observers and investors yet has not grown as much as expected. Customers seem reluctant to buy their computing this way. As we will discuss shortly, this is not to say that the subscription computing industry has a bleak future.

A company can learn much from this examination of the history of the industry, such as the following:

- Which, among the driving forces, can be strengthened for the industry to achieve its potential?
- Can and should this be done by one firm, a grouping of companies (as allies in a business war) or as an industry in aggregate?
- Which, among the restraining forces, can be removed or changed so that the industry improves its position and moves closer to its potential?

- Again, can and should one company (yours?), a group of companies and/or all companies in the industry attempt this?

Industry's Future

Some managers say that the pace of change makes it impossible to predict the future state of the industry. They say that technology, in particular, is changing so fast that any projection of the future is impossible. Perhaps, but rather than just throwing up our hands and saying that the future cannot be known, it is more useful to say that some aspects about the future are knowable with reasonable certainty by building on historical trends that show some consistency. Industry consolidation may be one such trend. Other issues, such as those that depend on technology, may be harder to assess but even here, scenarios or alternative outcomes may be established and probabilities of occurrence assessed for each among the alternatives. One could even take some of the scenarios to the extreme to predict possible boundaries for the future state. For example, while we do not know the precise impacts of technology, it is reasonable to follow Moore's Law[4] and ask yourself what would happen either if existing price-performance trends continue or in the extreme, what would happen if such as processing power, bandwidth and storage were virtually free. How would that impact the industry?

In short, while the specific nature of the future of the industry may be obscure, this need not affect planning, because one can assess probabilities for scenarios based on outcomes and plan for this range of alternatives, focusing more on developing strategic capabilities than strategic action plans. The capabilities provide for a wide range of alternative futures and limit the impacts of predicting a single outcome poorly.

Investors have seen the future of the industry and collectively have a comprehensive understanding of its outlook. They have to. Companies are no longer valued so much on the basis of their previous earnings as on their earnings prospects. And investors have also taken into account the industry's outlook as they determine the price-to-earnings multiples for individual companies. A review of reports from major investment houses provides clues on the future of the industry but may not answer some of the questions most important

[4] Gordon Moore, cofounder of Intel Corporation, said that processing power doubles, and costs for this power halve every eighteen months. More recently, he has suggested that this occurs every year.

to an industry participant. As examples, real estate developers would want to know the saturation potential for big-box stores[5]—how many square feet the marketplace can accommodate in total and in specific categories, such as lumber, hardware or consumer electronics. While they may be able to establish the rate at which new square footage is being opened, it is harder to establish a saturation level which will provide a ceiling of sorts on new construction and ultimately affect how companies such as Home Depot, which has been opening one big-box store each week, will be valued.

One way of thinking about the nature of the future is to put yourself there and look back to the present. Returning to the force field consideration, describe the current state of the industry and the potential three years from now. Consider issues such as industry sales volume, profitability and return on investment. How many participants can the industry accommodate, and how many will there be? What volumes will come from which specific distribution channels? And so on.

What are the main forces that will have driven the industry forward to the then-prevailing "current" state? What will the main forces restraining the industry be three years from now? Some of the driving forces you will have identified will be the same ones you reviewed earlier, while others may be new forces that will have been initiated in the next three years. For example, the Internet and e-commerce may have changed the industry profoundly and may have been important dislocations that did not appear in your consideration of the industry's evolution.

As a brief illustration, let us continue the example of subscription computing mentioned previously. In a few years, many computer manufacturers will have introduced this service mostly to get closer to their customers and to assure themselves of recurring revenues. Already, companies such as Dell, Hewlett-Packard and IBM have launched similar services, and others are looking at the opportunity. So what will the future look like? In all likelihood, the concept of subscription computing will have been legitimized by the major industry participants. Many more customers will pay a single monthly charge for computing as they would for other utilities such as telecommunications services, electricity and gas. As familiarity with the concept grows, the costs of selling would have declined for each customer, but the competition for each sale may actually raise the costs of selling. The main challenge for existing industry participants will be to develop sustainable competitive advantage against well-capitalized and experienced competitors with recognized brands.

[5] Stores with over 100,000 square feet, including Home Depot, Office Depot, Circuit City, Sam's Club and Best Buy.

Rather than compete directly, existing companies may choose to specialize in a few areas such as making existing company applications suitable for remote support, self-help Internet support systems or online support. Without a force field and a view of the future state of the industry, others may continue to compete with the larger companies now entering the business. It is likely that several companies that do this will fail.

Previously, you considered key success factors for participation in today's marketplace. Now consider the key success factors for participation in tomorrow's marketplace. What must any company, such as an undefined new entrant, do well in order to win in the industry future state you have described? Now, in your most objective way, consider how your company and the other industry participants are positioned in respect of these success factors. If you are more favorably positioned, the future could belong to you if you capture the opportunities and manage risks as you should. But then again, you have probably found a few companies better positioned in respect of some of the key dimensions of future industry success. These are the companies that could challenge you for your customers and need to be thwarted. They have lessons to teach, too, and should be targets for your competitive intelligence.

Planning to Win

The prior considerations will serve as a background for your planning initiative, which will identify the competitors on which to focus and transfer the profitable dimensions of their future to your company such as relationships with customers you want. We now consider the development of a plan to beat competitors—not necessarily all of them, just the right ones.

Figure 4-2 on page 109 outlines the approach for developing the plan to target competitors and help your company to win. The plan builds upon four individual assessments to arrive at a strategy and approach for competitor targeting:

1. Industry Assessment
2. Customer Assessment
3. Competitor Assessment
4. Company Assessment

We discuss the main components of these assessments and the central elements of the plan next.

Plan for a Plan

The first phase of the plan development is a preplanning stage, providing management with justification for the expenditure of time and effort and outlining the various components necessary to ensure that the plan, once implemented, delivers to management's expectations. This phase comprises the preparation for the assignment and includes the following:

- Ensure that executives are identified to sponsor the initiative and to potentially support the plan.
- Clarify the mandate for competitor targeting generally, and for this planning initiative specifically. This includes a clear statement of the rationale and strategic intent for a competitor focus and for undertaking this planning initiative. The statement of the business issues is to be resolved by competitor targeting, by this initiative, and by the benefits the company can expect from the pursuit of a competitor focus for shareholder value creation and from the implementation of this plan.
- Confirm the definitions to be employed by all project members concerning terms such as competitor targeting, competitive intelligence, CRM and relationship marketing so that all the team members and executives are using common terminology as they consider how best to defeat competitors.
- Form the team to work on the project, including who will lead the plan development. The appointment of a leader to implement competitor targeting can await completion of the plan. Define individual roles and responsibilities.
- Confirm success measurements—how the team working on the project will know it has achieved its mandate and met the requirements of the executives.
- Design the formats for any outputs to be delivered in the planning process.
- Determine the time and budget available to the project.
- Link this initiative to other relevant initiatives such as CRM and competitive intelligence. This question is sure to be asked before the competitor targeting plan is accepted.

Figure 4-2: Plan for Competitor Targeting

Plan for Competitor Targeting

Mandate development, executive approval, team formation, definitions, statement of objectives, timing, budget, format, approach, success measurements, linkage with CRM and competitive intelligence

Industry Assessment

- Industry review & outlook
- Assessment of industry forces
- Key success factors for participation

Customer Assessment

- Customer profitability
- Relationship quality
- Share of customer
- Customer selection
- Customer amenability
- Purchase decision-making unit, process & criteria
- Key customer success factors

Competitor Assessment

- Positioning of current & projected industry participants with respect to industry & customer success factors
- Shareholder value creation
- Capabilities & resources that enable positioning

Company Assessment

- Desired revenues and sources of the revenues by product, market, customer & competitor
- Competitive strengths & weaknesses

Statement of the Opportunity

- Development of "shadow customer plans" and "shadow strategic plans"
- Assessment of gaps between the company and the key industry and customer success factors, absolutely and relative to competitors
- Why pursue competitor targeting?
- Which competitors will contribute to the company's prosperity?
- What will be the nature of their contribution, such as which customers will be transferred from the competitor to our firm?
- How will this contribution affect shareholder value?

Future State

- Visioning
- Objectives
- Capabilities: People, Process, Technology, Knowledge / Insight / Intelligence systems
- Competing: Strategically, Tactically, Real Time

Change Mangement and Implementation

- Implementation planning
- Sponsorship and change agents
- Communications planning
- Measurements
- Pilot/Roll-out

Industry Assessment

The second phase comprises an assessment of the future state of the industry in which you participate, the current state of the industry and the likely transition of the industry to the future state. This phase concludes by asking the question previously noted: "What must *any* company (such as, but not specifically, your own) do to be successful in the industry future state?"

To answer this question, a thorough analysis of the industry should be undertaken, building on the work that will have been done. This assessment could consider issues such as those described in Table 4-1, which includes some questions you will already have addressed in your company and others that may not be needed. The intent here is to prompt the reader with some areas that may not have been fully considered.

Table 4-1: Industry Assessment

- Evolution and development of the industry to date, including an assessment of the major changes and the drivers of these changes
- The projected future state of the industry, including a comparison of current and future states for some of the following, as appropriate: Industry sales, operating profits, after-tax profits, return on assets and financial ratio analysis
- Industry concentration and relative market and segment shares in all product-market intersections
- Rivalry among existing competitors:
  - Number of market participants
  - History of strategic change and market share shifts
  - Proximity to market, labor and raw material
  - Unionized vs. nonunionized competitor assessment
  - Production mobility
  - Capacity—availability and utilization
  - Capital vs. labor—trends, trade-offs and costs per unit of production
  - Changing economies of scale and scope
  - Technology adoption and application internally, in the supply chain, for distribution and at the customer interface, including the role of the Internet
  - Promotion methods and expenditures, including relative shares of advertising expenditures (share of voice)
  - Pricing structures and methods

- Bargaining power of suppliers:
  - Supplier concentration and trends
  - Proliferation of innovation in the industry, and the changing role of suppliers in guiding the diffusion and price of innovation to their customers and endusers
- Threat of substitutes being introduced:
  - Emerging technical developments that have caused or may cause substitution for existing products or services
- Threat of new entrants:
  - Trends in offshore company participation in domestic markets
  - Relative ranking of profitability, return on investment in this industry relative to others
  - Company announcements of diversification intentions
- Bargaining power of buyers:
  - Purchaser concentration and trends
  - Trends in agreements, supplier-purchaser alignments, discounts
- Threat of takeover/ownership changes (which could cause some firms to take actions that run counter to their long-term interests):
  - Shareholder value assessment of companies in the industry
- Bargaining power of labor unions:
  - Trends in labor settlements, broad details of union contracts
  - Number of grievances filed and areas of coverage
  - Safety and other areas of union concern
  - Dues paid to unions
  - Union membership and trends
  - Financial health of unions
  - Issues associated with barriers to acceptance of management direction
- Bargaining power and availability of skilled technical and management employees:
  - Remuneration packages, employment contracts, signing bonuses
  - Number of graduates in key fields
- Threat of this industry receiving negative attention by special interest, political and lobby groups and social critics:
  - Number of positive, negative and neutral mentions of the industry in the press and the sources and timing of the references
- Threat of legislative or political action weakening the industry:
  - Number of positive, negative and neutral mentions of the industry in the Upper and Lower Houses of Parliament, the Congress and the Senate, or the seat of government wherever your company does business

- Bargaining power of middlemen (including dealers, distributors, trade representatives, agents and wholesalers) and retailers:
  - Number and profitability of middlemen
  - Trends, changing concentration
- Globalization of production, marketing, management:
  - Review of international media
  - Emergence of global production
- Other issues specifically relevant to your industry, such as adoption and use technology in key applications and processes, including CRM, the Internet for e-commerce and customer engagement, and vertical market portals

The issues raised here expand on the five forces for assessing industry profitability, the so-called Porter Model,[6] which noted that industry profitability is a function of the following five forces:

1. intensity of rivalry among existing competitors
2. threat of new entrants
3. bargaining power of buyers
4. bargaining power of suppliers
5. threat of substitutes being introduced

Porter's Model has as its foundation the assumption that the greater the company's power relative to the five forces, the better its performance over the long term. Seen this way, monopoly power maximizes company profitability. Market share is one way of considering whether a monopoly position has been achieved, but the more important measure is share of customer for the customers that are the company's most important.

While Porter has considered a selection of powers that constrain monopolization and threats that could do this, there are others that are also current and potential future drivers or constrainers of profitability. These relate to the firm's power relative to all its stakeholders (forces with an interest in seeing the company succeed) and all its competitive forces (those that have an interest in the company not succeeding to the extent it wishes). These issues include the following:

- the threat of takeover/ownership changes (which could cause other firms to prosper from the investments and assets of the acquired entity)

[6] Michael E. Porter, *Competitive Strategy*, New York: The Free Press, 1980.

- the bargaining power of labor unions
- the bargaining power and availability of skilled technical and management staff
- the threat of this industry receiving negative attention by special interest, political and lobby groups and social critics
- the threat of legislative or political action weakening the industry
- the bargaining power of middlemen (including dealers, distributors, trade representatives, agents and wholesalers) and retailers
- the threat and potential of new approaches to product and service distribution, transactions and, more generally, the application of e-business, the Internet and communications technologies throughout the value chain

While Porter considers bargaining power relative to customers in general, CRM has the potential to improve a supplier's power with *specific* customers, while the aggregate position of the supplier might remain modest or unchanged with noncustomers. Using technology and CRM processes to bond with individual customers has the potential to rebalance power in the customer-supplier relationship. While power has been shifting in favor of customers, with CRM and one-to-one customer relationships, there is potential for customers to have a greater stake in a relationship with suppliers.

When American Hospital Supply Company (AHS) first put computer terminals on the desks of purchasers of consumables in hospitals, it was a company with limited bargaining power and a supplier of undifferentiated consumable products for hospitals. Some of its competitors, such as Baxter Travenol (as the company was then known), were larger with more to offer customers, including proprietary capital equipment. However, once AHS's technology went onto the purchaser's desktop, bargaining power was changed dramatically in favor of AHS. The result was due more to an improved purchasing process and reduced access of competitors to buyers than because of an improvement in AHS's products or pricing. Purchasing agents had no interest in developing familiarity with the ordering and inventory management systems of more than one supplier. In 1985, Baxter bought AHS to ensure customer access for its medical technologies.

More generally, the complete management of the customer relationship through the principles of CRM has the potential to rebalance customer-supplier relationships and make the vendor not only more relevant, but potentially inextricable from the customer's supply chain. Seen this way, CRM not only helps companies get close to customers, it can limit customer churn and blunt the thrust of competitors into an account. As suggested by Figure 4-3, CRM is an integrated approach to bonding with customers. With CRM, the customer's boundaries have been extended until they reach into the supplier. This makes it challenging to unseat a company practicing CRM in all its depth and fully realizing the potential of CRM. Having said this, few companies are yet achieving the full potential of CRM, and gaps usually remain in several dimensions of the customer relationship. Once uncovered and exploited, these offer potential for a new supplier or one with a lesser position to unseat the incumbent. In short, weaknesses in competitors' CRM strategies, tactics and real-time marketing provide an opportunity for beating them and transferring share of customer to your company. (More about this in Chapter 6.) At this stage, note that it is more important to consider bargaining power relative to individual desirable customers rather than to customers as a whole.

Figure 4-3: CRM as Competitive Strategy

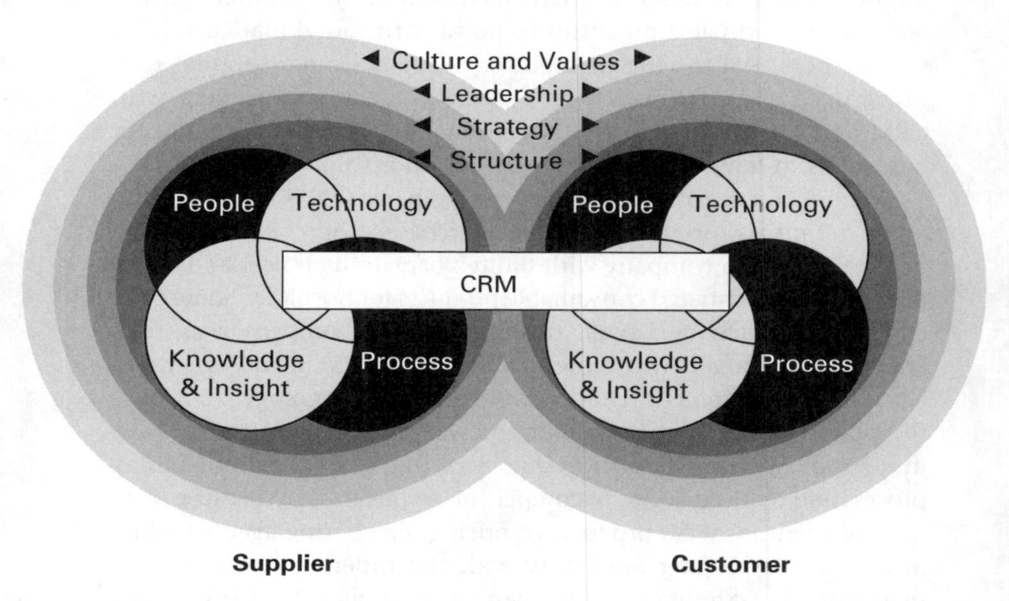

As we saw, your industry assessment should have a vision for the future state and with that in mind, evaluate the performance of individual companies in the industry. If you were to let the industry unfold without your intervention, what would happen to the individual companies? Now you should be in a position to establish hypotheses, which need to be reviewed when you examine specific firms. The industry assessment should conclude with a consideration of the likely future state of the industry, how that differs from the industry today, and what *any* company needs to do to be successful in the future state of the industry.

The conclusions from this assessment are the factors key to success in the future for those now in the industry and those that may enter it. If you were to start a new company to win in tomorrow's industry, what would you need to do to be successful? The answer to this question must avoid the usual platitudes and ensure that the company focuses on the main ingredients of winning.

Customer Assessment

This phase of the plan to target competitors considers the customers meriting priority attention by the company and includes answers to the following series of questions:

- Which customers should any company focus on in our industry?
- Which customers can we best bond with, including the current customers identified by our CRM initiative?
- What would *any* company need to do to win more or all of the business of the best customers in the industry? This question helps to identify offensive opportunities and suggests where your own company might be vulnerable in its own customer relationships.

Note that these questions differ from the important issue first explored in CRM, which initially seeks to identify the priority customers for the company to focus on, typically from among the customers the company is already serving and not necessarily the best customers in the entire marketplace. CRM often excludes competitors' customers from examination at the outset, which is potentially limiting.

The customer assessment should thus consider the following in this assessment:

- Customer Profitability
- Potential Prospect Profitability
- Relationship Quality
- Share of Customer
- Customer Mix
- Competitors and Their Relative Positions
- Customer Amenability
- Customer Bonding
- Purchase Decision Making

Customer Profitability

Customer profitability is established by reviewing which companies and customers make the company money. All costs should be allocated to customers, including those that are usually below the gross margin and contribution lines on the income statements of most companies such as sales and marketing, finance, customer service and support, inventory carrying and other costs not always attributed to specific customers.

Potential Prospect Profitability

The profitability of potential customers considers the profit potential from other customers in the industry by determining the type of customers they are and then comparing them to your existing business customers. The sales force can gather information to help the assessment comparison. Prospective consumers can also be equated to specific customers or customer clusters by using available scoring systems such as the risk scoring used by credit reporting agencies and risk assessors.

Relationship Quality

Measurement of relationship quality considers the current state of the relationships your company has with each of your current customers and prospects. This may require original customer research to fully understand how the customer views the company, its services, people and other capabilities, both in absolute terms and relative to competitors. In most cases, this research should be done by third parties to avoid possible internal bias, filtered comments or polarization of customers' perspectives.

Share of Customer

Assessing the share of a customer's expenditures the company has relative to the shares of competitors is the first step to discovering the company's current position and sets the stage for tracking how much this will change in the future. By paying particular attention to the main initiatives and areas of spending the customer is likely to undertake in the future, the company has an opportunity to focus its attention to gain customer share over time.

Customer Mix

Review the mix of customers in the firm's portfolio and select which customers the company will focus on. Where will the company invest? How can the profitability of less important customers be improved through more attention to management and even discipline? Which customer relationships appear to merit limited attention? And what should the company avoid if it wishes to build a profitable market position, customer by customer? If you have undesirable relationships with existing customers, perhaps those customers should be fired. Where the relationships do not yet exist or are weak, do not enter into them. Let competitors waste their time panning for gold in barren rivers. No matter how hard or how long they search, they will never become wealthy here.

Competitors and Their Relative Positions

Identify competitors that are already entrenched or are growing into the customers that are most important to the company. This assessment will aid the subsequent phase of competitor examination.

Customer Amenability

Assess the amenability of important customers regarding a relationship with any company, and yours, in particular. This will help clarify the dimensions on which you need to compete in specific accounts or how to win over individual consumers. Some customers may not want the type of relationship you want, and your company should not waste time on them. Educating your customer on the relative merits of a relationship can be lengthy, expensive and there is no assurance of success. Just as you cannot have a personal relationship with someone who does not want it, so, too, is it frequently futile in business to pursue a customer relationship when there is little possibility your customer will appreciate the potential.

Customer Bonding

Among those customers amenable to a relationship of the type you wish to offer, consider what a relationship means to them. What value do they want from you? Where do they wish to collaborate with you? How can your company become more relevant to the customer? Chapter 6 discusses dimensions of bonding that some customers might appreciate.

Purchase Decision Making

Examine the purchase decision-making unit, the process by which purchases are made and the criteria by which companies are assessed. Consider the positioning of the company and its competitors in respect of these criteria in the minds of the important customers. An approach for doing this was discussed in Chapter 3.

This phase concludes with an assessment of the main factors a company would need to do very well indeed in order to be successful with the customers and potential customers whom the firm considers as core to its future business. If you yourself were to start a business to serve the most important customers in the marketplace, with whom would you need to succeed, and what would you need to do very well to win them over?

Competitor Assessment

It is common for companies to consider their customer relationships with less rigor than fact-based management requires and it is even more common that the competitive perspective of the customer relationship is not objectively examined. Take the time to consider the competitive challenges in each of your major accounts. Include this consideration in account planning and in preparation for the targeting of a competitor's accounts as basic background to establish account objectives and focus and to plan to build your *competitive* position in each account rather than simply your position.

The customer assessments we described identified the key success factors for industry participation and the company's most important customers. In this phase, competitors are reviewed in the context of both of these considerations. Here we analyze what any company must do to be successful in the future state of the industry and how the various industry participants are positioned to succeed. The positioning is established by conducting an assessment of the capabilities of competitors in relation to the key success factors. For example, if in the future, companies must have even deeper financial resources to fund strategies that compete on scope with new products and technologies, how do the various industry participants fare with respect to their ability to finance growth internally and access capital?

This phase also comprises an assessment of the competitors' positioning with respect to the key customer success factors identified in the customer assessment. Here the task is to determine the rating of competitors according to the criteria your most important customers have emphasized such as those pertaining to vendors, products, services and relationship management. The best way to establish this is through individual customer research, either by the account management team or through a third-party consultancy that specializes in work of this type. Generally, the latter yields more objective results.

The data secured from the research can be examined to establish the relative strengths and weaknesses for specific competitors in each account to determine which ones represent the main threats and opportunities for your firm. These issues were reviewed conceptually in Table 3-4. The illustrated case that follows in Table 4-2 is for business forms. The focus here is on relationship formation with the customers of competitors and to a lesser extent, deepening of bonds and competing to transfer share of customer within existing accounts. The two concepts—penetrating new accounts and building from this base position—are discussed in Chapter 5.

Table 4-2: Positioning of Competitors with Respect to Key Purchase Criteria for Business Forms in (Account Name)

Key Vendor & Product Selection Criteria (illustrative)	Ranking	Rating (1-10*)			Weighted Rating		
		Company 1	Company 2	Your Company	Company 1	Company 2	Your Company
Price	30	5	8	7	150	240	210
Order shipped when promised	20	7	5	7	140	100	140
Problem rectification	15	3	6	5	45	90	75
On-line ordering and status review	10	5	5	6	50	50	60
Forms design skills	10	6	6	7	60	60	70
Inventory management	10	5	5	6	50	50	60
Other	5	3	5	5	15	25	25
Total	**100**				**510**	**615**	**640**
Relative value of you company (divide competitors by 640)					+25%	+4%	

* = 1 is very poor and 10 = excellent, from the perspective of the customer. (Thus, lower prices are rated with a higher number.)

A more complete assessment of the customer positioning would have required that the relative importance of decision makers in the account be weighted. A table such as Table 4-2 would then be prepared for each decision maker and the results weighted in accordance with the importance of that person. In Table 4-2, the vendor and product or service-selection criteria are established with each customer or account and then ranked according to the importance the customer places on each. A rating of your company and the competitors in respect of the criteria is then assessed, using a scale such as one to ten. The rankings and the ratings are then multiplied and added to arrive at an overall assessment of competitive positioning. To compare your company with the competitors in the account, simply divide the competitors' weighted values by your own.

In the case presented, your company has a value to the customer that is similar to Company 2 overall, but your firm derives much of its value from shipping business forms when you promise, while the competitor is perceived to have better prices. The competitor assessment should now examine why Company 2 is perceived to have lower prices. Do they indeed have lower prices or do customers just think that they are? This assessment will likely need to draw on competitive intelligence to provide a detailed review of the reasons why the competitor is seen to have lower prices. For example, it may require an assessment of their cost structure, margin expectations, channel markups, pricing structures and other dimensions.

The example presented is for a business-to-business marketplace, but if it is a consumer one, then the company can still assess the positioning of companies the customer considers to be substitutes by, for example, doing the following:

- Use a chart similar to that presented but modified for the individual consumer. Data will come from individual customer research (e.g., Internet-based surveys and real-time customer satisfaction measurement).
- Map the attributes of individual customers to profiles developed from market research at the segment or behavior cluster level. That is, by conducting research with consumers in specific segments or clusters identified from data mining and then profiling a typical consumer in each, the company can compare the profiles of other consumers to understand them better and predict what they might want or do.

Some companies often want to complete competitor profiles that describe the competitor completely and that gauge their strategies, strengths, weaknesses and much else. If you are thinking about developing profiles such as this, you might want to wait because it is important to understand how competitors have secured their positioning, and this assessment requires the completion of a portion of a competitor profile. A detailed profile can be a waste of time at this stage, especially if the competitor that is assessed is not your primary competition, is not seen by customers to be a substitute for your company, is not focused on priority customers or is otherwise unworthy of targeting. Rather, defer the development of a detailed profile for only those competitors to be targeted. For the rest, establish what you need to monitor about them to ensure that you are not blindsided. You can monitor as many competitors as you wish through competitive intelligence, looking for signs of change with respect to certain issues, but analyze just one or a few. In any event, you probably do not have the resources to do much more.

Having noted this, perhaps you will wish to complete a portion of a competitor profile anyway, possibly because you view this as an appropriate starting point in assessing competitors. Should you want to do so, you might consider some of the elements in Table 4-3 in your profile of the competitor's corporation overall or the specific divisions or product lines with which you compete more directly.

Table 4-3: Competitor Profile: Competitor's Corporation and Division

The Competitor's Corporation

- History and evolution of the company, including acquisitions and divestitures
- Mission and objectives (articulated and manifested—they may be different!)
- Description of organization, locations, staffing, key officers, board of directors, product lines and share of sales and profits derived from specific product/service offerings, regions, countries, channels, key accounts, people, categories of customers
- Forces acting upon the company:
  - Culture and leadership
  - Review of changes to key executives and the board of directors
  - Financial position, ability to self-finance, relationships with investors and lenders
  - Market analysis
  - Relationship assessment: customers, distribution channel intermediaries, end-users and suppliers, alliance partners, employees

- Competitive position (Five Forces analysis)
- Product and service teardown/reverse engineering assessment
- Distinctive capabilities: people, process, technology, knowledge/insight/intelligence
- Strategic direction: product and service categories, technologies, customer focus, competitors
- Efficiency and productivity
  - Innovation: patents, percent of sales from products or services not made three years ago
  - Finance and treasury: ROI, ratio analysis, cost of capital, market valuation of the company's shares and reasons for this valuation, leverage (comparison to industry), availability of additional equity or debt infusion, day's receivables and payables (and the implications for supplier and customer relationships)
  - Sales staff: Sales per person, recognition and reward, sales automation
  - Technology: Self-service capabilities for customers (e.g., customer support)

The Competitor's Divisions

- History (Why is it part of the competitor? How long has it been part of the company?)
- Relative importance to the corporation (current and historical)
- Key personnel at the division level (profiles) and the main backers of the division corporately
- Financial performance
- Dependency on key accounts, key people (technologists, marketers, etc.), products, regions, financial infusion
- Portfolio of products and relative emphasis
- Production: capacity by plant and overall, number of shifts produced per year, on-site warehousing, age and technology of equipment, labor vs. capital intensity, union relationships, quality of output (objective measurement and as seen by customers)
- Marketing: level of personnel, how organized (e.g., brand vs. market management vs. end user/trade organization), media (expenditures—in total and by type), agency—current and historical agencies and account personnel (profiles), advertising themes, positioning, consumer vs. trade promotion, total discretionary expenditures (percentage of sales, especially during economic downturns and upturns)
- Selling: number and quality of sales staff (experience, education), training, location of selling offices in relation to key accounts, major territories, approach to remuneration (base vs. commission vs. bonus), quotas, key people (profiles)
- Other relevant issues, such as those raised for the corporation overall

Before your company can expect to defeat the enemy, it should have a clear understanding of itself in relation to its history, present market circumstances and its destiny. A number of fundamental questions should be considered, such as why your company came into being in the first place and what value at the outset it was intended to create for whom. What was the founder's vision?

Akio Morita, the founder of Sony Corporation, said at the outset of its formation that his concept of the new company would be as "an innovator, a clever company that would make new high-technology products in ingenious ways."[7] For over 50 years, Sony has not strayed far from that road. Indeed, in Japan, Sony is prized as a pioneer in electronics. It is easier for companies to copy than innovate, and Sony has no shortage of imitators. However, while products can be copied, the brand Sony cannot. It has benefited from the value consumers associate with innovation.

On the other hand, when Bill Hewlett and David Packard founded in a garage the company that became HP, they began designing and making custom electronics in the hope that one of their custom products would be viable in a broader marketplace. This sprit of innovation helped build HP for decades, and when the company focused more on products and marketing than on innovation, the growth appeared to decline in concert. HP returned to a focus on innovation, although its recent acquisition of Compaq suggests it is also consolidating the industry in search of profitable growth.

Company Assessment

If customers are to be won from competitors, companies need a thoughtful consideration of the reasons for their historical competitiveness, including why they even exist today. Going forward, they need to establish the capabilities that will allow them to displace competitors. The intent of this phase of the work is to develop this understanding by asking and answering questions such as those described in the checklist that follows. Good questions are harder to formulate than good answers. Answers simply require marshaling of the facts and their assessment, but good questions require thoughtful insight.

---

[7] Akio Morita, *Made in Japan: Akio Morita and Sony*. New York: E. P. Dutton, 1986.

Table 4-4: Company Assessment

- What is our history and roots?
- What do we stand for that is absolute and timeless?
- Why do we exist?
- Why do we not have double the sales or profits?
- What is our destiny—the highest level of achievement we could possibly achieve?
- Would our founders value what we have achieved?
- Would our founders respect our present leaders?
- What do we have that competitors do not?
- Why do our best customers buy from us and not competitors?
- Why do some of the customers we want buy from competitors and not from us?
- Are our best customers more loyal to us than the competitors' best customers are to them?
- Do we give our best customers the best value we provide to any customer?
- Do we eliminate our worst customers?
- Do we change faster than our competitors?
- Have we demonstrated an ability to learn new things better and faster than competitors?
- Do we concentrate most on what we do well?
- Are we good at "unlearning"—undoing the people, process, technology and knowledge that was once appropriate but is now holding us back?
- Do we quickly cut the ties that anchor us to untenable situations?

One way of establishing useful questions is to consider what is holding the company back. For example, ask: "Why do we not have twice the sales we do?" "Why do we not have twice the market share we do?" "Why do the most important customers in the marketplace, the ones we want as the basis for our future, not buy exclusively from us?" A force field similar to the one used for the industry assessment could help further clarify your business, its reason for being and its strengths, weaknesses, opportunities and threats. That is, in addition to the issues noted in Table 4-4, a number of other questions bear consideration, such as the main barriers now ahead of the company. The force field for the company is illustrated in Figure 4-4.

Figure 4-4: The Force Field for the Company

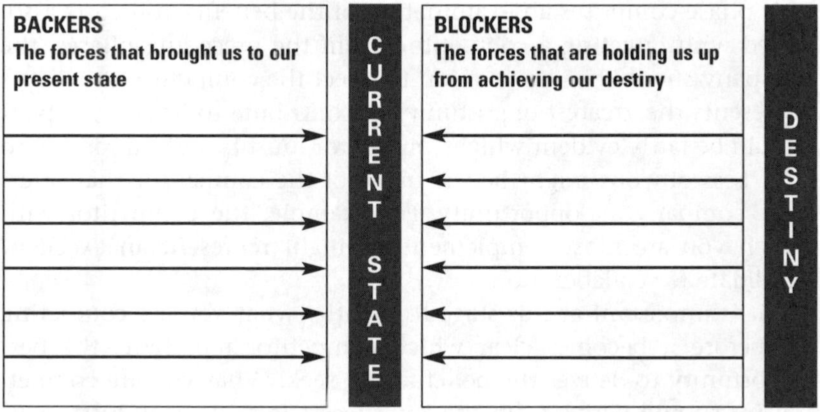

BACKERS
The forces that brought us to our present state

CURRENT STATE

BLOCKERS
The forces that are holding us up from achieving our destiny

DESTINY

Work through the forces in a management workshop or in one-on-one personal interviews with executives. For example, ask them to say what they think are the main forces that enabled your company to achieve its present market and financial position. They will probably respond with things such as leadership, culture, technology and so on. Then ask what forces are holding the company back from achieving the destiny of its founders. (If people can't remember or do not know what the founders had in mind, that may be worth considering, but at a later time. In this case, ask simply what management thinks is holding the company back from achieving its potential.) Management will likely respond with issues pertaining to leadership, culture, technology and so on. Yes, the things that often get a company to its present market and financial position are sometimes the very same things that are holding the company back from moving to the next level of growth or success.

A senior executive with a Japanese technology company once told me that this firm's main strategic challenge is to "overcome success," by which he meant that the company needed to unlearn many of the things that it was already good at and overcome these if it wished to arrive at a new level of achievement. In other words, some of the same things that had made the company successful were now holding it back, a verbal rendition of one aspect of the force field.

Statement of the Opportunity

This phase comprises an examination of the benefits and costs associated with targeting a competitor. From the preceding phases, the company should be in a position to select the competitor it believes represents the greatest opportunity to contribute to its prosperity. It should be fairly evident which competitor must be beaten for you to win. Less obvious might be the name of the competitor that offers your company an opportunity. For example, the competitor with which you are most complementary might represent an excellent candidate for collaboration.

It is important at this stage to identify what you are competing for before it becomes clear which competitor represents the best opportunity to deliver the benefits you seek. What you are competing for should derive from the key success factors for industry participation in tomorrow's marketplace. By now you will have conducted this assessment. You may be competing for one or a select group of customers, possibly including some in which a competitor is entrenched. You may be competing to become a contender rather than an industry leader in a given product-market space. And here second-tier competitors may be in your way. These are your primary competitors. You may be competing for the best ideas, financial and sales professionals or design and development talent, for example, in which the competition might be employers from outside your industry. In some industries, this competition may merit an even higher priority than winning the right customers or transferring share of the customer's future expenditures to your company.

Table 4-5: Selection Criteria for Competitor Targeting

Criteria	Competitor A	Competitor B	Competitor C
Largest "share of customer" among customers we want			
Largest "share of future spend" among customers we want			
Strongest position among "second source" suppliers to the customers we want most (barrier to our firm becoming a contender)			
Largest market share			

Most profitable sales			
Highest return on investment			
Largest shareholder value in our industry			
Developer of substitute technology or a potential major new entrant			
Strongest position in respect of key success factors for winning in tomorrow's industry (e.g., Internet)			
Company we can learn most from, to make us better			
Company with greatest brand equity or most differentiated in the minds of the customers we want			
Company that, if beaten, will confer on the contender the leadership position in the marketplace			
Company that, if an ally, would create a formidable alliance			
Company that, if acquired, would provide your company with additional ability to exploit the key success factors of the industry			
Company outside our industry that attracts the talent we need			

List the selection criteria for choosing a target, and score the competitors in respect of the criteria such as those listed in Table 4-5. If multiple criteria are to be used, weight them and score the competitors in respect of each. Then multiply the weighting by the scoring and add the result to arrive at confirmation of the relative importance of selected competitors.

Competitor selection is the most important aspect of competitive strategy. We have already considered choosing the best competitors on which to focus by exploring which customers your company needs to secure its future and so identifying the competitors that are also candidates for winning these customers. We have discussed company and competitor positioning in the minds of customers, an important consideration in the framing of competitive intelligence and strategy. Other issues associated with the competitor-selection decision were discussed in Chapter 3.

Now that you will have chosen the competitor you wish to focus on, your challenge is to know this company extremely well—well enough, for example, to do the following:

- Understand on which companies they are focused and where they make their money.
- Establish their dependencies (other than customer-based) and pressures for change such as the employees who are particularly important in their company, the financial resources they have available to them, the suppliers with whom they do business, the sources of their innovation and so on. Ask how their competitors, including your own company, are affecting them.
- Predict their customer, marketplace, innovation and other actions so that you can defend your position or get there first.
- Exploit their weaknesses generally or with the specific customers you have chosen.
- Learn from them so that your company can become faster or better.
- Ally or collaborate with them so that your companies can succeed together.
- Acquire them outright to gain control of certain lines of business or certain assets or capabilities such as brand names, customers, distribution channels, management and technical staff.

One way to develop this knowledge is to find out everything about the competitor and develop a competitor profile. As previously discussed, this has the potential to involve a huge amount of work, and the job may never seem complete. A better, more focused way to assess the competitor you have targeted is to develop a shadow strategic plan for the corporation as a whole and for their marketing plans for the product or service lines with which you compete. This will have the additional benefit of making explicit the competitive intelligence that you have in the company, both in formal systems and in the minds of employees so that you can know what you know and establish what you have yet to find out. In turn, this can serve to focus subsequent competitive intelligence. (See Chapter 5).

If your company is typical, when you prepare the shadow plans, you will find you know a great deal about the competitor in some areas and little in others. Most companies find they can describe competitors' financial condition but do not know much about the key executives who are driving the company. If business is people, these individuals must be known and understood. Do you know your counterpart (the person with your title) at your three main competitors?

Table 4-6: The Shadow Strategic Plan

Section	Purpose
Executive Summary	A brief overview of the competitor's plan for quick review by management.
Current State Assessment	Review of historical market and financial performance for the industry and the target company, the outlook for the industry (paying particular attention to scale and profitability), the key factors for succeeding in the industry, and consideration of the positioning of the target company in respect of the key success factors. The current state assessment should consider where the target company is today and what enabled the company to be successful at its present level. Develop product-market and product-customer matrices for their product, service, market and customer portfolios and assess the implications. Explore core capabilities, including people/leadership/culture, processes such as those for operations, customer acquisition and retention, technology in support of the customer, for the supply chain and for operations, knowledge/insight/intelligence systems that have enabled them to manage information for their business advantage.
Future State Assessment	Assessment of the vision, mission and principal strategies of the targeted competitor. Consider strategies in terms of capabilities such as those referenced for the current state assessment as well as strategies for customer selection, positioning/brand equity, value chain focus, product-market emphasis, technology/R&D focus, and strategies in respect of the main choices the company will need to make to be competitive. What is the future or end state for the company, as articulated by its management?
Transitioning	What will the competitor likely do to get from its current state to the destiny it has articulated or which it manifests by its actions, inaction or inertia? When might these actions occur, and what might precipitate them?
Projected Income Statement	Pro forma profit and loss statement

When developing a shadow strategic or marketing plan, use the format you presently employ for your company's own strategic and marketing planning. Perhaps the format for your marketing planning is similar to that presented in Tables 4-6 and 4-7, in which case some of the concepts presented here could be included with the development of the strategic and marketing plans. Of course, it can be very time-consuming to develop plans for many competitors. In Chapter 6, we discuss how to organize for competitor targeting so that you can manage the initiative without much additional investment of time or people.

Table 4-7: The Shadow Marketing Plan

Section	Purpose
Executive Summary	A brief overview of the competitor's plan for quick review by management
Current Marketing Situation	Relevant background data on the industry, including products and services, markets/segments, customer triage, distribution channels and the Internet, brand equity, positioning in respect of key industry and customer success factors, and competitor's competition
SWOT Analysis	A summary of the competitor's Strengths, Weaknesses, Opportunities, Threats and other relevant issues
Objectives	A presentation of the competitor's likely product-service objectives, outlining volume, revenue, market share, profit and return on investment objectives
Marketing Strategies	A presentation of the broad approach that will be used to address the plan's objectives: identifying (and modifying, if appropriate) customer focus, positioning, technology, product, promotion, pricing, distribution channels, service and customer relationship management
Implementation	Answers the questions: "What will the competitor do? How much will it spend? When will it seek achievement of the objectives? What will be the key milestones? Who will do the work?"
Projected Income Statement	Pro forma profit and loss statement

Considering your own strategic and marketing plans in relation to those of the competitor you are targeting, you may well establish gaps or differences in many areas. For example, if your visions of the business are similar, it is quite possible that your company and the target are on the same road to the same destination. In Table 4-8, we present vision statements articulated by CEOs in five financial services companies. These statements are quite alike. The companies seem to be headed in a similar direction, separated more by customer base, geographic market coverage and, to some extent, scope of service, than by differentiation of vision.

Table 4-8: Vision Statements—Five Financial Services CEOs

1. "Provide our customers with a level of service and price that will distinguish us."
2. "Sharpen operating efficiencies, and add value to the products and services we offer."
3. "Give the customer high-quality service that is not available elsewhere."
4. "Maintain the excellent service provided to clientele."
5. "Exceed customers' expectations through quality products and service."

Developing a Vision Statement

It is important that the company have a vision that is differentiated from those of competitors. It is easier for a company to adopt a vision statement that is similar to those of competitors than one that is different. Difference implies risk, especially if the vision proves to be wrong, inappropriate for the company or too hard to achieve. Yet, it might be riskier for the company to adopt a vision similar to those of competitors because this will keep the company locked in combat and will force it to focus on better implementation of the vision. Is your vision sufficiently differentiated? To find out, ask yourself if your best customers would recognize your company if they read only your vision statement, without any indication from which company it came.

In general, a good vision statement has:

- a clear destination, the attainment of which will be self-evident
- a customer and competitor reference frame
- a purpose to which employees are proud to commit
- resonance with stakeholders
- something unique

As mentioned, the vision statement should include consideration of competition so that the following are clear:

- which competitors are the priority enemies to be excluded from your vision of the future state of the industry
- which competitors are viewed as companies with which the firm will collaborate
- what attributes of value are to be transferred from competitors to your company, such as the considerations raised in Figure 4-5

Figure 4-5: The Targeted Competitor's Contribution to Your Prosperity

Gain some of their management or technical talent

Associate with them as an ally

Transfer some of their customers to your company and/or increase your share of common customers

Increase your company's share of a distribution channel also used by the competitor

Beat competitors of both your company and theirs

Acquire them outright, invest in them or acquire specific lines of business, plants, markets, know-how or brands

Technology adoption, especially at the customer interface and in the service of the important customer

Operations, product, quality, CRM process or structural improvement

New products or services concepts

Margin, turns and other opportunities to boost shareholder value

Managing stakeholders, investors and the "chain of relationships"

Culture, personnel and human performance improvements

The process for arriving at vision statements is usually to conduct management workshops at which the following happens:

- The industry and company facts are considered, and alternative destinations for the company are identified.
- The alternatives are reviewed, and management consensus is sought.
- The final vision is examined, and commitment is achieved, leading to changes in the various plans of the company.

Research and analysis is performed between workshops, followed by additional consideration at the next session. There are many things to avoid when crafting a vision:

- Do not confuse your vision statement with your mission. The vision is the destination. The mission is a stance based on company and stakeholder values and the implied direction. Using a

military analogy, the mission is more aki
mon cause a commander might communica
ture the hill from an enemy. The hill itself is th

- Do not pattern your vision statement after that of
pany. Because every company and situation is differe
pany's vision statement cannot substitute for that of ano
may not even be a suitable guide. If you have a book of visi
mission statements on your bookshelf, throw it away.
- Many companies have used the word "best" in their vision statements, which suggested that the company would be better than all competitors. While this has some appeal, visions of this type fail to describe what best means. In the increasingly crowded marketplaces in which most companies now participate, this shortcoming is a major one. If companies are not more specific, their vision will be nothing more than a hope. Hopes rarely come true.
- Use professional help in the development of the vision statement, but take care in selecting the consultants who facilitate these workshops. Consultants must be able to do more than facilitate meetings and secure management agreement. Consultants must bring content and context to the workshop to challenge management and help ensure that the vision is much more than a platitude.
- Be skeptical of the common wisdom that can dominate workshops. Depending upon when in the recent past a workshop was conducted, every management team could agree that there would either be an energy crisis or not, that commodity prices would be high or low, that there would be an excess or lack of skilled labor, that technology was too expensive to adopt widely or would be very inexpensive to use everywhere, that the company's business model need not focus on profits or that it should emphasize profits and so on. Wisdom is uncommon. The company seeking management consensus should take care that agreement does not substitute for insight and foresight.

Future State

By the time you are ready to conduct this phase, you will have a thorough understanding of the industry and its outlook, the position of your company and the targeted competitor in the context of the industry today and tomorrow. Now you need to establish how your company should respond to the opportunities to prosper at the expense of, or together with, the competitor you have targeted.

in the context of competi-
mpetitor you are targeting.
ill it be substantially differ-
n, what will the impact be

ment company, producing
right yellow construction
oviding ancillary services in
ich as financing and insur-
most disappeared in 1982,
firm undertook a compre-
uidance from companies in
onsumer durables market-
places. In developing its strategic response to unfavorable market conditions, Caterpillar paid very close attention to competitors. When it moved to reduce costs, restructure, automate, consolidate and expand the scope of its product line to fill in niches, there was considerable competitive context in their decision making. Competitors such as International-Harvester, Allis-Chalmers and Bucyrus-Erie failed, but Caterpillar went on to confirm its position as the leading equipment company. This is not to say that Caterpillar specifically targeted individual companies to create prosperity for their firm, but there was clearly excess industry capacity at the time, and the largest company in the industry has the responsibility to manage this capacity. That is, a company such as Caterpillar should establish the industry capacity and manage its own business *and that of their competitors* to this level. This will help ensure the profitability of the industry for all remaining participants.

Competitor-Related Objectives

In addition to envisioning a future state for the company, the firm should establish objectives that pertain to the targeted competitor. What volume of sales will be derived from the defined enemy? How much shareholder value will be yielded by the competitor to the benefit of the company? Which customers will be transferred to the company? What share of customer will be achieved in the customers that matter most? Figure 4-5 identified a number of ways that a competitor can create value for the company. The following objectives could be established in respect of those areas in which your company intends to prosper at the expense of the competitor:

ht, invest in them or acquire specific lines
markets, know-how or brands.
both your company and theirs.
any's share of a distribution channel also
tor.
heir customers to your company, and/or
of common customers.

as an ally.
management or technical talent.

eeded to attain objectives such as these,
eeded in any event for the company to
ics and real-time initiatives to beat the
d. The following are some of the capabili-

mension of your business must be better
u are targeting at all levels. As mentioned in
time you are hiring, ask if this person is bet-
art in the targeted company. If not, hire the
titor. Making people a priority in your busi-
dering alternative processes for creating the
doing so in a manner that is better than

In this way, you can be sur
people your company needs t
Consider using the principles of
yees as well as your customers.

—This is the manner in which triage
ged, retained and managed for greater value
ly, how the relationship is governed. Beyond t
in your company should outperform those of t
petitor in respect of intent (such as an ability to
new and mutual value with important, chosen
tiveness and efficiency, including the processes t
sion of the products and services customers want

- *Technology*—Beyond the traditional roles of mana
trol, technology clearly has a central role to play i
enterprise and ensuring individual customers
they want, as and when they want it. Ask how te
ate the "self-service" company for the customer
nent of the value chain. Starting with the end cu
technology be deployed to cater to their individ
over a lifetime of purchasing? For example, can
center for after-sales service with an on-line self-
customers can help themselves before they call?
the customers in. Give each of them the opportu
value they want. Use technology to do this econ
- *Knowledge, Insight and Intelligence*—This entails
managing the data and intelligence of the busi
knowledge, insight and predictive ability neede
tomers and competitors for profit. Market, cus
petitive intelligence cannot be treated as separat
fragmented initiatives or systems in the organiz
data should be made available to those who ne
an Intranet. Suggestions about competitive int
cally, are presented in Chapter 5.

Capabilities place an upper limit on organizatio
customer engagement and responsiveness. Organizat
resources may deploy them quite differently, leading
entiated capabilities. Charles Schwab has consisten
an ability to push the limits on developing a customi
and interactive customer experience. Schwab was
1986, yet it is a brokerage leader with 3 million ind

and over $850 million in on-line revenues. Some of its competitors focused on investing in bricks and mortar, such as opening new offices, while Schwab invested in customer knowledge and insight and processes for helping individual customers on-line. Schwab's vision is to "create a rich investing experience, touch investors in more ways and reach deeply into their lives with the help, advice and tools they need to make informed investing decisions." [8]

To that end, the firm initially focused on giving customers' communications a personal look and feel. This personalization included, for example, stock quotes, charts and other information, asset allocation models and customized news. Much of this was "pull," with the customer personalizing the information him or herself. Schwab has now developed a "push" system, which uses an assessment of each customer's portfolio, watch lists, transactions and investment positions to e-mail timely information the customer can use. The information service takes one-to-one marketing to a new level by making extensive and novel use of intelligent e-mail communications solutions. In so doing, customers become intangibly locked into a learning relationship with Schwab, which is becoming better and better at serving each one uniquely, raising barriers to switching. Schwab has demonstrated how technology, customer knowledge and insight and processes for customer engagement can set themselves apart from competitors.

With the right capabilities in place, approaches can be formulated to beat the competitor you have targeted or to otherwise ensure that the competitor contributes to your prosperity. Chapter 7 provides discussion in this regard, but it should be noted that the strategies, tactics or approaches to real-time competition that your company will choose to follow cannot be discerned from items on a checklist. Rather, you will need to proceed down the planning path with senior management workshops at key milestones to ensure that the process is yielding the results you expected. A workshop is also suggested for the development of strategies to prosper with, or at the expense of, the competitor you have targeted.

Change Management and Implementation

At this stage of the planning process, you will be in a position to determine the specific steps to achieve your competitor targeting objectives. This will require good project management skills, a challenge made no

[8] Charles Schwab Web site information – www.schwab.com, 2001.

easier by the fact that you may be the first person to plan and implement a comprehensive competitor targeting initiative in your company. If the challenge seems great indeed or you do not particularly wish to don a suit of asbestos to deal with fiery comments from recalcitrant or negative management, consider outsourcing the initiative to a consultant with experience in competitor targeting and the management of large and complex senior-level engagements.

The overall project should be broken down into subcomponents such as IT, people, knowledge and process. Sponsors should be sought for the overall process and for each of the subcomponents. The sponsor should appoint a change agent responsible for the planning of the implementation and management of his or her area of responsibility. The detailed planning for each area should confirm the scope of the exercise and describe the tasks, responsibilities, timing and costs associated with implementation.

Implementation will benefit from thoughtful communications of the initiative within the company and to its customers and suppliers. It may also be appropriate to send a message to the competitor you are targeting as part of a process to manage it. For example, in an industry in decline, such as receiving tubes[9] in the mid-1960s, the leader has the potential to cause marginal players to leave the industry by effective public communications that send them appropriate messages. Companies in the receiving tube industry, such as Westinghouse, General Electric or RCA, could have been encouraged to leave early or in an appropriate schedule if a competitor such as GTE-Sylvania encouraged them to do so. Perhaps through the media, GTE could have communicated that it had reinvested in new processes, was driving costs down and was committed to the industry as long as there were tubes to be made.

That firm could also directly or indirectly welcome specific competitors to sell their assets and/or license their technologies or processes to make it easier for competitors to leave the industry. In short, the company that wants to be the leading consolidator in an industry in decline can use the media and other communications to its advantage. Being the last iceman, as GTE-Sylvania would have been, can be profitable, particularly if it is recognized by competitors that the industry holds no promise and it needs to leave. Equally, the first company to leave an industry, if it does so before others realize this is not a very attractive industry in which to be, has the opportunity to reap a higher reward than those that leave subsequently.

---

[9] Called valves in the UK. Receiving tubes provided signal amplification and were a higher power alternative to the transistors that replaced them in many applications.

Sending encoded messages such as that just described is not just for industries in decline. In growth and maturing industries, too, there may be opportunities for companies to manage their competitors through the media. More typically, companies want to build awareness and interest in their product or services and pay less attention to competitors earlier in the industry life cycle. This may be a mistake. For example, they may save press releases of contract awards and announce several at once to send a message to competitors that they are very committed to a specific geographic area, which, when linked to other actions such as pricing and hiring, may lead to regional dominance.[10]

Internal Communications

There are barriers to having a competitor targeting initiative adopted within the company, just as there would be for most projects. Communications of the project's intent within the firm could be met with the usual naysayers who congregate by the watercooler or lean over cubicle walls, Dilbert-like, to decry the flavor-of-the-minute project, one that will surely be replaced shortly by something of equal endurance. Attitudes such as these, if they exist in your firm, will need to be dispelled quickly by the president or other executives. Often, though, only the president can sway the entire organization on an issue of major importance. Have him or her issue a white paper describing the initiative and putting his/her authority and reputation into making this work. This should not be hard.

Chapter 1 provides a basis for some of the main points in the white paper such as what competitor targeting is, the main benefits for the company, the reasons the company is investing here and who will have what responsibilities to make this happen. If the president wants it done, it will occur. Do not proceed with this initiative until you have a senior champion and his or her public commitment. If the president, general manager or other senior executive is unwilling to commit, you should communicate, communicate and communicate again with them until he or she is finally willing. This executive's support will help open doors to the project, ensure that it is staffed with personnel best suited to the work and that there is broadly based support to ensure that insight, effort and intelligence flow into the initiative.

There is a saying in management consulting that organizational change does not occur until the pain of staying where you are is greater

[10] In military jargon, this is termed hegemony.

than the pain of change itself. Change management specialists talk in terms of the burning platform and the need to jump off it before being incinerated. So, where is the burning platform in competitor targeting? If this is simply a good idea, then it will compete with many other good ideas in the company and perhaps be relegated to the back burner, where it will remain until a more persuasive case can be made to elevate its importance. That does not happen often; once a project is on the back burner, it rarely moves forward again.

You need to identify the reason your management and staff should come with you on this journey and then articulate this effectively. Possible reasons could include a desire to do the following:

- Blunt competitor's CRM initiatives before they become too entrenched in their customers' supply chains.
- Deliver yet new revenues.
- Take CRM to the next level.
- Survive.
- Win all the best customers as you roll out CRM to noncustomers.

Another consideration is: What if competitors target us? Are we better off to contribute to their prosperity, or should we be proactive now to ensure that the reverse occurs and that they help to make us better, stronger and wealthier?

Governance

The management and governance of the process by which the competitor will be targeted should be formally established. Consider putting together a team to serve essentially as an internal board of directors for the initiative. Some companies draw these personnel from the senior management and assemble a team that given the task of approving the competitor targeting plan and budgets and periodically reviewing the progress in respect of implementation, say once per quarter.

Measurements

Measurement of the progress of the initiative should be part of the project planning and implementation process. In addition, a number of key metrics could be put in place to ensure that the company is deriving strategic value from what will likely be a material investment. Selected strategic measurements are described in Table 4-9.

Once implemented, provision should be made for assessing the impact of the overall endeavor on your business, including an assessment of the extent to which the original goals and objectives have been attained.

Table 4-9: Key Measurements for Competitor Targeting

Your Company vs. Targeted Competitor, by Time Period:
• Revenues by important (chosen) customers—share of customer considering all spending customers make on goods and services of the type your company could provide, whether or not it does so now • Revenues and operating profit per employee • Revenues and operating profit per customer account • Cost of capital/hurdle rates of return • Shareholder value • Customer satisfaction, intent to repurchase, and level of bonding attained by customer • Costs to serve, with allocation of all costs to customers, to the extent possible. (e.g., presale, during sale, postsale, cost of goods, carrying costs on receivables and inventories etc.) • Share of future comprising the share of customer business you expect your company and the competitor will derive • Share of revenues represented by core versus noncore customers

Implementation could be designed in a pilot program to focus on one line of business and competitor to demonstrate the benefits of competitor targeting before a more general rollout of the initiative. But it should be noted that while the analytical and some of the process components of the initiative can be done this way, competitive advantage will likely require commitments to capabilities such as technology, that will have application beyond the pilot program. To this extent, if your company believes it really does need to prosper with or from competitors, it will likely need to commit more generally to the initiative than in a pilot program or not at all.

This chapter provided a framework for planning to beat specific competitors and showed how to do research and develop a plan that will deal with many of the important competitive barriers a company faces in the marketplace. In Chapter 5: Competitive Intelligence, we will provide new frameworks and considerations to help a company formulate winning competitive strategies. Some of these concepts will have more applicability to your business situation than others. For your further consideration, we have identified a number of areas in which strategy can vary and selected alternatives that can help a company target competitors and gain customer share.

CHAPTER 5

Competitive Intelligence

***"We can learn even from our enemies."*[1]**

—Ovid

Competing strategically, tactically and in real time requires a thorough understanding of the competitors you want to beat, whether they are serving your core customers or in the marketplace more generally. This, in turn, creates a need for strategic, tactical and real-time intelligence to make your company more competitive—competitive intelligence, the subject of this chapter. If your current interest is less in the execution of competitive intelligence than in the concepts that deploy the intelligence, you might want to delay reading this chapter until you need the information presented here.

Competitive Intelligence Defined

Competitive intelligence is the process of obtaining and analyzing publicly available information to achieve the objectives of your company by facilitating organizational learning and improvement, differentiation and competitor targeting. This should assist the company to do the following:

- Understand strengths and weaknesses relative to specific competitors and the opportunities and threats they represent and predict what they will do next.

[1] Publius Ovidius Naso, *Metamorphoses*, 43 BC – AD c. 18.

- Improve and differentiate strategies, positioning, operations and financial performance.
- Compete for scarce input resources—people, time, money and knowledge.
- Win in respect of key success factors such as customer relationships, customer access, customer influence and channel support.
- Avoid the mistakes competitors are making or might make.
- Maintain or increase share of customer, and/or win over competitors' customers.

As noted, competitive intelligence is not an outcome or the content itself but a process geared to making the company more competitive with inputs, outputs and sequences of activities. It is a way of finding answers to questions about competitors. The conduct of competitive intelligence does not and should not seek to identify the questions to be examined. For example, one company watched Procter and Gamble (P&G) launch a tooth whitening product called White Strips in the US and wondered if it would do likewise in Canada. From this starting point, competitive intelligence could determine if P&G had applied for regulatory approval for the use of peroxide, if dentists had been informed of the new product and the timing of the introduction, if their usual suppliers were gearing up to produce and so on.

Most companies start a competitor examination without thinking about the main questions that they must answer if they are to win in the marketplace. Looking to identify questions from a mountain of intelligence is not unlike looking for the proverbial needle in a haystack. You might find it by working your way through the hay, but you would have been better off thinking about the best way to get the needle before starting. Not surprisingly, managers who do not ask the right questions before looking for answers often complain they do not have enough people to do the work.

One way of considering the process of competitive intelligence is described in Figure 5-1 on the next page.

Historically, competitive intelligence has helped companies build their market position by better understanding competitors and their strategies and tactics. Now, with one-to-one marketing, companies need to consider more than their competitive market or market segment positions. Attending individually to core customers brings with it an attendant focus on specific competitors and their relationships with these same customers. Here, competitive intelligence is used to build share of customer.

Figure 5-1: Competitive Intelligence (CI)

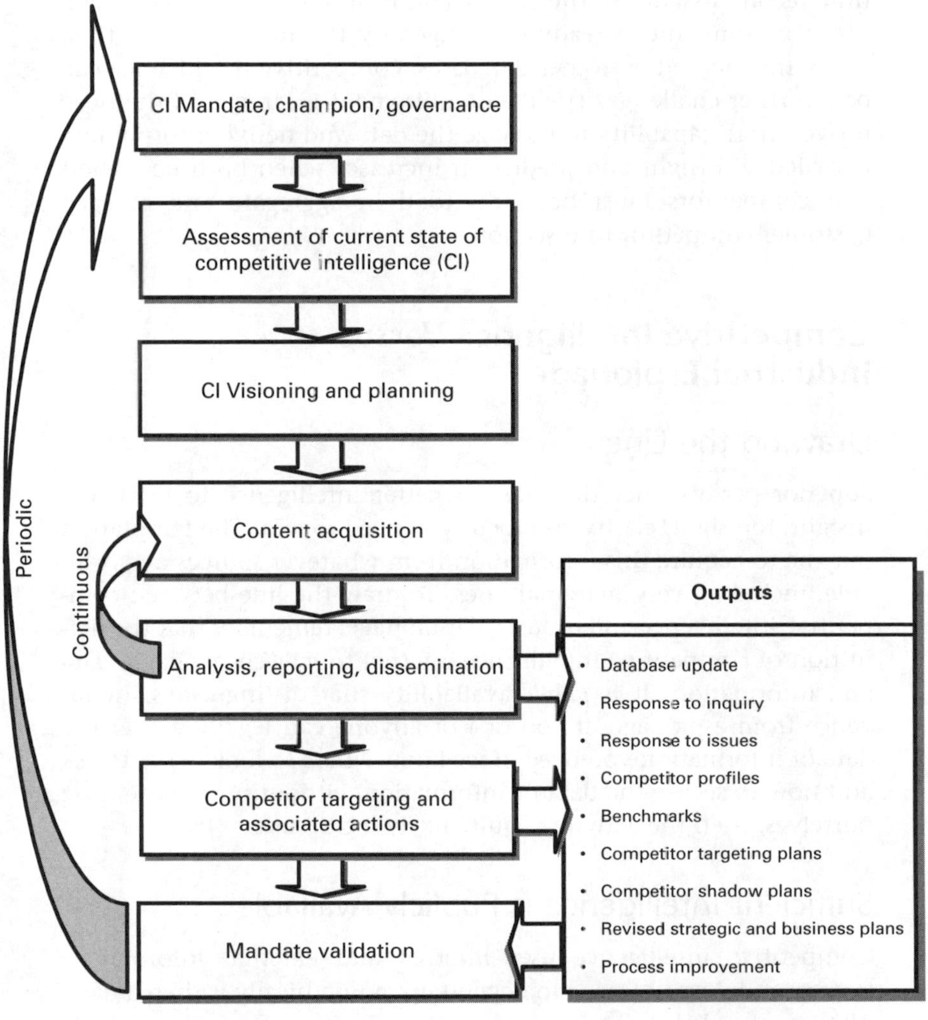

CI Mandate, champion, governance

Assessment of current state of competitive intelligence (CI)

CI Visioning and planning

Content acquisition

Analysis, reporting, dissemination

Competitor targeting and associated actions

Mandate validation

Periodic

Continuous

Outputs

- Database update
- Response to inquiry
- Response to issues
- Competitor profiles
- Benchmarks
- Competitor targeting plans
- Competitor shadow plans
- Revised strategic and business plans
- Process improvement

Competitive intelligence and competitor intelligence are not the same thing, although some people use them interchangeably. Competitive intelligence is geared to making your company more competitive and can thus include data from customers, channel intermediaries, other stakeholders and even noncompetitors who can help you outperform targeted competitors, making your company more competitive. Competitor intelligence is strictly intelligence about competitors, and it is thus a subset of competitive intelligence.

Competitive intelligence provides strategic, tactical and real-time reconnaissance of the enemy and facilitates competitor targeting. For companies already challenged by the integration of their many fragmented customer databases, competitive intelligence can be a further challenge. The data requirement is large, and the need for yet more capability to manage the data and derive information, knowledge, insight and prediction increases when both customers and competitors must be understood in aggregate and at each customer-competitor intersection.

Competitive Intelligence Versus Industrial Espionage

Drawing the Line

Superior performance depends on better intelligence to drive the insight, foresight, clarity and focus you need to win. The temptation may be to acquire this information from whatever sources are available, including very marginal ones. To draw the line between competitive intelligence and industrial espionage, remember that the definition of competitive intelligence referred to *publicly* available data and information. It is *public* availability that distinguishes intelligence from espionage. If you or I or anyone can legally gather the data or information you need, if we know where to look, what to ask and how to secure the data or information without misrepresenting ourselves, then the activity is quite likely legitimate.

Sufficient Intelligence Is Publicly Available

Competitive intelligence uses internal and external information sources and does not need to depend upon unethically gathered data. All that is needed to obtain a competitive advantage is readily available from a wide variety of legitimate, publicly available sources. No one needs to crawl through the competitor's plant in the dead of night clutching a flashlight and spy camera. The information you need is probably in the public domain, and it is certainly easier to obtain than by going the spy route. Even in the super-secret world of intelligence agencies and military and space programs, there is considerable use of public information. According to Admiral Ellis Zacharias, Deputy Chief of US Naval Intelligence in the Second World War, the US Navy obtained 95 percent of its intelligence from public sources and only 5 percent from borderline and secret sources.[2]

Some Companies Have Demonstrated Questionable Ethics

In spite of the fact that virtually all corporations consider their executives to be honorable, there have been significant cases suggesting that data are not always obtained from publicly available sources. For example, reports document the following:

- in the consumer products industry:
  - an attempted exchange of the marketing plans of a toothpaste manufacturer for cash in the men's washroom at Kennedy Airport
  - the alleged overflying and photography of a new P&G cookie manufacturing plant perhaps to determine plant layout, capacity and technology
  - also in the cookie wars, a competitor alleged to have been seen snooping through packaging material at a manufacturer that supplied two rivals
- in the petrochemicals industry, the overflying and photography of a new plant to determine the design, flowrates and by-products (advanced photography of the type previously found in the aerospace and spy industries have long been in the public domain)
- in the automobile industry, the removal of GM's company confidential documents by a former executive, who may have made this available to his new employer
- in the computer industry, the theft by a competitor of IBM's micro-code data
- the alleged orchestrated eavesdropping on executives flying first class on transatlantic flights aboard a European airline in an attempt to help domestic companies gain advantage over foreign competitors

[2] E. M. Zacharias, *Secret Missions: The Story of an Intelligence Officer*, New York: G.P. Putnam's and Sons, 1946, pp. 117-18.

Staff May Make Errors of Judgment

Even the most ethical of firms may have unethical employees who can damage its reputation. An attractive female employee of a major aerospace company told me that she visited a restaurant near a large competitor seeking to gain competitor information. At the end of the day, the competitor's workers entered the restaurant, and this woman engaged an eager man in conversation. After pleasantries, she steered the discussion to her areas of interest and believed she would soon obtain the required information when the "competitor" flashed his FBI badge and asked her to explain her interest in secret information. It took some considerable reassurance to convince the federal investigator that she was not a foreign spy.

Executives May Want to Win Too Much

Early in an engagement to help a company to defeat a specific competitor, I stood behind the president at the window as he gestured to a nearby building. "There," he said, "are the offices of [the competitor]. Their garbage bins are at the back. Why don't you just go through their material and see what you find?" No mention was made of dumpster-diving as an unethical and quite likely illegal sport. In my mind's eye, there was a picture of me on the front page of the newspaper, computer printout in hand, peering out over the rim of the garbage bin. I discouraged the president from this course of action and wondered why he was so motivated to beat this particular competitor. It turned out that the rival had been founded by a former executive who had taken customer lists and other confidential material when he left. What made the competition even more personal was the fact that he had also absconded with my client's wife!

Much more could be said about industrial espionage. The intent here is simply to focus the reader on publicly available sources of data and information to make your company more competitive. Most of the answers you are looking for can come from sources other than competitors. Some information will need to come from competitors themselves but not in an underhanded way. Leave contact with your rivals until the last step in your intelligence initiative. It may turn out that you never need to actually contact them and, if you do, ensure that the contact is well planned, well rehearsed, well documented and vetted by your lawyers and advisors.

Three Sources of Competitive Intelligence

All sources of competitive information may be categorized into three groups:

- Individuals in Your Own Company
- Third Parties
- Competitors

Individuals in Your Own Company

A vast amount of information already exists within your firm—perhaps as much as 80 percent of what you need depending upon the size of your company and the level of awareness and sensitivity of the staff to the subject matter. Most of your employees have monitored competitors informally throughout their careers. Now you want to make this informal knowledge formal by documenting, archiving and sharing competitive insight and finding new ways to systematically defeat a targeted competitor, especially in your core customers. Now you are making competition central to strategy development, not a peripheral element that an informal monitoring would suggest.

Much of what you need to know about your competition may already be available inside your firm, which is a friendly source of information and the least costly. Start your search for internal information by understanding who knows what about your competitors. Take an inventory of the internally available information by asking people in person, using forms, an Intranet site or newsletters to drive internal traffic to the site. An incentive to help is always useful. One company awards a computer to the person providing the most help within a specified period. Once you understand the availability of specific types of competitive information within your company and have formulated key questions about your competitive environment, identify the likely employees who could provide the answers you need, and set up appointments to review the information in their possession. Conduct interviews with them.

Table 5-1 could help prompt a review of some of the areas you may wish to cover in your discussions, depending upon the issues that are of most relevance to you. Obviously, the questions to be asked will depend on what it is you are trying to find out to guide your targeting strategies and tactics, and how you are going to use the intelligence.

Think about the key success factors for participating in tomorrow's industry and how the competitor might approach these issues. Consider formulating hypotheses and confirming these in the interviews. Reflect on how the rival might respond to the main thrusts you are planning. Review their financial condition and how they might be pressured to act. What other factors are driving change at the competitor? New executives? Declining profit margins? Unhappy shareholders? As with all research, asking the right questions is a vitally important component of gathering good intelligence but there is no mechanical approach for guiding this process. Hopefully, many of the issues raised in this book will serve to prompt you and others working with you on this engagement to ask the right questions.

Table 5-1: Internal Sources of Competitive Information

Departments/Personnel	Typical Areas of Current or Potential Competitive Knowledge
President	Insight developed into targeted competitors as a result of networking, exposure to analyst's reports, consultant's advice and other sources, even including playing golf with the executives of competitors or working on industry association committees or charity events with them
Engineering	Reverse engineering of competitors' products; cost of production; technical excellence relative to our offerings; direction of technology
Finance and treasury	Cost of competitors' funds; relationships with financial community; financial analysis
Human resources	Key performance criteria; knowledge and skills gaps; key executives in competitors' companies —profiles, behaviors and other attributes; organizational culture and structures; employees within your company who have worked for competitors
Information centers	Published data; informal librarian network
Manufacturing	Assembly methods; labor to capital ratios; unionization; labor rates; state of employee relations; key manufacturing weaknesses, strengths

Marketing	Media expenditures: strategy, level and nature; core customers; relationship marketing strategies; customer share performance; competitive product, service and solution strengths and weaknesses; barriers to increasing core customer share held by competitors; strategic direction
Procurement	Relationships with strategic suppliers; estimated costs of obtaining key components; specific sources
Public relations	Level of "unpaid" media exposure; media relationships; strategies articulated
Research and development	Core technical competence; emerging technologies under development
Sales	Relationships with core customers; types and timing of programs; usual reflex actions to our/other competitor initiatives; key sales staff profiles; sales culture

Third Parties

Third parties are people and organizations outside your company that know about the competitor you are targeting. They are the next major source of competitive information. Many are likely to be friendly contacts because you already deal with them, perhaps making them amenable to helping you with your information development.

Table 5-2: Third-Party Sources of Competitive Information

Third Party	Typical Areas of Competitive Competence/Knowledge
Advertising agencies (yours)	Competitors' media expenditures, positioning, communications, customer and product/market strategies
Bankers	Competitors' financial dealings
Consultants	Competitive intelligence programs; competitor profiles; specific information as well as process facilitation for the entire competitor targeting exercise

Customers	The ultimate information source: for competitors' positioning, new products, services, solutions and programs; e-business strategies, favorability regarding purchase intent; attitudes, awareness and much more
Distributors	Trade programs; distributor margins; support received from competitors and given to them by the distributors
Trade or general press	Loquacious sources of general competitor insight
Equipment manufacturers	Installed base; technology employed; productivity rates
Financial analysts	Business, financial and product/market strategy; understanding of stock valuation and reasons for discount or premium vs. your company
Government	Usually helpful about overall industry rather than individual competitors
Labor unions	Contracts, labor conditions
Lawyers	Interpretation of court rulings involving competitors; assessment of proclivity of competitors to use legal means to achieve business ends
Patent attorneys	Patents issued to competitors and the strengths and weaknesses of the patent filings
Previous employees	Focused competitive insight
Suppliers	E-business direction, costs, quality and amount of inputs; competitor procurement packaging, other priorities; recent requests for offerings not usually supplied
Trade associations	Shipments; focused competitor information

Currently, representatives of organizations such as these are asking your company for information. Consider how you can make this more of a two-way street. For example, when financial analysts contact the senior financial officer in your firm, they should be asked pointed questions, much as they ask you. If they want to know the financial projections for the company, the CFO could note that this data will be provided and that he or she then wishes to discuss the firm's position in the context of the industry. In the ensuing conversation, reference to specific competitors can be made.

The advertising agency should be expected to develop competitive positioning discussion papers and to assist in identifying key questions to be resolved about competition. For example, many companies track their "share of voice," which means their media expenditures are divided by media expenditures from all industry participants. This is a good measurement and made better if the share of voice numbers are compared with share of market performance to see correlation. The agency could also assess the share of voice of the company relative to targeted competitors and develop shadow media and positioning plans for the targeted company. Then, the company can plan its own media and marketplace positioning.

Lobbyists, public relations agencies, lawyers and other professionals employed by your organization may also be able to add value to a competitor targeting initiative. For example, lobbyists could be asked to identify the issues a targeted competitor is pursuing, how it is doing this, which lobbyists it is using and what the outcome might be for the competitor.

Former employees of competitors, particularly those who work for your own organization, should be sought out and interviewed. Your human resources department can help by identifying who to contact. (If it cannot, which is sometimes the case, its information systems need some changing.) Former employees of a company should be routinely interviewed, whether as part of an acquisition due diligence or a competitor targeting exercise, to assess relevant issues. One does need to be aware, though, that disgruntled former employees, while motivated, may have agendas that bear consideration.

Competitors

Competitors say a great deal about themselves for one of two main reasons:

- Personal Ego or Corporate Prestige
- Public Disclosure

Personal Ego or Corporate Prestige

You may wish to obtain items such as speeches, media interviews, curriculum vitae and other relevant personal information on a competitor's senior executives. These can be provided to a psychologist for as detailed an evaluation as is possible with published material, although this sort of arm's length assessment is controversial. What it can do is establish additional questions or issues to be further examined using CI. For example, profiles of senior executives could help you identify patterns of behavior and decision-making processes in the competitor, information that could be employed to strategic or tactical advantage in the market. For example, these types of profiles could help you learn the following:

- What do they do under stress? For example, watching how they play golf might help you predict what they would do in a takeover attempt. Are they calm, or do they get emotional easily? Do they keep an accurate score, or do they forget to count some strokes?
- Do they challenge the status quo or accept it? These are important issues when you consider their response to an introduction of a new product or a change of price.
- Do they have intellectual or psychological "blind sides"? In other words, do they generally not appreciate certain areas or activities very well? For example, if they are financially strong, do they fully appreciate, recognize and reward their people? If not, might some of their better people be enticed to join your company?
- Do they have comfort zones to which they gravitate when under pressure? Often, these zones of comfort are the areas with which they are most familiar such as the work they did for the longest period of time before their present position. The senior executive of a major packaged goods firm developed his career from operations. Whenever he was in town, he was to be found walking around the factory at which he was once plant manager. If you wanted to target this company, it would be helpful to understand the president's operations experience and the support he would likely accord products made at this factory.

Public Disclosure

Information disclosed by competitors is frequently published and may be obtained via on-line search procedures from the company's own Web site and others or from a clipping service. Some people visit chat rooms or even start chats with a view to benefiting from the insight of company insiders. One particularly helpful US source for learning precisely what executives communicate is The Wall Street Transcript (www.twst.com), which collects verbatim responses of senior executives to the questions of financial analysts. This helps not only in understanding the strategic direction of competitors, but could help profile the senior executives. The verbatim nature also can help one understand what is not said as much as what is. Additionally, the reader can learn the communications styles of competitors' executives.

Other sources can be helpful, too such as Research Bank Web from Thomson Financial, including Investext (www.investext.com), although this is a paid subscription service. Over 600 full-text databases are available for searching at Dialog Corporation, a Thomson Company, at Dialogweb (www.dialog.com). This can provide much more than what competitors themselves say—it is a gateway to an enormous resource on company and industry information. Lexis-Nexis (www.lexis-nexis.com) provides a similar gateway to a large number of databases. The firm claims to have access to over 30,000 sources. In this era of content proliferation, the number of potential sources of information is obviously vast and growing, and this could be the subject of a book in its own right.

Competitors' communications may be captured in sources such as those identified in Table 5-3.

Table 5-3: Competitors' Communications

- Advertisements
- Annual reports
- Company newsletters
- Court cases
- Filings with agencies and boards such as environmental, health and safety, municipal or city planning, equal employment and labor relations
- Financial filings with regulatory authorities or the government
- Financial press
- Local or regional press
- Magazine articles
- Patent filings
- Popular press
- Product literature and brochures
- Recruitment advertisements
- Regulatory hearings
- Technical papers

Review what competitors communicate for information about their activities and plans, especially when these have a bearing on your core customers. For example, a competitor may announce that it is about to launch a new, more advanced product, which might cause customers to defer purchasing. Your competitive intelligence could establish that the competitor would not be ready to launch for some time, or it could identify specific shortcomings with the new product. Then you can communicate with your customers to encourage them to buy now.

Competitors' advertising and direct mail is particularly informative because it presents the results of their market and customer research, strategic thinking, targeting, selling propositions and positioning all in one brief piece of celluloid, paper, magnetic tape or whatever. However, by the time you see the advertising or direct mail piece, it may be a little late to do much except take short-term, reactionary measures to defer the impact of a competitor's thrust until you have had time to address the issues raised in the advertising. Legal avenues are used to blunt a competitor's thrusts such as demands that they produce evidence of advertising claims. Less litigious responses to their advertising could include your own advertising, communications of research you have conducted, and coupons and promotional pricing to encourage customers to buy from you now or achieve other business objectives.

Companies say a great deal about themselves in annual reports and financial filings with regulatory authorities such as the Securities and Exchange Commission (SEC) in the US, the Corporations Directorate of Industry Canada[3] and Companies House in London, England. SEC filings are available on-line from the EDGAR database (www.sec.gov).[4] Much of this is helpful in the development of a competitor profile but the usual market and financial emphasis is on what has already occurred, not on the future. To arrive at an understanding of what the competitor will be doing next, you need to examine sources that provide an earlier warning of their intent. These could include strategies announced by their executives and close examination of concept development and early stages of commercialization. Information such as this can come from technical papers presented at conferences, patent filings, local or regional newspapers or the trade press. Engineers and scientists often seek peer group approval at conferences at which they discuss the nature of their work, and that can be a good indicator of future investment emphasis in that company. Your own technical staff should be directed to obtain relevant information at these events.

[3] Various provinces also provide company information such as the Companies Branch, Ministry of Consumer and Commercial Relations, Province of Ontario.

[4] The SEC requires all public companies (except foreign companies and companies with less than $10 million in assets and 500 shareholders) to file registration statements, periodic reports, and other forms electronically through EDGAR. *Source:* SEC Web site (www.sec.gov/edgar.shtml), 2001.

Patent filings are another good source of future market if not customer-specific activity. Not all patents should be treated equally. For example, companies in the pharmaceutical industry are known to patent discoveries that may not result in commercial drugs, perhaps in the hope of developing workable products later on. Patent searches will nevertheless indicate the direction and areas of emphasis of a competitor's research and development program, even if the specifics are not always clear evidence of preparation for new product launches. While the patent process is lengthy, some country jurisdictions may publish information earlier than others. I have found early patent information in Belgium, for example. You may want to use a patent attorney if this is an important area of investigation for your company.

Because of the rapid pace of technological change and ease of duplication of the benefits of patents, some companies prefer speed over monopolization and go without patents to develop a strong position in the minds of core customers before competitors can respond. This is particularly evident in the commercialization of electronic products and software.

Local and regional newspapers monitor issues that affect their constituency. Companies often choose to locate in a town, believing labor there to be more loyal or hardworking than in larger cities. The local newspapers, or indeed the community papers in the cities, monitor the companies that most affect their tax base, level of employment and quality of working life. They tend to report more detail than national papers on the activities of the companies that are important local employers.

Early Warnings

As an example of what not to say, a client pursued complete stealth in their electronics initiative—complete stealth, that is, except for granting an interview to a community newspaper that fully profiled the project. There was even a photo of the president with his arm draped around one of the secret machines that had been installed. The commentary described the objective of the project, the number of machines that had been bought, the productivity of each unit, how much employment would be added to the facility and more. Several competitors would have benefited from the information. Today, the company is not the leader it once was. Whether or not it could have retained its leadership position is questionable in any event, but certainly it was not aided by the president's disclosures.

On another project, by reading local press, I was surprised to find considerable congressional interest in a competitor's plant, one with significant local employment and proprietary technology. The local congressman went on record that he was against the Department of Defense's interest in having two sources for major contracts presumably because the plant in his district had a major contract, and employment would be undermined by second sourcing.[5] Following up on the contacts revealed in the article led to an understanding of the extensive political support available to the competitor—an area our client had all but ignored. It has since developed a very strong ability to manage its political affairs.

Competitors blurt out much to damage their future prospects. Few are alert to the wartime saying that loose lips sink ships. To illustrate, a few months before Colgate was about to introduce its toothpaste in a pump, an article appeared in a mass circulation consumer affairs column that discussed the pump project, the target market, the media expenditures and frequency of airing, the pricing of the pump and the coupons that would be issued. I received a coupon as promised a few months later. As a brand manager for Crest, Colgate's major rival, this would have presented me with valuable information which would allow me to do the following:

- Find out whether my core customers and retailers saw any merit in having toothpaste dispensed in a pump format and, if they did, the specifics of their needs.
- Develop tactical approaches to blunt Colgate's thrust, perhaps by "pantry loading" core customers with significant incentives to purchase high volumes of Crest for future usage, which would likely lessen their interest in trying the Colgate pump when it was introduced. That is, a customer with a lot of Crest toothpaste in their bathroom cabinet would be less likely to try the new Colgate product.
- Develop strategies to supply core customers with Crest's own pumped product now that time has been bought by the two tactics described above. This could include the purchase of machinery and packaging or having the product produced under contract packing agreements.

---

[5] Contracts often have a lead supplier that obtains the majority of the volume and a second source that obtains less business. Because the second source supplier has a production capability, it can gear up to make more at short notice, if the main vendor cannot provide the needed volumes.

Recruitment advertisements provide an immediate early warning about the skills the competitor thinks it needs. Sometimes it can reveal an entirely new strategic direction. Through the monitoring of employment advertisements, a client became aware of the decision of a supplier to the automotive aftermarket to get out of the production end of the business, moving instead to company-owned service outlets. By studying the advertisements, the client was also able to establish the geographic coverage of this program, which was at the time principally in the US south. This led our client to consider also providing consumer services as well as products, although the precise location of the rival's initiative was of less initial interest.

Government Filings

Filings that companies must make with specific government departments can often be accessed under the so-called sunshine[6] provisions by which governments open their files to public scrutiny in countries such as the USA, Canada and the UK. The information that can be gleaned from examination under these laws can be more than useful; it can make a fundamental difference to the competitiveness of a company. For example, in an early, celebrated case, the *Freedom of Information Act (FOI)* was used by a competitor to gain knowledge and design details without incurring high research and development costs. Air Cruisers had filed a design for a 42-person inflatable life raft with the Federal Aviation Administration. Approval, it thought, would give it a competitive advantage. Although approval was granted, a competitor, Switlik Parachute Company, apparently obtained portions of the Air Cruiser submission using provisions of the *FOI Act*, under protest by Air Cruisers, which had learned of Switlik's interest in procuring what it considered confidential technical documents. Switlik designed its own raft and won a major European contract award in competition with Air Cruisers.[7]

The *FOI Act* is not supposed to reveal trade secrets and commercial or financial information that is privileged or confidential. In practice, it sometimes does. Make applications for FOI filings through third parties who do not need to advise who their client is. A direct filing of your own is subject to a reverse FOI search, which would reveal you as the party seeking the information. When applying for

---

[6] Likely called sunshine because the information is not kept in secret (dark) files.

[7] B. Schorr, "How Law Is Being Used to Pry Secrets from Uncle Sam's Files," *Wall Street Journal*, 9 May, 1977, p.1.

government documents, you will usually need the support of the employee who works for the government and administers the information you need if you are to get exactly what you seek. If you ask for documents that do not have the information you want, the government employee can guide you to potentially more useful documents. Try to gain cooperation without making reference to the provisions of acts that require the employee to assist. This will help to expedite the process without resorting to time-consuming provisions of the legislation. Know what you want before you call. Can you describe the record or information you seek? Do you know the contract numbers or the numbers of the forms? (Much information of this type can be identified within your own organization by establishing what forms your company files with which government departments.) This will prevent the phenomenon of endless referral loops, which often follows undirected requests for information to the government, any government.

Gathering Published Information

Published information is generally a low cost source of intelligence. In the following, we discuss a number of considerations in the gathering of published information, which is also called secondary research.

Primary or Secondary Research?

Secondary research comprises material such as research reports and articles that are published, while primary research is gathered directly from sources, using interviews and surveys, for example. Secondary research, although an important competitive information source, is relied on for too much competitive insight by most companies. Many researchers like to spend time at their computer screen looking to the Internet and other on-line sources to provide the revealed truth. This is not surprising since published information is readily available, easy to organize, and does not require interpersonal contact, which some researchers or analysts prefer to avoid, especially when obtaining sensitive information. Published material, however, often suffers from significant deficiencies, particularly the fact that the data have been gathered for purposes other than your own, often to inform and entertain a mass audience. As such, it often lacks the clarity and insight you need to assemble your own strategic conclusions. Resist the temptation to gather mountains of published material, thereby deferring other research and the development of conclusions and implications for your company. Get out from behind your desk and ask the specific questions to which you need answers.

Secondary Sources

Having said this, published information nevertheless must be obtained in any integrated intelligence operation once internal staff have been debriefed and their own published sources accessed. Start at the most general of sources and work to the progressively more specific. The following is an appropriate order to review:

- company-produced literature such as product brochures, employee/mass publications
- competitors' Web sites
- directories and indexes for background company information
- directories published by financial brokerages to identify the companies they cover
- financial filings, annual reports
- indexes for articles published about the competition
- key publications, which should be subscribed to and monitored on an ongoing basis
- on-line databases to search specific key words associated with core customers, products, services, personnel, advertising, technical and other information to answer the questions you will have formulated
- third-party, "off-the-shelf" studies

"Snowball research," as its name implies, will result in additional publications (and relevant personnel to interview) being identified from the research process itself.

Clearly, the Internet provides an excellent opportunity to develop data and information about competitors. There are standard search methods such as those that use the major portal search engines, which yield data on various Web sites, for example. And obviously, the competitor's own Web site provides much news. New tools are becoming available to search for competitor's pricing and other data. These so-called shopping-bots scour the Internet to learn more about competitors' prices.[8] Some companies use the Internet in

[8] For example, on-line software called Net Periscope (www.onx.com) watches competitors' prices on the Web. Price comparisons are also available at www.mysimon.com and www.dealtime.com.

novel ways, visiting or even setting up Web sites and discussion groups or threads to solicit comments about competitors. It is not uncommon for sites incorporating the competitor's name and negative words such as "sucks" to have extensive diatribes on the enemy, and some of it may be of use.

Internet-based research is a large and fast-changing arena. The reader is referred to a number of books on the subject.[9] Again, be reminded that the Internet can provide data of value but also much that is useless. It is a time-consuming channel to explore. You would do well to bookmark the most relevant sites and use the data you secure with caution, helping to frame or refute hypotheses rather than serving as definitive evidence. Later in this chapter, we discuss how to develop reliable information by validating it and confirming its accuracy.

Telephone Interviews

As has been mentioned, competitive intelligence is a process of finding answers to questions that will help your company attain its business objectives such as those that may be achieved by competitor targeting. Some of these questions may be answered from secondary sources but, often, primary research sources will be necessary to supplement the information gathered. So, by the time you are ready to conduct interviews, you will have obtained much published material. Depending on the questions you are seeking to answer, you should now be familiar with the competitor's core customers, the intersection of these customers with those your company values most and many key issues your competitor faces. Now comes the part that is hardest for some people: telephone interviews.

If you or your staff are a little hesitant about conducting telephone interviews, consider hiring professional researchers and consultants. They can prove less expensive than training your own staff and may provide better results the first few times you use them. But remember that once they leave, so does their expertise. If you want to develop an intelligence center of expertise in your company for the longer term, consider investing in training first.

[9] For example, Helen P. Burwell, *Online Competitive Intelligence: Increase Your Profits Using Cyber-Intelligence*, Tempe, AZ: Facts On Demand Press, 1999.

List Interview Candidates

Develop a contact list of individuals who may be able to provide the insight you need. You will need to supplement a list developed from internal, personal and published sources with contacts identified from the following:

- *Trade directories*—Every industry has directories that identify many of the key decision makers, company information and telephone numbers, among much else. This is usually more helpful than using the Internet because all the companies are grouped together in a logical way such as by Standardized Industrial Classification (SIC) code.
- *Articles*—Milk them for all the names you can. Articles, particularly in trade journals, will frequently quote sources who would be helpful contributors to your project.
- *Authors of relevant articles*—Contact authors who have written about the issues you are examining to understand what additional information they have, who their sources were and who else they know who could help you. Usually, the authors have not included all sources in their articles.
- *Friendly and unfriendly sources*—Categorize your contacts according to their level of friendliness. Friendly sources would include your suppliers, government agencies, trade associations and your distributors and agents. Sources likely to be unsympathetic to your information needs include specific competitors and those companies or individuals that depend heavily on competitors for their livelihood such as sole-source suppliers of products or services. Contact friendly sources first, both to find out what they know and to obtain referrals to others.
- *Cold calls*—Cold calls made to a company's switchboard for the name of a person without an introduction or prior information should be the last approach to consider because it may prove most difficult to secure cooperation from the respondent.

Plan the Interview

Before you call anybody, prepare an interview guide and a respondent profile. An interview guide is required to make sure that you identify the main issues you would like addressed in the course of the discussion. The guide (or guides, if you are calling several different categories of respondents) does not have to detail the precise phrasing of the questions nor their specific order. By having a listing of the issues, you will know when you have succeeded in the interview and when your discussion is complete. Do not attempt to follow the guide rigidly—a successful interview should allow some leeway in the issues that are covered if it is to reflect the areas that are perceived as important by the respondents. After you have conducted a few interviews, you should update your guides to reflect the knowledge you now have and the outstanding issues that remain to be resolved. Only if you are seeking confirmation or validation of responses should you consider asking questions of one respondent that you have previously directed to another. Either ensure that your questions reflect greater depth or stop interviewing.

To ensure that your contacts yield considerable information over an extended period of time, you will need to call some of the respondents back periodically to obtain updates, verification, hypotheses review or to ask directed questions about key issues that may arise in the future. You should systematize your contact network by preparing respondent profiles. This will enable you to remain familiar with the key items of interest to the respondents and to do small favors to help them and cement your relationship, such as sending articles or information in which you know they will be interested. At the end of each interview, prepare a form to assess the conclusions from the interview and what actions should be undertaken. Also, update the respondent profile as indicated.

Structured and Semi-Structured Interviews

You need to decide what type of interviews to employ. There are two basic types: structured and semi-structured. In structured interviews, respondents are asked fixed questions one after the other. These are prepared in advance and asked in a prearranged sequence. This type of interview yields information that is comparable from one interview to the next. This is similar in approach to a mail questionnaire and may be carried out using the telephone. The disadvantages include the rapid tiring of respondents, inadequate depth of information and no opportunity for the learning achieved by the research to date to be built into the questions. Especially in business-to-business research settings, structured personal interviews are not recommended and should be used only rarely for telephone interviews.

A better way is to use semi-structured interviews whereby the interviewer is directed by a guide, but the timing, format or nature of the questions is left up to the skill of the interviewer. A truly successful interview should leave the respondent feeling that he or she has just engaged in an interesting discussion rather than a rigid question and answer session. The key is to let the respondents talk about what is important to them while aiding their recall to ensure that they cover the topic for which you have planned a response.

Good and Bad Interviews

There are good and bad interviews. Some will be the fault of the respondent, and some the interviewer's. For example, almost anyone can chat with other people, and, if enough discussions are held, a vast amount of data will have been collected. However, this is not the purpose of the intelligence operation. Good interviews must be highly directed and yield correct, accurate information relevant to the research objectives and obtained with the minimum number of interviews consistent with obtaining this information. Good interviewing practice may or may not come naturally to you. Each person develops his or her own style according to his or her personality, but many of the important skills can be learned such as how to listen and how to draw out what you need to know. Interviewing is time-consuming and, at times, frustrating. But perseverance and dedication will likely yield the results you seek.

Preparing and Conducting the Interviews

If you are going to do the interviews yourself, here are some thoughts to bear in mind.

Prepare Mentally

Remember, almost nobody is going to hang up on you. Most people are pleasant and cooperative, and several will consider that they will gain from speaking with you perhaps because they want to talk about their work or want to learn more about their industry from you. If people do hang up, understand that this may have as much to do with the timing of your call or their own personality as your introduction, subject matter or style.

Resist making assumptions about what people will tell you. Ask and you may uncover a considerable amount of information. At first read, this may seem obvious, but many researchers assume that a respondent either does not know or will not tell even before posing the question.

Do Important Interviews Last

The quality of your style will improve with time, so start by doing the less important interviews first so that you can warm up, adjust your approach and gain confidence.

Introduction

Introduce yourself and your reason for calling. Be honest, and do not misrepresent yourself. State right away that you are not seeking to sell anything, but would like to share views about issues of mutual interest. Provide a benefit to the person to participate in the discussion. One benefit you can offer is to share information where you can. Do so early on in the interview so that the individual understands that he or she has much to learn from you as well.

If someone has referred you to this person, mention who it was even if the contact is not very well known to you. Such a bridge improves your credibility and acceptance.

Prequalify the respondent to ensure that this is indeed the right person to be answering your questions. For example, if calling to find out about aspects of a company's call center equipment, you might have decided that the person who buys the equipment should be answering your questions. You might inquire, "Mr. Jones, are you responsible for purchasing call center equipment for Acmnex Corporation?" [10]

Ask if the person is busy. Such a basic courtesy is often overlooked and could lead you to making an incorrect assumption about the brevity of the interview or the quality of the discussion. If the person is busy, "in a meeting" or if you get his or her voice mail, leave a message and mention a time when you will call again. You are imposing an obligation if you expect the respondent to call back. The best time to call busy people back is early in the morning while they are alone at their desks and take their own calls. I suggest calling before 8 a.m. You might want to block caller identification if you think that this might cause you to be screened out before you have an opportunity to present your reason for calling. Consider, though, that some people do not answer blocked calls.

Relating to the Respondent

Relate to the respondent as a peer because this is the best way to ensure high volumes of quality information transfer. You are proud

[10] All names are chosen at random for illustration purposes only.

of the company for which you work and may be thinking something like: "I am calling from CorpusMaximus, the world's most profitable corporation, and I decided to talk with you even though you obviously have a less important job in a much smaller company than mine!" Resist the temptation to appear overbearingly powerful (even if you are!) or meekly submissive (which is usually transparent because you are not or you would not be engaging in this assertive program in the first place).

Asking Questions

Simple open-ended questions are at the heart of good interviewing technique. Yes/no answers in interviews are often not very useful. The good interviewer should begin all questions with one of the following six words: who, what, where, when, why, how? For example, in an inquiry to establish if a company is experiencing financial problems, you might say "I understand that Acmnex is stretching out its payables. Do you know why they might be doing that?"

Do not ask questions with great intensity or in a rapid-fire manner because this will kill the interview within a few minutes. Goodwill may enable the respondent to get past an initial onslaught, but in a few minutes, patience for one-way information transfer usually is exhausted. Whenever possible, ask the respondent to quantify responses and obtain detailed explanations for the conclusions or information provided. People tend to offer only qualitative statements, but these usually do not yield the insight you need. A comment such as "we are dependent on sales to the mining industry" could be met with the response "what percentage of your company's total sales last year were from the mining industry?"

Clarifying Answers

When people do not know the exact answer to a question that has a number as an answer, try to narrow down their range of uncertainty. The result is usually good enough for your purposes. Ask if the number is likely greater than—or less than X. This provides bounds to the uncertainty. You can confirm and narrow down the spread even more in subsequent interviews.

Cross-reference statements made in the interview with others presented by the respondent earlier in the discussion and with information available from other published sources or interviews you have previously conducted. For example, you might say, "Can you help me clarify my understanding? Earlier in the interview you said your inventory turns were about twenty last year and that your average inventory levels have been about $40 million. This suggests that your annual sales would have been in the area of $800 million last year, but you said your sales were about $500 million. Is there something I am missing in my understanding here?"

Restate key responses to make sure that you understand and that there is no more detail the respondent wishes to add. For example, if the respondent says, "I buy about half my widgets from Company A," you could respond, "You said earlier that you buy a total of 2,000 widgets per year. Is it correct to say that you buy about 1,000 each year from Company A?"

Eliciting a Response

If you are having difficulty obtaining a response to a key question, you might use the knowledge you have available and seek confirmation of a hypothesis by taking a stab at the answer. For example, if you wished to know which customer was most important to a competitor you are targeting, you might say something such as the following to a person who should know, such as a mutual competitor of your target: "I understand that Acmnex works very closely with Hugmir Enterprises. Is this your information, too?" Many people feel uncomfortable when an inaccurate perception exists in the minds of others and will immediately leap to correct your erroneous understanding or confirm the one you do have. Then you have an opportunity to expand and deepen your insight. This is not to say that you would deliberately make a misleading or false statement to get a rise out of the respondent. The intent here is to clarify slim evidence or your suspicions.

To induce a respondent to go deeper into a subject when he or she thinks that the end has been reached, bridge to an in-depth question by suggesting that you may have missed something or wish to clarify specific points. For example, "You said earlier that Acmnex was experiencing financial problems because its management was either incompetent, unethical or both. Can you provide any specific examples of either situation?"

Occasionally, the interview may go silent as the respondent decides how or whether to answer a key question and you establish how best to direct the interview from then on. In moments such as these, keep quiet. Let the silence continue, and continue. Your respondent will inevitably rush to fill the void, often with particularly revealing material.

Timing of Key Questions

Time the placement of key questions. Telephone discussions of ten to fifteen minutes are common with middle- to senior-level line managers. Few managers have time for much more than that anymore. Consider that interviews that are longer than fifteen minutes are atypical bonanzas, while shorter interviews could mean that you either have a poor respondent, insufficient benefits to offer or an inadequate interviewing style. Around the three to four minute mark, the respondent should be warmed up and ready for your main question(s). If you try to present it too early, you may get a truncated response or none at all. If you wait too late, you may never have the chance. Slip in the question without fanfare or tremulous voice and move on once you have the response you seek without dwelling on the subject.

Concluding the Interview

Conclude the interview by asking, "Is there anything I can tell you that you would like to know?" This usually brings respondents back to the issues in which they are most interested and leaves the last impression that you are helpful and cooperative. Ask if you can call the respondent back at a later time to go over some of your main findings. The person will likely be flattered and more than willing to participate. This could open the door to an ongoing relationship. Lastly, obtain referrals to others who may know about your particular areas of interest.

Overcoming Pitfalls

Even with these techniques, you are likely to experience several pitfalls that must be overcome. For example, an efficient assistant screens you. It may be difficult to articulate your mission and persuade this person of the value of your cause. Try stating your name, company name and the fact that this is an important matter related to your industry that you would like to discuss with the boss. Brace yourself for not getting through all assistants. If told he or she is "out of the office today," you could respond by asking that your name and company name be recorded and placed on the employer's desk, and ask when would be a good time to call again.

Occasionally the respondent may indicate that he or she is not interested in discussing this subject matter. Ask what his or her concerns are, and try to address them. For example, the respondent may not want to discuss confidential data, and you can assure him or her that no confidential data need be disclosed to you. If you are still unable to resolve the issues to his or her satisfaction, thank the respondent and conclude the discussion. Recognize that a disproportionately small number of people yield the vast majority of the insight you need—perhaps 90 percent of what you need to know is supplied by 10 percent of the people you interview, so do not be discouraged if you lose a few respondents along the way.

While you are conducting a telephone interview, the respondent may mention that someone has just entered his or her office and asks, "Would you hold for a moment?" This may well happen a second, third and fourth time. Hang onto your patience and ask if this is not a convenient time to talk, could you call back at a later, more suitable opportunity. Make sure you nail down a definite time to call before concluding the discussion.

Your respondent may be argumentative. Do not respond in kind. Try to establish if you have given the person a reason for relating to you in this way or if it is just naturally the respondent's personality. If you have caused this reaction, try to cover your previous remark, but if this is the person's style, relate in softer tones, ask open-ended questions and emphasize the insight or wisdom of his or her responses. A characteristic need of argumentative people is to be right all the time. Although you may be very knowledgeable about the subject matter, do not appear to be a know-it-all. Respondents have little desire to share information with someone who already appears to be in possession of all the facts. And no one likes to be trampled underfoot.

If the respondent starts talking in tangents, gently return the individual to your areas of interest. In every interview program, someone will present an emotive argument about the economy, the weather or the politics of the day. Confirm that you have heard the respondent's argument and then return to a point about which you would like to know more. Say something like, "That's interesting, Mr. Bloggs. Returning to a matter you raised earlier ..."

Above all, listen. Speak no more than 20 percent of the time. If you are talking much more than that, you are being interviewed! Take notes. Do *not* tape record the conversation without alerting the other party and, because this usually establishes a barrier to communications, it is a very bad idea in general. As should be apparent at this stage, interviewing executives for purposes of competitor targeting may borrow on some marketing research skills, but it is very different. It is essential to provide training to the people who do this or, as is the case with all professionals, it may be cheaper to use external services rather than attempting this on your own.

Personal Interviews

Many of the suggestions for conducting effective telephone interviews, discussed above, apply equally for personal interviews. Three key differences exist for the following:

- Setting Up the Interviews
- Physical Environment for Interviews
- Information-Gathering Details

The ultimate rule is to make sure that the interview warrants a personal visit because this is an expensive way to gather information.

Setting up the Interviews

Whereas you should be able to conduct and document many telephone interviews in a day—doing ten to fifteen is not uncommon—you will be able to conduct only a small number of personal interviews. Identify whom you plan to meet in person and whom you will contact by telephone. Generally, senior respondents should be offered the courtesy of the choice between a personal meeting or a telephone discussion. Ideally, the personal interviews will be done by a researcher with seniority that is at least equal to the respondent.

Group the personal contacts together into a single geographic area, and have at least four names to contact for every day in which interviews are to be held. Make interview appointments three to four weeks in advance by saying, "I will be in your area on (month, day) and would like to meet with you to (review benefit)." The benefit for meeting with you could be to review issues of mutual interest in the industry. Try to set the time rather than have the respondent choose it. This way, you can plan the sequence of interviews better. Establish whether you can meet for breakfast, lunch or dinner, and failing that, if the individual is unavailable, whether someone else from the respondent's company can stand in for this person.

In general, avoid falling into the trap of setting up interviews for the times when only respondents are available. This can consume a lot of your time without yielding many completed interviews. If a respondent chooses an inconvenient time, thank him or her for the opportunity to meet and then offer two or three other times that work better for your schedule. When a particular respondent is absolutely vital for the project, you might want to make an exception and see him or her when the opportunity is offered. Respondents are usually flexible and rarely insist that the only open time period for the next several weeks is the one they mentioned. When you contact the individual to set up the appointment, you may be told that "you have no more than thirty minutes" for the discussion. Some respondents even display a clock prominently in front of you. Do not be concerned about this. When you conduct the interview, it is highly unlikely that the respondent will cut you off after precisely half an hour. Likely, he or she will be most intrigued and your interview could well last longer. However, you should make sure that the key issues are covered by the thirty-minute mark just in case your interview is terminated.

Physical Environment for Interviews

When you enter the respondent's office, take cues from the environment to establish rapport and gain insight. For example, if the person has a picture of a vintage car proudly displayed, ask if he or she has a car like this. If there is a signed picture of the person with a celebrity, such as the president of the US, ask when this meeting took place and what it was about. Usually executives will conduct a meeting such as this at a small table in their offices or in a nearby meeting room. Locate yourself at the table so that any window in the room is not directly behind either of you. This avoids the possibility that you or the respondent will squint into the light. That limits impressions of facial expressions and body language and provides an advantage of one person over another, the exact opposite of what peer-based communications should be achieving.

Try to ensure that the respondent has his or her back to the office door so that anyone entering the office will see the respondent's back and will be discouraged from interrupting the meeting. Even better, close the office door when you enter to further reduce this likelihood. If the respondent takes a telephone call early in the meeting, you might ask if it would be possible for calls to be forwarded to the assistant or voice mail for this brief period.

Information-Gathering Details

By watching the respondent closely, you can establish which areas the person is particularly sensitive about. Perhaps the individual will cross arms and or legs, put a hand up to cover or partially obscure his or her mouth or have a change of facial expression. By registering these signs, you can come back later in the interview to explore the reasons further.

Do not ask to tape-record the discussion as this increases formality and heightens the respondent's anxiety. It is a good idea to take notes in your interview, but ask for permission first, as a matter of courtesy. (I have never had anyone object.) Keep notes in the interview as verbatim comments to avoid introducing biases or conclusions too early. Do not use big clipboards or leather bound portfolios. Make note taking informal and unobtrusive. Write quickly; otherwise the respondent may lose his or her train of thought waiting for you to complete a sentence. Use an inexpensive pen to avoid creating an inappropriate impression. This is not the time to flaunt your expensive Mont Blanc. Immediately after the interview is completed, fill out and expand these notes to ensure that the maximum amount of information is recorded.

Personal interviews have important advantages over those done by telephone because they typically offer a longer opportunity for information interchange, and they allow the interviewer to interpret facial expressions and body language. When people cast their eyes upwards during a discussion, they are often trying to recall details, but if they look down when thinking or speaking be careful. Police usually take this as a sign that the person is less than fully forthcoming or may not be telling the truth.

Personal interviews allow for review and debate of visual material such as sales and organizational charts, sketches or published materials. Go to personal interviews with material such as this in your briefcase.

Trade Shows

When competitors gather at trade shows and present their products to the world, they offer a unique opportunity to gather competitive intelligence directly. A few tips on conducting your intelligence operation at a trade show are as follows:

- Before going to a trade show, do your homework. Who is likely to be there from the competition or from organizations that know the competitors you are targeting? What is their background and areas of expertise? What products are they likely to be exhibiting? Prepare and commit to memory the key points from an interview guide. When you interview a respondent in a booth, go through the guide you memorized. Do not take notes, but commit important details to memory.

- Before approaching competitors' booths, do some reconnaissance, surveying the layout, organization and staff complement at the competitors' exhibits. Identify who it is you wish to interview.
- Visit their booth at a time that would be convenient for the respondent to answer your questions in detail, which usually means visiting in off-peak hours.
- Select respondents who appear to have had limited training or experience in dealing with the public. These people are often found putting unnecessary "final touches" to a piece of equipment or sitting in front of a computer. They seem to be studiously avoiding contact with the public. Often, they are the technical gurus who are present primarily to answer technical questions. Usually, after you encounter initial resistance from them, they become very helpful indeed, not just on technical matters, but regarding many other aspects of the company.
- Do not misrepresent yourself. Some people remove their name badges in order not to discourage conversation, and they believe that there is no need to identify themselves at a public forum such as a trade show. Actually, respondents are less likely to be helpful if they do not know whom they are talking with. Leave your name badge on and introduce yourself in a straightforward manner as someone who has much interest in the company (or a mutual competitor, say) and their specific accomplishments or directions. If you think this will not yield the results you want, you might think about having interviews done by third parties.
- Keep your own secrets confidential, but be prepared to provide information of mutual interest. Practice how you would respond to challenging questions such as, "Sure I would be pleased to discuss our new services in this area. Is your company planning to introduce similar services in the next year or two?" Provide a direct, honest answer such as, "Yes, we are considering entering this market space as are most of the other companies in the industry." When talking with a rival, try to avoid using the terms "competitor" or "competition" as these can cause respondents to shy away. The term "another company" is better.
- Start with a review of products on display, and then branch out to a discussion of issues that are more relevant to you. Pick up product literature and other published material along the way.
- After concluding each interview, go to a remote area of the hall and immediately record your findings on index cards or a handheld

tape recorder. If you delay, you may forget many of the salient details even though you may think that you will not. Do not use a tape recorder surreptitiously.

- Make an overall assessment about the quality and positioning (both in the hall and from a marketing perspective) of the competitor's trade exhibit, presentation and individual staff. Compare this to your own and decide what you need to improve for next year. You may be aided in your perception of relative quality by anonymously interviewing trade show visitors, having the key buyers interviewed by third parties (assuming they already know you) and doing traffic counts at the same time at all competitive booths (How many people are in the booths? How long are they staying there?). Some companies put a third-party tail on key buyers to understand where they spend their time, how much time they spend there (using stop watches) and with whom they talked.

Doing an effective interview at trade shows may be limited if you are, or think you are, known to the competitors or if you feel uncomfortable about doing the interviews yourself. In situations such as this, you may consider hiring third parties to do interviews for you. Make sure you understand the tactics they will engage in and that they will represent themselves legitimately and in a manner with which you are comfortable. Obtain a detailed proposal that identifies their approaches and ask for references before you engage them. Provide guidance at the outset of the engagement as to what you consider acceptable practice and what they are not to do. Even if you and your company's legal representative cover many issues, the third parties will need to demonstrate judgment in the conduct of their work. You will need to be sure that you trust these people with this sensitive assignment.

Information Validity and Accuracy

Intelligence has the potential to generate data and information of a breakthrough nature—but, is it believable? When it is apparently in conflict, which source is right? Is the critical information correct? This can be established by validating two main factors:

1. Source
2. Data

Source

The validity of the source can be determined by the quality of the information that has been previously provided. Consider the reasons the source might have for providing you with the information. For example, disgruntled former employees, ex-suppliers and jilted acquisition targets usually make unreliable sources. Ask yourself whether or not the source possesses the information claimed. For example, if a purchasing manager is discussing plans for market entry, is it likely he or she would have information at the level of detail being discussed? The credibility of the source can be determined by asking questions for which you already have the answer. If the answer differs, find out why. Informal character references from others can also help ensure an accurate assessment of credibility.

Data

The validity of the data can be determined by cross-referencing it to other sources. If the data were from a print source, confirm them by asking focused questions in interviews. If the data were provided by people, check it with others. Always scrutinize the data provided by the source by comparing it with information provided elsewhere during the interview.

If you suspect that the source is not in a position to know the information being supplied, make sure that you are not being deliberately misinformed. When companies or secret service agencies seek to misinform others, they spread false information to a number of people. When this disinformation is repeated by rote, it can sound identical. If you check with multiple sources at the same time and they all respond with exactly the same story, without variation and with no more or less color, it is possible that you are indeed being drawn into a competitive trap of some sort. It happens.

Keeping Your Secrets Secret

You would obviously like to minimize the amount of intelligence a competitor can conduct on your own organization. Perhaps you are now thinking of implementing or enhancing your company's traditional security systems to limit information theft and compromise, and you should. For example, what happens to your computer printouts, photocopies and refuse? Do staff engage in practices that make them a security risk? When were your offices last swept for electronic listening devices? Is the most sensitive information typed on a secure personal computer, or can competitors pick up the emissions of small amounts of radiation from a distance? For some time now, it has been possible to monitor the radiation from your computer and wireless networks. So-called tempested computers shield radiation, but few companies use them, just as encryption for wireless networks is not usually turned on, in part because firms are unaware of the risks.

I suspect, however, that much more information leaves the company via e-mail, from the Web site, over the telephone, in conferences and in personal discussions than is ever stolen by intruders foiling guards, getting through authorized access zones and defeating identification systems. Many firms spend considerable time and attention on the wrong risks, seeking to perfect a physical security system that limits illegal activity, for example, while few have programs to minimize the loss of information by sensitizing employees and managing communications with outsiders.

A program to counter competitive intelligence requires that you define what secrecy means in your company. Many organizations are quite prepared to share much vital information with employees because they want the commitment that comes with the openness and a more complete understanding of the objectives and performance of the firm. Others prefer to operate on a need-to-know basis, screening information from those without a legitimate requirement to be in possession of specific information. Competing in real time means employees need rapid access to the right information, and denial of that can limit competitiveness if it is rigidly enforced.

Plan for Keeping Secrets Secret

It is appropriate to designate information according to its competitive sensitivity. Three or four levels of coding would enable different secrecy requirements to be reflected in a security plan. Your security plan should recognize that the key resource most organizations mine, process and inventory is information, and it should thus seek to protect this asset. The plan should identify the key information that you wish to protect. Generally it is that which has the most impact on your organization's future such as technology under development, investment plans, capacity addition, equipment procurement, new business start-ups, acquisitions, divestitures and strategic, financial and operating plans. This would receive the highest level security access coding. Make a list of the people who might divulge information such as current and past employees, suppliers and unrelated individuals. You should also examine how this information could find its way into the hands of competitors such as inadvertent transmittal. This is usually the result of not being sufficiently sensitized to the importance of the information, the techniques employed by interviewers, communication to one audience that could be accessed by another (such as saying something in a trade publication that can be used differently in regulatory hearings) and so on.

Each of the possible sources of information leakage must be targeted to ensure that proper sensitivity exists. This is particularly important for technical personnel who derive esteem from peer group acceptance at symposia and industry conferences and have been known to blurt out information that can be harmful to the company's longer-term interests. Employees should also sign nondisclosure agreements so that those who leave will not be involved in information hemorrhage. Employees must be briefed on the handling of interviewers, and senior executives who communicate with the media need to get professional media training so that they do not discuss sensitive issues and know how to manage such a discussion appropriately.

Security plans must establish the communications reception and delivery responsibilities of different levels of employees and ensure that each category of people knows what information they should communicate with whom and that they receive only that which is appropriate to their security level. For example, receptionists, call center operators and other frontline personnel should know how to direct callers without disclosing any information, including the names of executives. Here, screening questions would be asked such as, "Why do you wish to know the names of these people?" Responses which are not in the company's interests would be met with prepared answers which politely reject the approach for information or steer the person to alternative sources. Again, the employee policy and procedure manual can help to reinforce key points here and can include a code of conduct.[11]

Appoint overall information gatekeepers such as PR personnel whose responsibility it is to field calls from the media, consultants and others whose direct business purpose is unclear. If appropriate, these PR people will either deal with the information request themselves or

[11] See The Society of Competitive Intelligence Professional's Web site for a good example of a code of conduct—www.scip.org

channel the individual to the right person. The switchboard operators need to have a brief checklist to help them decide when to send incoming calls to the gatekeeper. This checklist could be prepared by the department responsible for competitive intelligence if there is one, or human resources if there is not. Procter and Gamble's headquarters in Cincinnati, Ohio, appears to have such a mechanism, which effectively screens, manages and directs calls from external parties. One company for which I worked did not. The media contacted a plant manager who, flattered by their interest in his business, proceeded to discuss contentious issues, which were subsequently printed in a mass circulation paper. The plant manager left the company and the rules of dealing with the media were changed.

After developing and implementing your security plan, you should test how well aspects of it work. Call up your own switchboard, and try to establish who is responsible for new product development at your company. See how they handle the call. Conduct interviews with the people to whom you are channeled such as human resources personnel, and keep notes so that you can upgrade your security plan. Conduct an on-line database search on your own firm, and review the Web site of your company, imagining that you are a competitor. You may find opportunities to focus and tighten information security.

More generally, whatever the safeguards, satisfied employees are unlikely to leak competitive intelligence, while disgruntled employees represent a security risk. There is a link between employee satisfaction and data security, which is another good reason for developing relationships with individual employees. Lean companies have left employees to manage their own careers with much less career guidance or personal attention, making the company more vulnerable to employee loss and data leakage.

Customer and Competitor Databases

Just as companies develop customer understanding and predictive abilities in support of CRM by establishing customer profiles, undertaking customer research and implementing data mining and predictive modeling, competitor targeting needs much data, too. For example, competitor targeting benefits from data about competitors and customers including initiatives that will make specific customers into competitors, how customers think of your competitors and competitors' initiatives in your accounts.

Table 5-4 provides an example of a customer information file and includes selected competitor data that you might want to consider for capture and integration with your customer data for business-to-business relationships.[12] One of the main impacts of technology has been to turn individual customers into markets that companies can assess, penetrate and develop. In marketing to individual consumers, there are some similarities to business-to-business marketing, so that some of the business-to-business considerations presented in Table 5-4 could also be adopted for consumer information files.

Data for the customer information files are derived directly from such things as questionnaires, interviews and customer contact (with the company's Web site and call center, for instance), merging external marketplace databases with internal ones or inferred through demonstrated behavior and preferences.

Table 5-5 on page 185 describes selected fields for a competitor information file other than the customer-sourced data mentioned in Table 5-4.

Table 5-4: The Business-to-Business Customer Information File

Identification – Account or identification number – Company name – Main telephone number – Customer has reviewed company's data procurement, disclosure and archival policy: Y/N and date of review/person reviewed with[13] ***Customer Rating*** – Customer categorization in terms of value to your company – Bonding level presently occupied by customer – Bonding objective and time frame	***Competitor Usage and Overall Satisfaction*** – Companies currently supplying customer – Duration of relationships of each competitor (and your company) – Relationship matrix, showing the various decision makers of the customer and the relative positioning of each competitor with each purchase decision maker or influencer – Expenditures by customer with each company, by line of business – Share of customer calculation (this period) – Share of customer (last period)

[12] You may wish to read Terry G. Vavra, *Aftermarketing: How to Keep Customers for Life Through Relationship Marketing*, Homewood, Ill.: Business One Irwin, 1992, for additional considerations for consumer-focused customer information files.

[13] This may be helpful or have other implications for the retention of data control and security. Discuss with your legal advisor.

- Satisfaction rating (CSI) for each supplier
- Dissatisfaction rating (CDI) for each supplier[14]
- Major upcoming initiatives and associated supplier expenditures
- Favorability rating (FRI) for each supplier[15]
- Share of future calculation for each supplier[16]

Background

- Business demography
  - Industry classification code (SIC)
  - Employment levels
- History of company
  - Date first incorporated
  - Date first started making relevant products
  - Corporate affiliations and interownerships
  - Linkages of ownership, investors or Board members (if any) to competitors or your company
- Geography
  - Head office
  - Regional offices
    - Manufacturing locations
    - Proximity to your company and to competitors
- Sales, profitability and cash flow
  - Size – total sales
  - Growth rate – total
  - Size, relevant products
  - Growth rate – relevant products
  - Profitability – overall
  - Profitability – relevant products
  - Cash flow, overall
- Financial position (relevant ratios, from financial statements) It could include:
  - Return on investment (ROI)
  - Operating profit on net sales
  - Asset turnover: sales/assets
  - Current ratio: current assets/current liabilities
  - Stability ratios such as debt/assets
  - Overhead: general, selling and administration/net sales
  - Coverage: times interest earned
  - Growth: sales growth/asset growth
- Market position
  - Market size for customer's products
  - Market segment participation

---

[14] Some companies track and monitor only customer satisfaction ratings, using customer satisfaction indexes (CSI). An equally important measure is customer dissatisfaction, especially inasmuch as this provides a basis for attacking or otherwise managing specific competitors. Sometimes measuring the inverse of the desired outcome provides much guidance, a customer dissatisfaction index (CDI) in this case.

[15] Favorability rating index (FRI) is a measure of the intent of customers to buy from your company and competitors for their next purchase decision.

[16] Share of future incorporates current levels of spending and projected levels of expenditure for each among the major investment or procurement decisions, identified previously.

- Market share (current period, past period)
- Customer's major end customers
- Positioning of the company with its end customers

Presale

- Number of "touches" or contacts prior to purchases
- Types of information sought
- Channels of communications initiated by customer (telephone, Internet, interactive voice response, etc.) by type of information sought
- Contact history – nonpersonal
- Offers and promotional material sent directly, by date
- Sensitivity to different media, assessed according to response to specific offers, promotional material, advertising
- Sensitivity to different media, assessed according to respondent's stated preferences in magazines, television, etc.
- Medium that contributed to first purchase such as telemarketing, Internet, personal referral, television advertising, direct mail solicitation, etc.
- Call history – personal sales calls, by date, by audience
  - Call reports
  - Competitive activity in the account (new products, promotions, relationship development or other)

Purchasing

- Purchase behavior
  - Specific items
    - For first purchase and all subsequent purchases: specific items or services bought by categorization code such as SKU number, by department
- Usage
  - Rate
  - Application
- Recency (R)
  - Date of customer's first purchase
  - Date of all subsequent purchases
  - Date of last purchase
- Frequency (F)
  - Frequency with which purchases are made (per day, week, month, year)
- Monetary value (M)
  - Amount spent on customer's first purchase
  - Amount spent on all subsequent purchases
  - Amount spent on last purchase
  - Margin derived from customer's first purchase
  - Margin derived from all subsequent purchases
  - Margin derived from last purchase
  - Average expenditures
  - Average margin on expenditures
- RFM (recency, frequency, monetary value) for specific competitors
- Financing
  - For first purchase and all subsequent purchases: method of payment for goods or services bought: cash, credit card, store card

Decision Makers

- Names
- Titles
- Our staff who have relationships with these people
- Scoring of quality of relationships we enjoy
- Relationship scoring we plan to achieve, by person
- Scoring of quality of relationships specific competitors have
- Relationship scoring objectives we establish for specific competitors

Decision-Making Process

- Decision initiators
- Decision influencers
- Decision makers
- Decision confirmers
- Executors of decision
- Purchase cycle
- Time required to make decision, by type of decision:
  - New buy
  - Project, system, solution, program, product or service
  - High involvement/strategic vs. low involvement/low impact
  - Modified rebuy
  - Rebuy (standard repurchase situation)
- Month when decisions are initiated, by type of product
- Month when decisions are final
- Criteria and positioning
- Vendor-selection criteria
- Product-selection criteria
- Key selection and patronage criteria, overall company
- Key selection and patronage criteria, specific departments or product lines
- Perceptions of our company in respect of criteria[17]
- Perceptions of competitors in respect of criteria
- Opportunities to improve positioning, by major area of purchase
- Opportunities to reposition competitors, by major area of purchase or procurement decision
- Opportunities to improve positioning, overall
- Style
- Process by which business is contracted
- Formal proposal development
- Informal relationships
- Receptivity to proactive value addition
- Perception of customer regarding company and competitor's style and manner

Influences

- Factors influencing level of business contracted
- Business cycle
- Derived demand dependencies

Postpurchase Behavior

- Services required
- Items returned
  - Condition in which returned
  - Purchase amounts of returned product
  - Tone and manner of return
  - Customer complaint frequency, recency

[17] Criteria referenced here apply to the specific purchase situation and may vary according to the situation or nature of the procurement.

- Customer satisfaction with issue resolution
- Elapsed time between product purchase and return

Channels

- Intermediaries used for product, type and name
- Intermediaries used for service, type and name
- Customer satisfaction with channel intermediaries
- Opportunities to enhance aspects of intermediary performance
- Channel selection and support criteria for products, services and company
- Channel satisfaction with company and competitors

Pricing

- Pricing history
- Pricing expectations
- Win/loss assessments: prices of winning vendors
- Reasons customer says was behind win/loss decision[18]
- Pricing structures preferred
- Competitor pricing, by product line
- Competitor value-added (pricing and nonpricing dimensions appreciated as valuable by the customer)

Predicted Behavior

- Product or service expected to be bought next
- Decision maker for next purchase
- Value of purchase
- Decision maker's expectations of supplier preceding purchase:
  - Call frequency
  - Benefits
  - Presentations
  - New value to be mutually created
  - New value we are expected to create
  - Process changes
  - IT linkages
  - Training
  - Other
- Media of primary influence
- Ancillary services that customer may purchase together with the product
- Vendor preference, if any
- Current incumbent, if any
- Positioning of incumbent or other challengers in respect of forthcoming procurement

Creditworthiness

- Debt history
- Receivables on account
- Day's receivables
- Payment schedule
- Credit scoring and rating
- Competitor's payment terms

Selected Relevant Information

- Customer's customers
- Business strategies
- Key initiatives
- Account planning

[18] This should be sourced with the respondent and date of response described. Some respondents may prefer not to talk about issues other than price, and some sales personnel may encourage this. The company may wish to have this assessment undertaken periodically by an executive with the company or third-party consultants.

Table 5-5: The Competitor Information File—Selected Fields[19]

Overview

- Company name
- Web address
- Mission and objectives
  - Articulated
  - Manifested
- Core capabilities
  - People
  - Process
  - Technology – including IT, ERP and CRM technology infrastructure
  - Knowledge management and customer insight
- Distinctive competencies
- Organizational structure
- Positioning
- End users
- Channel intermediaries
- Suppliers
- Employees

Geography

- Head office address
- Head office telephone number
- Regional and international locations
- Regional and international telephone numbers
- Manufacturing locations

History of Company

- Date first incorporated
- Date first started making relevant products
- Corporate affiliations and interownerships
- Acquisitions and divestitures

Main Stakeholders and Their Roles, Commitments or Exposures

- Investors
- Owners
- Board of directors
- Management – overview (detail below)
- Employees – number, cultural comments
- Labor unions
- Financial institutions
- Knowledge capital suppliers – consulting, accounting and advertising
- Equipment suppliers
- Raw material and consumables suppliers
- IT vendors
- Channel intermediaries – including volume and percentage of sales moving through each intermediary
- Customers – names, relative importance (detail to follow)
- Media – advertising, direct marketing and other agencies
- Political and regulatory supporters

Financial Stakeholders

- Nature and structure of ownership

[19] These fields are provided for your consideration. Depending on your busines, you would likely need to add extra fields and delete some of those mentioned here. Whatever fields you use, track all sources and dates, for subsequent verification if needed and to facilitate follow-up and additional information provision.

- Sources of debt
- Relationships with key providers of funds – including brokers, shareholders, bankers
- Availability of additional equity or debt infusion

Personnel – Company

- President, by year (with phone, fax, e-mail addresses)
- Vice presidents or general managers – lines of business, by year (with phone, fax, e-mail addresses)
- Vice presidents – Head office staff functions, by year (with phone, fax, e-mail addresses)
- History of previous positions for key executives within the competitor and prior companies
- Executive compensation, including salary, options, bonuses
- Staff compensation
- Analysts' assessments of executive performance
- Characterization of culture and culture changes

Performance – Company (By Year)

- Sales
- Operating costs (with relevant cost components
- Operating profits
- Return on capital employed (ROCE) or return on investment (ROI)
- Stock price
- Price-to-earnings ratio (P/E ratio)
- Employment
- Revenue per person
- Operating profit
- Day's receivables
- Day's payables
- Cost of capital
- Operating profit on net sales
- Asset turnover: sales/assets
- Current ratio: current assets/current liabilities
- Stability ratios such as debt/assets
- Overhead: general, selling and administration/net sales
- Coverage: times interest earned
- Growth: sales growth/asset growth

Sales, Profitability and Cash Flow (By Year)

- Size – total sales
- Growth rate – total
- Size – relevant products
- Growth rate – relevant products
- Profitability – overall
- Profitability – relevant products
- Cash flow, overall – source and use of funds

Divisions (Repeat for Each Division)

- Description of line of business
- Product and service categories
- Portfolio according to market attractiveness – competitive position matrix (stars, cash cows, dogs, question marks)
- Size – sales, by division, by year
- Growth rate – sales, by division, by year
- Market segments - sales, by end-user segment such as geography, demography, psychographics and end-user industry

- Market share – by segment, by year
- Customers
  - List
  - Relative importance (sales)
  - Scope of product sales, service (breadth of range)
  - Profitability (using costs, below)
  - Share of customers' expenditures
  - Relationships, by key stakeholder, by customer
- Value chain costs, including cost to serve – components of cost for value chain of main products or services

Value Chain

Conceive/Design/Develop

- Patent filings, focus of research and development
- Resources – people
- Level of internal funding
- External funding as available
- Productivity
- Customer satisfaction assessments that have a bearing on this component of value chain

Production and Quality Management

- Facilities – location, size, age, focus/specialization
- Proximity to major customers, markets, suppliers, channel intermediaries, labor
- Integration – scale and scope
  - Other company facilities
  - Suppliers' facilities
- Capital to labor ratios per unit of output
- Labor
  - Cost and quality, by skill level
  - Age
  - Turnover
  - Unionization
  - Labor relations
  - Training
- Quality assurance
  - Incoming
  - In process
  - Final assurance

Sales, Marketing and Distribution

- Sales (company – repeat if agents, brokers)
  - Number of sales personnel
  - Skills
  - Location
  - Territorial coverage
  - Focus – industry, customer, geography
  - Compensation plan
  - Effectiveness
- Marketing
  - Number of marketing personnel
  - Skills
  - Educational background
  - Media
    - Expenditure
    - Share of voice – spend as percentage of industry
    - "Push" vs. "pull" spending – trade vs. consumer
    - Product and company positioning
    - Support for product claims
    - Alignment with

- Purchase criteria
- Purchase process
- Competitive environment
- Regulatory/social/legislative environment

- Independent media tests of competitor's executions

– Distribution
- Channels used
- Number, key intermediaries by name
- Dispersion – geography, segment, customer
- Relative importance – percentage of volume, profits (estimated)
- Quality
- Type
- Strengths of intermediaries
- Margin – by stage of distribution
- Inventory turns
- Channel partner compensation structure
- Cooperative advertising
- Floor plan financing
- Training
- Support
- Alignment of strategies
- Warehousing locations
- Transportation
- Policies
  – Order size
  – Shipment
  – Return
  – Other
- Satisfaction of intermediaries with competitor – independent assessment

– Internet
- Strategy
- Positioning
- Uniqueness of customer experience
- Information provision and other value-added
- Clicks and bricks: Internet relative to physical channels
  – Partitioning – product, service
  – Integration
  – Relative importance – sales, product line, market segment, customer
- User interface
- Benchmark performance
- Policies and procedures
- Returns
- Payment

Finance

– Cost of funds

– Availability

– Structure

– Strategy

– Return on investment
- Earnings as a percentage of sales
  – Net income
  – Costs
    - Cost of goods
    - Operating expenses
    - Depreciation
    - Interest
    - Less other income
- Asset turnover
  – Total investment (assets)
  – Fixed assets

- Current assets
  - Inventories
  - Cash
  - Accounts receivable
  - Marketable securities

Management

- Planning
- Organizing
- Leading
- Controlling
- Employee-centric
- Culture

Product Lines

- Description
- Performance (expand as necessary)
- Associated services

Financial Position *– relevant ratios from financial statements. Could include measurements selected from those in respect of customer analysis – Table 5-4. Also, ratios in respect of:*

- Liquidity
  - Current ratio: current assets/current liabilities
  - Quick ratio: (cash and near cash + accounts receivables)/total current liabilities
  - Day's receivables: (accounts receivables/net sales on account) x 365 (could be an indicator of customer relationships)
  - Day's inventory: (inventory/cost of goods sold) x 365
  - Day's payables: (payables/cost of goods sold) x 365 (could be an indicator of trade relationships)
  - Financing operations: sales/working capital
- Stability
  - Current liabilities/assets
  - Long-term debt/assets
  - Debt/assets
  - Sales/assets
- Profitability
  - Usual measures such as profit/sales, operating profit/net sales, net sales/total assets, net profit/average equity
  - GSA (general, selling and administrative) expenses/net sales
  - Break-even analysis: fixed costs/contribution margin
- Coverage
  - Times interest earned: earnings before tax and interest/interest
  - Interest service: (cash flow from operations + tax + interest)/interest
  - Current service: (cash flow from operations)/(current debt + lease obligations)
- Sustainable growth (internally financed, without revising or jeopardizing capital structure)
  - Sales growth/asset growth
  - Growth factor (GF): (net income/net sales) x (1 - ((preferred dividends + common dividends)/net income)) x (1 + (total liabilities/total net worth))
  - Sustainable growth rate: (GF/((total assets/net sales) - GF)) x 100%

Pricing	***Selected Relevant Information***
– Pricing history	– Competitor's competitors
– Pricing structures	– Business strategies
– Win/loss assessments: prices of winning vendors	– Key initiatives
	– Other, according to the main strategic issues being examined in your company
Creditworthiness	
– Debt history	
– Receivables on account	
– Payment schedule	
– Credit scoring and rating	

Data of the type presented in Table 5-5 will need to be supplemented or refined according to the needs of the user. If the intent of the competitive intelligence is to make operating personnel more competitive, for example, pricing and other relevant information will need additional fields. Executive management would expect more data on the strategies of competitors and early warning in respect of changes in their strategies, including replacement of executive management or changes in how they manage, infusion of funds, refocusing of their resources and so on.

Some Technology Considerations

As technology is fast-moving, specific applications and vendor approaches for developing tactical and real-time implementation may not endure as long as the concepts for so doing. While the intent here is not to develop a detailed consideration of implementation, as you decide what data fields to maintain and how to integrate customer and competitor data with your existing technology environment, you may want to assess the following four points:

1. There are business intelligence modules available from existing enterprise resource planning (ERP) system solutions providers. (Some of the better-known ones are SAP, Baan, Peoplesoft and i2.) It should be noted that some of these modules are presently underdeveloped, and they will need additional work to accomplish what it is you want. Additionally, the company implementing a standardized module should also be prepared to adjust their

expectations to align with what it is the vendor thinks they should provide. As you know from your initial ERP implementation, in all probability you will find yourself accommodating their solution more than the other way round.

2. Alternative competitive intelligence software is available from purpose-specific vendors such as Wincite (www.wincite.com). As is typical with packaged or semi-customizable solutions, some packages may not integrate well with your legacy environment and your strategic focus on competitor targeting.
3. "Data cubes" draws data from existing databases present in your company, which can allow you to review and consider the data in many ways, slicing, dicing and drilling down to find meaning. Enterprise decision support tools that can facilitate this and do more such as ad hoc queries, analysis, data mining, reporting and visualization (graphical presentation) include Powerplay (www.cognos.com) and Business Objects (www.businessobjects.com).
4. Reporting tools can allow companies, especially smaller ones, to extract and present data from their existing databases such as their accounting systems including such widely used applications as Simply Accounting and Great Plains. One such reporting tool that is in fairly wide use is Crystal Decisions (www.seagatesoftware.com).

The data warehouse is a key component of a learning relationship, and its updating is important if real-time insight is to be derived from the data and immediate actions initiated to boost a company's competitiveness. For example, if a competitor lowers its prices in a specific account or territory, your firm obviously needs to know this right away so you can decide how best to respond. Increasingly, customers and channel intermediaries provide the data companies need, helping to keep the database current. Companies can give their customers Internet access to their data warehouses.[20] Some among a company's best customers merit a high degree of alignment and openness including mutual data sharing and planning.

At this level of bonding, companies can provide access to databases and expect access to the customer's databases, facilitating updating of fields relevant not only to customer understanding but also to ensuring the competitor is defeated in the account and more generally. While some IT managers oppose the sharing of customer information in this way, others argue that opening up the company's database

[20] One source for selected additional data warehousing considerations is Mark Madsen, "Warehousing Meets the Web," *Database Programming and Design*, August, 1997, pp. 36-45.

to its best customers is a way to increase bonding and aid differentiation, especially if competitors are unwilling to share in a similar manner. A number of tools are available for presenting internal information on the Internet including some of those already referenced.

Your Employees and the Intelligence Program

Communicating the CI Initiative to Employees

Commitment by management and staff to the competitive intelligence process is vital if the organization is to become truly competitive relative to the targeted enemy. Before the vast storehouse of competitive information within a company can be accessed, some barriers in the minds of potential internal contributors must be removed, including the following:

- uncertainty about how the information is going to be used
- skepticism about competitive intelligence and the results that can be obtained from the process
- insufficient time, budget, human resources and a low priority allocated to competitive intelligence in relation to other required activities

Some providers of information about competitors may feel that it could be used to judge their performance relative to competitors, and because they are reluctant to compare performances, they may withhold information. At the outset of a competitor targeting initiative, there are likely to be skeptics who doubt the usefulness and validity of the program. Perhaps these are people who doubt anything new because they have been through too many new flavors of the month that promise salvation of the company only to be subsequently discontinued. Whatever their reasons, they need to be convinced of the merits of competitive intelligence and how competitor targeting can make an important contribution to the continued growth of the firm. If communications do not yield commitment, compliance can usually be obtained by tying performance reviews to aspects of CI. For example, for a marketing manager, the result area in the review could be the development of a targeted competitor's shadow marketing plans.

Many of those most able to supply the needed information may feel that they do not have enough time to comply now and too little human and financial resources to provide ongoing support to a program, especially if the initiative does not affect their performance evaluation. Barriers such as these can be lowered or eliminated if a senior executive of the company communicates effectively the urgency for competitive intelligence to the employees. At the outset of the program, that executive may not fully appreciate the benefits of investing time, attention and budget here, and you may need to lead this person to the conclusion that an integrated program of competitor targeting and competitive intelligence could increase shareholder value (and not incidentally, their own remuneration). Moreover, if competitors target your company's core accounts while you allocate resources elsewhere, not only will opportunities be missed, but competitive threats will surely grow.

Senior management may still be unconvinced, and because competitor targeting may be a new concept to the company, funds allocated to it will likely come under close scrutiny. Executives may want to know what the payback will be on such an investment. Considering the lifetime value of customers and putting customer share objectives in the context of lifetime value could result in an assessment of the affordability of the initiative, with the associated timing leading to the development of a payback schedule. However, deeper commitment will likely be obtained if executives buy into the concepts in much the same way as they presumably think that financial planning and marketing planning are good things to do, even in the absence of financial analysis to prove this. I am not aware of a single firm that has examined the paybacks on the huge amounts of time and money committed to planning, but virtually every major company does it.

Management, once persuaded of the merits of the need for competitive intelligence to contribute to competitor targeting, should now issue a "white paper" to the organization, which provides employees with the following information:

- the pledge of commitment to competitive intelligence to support a competitor targeting initiative
- the reasons for this focus
- the objectives of the program
- the responsibilities for internal coordination
- expectations of employees
- timing of the initiative and key milestones

Reportedly, GTE's president did something like this when implementing a visionary competitive intelligence initiative, one of the first to be company-wide.[21] That program and the experiences of other companies since then contain some lessons[22]:

- *Target competitors*—While the white paper was well executed, the initiative at GTE covered data development for too many companies, insufficient targeting of a few specific competitors and did not focus on the company's key customers. As a result, it was less likely that the program would deliver competitively superior results.
- *Ask questions before looking for answers*—It appears as though the company spent more time on information gathering and technologies for data management than on defining what needed to be known. The result was that much data was gathered and archived, but the answers to the right questions would only be developed by chance in this way.
- *Centralize capabilities*—The program was rolled out to many divisions and product lines simultaneously. The data input and warehousing was centralized, but with an enormous amount of information to manage, the initiative collapsed. It would likely have been better for the corporate group to centralize system and capability development including technology (such as Intranet Web site development[23]) and training of employees in the conduct of competitor targeting and competitive intelligence.
- *Decentralize information input, management and use*—GTE centralized information input, management and use. Most companies find they achieve better results by having the data gathered and analyzed by the people who have most to benefit from CI.
- *Focus on initiatives that provide most yield for the company's shareholders*—Typically, this means the company should concentrate first on strategic competitor targeting, then tactical and real-time competitor-centric initiatives. GTE seemed to cover a large number of competitors, divisions and product lines simultaneously which would have made it hard (or even impossible) to use this intelligence effectively.

Whether or not these considerations apply to your company obviously bear independent examination.

---

[21] GTE's initiative was called the "BEST" program.

[22] Comments made here are derived from publicly available documents. GTE's experience was similar to that of many other companies and is used here for illustration and learning purposes only.

[23] Although Intranets were not in use at that time in industry, today they would be an appropriate area for capability development.

Securing Support

A critical part of any intelligence program is to ensure that your own employees support your intelligence efforts. In addition to the communications discussed earlier, this can be aided by doing the following:

- Develop a reward and recognition system.
- Develop punishments for non-compliance.
- Provide clear, succinct direction, explaining what information is required, from whom, by when and developing an effective approach for timely reporting.
- Establish a method of publicizing the program and communicating with employees.

Management must develop a formal positive and negative reward system. Perhaps the most effective way of doing this is to incorporate competitive intelligence objectives into job performance objectives and annual reviews. People should be rewarded for the competitive information they generate in their areas of expertise, especially if it helps them do their job better and if it contributes to the objectives of the overall program. For example, sales staff should be required to submit competitive data sheets using forms you designed to reflect your information requirements. Those who do not should be penalized in the performance appraisal process. Those who perform well might receive commendation both in the annual review, in an information bulletin and be recognized with a direct incentive such as a certificate from the president and a prize for the most valuable and consistent supplier of competitive intelligence. The award need not have large monetary value to secure cooperation. One method is to award the winner a trip but some companies report that vacation schedules can complicate the use of this prize and have chosen to make other awards such as computers. You may even want to have an annual competitive intelligence award for individuals who have consistently provided information to help the company with the competitor targeting exercise.

For the intelligence program to be successful, you need a well-developed system for asking focused questions of specific employees. Establish who the key contacts are for specific categories of information. Areas of expertise are quite easy to establish because most companies are organized functionally, but the information you need frequently cuts across functional lines. Hopefully, your human resources group will be able to inform you which employees have the insight you need and which have worked for competitors. If they cannot, do what you can to ensure that they modify their data capturing so that they can provide information of this type in the future.

Consider setting up a physical or electronic newsletter to provide positive feedback on some of the results you are achieving. (However, be alert to the impact such a newsletter could have if a competitor obtained a copy somehow). The newsletter could include insight into competitive activity, your information requirements, what your company is doing to beat the enemy and cases in which employee information has helped the company. If you have questions that require responses from large numbers of employees or an obscure requirement that you believe someone out there might know, you can broadcast your need in the newsletter and indicate who employees should contact and when. To establish urgent answers to vital questions, you may wish to use the company's e-mail system and issue a general inquiry or have a question of the day when employees sign onto the network.

Planning Competitive Intelligence

Competitive intelligence requires an internal plan to confirm, manage and lower what can be impossibly high expectations of the initiative at the outset. The plan will also ensure appropriate resourcing, budgeting and timing for the initiative. Table 5-6 provides a framework you might want to consider as a starting point for the format of your plan.

The CI plan should have a clear charter that describes the mandate for the initiative, how competitive intelligence links to competitor targeting and CRM and the roles of each person. The mandate is important if the manager is to use resources well and distinguish between what is within and what is outside the scope of the initiative. For example, one mandate could be to develop capabilities for each function in the company to assess and improve its performance relative to similar functions in a targeted competitor. Capabilities could include development of the Intranet, training and codes of conduct. For such a company, the actual competitive intelligence would be the responsibility of the users.

The plan should identify the users and the standards of service that are to be provided. The types of users of the outputs and processes have substantial impact on the nature of the system. Senior executives typically need strategic systems, and operating personnel prefer more tactical and real-time capabilities. For example, one company might cater to executives with ad hoc strategic projects, while another might have a department serving sales personnel with CI content such as pricing.

How the CI will be conducted should be identified, describing what kinds of outputs will be provided and how often. One company provides executives and others who want to be on the distribution list with a Friday Report, which summarizes news on targeted competitors that has appeared during the preceding week. Then it should provide details on implementation, identifying who will do the work, how they will be managed and how their performance will be measured. If CI is to support internal constituencies, one area of measurement for consideration here is the satisfaction of internal users.

The CI process should be charted, describing what information is to be used and how this is to occur. Technology considerations are important for a CI system, and the plan should identify what these are and how they will aid the initiative. As mentioned, business intelligence tools include Cognos' Powerplay, while intelligence dissemination and other capabilities use tools such as Wincite. The technology discussion should also pay attention to tools for gathering intelligence in real time on the Internet and the integration of this initiative with the company's existing technology infrastructure, including CRM, sales force automation, call centers and ERP systems. The plan should note whether or not the ERP vendor's business intelligence modules are to be adopted by the firm and the reasons for this.[24]

A planning document such as this can help bring together the various components of competitive intelligence and align it with competitor targeting and other aspects of business intelligence including customer intelligence and sales force automation.

[24] Enterprise Resource Planning systems automate the accounting systems, business rules and processes and e-business of the enterprise.

Table 5-6: A Framework for an Internal CI Planning Document

<table>
<tr><td>Charter
• Mandate
• Linkage to competitor targeting and customer relationship management
• Role</td></tr>
<tr><td>Objectives
• What will be done for whom with what intent by when
• Success measures and service standards</td></tr>
<tr><td>Approach
• High level method, categories of output, frequency of delivery</td></tr>
<tr><td>Implementation
• People
– Managing the implementation
– Managing the completed implementation
– Staffing the function
– Internal training
– Tracking performance: real and perceived
• Process
– CI process architecture: what is to flow from whom through whom to whom - inputs, outputs, sequence of activities
• Technology
– What level of technology for what purpose. Review of Intranet sites, data warehousing, mining, predictive modeling and other tools such as those that scan the Internet, and tools for business intelligence and information dissemination
– Integration with legacy and ERP systems, customer and marketing information systems, sales force automation and other preexisting and planned technology implementations, such as call centers
– Converting paper-based competitive intelligence into electronic documents (many successful strategic CI implementations start by confirming data flows and use in paper-based systems)
• Internal Communications
– High level communications plan: who will message what to whom
• Transitioning considerations
– Especially for technology, existing outputs and processes</td></tr>
<tr><td>Budget, Timing and Responsibilities</td></tr>
</table>

This chapter discussed competitive intelligence and its conduct in support of competitor targeting. We noted that companies should have policies in place to ensure that any CI done by the firm or contracted to third parties is handled in an appropriate way. Much detail was provided in the methods and approaches for gathering data on competitors. We described pitfalls that some companies face and how to overcome these, including how to ensure that internal stakeholders support the initiative, how to decide who should do what, and the importance of actually having a plan for CI. We suggested approaches to plan a competitive intelligence initiative. We now review strategies and tactics for targeting and beating competitors.

CHAPTER 6

Competitor Targeting Strategies

"In war nothing is impossible, provided you use audacity."[1]

—General George S. Patton

This chapter discusses various strategies and tactics for targeting selected competitors. We build on the principles of CRM and offer new suggestions for strategies to gain customer share. At this stage in the process of winning, the objective of the competitive initiative has been clarified, the key competitors have been identified, the plan has been prepared and data gathered and analyzed. Here we discuss bonding with customers in a competitively superior manner and other strategies and tactics for beating individual competitors. Of course, the ideas presented do not apply to all the competitive situations you face, but the considerations we do explore should serve to complement aspects of your competitive thrusts.

The Battlefield in the Mind of the Customer

Ultimately, the mind of the customer is the battlefield to be won by competitors. It is there that the battle for dominance rages and there that one company must gain supremacy over another if it is to win

[1] George Smith Patton, *War as I Knew It*, Boston: Houghton Mifflin, 1995 (originally published in 1947).

and keep the customer and deepen the bond over time. In the era of technology and engaging customers one-to-one, the battlefield is in the mind of the *individual* customer. The winning company will understand this battlefield better than its competitors and will be better able to manage its position than they are.

In Chapter 3, we discussed the company's competitive position with the firm's most important customers. The question to be answered now is why the company has the position it does and what it can do to improve it. Product, vendor and relationship criteria can be broken down into the two main challenges faced by many companies: 1) relationship formation; and 2) deepening the bond and further developing the relationship. These challenges are within your company's current customers, your competitors' customers and the customers you both share.

Relationship formation obviously occurs when the company sets out to secure business from the customer. It also happens throughout the company's association with the customer as decision makers come and go and the firm has to continually renew relationships with individuals. When companies fail to do this, they open the door to competitors. By tracking a targeted competitor's customer relationships, a company can know when the time is right to approach specific decision makers. It is common for companies to commission research to assess the relationships of competitors and to use these data to plan their approaches to the competitor's most important accounts or customers that the company considers potentially important.

The development of competitively superior relationships requires that the company deepen its bonds with its most important customers faster than targeted competitors do. We discuss customer bonding next.

Customer Bonding

Figure 6-1 describes the seven ways customers bond with their suppliers. We discuss each briefly below.

1. Structural Bonding

In structural bonding, the customer and the company are operationally and structurally linked or integrated, often employing technology to facilitate the interaction. For example, the customer that is able to check the inventory in a supplier's warehouse or purchase on-line is

Figure 6-1: Dimensions of Bonding

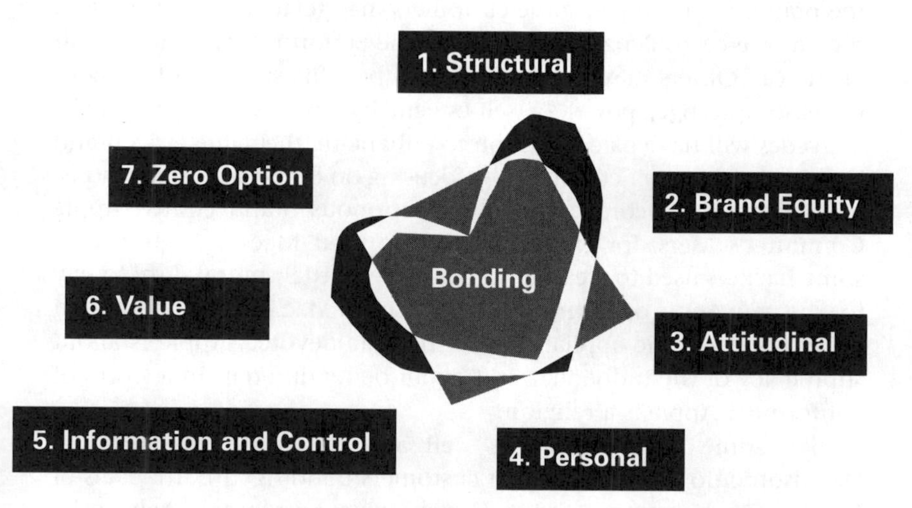

more likely to be bonded to the company than the customer that is unattached and easily able to switch suppliers. Often familiarity with the technology and/or its user interface can present a barrier to switching.

Structural bonding may be intensified when the company has aligned its technologies, people and business processes with customers, and even integrated them with the customer in a manner that raises switching costs, time, knowledge or risk.

Structural bonding needs strategic alignment to bring about and accelerate the integration of organizational capabilities. Companies that plan together, make money together. Proactive and joint customer-supplier innovation has the potential to further deepen structural bonding. A castings company supplying the auto industry independently advances ideas for auto companies to consider, which helps increase their win ratio for these and other opportunities. For example, the firm recently showed a car company how to make its product lighter by combining a number of forged engine parts into a single lightweight casting. The car company adopted their suggestions, putting the vendor in a position to supply many such castings over the life of the vehicle and in the process, insulating them from competition.

2. Brand Equity Bonding

Brand equity bonding includes the value a customer derives by relating to the product directly. That includes both the brand's functional attributes and the emotional or nonfunctional attributes captured in the brand. For example, some customers may relate to an auto brand such as Mercedes Benz because of the fine performance, fit and finish of the car. Others may derive emotional benefits such as a feeling of increased prestige, power or self-esteem by owning such a vehicle. Mercedes will have paid attention to enhancing the value of its brand in the minds of their customers by focusing on both these dimensions.

A number of companies enjoy enormous brand equity. Apple Computer's users, for example, embrace their Macs so tightly that some hackers used to stealing software feel it their moral duty to pay for the new Apple operating systems. Using a Mac is much more than using an electronic appliance. For the Mac devotee, Apple is about supremacy of the individual. It is about being different in a world of conformity. Apple is a religion.

For some of the same as well as different reasons, Harley-Davidson enjoys the benefits of customers bonding at both levels of function and emotion. Today, Harley owners are more likely to be business executives in search of their free spirit or youth as hard-core bikers, but both types bond with their bikes as symbols rather than as transportation. There is emotion in the Harley brand, something its competitors have yet to capture. How else to explain the number of people who obtain a tattoo of the Harley logo?

In the arena of goods and services, perhaps the most extreme example of brand relevance is the narrow customer profile attracted by Porsche. The German sports car company has found that customers who buy a Porsche have always owned one—in their minds, at least. Even first-time buyers have always imagined themselves in a Porsche.

3. Attitudinal Bonding

Attitudinal bonding occurs when customers bond with the company because of its professionalism, skills, customer focus, values, culture and responsiveness. Customers of banks and other services often bond at this level because they expect both technical skill and professional courtesy. Few customers would want a friendly yet incompetent banker. One of the reasons customers bond attitudinally with a specific supplier is that the company's culture may focus more on the customer than that of competitors. Contrast the cultures of Wal-Mart with their competitors and you have one explanation for the faster growth of the former.

Companies like Wal-Mart, with customer-oriented cultures, often also value their individual employees highly because it is challenging to develop lasting bonds with customers if employees do not feel good about their work.

4. Personal Bonding

Personal bonding occurs when customers like to work with specific people and will do so regardless of the company with which they work. Individual consumers prefer certain hairdressers, travel agents, consultants or accountants. Similarly, businesses bond with some reps regardless of the companies they represent, focusing their attention on the individual who is at the frontline creating business value. Here the organization behind the individual is less important. There is a risk that the company can lose the customer if the favored employee leaves, and this happens often in many industries. The answer is to make the company a magnet for high performance people, not to build walls around the firm that makes it difficult to leave. Additionally, companies can avoid such losses by focusing on building bonds with both employees and customers, and having many among their staff develop personal bonds with their customers.

Personal bonding occurs at multiple levels in the organization—from the most senior executives and the board interacting with their counterparts in a customer's organization to the payables and receivables personnel and processes working together. Personal bonding can represent a barrier to switching because people buy from people they like, all else being equal. Whenever a customer's executives have endorsed a supplier, personal bonding is also more likely to take root.

5. Information and Control Bonding

Information and control bonding means that customers benefit from the reporting and other information systems that can help them with operational and financial management. For example, companies such as UPS and Fedex have invested heavily in elaborate track and trace systems for their parcels. Customers can learn where a parcel is at any time, which helps reduce the customers' fear of the parcel going astray. American Express provides detailed reporting tailored to the needs of customers for expense tracking and other purposes such as taxation.

Information and control bonding can make it difficult for competitors to copy because of the large capital investment needed to provide customers with the information they want, when and how they want it. Often, the first company to invest in providing customers with better and more timely information has a significant opportunity to beat competitors, especially when the information and control can be customized to each customer's preferences and situation. As happens in a number of industries, one digital media company provides all its important customers with their own Web pages to review the status of the production processes and account information. In a consumer setting, eBay provides its customers with auction information allowing for real-time auction management.

6. Value Bonding

Value bonding occurs when customers repeatedly derive the value they seek from their suppliers and have every reason to believe that they will continue to receive this value over an extended period. Customer loyalty programs such as those that provide gas and airline consumers with points or rebates, fall into this category because they offer additional financial and in-kind incentives to continue buying from the supplier.

Value bonding can occur as a result of the supplier being obsessed with quality and/or being guided by delivering high value for specific prices. In an approach pioneered by Southwest Airlines, some airlines have expanded rapidly by keeping their planes in the air longer each day, using regional airports where the tariff is lower and managing their costs in a variety of other ways. They then pass on the benefits through lower prices to their customers, resulting in yet more passengers. Even before the impact of the September 11, 2001 tragedy was felt across the entire industry, many airlines had insufficient load factors to be profitable.

Value bonding can also occur according to the focus of the vendor on mass customization, which has the potential to create unique value for individual customers not available elsewhere. For example, incorporating technology for mass customization of consumer financial services, a financial institution has the potential to engage you at the counter or automated teller machine and add value to your transactions, perhaps recommending alternatives better suited to your requirements. If you have extra cash in a savings account, why not put that in a term instrument? If you have peaks in your cash balances for just a few days at a time would you like information to secure higher yields from this short-term money?

7. Zero Option Bonding

Zero option bonding occurs when you have no choice but to do business with a company or organization. Examples include the federal, state or local governments in areas such as social services, taxation and even defense. If the organization treats their monopoly position as a trust, customers may be more inclined to reward it and help it retain its preferred position. Otherwise, customers might push for break-up of the company or encourage regulators and other stakeholders to reregulate industries to increase competition. The zero option bond no longer exists in reregulated industries such as airlines, electricity, financial services, telecommunications and transportation. This bond continues in a number of instances such as de facto monopolies created by patent protection, when provided for by law such as for mail, and when companies control the availability of scarce raw materials such as for diamonds.

The zero option can also apply when suppliers have made a financial investment in their customers, making the supplier preferred under all but the most extreme situations of poor performance or insufficient product line. This is certainly one way for companies heavily dependent on a few customers to secure their future. In the hotly contested Canadian photographic retail film industry, in which Fuji and Kodak are locked in intense competition, Fuji acquired Black's Cameras, one of the largest volume retail camera and film chains, which helps Fuji to maintain its strength in this important channel.

In some industries, customers may wish to change suppliers but may not do so because of the high costs or perceived risks of switching. Structural bonding may have increased these costs and risks, but the costs of switching can be materially increased if customers really have no choice but to remain with the supplier. For example, specialized on-line transaction processing software used in industries such hotels, retail, libraries and financial services, once successfully installed and accepted by the users, is usually not rapidly replaced with competitors' systems. The costs and risks of conversion are very high, so customers often wait until the reasons to change far outweigh what will likely be a challenging conversion. Recognizing this, some software companies have built their businesses profitably by acquiring competitors with large customer bases and then earning out their investment by cutting costs associated with marketing, support and new software releases rather than investing for growth and in customer relationships.

Bonds with Other Stakeholders

While the battlefield may ultimately reside in the mind of the customer, there are a number of other locations in which supporting battles are to be waged for the war against a specific competitor to be won overall. These battlefields include the following:

- ownership, including ownership changes that could enhance or disadvantage your company and the targeted competitor
- labor, including labor unions and the marketplace for new employees such as skilled technical and management employees
- the broader community and government, including regulators, social critics and special interest and lobby groups such as those associated with the environment, safety and public health
- distribution channel intermediaries, including dealers, distributors, trade representatives, agents, wholesalers and retailers
- technology adoption, including new approaches to product and service distribution, transactions and, more generally, the application of e-business, the Internet and communications technologies throughout the value chain
- members of the targeted competitor's arm's-length business network, including alliance partners, complementary suppliers, and coinvestors in development and other initiatives
- suppliers of strategic inputs such as capital (banks, investment houses), factors of production (equipment, technology, parts, subassemblies, components, ingredients, packaging etc.)

If a company successfully thwarts a competitor in many or all of these subbattlefields, it has a much greater potential to win overall in the minds of individual customers. In some cases, winning can mean denying choice to a customer, whether by acquisition of a competitor, alignment with distribution channel intermediaries or suppliers or other means. In the era of the Internet, it is harder to limit access to channels since customers can often gain direct access to competitors.

Beating Competitors Strategically

Having charted the mind of the individual customer, you begin to understand your positioning. The challenge then is to develop strategies to advance the positioning to your advantage and possibly to your competitor's detriment. This may sound complex and challenging, and it can be (although companies sometimes unduly complicate the answers to their competitive issues), but there are challenges that must be overcome first if winning competitive strategies are to be developed. These include:

- having leaders invest the time needed to develop competitive strategy
- implementing and sustaining the strategic initiative

In the time-compressed lives of most leaders, it is common that managers will sequester themselves at a retreat to review strategic plans assembled by others, typically their subordinates. They will then make observations and suggestions for improvement, but will not often take the time that is really necessary to, for example:

- consider how the future could evolve
- identify the main strategic questions to be answered
- develop a vision for the company's future position
- establish the resources and capabilities needed to secure the desired position
- craft the strategies to accomplish the vision

Although little time is spent on the most important decisions a company will ever make, even less is spent securing alignment among the members of the management team on the main strategic issues. There are two types of strategies for the company: 1) those that are articulated by the management team; and 2) those that are implemented by the company. Without alignment of the management team, the strategies that are articulated are rarely implemented, and the company continues on its strategic trajectory, guided more by momentum, marketplace happenstance and buffeting by competitors and regulators than by management will and intent.

A company should appreciate its competitive position relative to targeted competitors and the potential for this to change in order for it to develop strategies to win. One way of considering relative competitive position is the differentiation a company has in the minds of its most valuable customers. The potential for this differentiation to change can be assessed by comparing competitors' vision statements to that of the company. Based on this, Figure 6-2 suggests four main strategic alternatives in the battle for the customer. These vary according to the differentiation of the company as a whole, its products, services and solutions or customer relationships in today's marketplace and the extent to which the vision of competitors are similar to those of the company. In taking this view of competitive strategy alternatives, we repeat that competition is a relative consideration, so a consideration of the current state and future state (which the competitor would accomplish if it achieved its vision) must also be compared with that of the company rather than an absolute review.

As shown in Figure 6-2, the four main strategy alternatives for competing may be categorized as (in no particular order):

1. Best Route
2. Cut and Thrust
3. West Versus East
4. Nelson's Telescope

Figure 6-2: Competitive Strategies

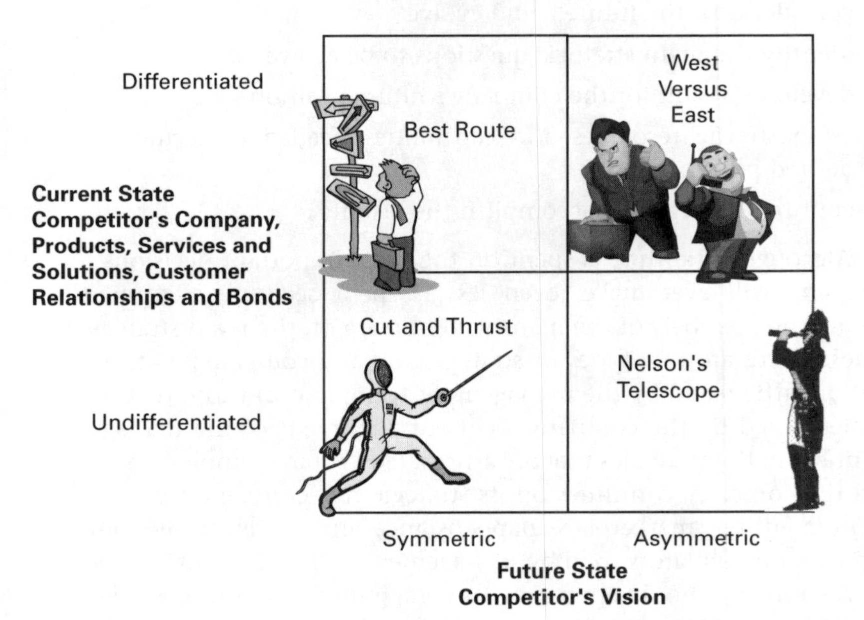

Best Route

Best Route competitive strategies apply to those companies that have similar, symmetric visions for their companies in the longer term, and at present, have differentiated their companies, products, services or solutions, or customer relationships as seen by their most valuable customers. The question here is which company has the best route to the future given their different starting points. An example is the case of Cisco and Nortel Networks. Both have seen themselves as vendors of equipment for tomorrow's Internet, yet their starting points are very dissimilar. Telephone operating companies, in particular, are likely to see the companies presently as somewhat different in terms of their offerings and capabilities, yet both were headed in the same direction until the stock-market melt-down changed the near-term focus from growth to survival. Here are the publicly stated visions of Nortel and Cisco:

Nortel Networks

Within 10 years, virtually all communications—voice, video and data—will take place via the Internet, over a unified network. ...Nortel Networks is creating a high-performance Internet that is more reliable and faster than ever before. It is redefining the economics and quality of networking and the Internet through Unified Networks that promise a new era of collaboration, communications and commerce.

Cisco

Cisco's vision is that the Internet will transform the way people work, live, play and learn. Today, change is happening faster than ever before, and Cisco helps companies turn that change into a competitive advantage by helping them become agile ...Cisco is the worldwide leader in networking for the Internet ...[Cisco will] shape the future of the Internet by creating unprecedented value and opportunity for our customers, employees, investors and ecosystem partners.

When two companies are headed in the same direction, the question is which of them will achieve their vision. This, in turn, depends less on the strategies of each firm and more on their execution of the strategies, the route they take to their destination.

Cut and Thrust

In this case, the starting points for the competitors, as perceived by the most valuable customers in the marketplace, especially those coveted by your company, are the same. The destination envisaged by their visions is also the same. The competitive strategies will likely appear very similar and be characterized more by day-to-day combat, tactical and real-time maneuvering, working with one another in a complementary way or aligning with allies that are not directly competitors than by fundamental differences in strategy. This is a particularly intense battlefield that is described as cut and thrust because it is often excellence in execution that separates the victor from the victim. The challenge is to retain some competitive order while the battle rages or risk the destruction of profitability for all.

The ongoing battle for supremacy between Coke and Pepsi illustrates competitive strategies of this type. One way to advance their competitive positions is to differentiate in areas such as positioning, acquisition of niche companies and development of new products. Another way to compete would be to have a very different vision for their companies, perhaps one that has less to do with sweetened water. However, both firms have been trying to develop such a breakthrough for years, so far without success. Were they to develop a basis for collegial coexistence if not collaboration, perhaps the profitability of both firms could be materially improved.

Some wars have been motivated by the pursuit of regional "hegemony," by which countries seek to dominate a given geographical area with the consent of allies.[2] The Axis countries of World War II prepared Japan for control of Asia and Germany in Europe. In the late eighteenth century, France had hegemony over Germany; Spain had hegemony over Italy for two centuries, ending in the seventeenth and so on. In business, some companies seek hegemony less by tacit agreement than by swapping assets with their competitors. For example, Ernst & Young and KPMG traded offices in the Canadian marketplace. Also in Canada, Rogers Cable and Shaw Cablesystems traded some cable television markets with one another to build their regional positions, and several consumer products companies have swapped brands such as for cookies and breakfast cereals to strengthen their positions in certain shelves of the supermarket.

In short, hegemony seeks accommodation for mutual advantage. If that cannot be found and companies are determined to overcome the enemy, battles will be increasingly of a cut and thrust nature, an intense skirmish at close quarters. In this type of combat, the winner will be the company that does the important things just a little bit better than the competitor.

A preferred approach is to develop differentiation, even for products for which this has been tried. For example, in the case of Coke and Pepsi, this has proved very difficult; some assume it to be virtually impossible for commodities like coal. Gasolines have not been materially differentiated, yet they, like coal, come in many different

[2] Hegemony means dominance, influence or authority over others. Hegemony does not seek capitulation or compliance through military force but seeks to change perspectives of the populace and manage the culture of the country through persuasion and propaganda to secure consent.

levels of sulfur, which can affect the nature of the discharge to the atmosphere. Some customers might appreciate these differences enough to buy from a particular company. Of course, there are as many ways to differentiate a product, service or solution as there are customers. Customers expect an offering from the company that they find valuable. The core of one-to-one marketing asserts that individual customers merit unique focus by the company wanting to be especially relevant. Customers should be differentiated before products or services. Companies then concern themselves with how to deliver the special relevance. Differentiation is so important that we pay attention to it later in this chapter.

West Versus East

In this situation, customers see companies and their products and services to be quite different. Companies also have quite different visions for the future and their place in it. Given these differences, it is likely that the companies will not grow in a similar manner and that one will triumph. In the Cold War analogy, this situation may be described as West Versus East, whereby each side had a different vision and was seen to be quite different by the world's citizens. This can happen in business, too.

Take the case of Commerce One and Ariba. These two companies provide the software over which business-to-business (B2B) electronic commerce is transacted. They enable electronic marketplaces, manage transactions and facilitate procurement over the Internet. B2B is expected to be the main area of opportunity for e-commerce, and both companies are competing for preeminence as solutions providers, especially for so-called vertical market portals. Using portals, companies within a given industry can buy and sell, either directly from one another or through on-line auctions.

Ariba and Commerce One have different roots, solutions, strategies and visions. For example, Ariba's approach to portals is to provide B2B solutions and services to all companies without directly forging alliances with any firms that use the software. Ariba wants to be able to sell to all comers. Commerce One has a different strategy, focusing on developing a relationship and forming a formal network with the major companies in an industry that will be users of the platform on which commerce is to be conducted. For example, Commerce One is a partner in Covisint, an e-commerce exchange for automobile industry sponsored by GM, Ford and DaimlerChrysler. It is also working with aerospace industry participants such as British Aerospace, Boeing,

Lockheed Martin and Raytheon in sponsoring Exostar, an e-marketplace. In the electric and gas utilities and pipeline sectors, power companies such as Cinergy, Consolidated Edison, Duke Energy and Ontario Power Generation are working with Commerce One on an e-marketplace called Pantellos. While Ariba and Commerce One are nominally in the same product-market space, their differences are sufficiently pronounced that it is likely one will succeed materially more than the other. Which one will succeed most, though, is unclear.

Nelson's Telescope

Horatio Nelson was second in command of the British fleet that engaged the Danes at the Battle of Copenhagen in 1801. Sir Hyde Parker, his superior, signaled to him to stop fighting, but Nelson, holding a telescope to his blind eye, said he could see no signal and continued fighting, winning the battle (luckily for him). Nelson would not see what Parker wanted him to. In business, when companies are seen to be similar by their customers but have different visions, it is quite possible that some companies have inaccurate or unrealistic visions. They continue the fight in the blind hope that they are nevertheless right or that their skill and effort will be sufficient to triumph. Such companies can succeed or fail spectacularly.

Britannica, that venerable vendor of weighty tomes, would not change its focus on physical books when Microsoft launched the relatively lighter-weight, CD-ROM-based Encarta from Funk and Wagnalls. Even when it was clear to all that customers preferred a CD version of an encyclopaedia, Britannica moved slowly. It did not want to offend a sales force focused on hard-won, foot-in-the-door sales. Britannica's sales disappeared overnight as though the collective doors of every household in the world suddenly slammed shut. Britannica (the company) was sold and has since reemerged as a portal. The opportunity had been there for Britannica to compete on scope by offering its customers more than physical books, but to do this, Britannica needed to change its vision and abandon its commitment to an untenable business model.

The strategic challenge here is to differentiate the company, its products, services and solutions or relationships in the minds of individual customers while affirming the accuracy of its vision. In industries, especially ones in which companies have similar perceptions of the future, there is an opportunity for the industry to be ordered. When the vacuum tube[3] industry entered into its declining phase, it

[3] As mentioned prevously, these are also sometimes called receiving tubes or valves.

was clear to all that this forerunner to transistors and integrated circuits would be displaced for consumer applications. Companies could make plans to retire industry capacity in an orderly manner while looking for growth and competitive advantage in the new regime. Industry participants aligned their visions to the reality of marketplace demand for receiving tubes and exited the industry in a manner that rewarded early leavers and those that stayed behind to make tubes for themselves and the departing companies.

Competing on Scope

Companies with limited product differentiation can still become more important to customers by competing on scope—providing customers with what they want to buy rather than what companies have historically made. Competing on scope can create differentiation for companies and provide a differentiated vision, too. This strategy can provide a way to enter the West vs. East quadrant where companies have an opportunity to compete very effectively against competitors that may still be focused more narrowly on specific product or service attributes, for example. For companies already in the West vs. East quadrant, competing on scope can set them apart from competitors by further differentiating visions and the depth and breadth of the ranges of products and services provided. According to this approach, companies are much less concerned about whether or not they make every product or service or the profit of each one, but are focused instead on the profitability and satisfaction of individual customers. This may lead them to supply whatever the customer would expect from such companies, whether or not these firms have previously made these products or provided these services.

Competing on Scale for Market Share

In previous eras, companies competed extensively on scale. The view was that size would bring rewards to the large company in a number of dimensions, mostly derived from greater power in relation to customers, suppliers and intermediaries, and relative to competitors. There was much evidence that market share advantage, a measure of relative competitive scale, translated into relatively more profitability. All this is not particularly surprising given Porter's Five Forces model, which we have already seen. As a company builds market share, it extends itself toward a monopoly position, which is achieved when its share is 100 percent.

Those that have attained near monopolies through, for example, pharmaceutical patents, control of computer operating systems or regulatory approval of a single supplier of cable television or telephony in a region, have often secured considerably more profitability than companies without this share advantage. For example, wireline telecommunications companies with monopolies for local service tend to be more profitable than the wireless carriers they spawned that compete in open markets. This is not to say that monopolies remain profitable forever. Just when companies control aspects of a product-market, substitutes often emerge to challenge their strength.

Thus, pharmaceutical companies face challenges from other compounds that achieve similar benefits such as the emergence of alternatives to Bayer's Aspirin headache medicine. Other examples of monopolies that disappear are pharmaceutical companies contending with generic manufacturers when their patents expire and operating system software companies such as Microsoft and Apple facing challenges from the Internet and open operating systems such as Linux and Java. Regional monopolies in cable television are challenged by technologies that deliver television signals in new ways such as via satellite or over the Internet.

Increasingly, companies are finding that competing on scale, if achieved, provides some respite from competition, but the duration of the benefit is dwindling as technology proliferates and industry structure changes, together eroding certain types of commanding market positions. Being bigger is not necessarily a basis for building a business, as can be seen from Daimler's acquisition of Chrysler and the inability of some share leaders such as General Motors, to translate their market leadership into significantly higher returns than some among their smaller rivals. Rather than use scale to ensure longevity and enhanced performance, some companies are turning to competing on scope.

Competing on Scope for Customer Share

Competing on scope is a customer-centric approach to build customer share just as competing on scale was one way to create the efficiencies needed to increase share of market. As mentioned above, competing on scope means that companies seek to provide their important customers with the products or services they consider should be logically supplied by the company. It means that the company becomes the most *relevant* supplier to the customers it has chosen to focus on. More than this, it means that companies with scope economies have a number of other competitive advantages. By virtue of a close working relationship, they know what the customer needs next and can position to address this need in advance of competitors. A number of companies have put employees at customers' premises to provide better service and gain customer intelligence that gives them an advantage for upcoming business opportunities.

Companies that compete on scope cannot easily be replaced by a competitor. Major accounting-consulting firms compete on scope, seeking to be a one-stop shop for their customers. The firms become bonded within their clients, and this creates barriers to switching. Even when alternative suppliers that may do more specialized work appear, firms that have wide presence in the account are generally able to retain their position. Competing on scope is hard to do mostly because processes become more complex, and few companies are willing to tolerate increased complexity. But for those companies able to do this, the benefits are well worth the effort. These include things such as profiting from a broader base of sales in the account, helping to specify new procurements, lower business development costs, and having a forgiving environment for product testing.

Clearly, not all successful companies have chosen to compete on scope, but many are challenged by "scope creep" as customers ask them for more and different products and services, and the company does what the customer wants. Some companies continue to use the ways of the past to build their future businesses. For example, some firms seek to build scale and profitability by:

- adjusting their mix of products and services so that they have the most profitable portfolio (even though some of their most profitable customers may want some of the less profitable products, putting the relationship as a whole at risk)
- selling more of what they make and insisting that they make what they sell
- restructuring their industries by engaging in practices such as acquiring competitors

Inasmuch as these strategies continue to work for the company, they obviously merit continued consideration. For those enterprises facing flattening revenue and profit growth and intensified competition, competing on scope rather than scale and mix may offer a way forward. Figure 6-3 describes the evolution of businesses in several industries, as they shift from scale to scope competition.

Figure 6-3: Competing on Scope

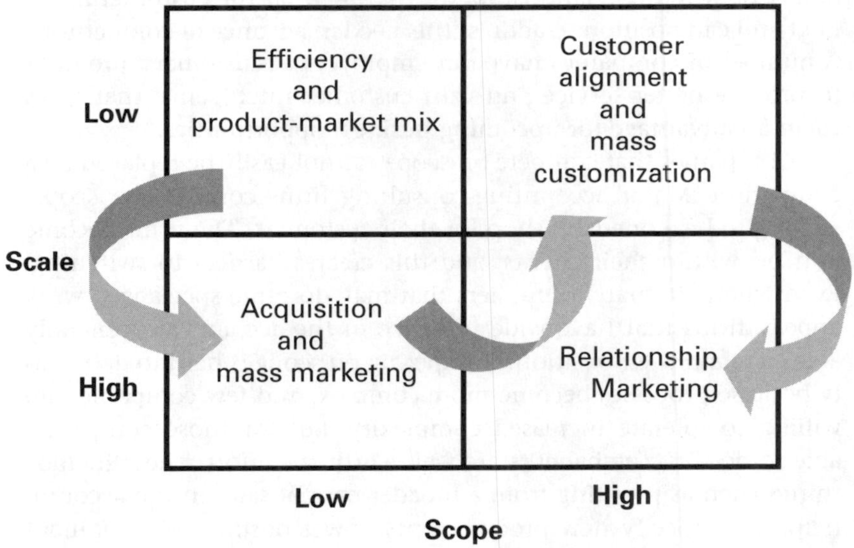

New Meaning for Focus

One of the earliest challenges in shifting from competing on scale to scope is the redefinition of the term "focus." In most companies, focus means concentrating on the *products or services* that generate most profitability for the company. When the firm starts to compete on scope, focus, defined this way, becomes difficult indeed. Competing on scope means that the company provides important, chosen customers with the products and services they expect to buy from their supplier. This puts pressure on the supplier to make available a broader range of products and services.

Thus, a vertical market software company that provides software to libraries can be challenged to expand the solution to include, for example, software customization, computers and peripherals, products and software made by third parties and network services, among much else. The result is that customers receive an integrated solution and can work with a single vendor, which simplifies their lives. On the other hand, the software-turned-solutions company must cope with challenges to its internal processes as it assembles the value the customer wants. The supplier's executives are likely to prefer more product focus to simplify their lives but, in reality, must accept greater complexity in their processes so that the end customer gets what he or she wants.

Focus, in the era of scope competition, means concentrating on specific customers. In this context, then, focus on customers can and often does result in lesser focus in areas such as processes and product profitability. It is entirely appropriate for companies to retain some products or services that lose money if their best customers want these included as a condition for doing business with the company.

Competing on Scope and Scale

Companies that compete on scope evolve from management of their product-market mix for greatest profitability to growing either internally or by acquisition according to their existing model to build scale. Then they evolve into mass customizers and one-to-one marketers, aligning with the customers they have chosen to serve them with a broader range of products and services. This transition can be difficult because this is where processes are changed, new suppliers secured, brands repositioned and extensive training undertaken in areas such as up-selling and cross-selling (what relationship marketers call "lift" and "shift"). Once the chaos is reduced or the tolerance for it increases, the company can embark on growing by both scale and scope, leading to the fully developed relationship marketing company. People often ask which companies fall into this category today. Simply put, I am not aware of any. This is the nirvana for which many are striving.

When competing on scope, there is a potential and even a likelihood that companies will stray into unfamiliar territory and could face unanticipated risks. Companies need to be very clear about the value chain components they control and those areas they consider best undertaken by others. Competing on scope not only creates a new competitive set, it challenges the notion that companies must control their value chain end-to-end. Competing on scope means that companies must manage the processes by which value is created for the customer, not necessarily every aspect of the value chain.

New Competitors

The implications for competing on scope on competitor targeting are profound. With scope competition, your set of competitors changes.

When you begin to supply products and services your customers consider logical for you to provide, the boundaries of your product market may extend to include nontraditional competitors. This leads to the discussion on convergence that follows.

Convergence

When the verb converge was coined in the seventeenth century, it was used to describe the tendency of two lines to approach one another, as tributaries of a river flowing together. Usage in the twentieth century and since has been broader such as the coming together of fields of endeavor. In business, convergence has a number of distinct meanings such as digital convergence and industry convergence.

Convergence can be one manifestation of competing on scope and is a way to propel companies into the West vs. East quadrant where they may have good prospects for success. However, companies pursuing convergence strategies should recognize that digital and industry convergence may cause divergence of customers, markets, channels and products, resulting in a different set of competitors.

Digital Convergence

Digital convergence means the coming together of sound, video and data for the purposes of transportation, processing, routing, storage and retrieval. Once what we see and hear is converted into digits, computers can store, process and transform these and other data such as text and numbers and communicate them at high speed to other computers and people. With digital convergence, the data streams from various originating sources flow together as a series of ones and zeros down a common pipeline such as the telephone lines. At either end of this pipeline are the products and services that facilitate the flows and which enable the processing, compression, manipulation, presentation, storage and retrieval.

Digital convergence has made competitors of companies traditionally engaged in different areas of communications, carriers, content and computing. Now these firms provide products or services from one or more of the other areas to customers that want a broader set of solutions as suggested by Figure 6-4.

Figure 6-4: Digital Convergence

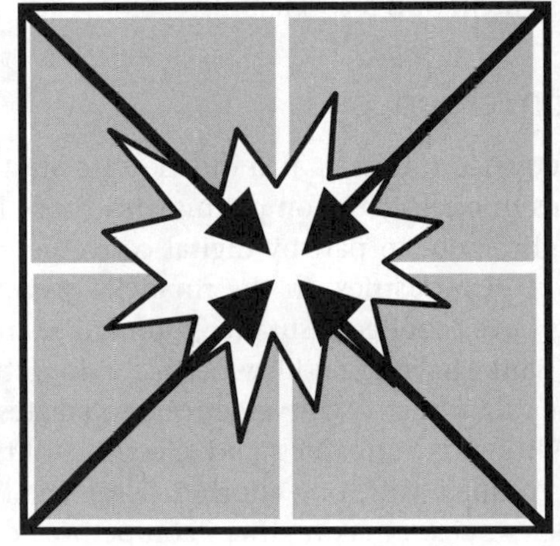

America Online's (AOL) interest in acquiring Time Warner in January 2001 is a case of an Internet carrier or portal company wanting content and broadband access for its customers. Through Time Warner, AOL has the potential to provide customers with tiers of information and to stream them and other content as broadband capabilities become more widespread. When Time Warner, in turn, seeks to acquire other content companies such as in the music recording industry, they create huge potential for AOL to compete on scope by giving customers the content they want in a wide variety of media, from print and broadcast to music and video. By acquiring Time Warner, AOL differentiated its company from Yahoo!, with which AOL had been compared often. AOL moved into the West vs. East quadrant with a favorable position against Yahoo! which had taken the position that they would not acquire content companies. With Time Warner, AOL has obtained a strong recurring revenue stream and a basis to continue its growth and compete on new fronts. It will need the additional resources. Digital and industry convergence, which we will discuss next, has now given AOL a much tougher competitor, Microsoft.

In another example, Rogers Communications has entered into arrangements with some of its competitors in the cable television industry to offer the products and services of one another.

Companies such as Rogers want to provide a variety of media, entertainment, Internet, cellular and communications services to customers, with invoicing on a single bill.

Industry Convergence

Industry convergence means that industries are starting to be more alike, with firms in one sector competing with those in another. This has been brought about in part by digital convergence, deregulation and reregulation of industries. In the financial services industry, for example, banks have acquired insurance companies, and now compete in that sector. Banks have done likewise in the investment brokerage industry. In the utility sector, convergence also creates nontraditional competitors, with gas companies and electric utilities increasingly positioning to compete with one another. Some utilities also provide communications services, making them competitors of the telcos.

Mergers and acquisitions are accelerating industry convergence, with carriers acquiring content companies and broadcasters, for example. Cases in point are AOL's acquisition of Time Warner, already mentioned, and Bell Canada's purchase of Canada's second largest television network, CTV. Companies are also creating new entities as an alternative to acquisition to compete in the new areas enabled by digital convergence and changed regulations. For example, a major Western Canadian cable television company, Shaw Communications, has established an entertainment company, Corus Entertainment, to produce content as well as distribute it. The shift from distribution to content ownership is an increasingly common theme for interactive service companies, broadcasters and cable companies. Some content companies are also acquiring distribution interests such as MGM's investments in four national cable networks[4] and investments in fourteen television channels.

Very large convergence companies are emerging to participate in multiple media. AOL Time Warner, for example, has business units that include America Online in interactive services, network companies such as Turner Broadcasting and Home Box Office, a publisher—Time Inc., moviemakers Warner Bros. and New Line Cinema, and Warner Music Group and Time Warner Cable, with their obvious areas of interest.

Companies such as AOL Time Warner face a new array of competitors as they enter into new lines of business. AOL now competes

[4] Twenty percent ownership in American Movie Classics (AMC), Bravo, The Independent Film Channel (IFC) and WE: Women's Entertainment (formerly Romance Classics).

with Rupert Murdoch's publishing empire, for example. It is possible that very large convergence companies will emerge in the future to provide a wide range of services such as property security, financial, telecommunications, cable television and entertainment services to distinct market sectors or specific consumers. The challenge for companies broadening their business base using convergence will be to create new value for customers that is competitively superior to more specialized companies that have remained within the industry boundaries. If they cannot, they will go the same way as the conglomerates of the 1960s. They will be broken up into smaller units that make more sense to customers and investors.

Customer, Market, Channel and Product Divergence

Industry convergence can cause divergence of customers and markets. To return to the AOL Time Warner example, AOL obtained an entirely different mix of customers such as kids and businesses, not to mention lines of business, when it acquired Time Warner. Products and services fragment in response to the enabling effect of digital convergence and industry restructuring. Consider the many new technology products and services that many consumers now take for granted such as pagers, cell phones, on-line auctions, health information, e-mail and increasingly Internet gambling. As products and services fragment, so do market segments until the ultimate market segment, that of the individual consumer, is reached. This is where CRM comes into play.

Market segment fragmentation brings with it an associated fragmentation of distribution channels and channels of communications. Consumers, for example, may buy personal computers over the Internet, by telephone, from independent and chain computer dealers and at mass merchandisers among other channels. Marketing communications may be one-way such as traditional mass media vehicles, including television, radio, catalogs and print media, and, increasingly, two-way such as the Internet, call centers and fax-back services.

In the area of products, digital convergence brings about divergence. While there are examples of convergence products such as television sets that function as game terminals and Internet appliances and computers that have TV cards and games, customers usually prefer having appliances that do one specialized task only. This is evident in the many wireless products consumers use ranging from pagers to cellular phones to wireless data communications devices.

Convergence is bringing with it fragmentation in other areas. For example, as companies find new ways to capture the opportunities associated with technology and convergence, new industries are being created such as computer telephony integration (CTI) formed by a merging or redefinition of the computer and telephony boundaries. New companies are also being created to benefit from convergence opportunities. For example, companies such as Siebel have emerged to provide customer contact and call center automation, employing computer, networking, Internet and telephony technology.

The technology environments within which the companies are participating are also fragmenting. While Microsoft has dominated the operating system environment for personal computers, it has less relative strength in the Internet arena, where Sun Microsystem's Java has been strong competition for Microsoft's ActiveX. Hand-held devices have different operating systems, too, and Microsoft's strength on the desktop has not translated into dominance in the mobile arena such as the firm's Windows Lite/CE environment.

Strategic Impacts of Convergence

The strategies being pursued by the companies marketing technology products are also proliferating. Some computer companies such as Dell and Gateway, seek out their customers directly, while other successful firms such as HP, mostly employ indirect channels of distribution, reaching their customers through a network of computer dealers and other retail channels.

There have been many alliances among companies seeking to capture convergence opportunities and spread their market and R&D risks while retaining the capability to address opportunities as they emerge. Well-known alliances include ventures such as MSNBC, the alliance between Microsoft and the NBC network to provide broadcasting on the Web. Hewlett-Packard has built its business using alliances with a wide variety of companies such as Andersen Consulting, Cap Gemini Ernst & Young, Cisco, EDS, Intel, Nokia, Nortel Networks, Oracle, PeopleSoft, SAP and Samsung.

Differentiation

Vendors and products are proliferating, and one of the byproducts is declining differentiation of both companies and their products and services. This is compounded by a number of other factors that erode differentiation, including customers who become sophisticated buyers very quickly in addition to the loud general clamor in the marketplace where companies with similarly deep pockets spend what it takes to position themselves favorably. With declining differentiation comes increasing price competition, which cannot simply be avoided by a focus on customer relationship management. Declining profitability is often the result of this scenario, but this need not be so. Opportunities exist to restore differentiation relative to specific competitors, in dimensions that are important to the customer. It is important to restore differentiation for companies wanting to position themselves favorably in the West vs. East quadrant.

The Company and Its Brand

As companies compete on scope, the range of products and services expands, and it becomes more difficult to differentiate every offering. While technology can assist here such as by providing content that aids differentiation on the Internet and by communicating with individual customers, it is important for the entire company to be differentiated from a targeted competitor. This differentiation increases the margin on sales and makes it easier to launch new products and services. As importantly, it keeps customers coming back for more.

For your company to be perceived as unique or at least very different from the competitors you have targeted, it should be able to make a statement of relevance to the customers you have selected in terms of their main vendor-selection and support criteria. All else being equal, significant size and, to a lesser extent, fast rate of growth become important bases for differentiation, just as large and rapidly mobile armies tend to do best in battle. Buyers seek the reassurance of dealing with the largest and fastest-growing companies, exemplified by an old saying in the computer industry that no one ever got fired for specifying IBM. Today, scale seems less important than dominance of a relevant position. So, for example, Oracle, although large, has grown at the expense of other companies that were nominally in its product space by focusing on its ability to enable companies that wish to do business on the Internet.

Purchasers tend to associate good attributes with companies that have a scale and other characteristics similar to their own. Thus, large companies tend to buy from large suppliers, requiring smaller companies to prove themselves. Increasing centralization of purchasing authority in the hands of fewer decision makers in large companies makes it even more important for the supplier to be seen to be operating on the same scale as the buyer.

In consumer markets, large companies also occupy the high ground in the minds of their purchasers. Although small restaurants may serve a better hamburger, for example, many consumers still visit a major chain because it is a less risky purchase. The size, cleanliness and product quality at least will be uniform, if not particularly exciting in some cases. Rather than compete on the same battlefield as large companies, small firms would do better to emphasize their mobility, flexibility, speed, customization, personal service and responsiveness, areas in which large firms can be weaker performers. Small firms may also benefit by supplying larger companies and helping them to compete on scope, as discussed earlier.

Differentiating a company requires an understanding of the benefits it can bring to customers. For example, in the commission-hungry world of car selling, few customers want to be put through the combative process dealers use to secure a sale. GM's Saturn division does things differently, selling cars at a fixed price and rewarding salespeople without using straight commission. With no price to haggle over, customers can be more focused on the product, and the salesperson can pay more attention to customers' requirements.

Brand Equity

The value of the brand to the customer over and above the core functionality needed for marketplace participation may be termed the brand equity. This additional value is the goodwill consumers are willing to pay to obtain a specific brand over another that is the same in all respects except for the name. In both consumer and business-to-business markets, the brand itself has considerable power to influence the purchase decision. If customers are engaged by the brand alone, this represents the main vehicle by which the company forms a relationship with its customers and sets itself apart from competitors.

Brand equity can be seen in terms of two categories of attributes:

1. those that describe the functions the product performs
2. emotional or other nonfunctional attributes captured in the brand[5]

---

[5] Additional perspectives on brand equity can be gained from David Aaker's books, *Managing Brand Equity: Capitalizing on the Value of a Brand Name*. New York: Maxwell Macmillan, 1991; and *Building Strong Brands*. New York: The Free Press, 1996.

Typically, companies focus most on building a physically better product, in search of the proverbial better mousetrap or improving their services in some way. They often pay insufficient attention to the emotional appeal of their products. Chrysler makes great minivans and makes a persuasive rational case for buying their product by emphasizing features, benefits and prices. It notes it is the largest seller of minivans. Sales of Ford's Windstar were expected to suffer when Chrysler introduced its newly redesigned product. Actually, Ford's sales went up as it built the emotional value of the brand, saying, in effect, that families would be safer in the Windstar, a claim they supported with government crash tests results. In most companies, the opportunity remains for marketers to bond with their customers on an emotional level, which can be an important basis for differentiation, especially when customers feel no emotion toward your competitors, too.

Differentiating the brand with consumers can also indirectly differentiate the company and solidify relationships with business intermediaries and partners. When Intel, the largest manufacturer of microprocessors (chips) for personal computers, branded "Intel Inside" with end customers, it created value for manufacturers of personal computers and also made it more difficult for these companies to buy from competitors such as Cyrix, AMD and others. Intel ended up dominating the marketplace.

Brand equity has the potential to be, for both business and consumer markets, the equivalent of the encyclopedia salesperson's foot in the door. It provides a more receptive opening to the mind of the customer and a basis for achieving a higher share of the customer's business. If the Moore business forms company stands for just "business forms" in the minds of their customers, they obviously will have considerably more difficulty penetrating accounts and becoming a more broadly based supplier than if their firm was positioned more broadly such as "providers of information solutions." Once a very large company, Moore's challenge has been to find new sales to replace the declining volumes in business forms. The trouble is, the marketplace is crowded with very competent technology vendors, making it hard for Moore to set itself apart.

Insufficient brand equity and differentiation can also impede the development of opportunities. When Singer wanted to offer more than sewing machines through its several thousand outlets worldwide, it chose to purchase companies in the consumer electronics arena such as Marantz and Sansui, rather than try to extend the Singer brand to this category. Perhaps it felt that most consumers would identify Singer with sewing machines and their service rather than with a more broadly based brand. Sony has no such difficulty doing precisely that. Most consumers likely see Sony as builders of leading edge, quality electronics. The Sony brand has been an umbrella for the firm to broaden its product line in the fast-paced consumer electronics, entertainment/games, services and software/content arenas.

Brand equity can increase the firm's revenues sometimes even in areas unrelated to its main business. This is being appreciated in emerging or newly deregulated industries such as electricity, where the notion that electricity is a commodity without differentiation potential is being challenged. Enron, an electricity wholesaler that does not own generating assets, has invested heavily in mass advertising to brand itself as a supplier of energy. Enron will likely find that its investment will pay off as markets become more open and new industrial, commercial and residential customers, now aware of the Enron brand, are prepared to consider Enron as their supplier. Having formed relationships with customers for electricity, Enron could then supply natural gas, communications, security services and even cable television services. This is the opportunity afforded by convergence, and brand equity opens the buyer's mind to a company wanting to participate in new arenas.

In addition to sustaining and expanding a business, high levels of brand equity contribute significantly to its durability. Procter & Gamble has demonstrated the enduring power of brand equity and differentiation. Ivory soap was first sold in October 1879. Its positioning as a floating soap that is "99-44/100 percent pure" was established shortly thereafter by Harley Procter and has remained essentially unchanged since. P&G was among the first companies to establish brand managers to safeguard and advance the brand relative to competitors, internal as well as external ones. Its brands have proliferated to include, in the laundry category, for example: Bold, Bounce, Cheer, Downy, Dreft, Dryel, Era, Gain, Ivory Snow, Oxydol and Tide.

Differentiating Relationships

If your company and your targeted competitor both want relationships with the same customers, to win share of customer, the company will have to succeed in setting the relationship apart from that of the competitor. This, in turn, will require that the company deliver the value and relevance the customer wants. Delivery of value has been addressed to some extent by product and service differentiation, but it is more than that. Value includes giving customers the opportunity to assemble the components of value they want and pay for those separately, with pricing established not just according to what customers buy, but also based on who they are. If a company is to differentiate its relationship, it will thus need to position itself uniquely to each customer in an ongoing dialog based on learning, differentiated according to the eleven Cs of relationship marketing, which replace the 4 Ps of traditional marketing.[6] The eleven Cs of relationship marketing differentiation are:

1. Customer Differentiation
2. Category Differentiation
3. Capability Differentiation
4. Cost, Profitability and Value Differentiation
5. Contact-to-Cash Process Differentiation
6. Collaboration and Integration Differentiation
7. Customization Differentiation
8. Communications, Interaction and Positioning Differentiation
9. Customer Measurements Differentiation
10. Customer Care Differentiation
11. Chain of Relationships Differentiation

Customer Differentiation

Companies employing the principles of CRM differentiate their customers, choosing which merit priority attention. They ask themselves questions such as, "Which customers will be served (those of your company and those of the targeted competitor) and what bonding and other objectives are to be achieved with each?" In addition, the company might consider which customers will *not* be served, which should be fired as customers and what the rules of engagement are to be used for each customer or tier of customers.

When considering customers, also review who the decision makers are *or could be* within a customer. That is, while some companies differentiate customers according to the buying organization as a whole, the potential also exists to do the same for specific buyers and decision influencers within each account. For example, as the decision-making

---

[6] From my book, *Relationship Marketing: New Strategies, Techniques and Technologies to Win the Customers You Want and Keep Them Forever*, (Toronto: John Wiley and Sons), 1998.

process matures together with an increase in buyer knowledge and sophistication, typically the decision maker becomes more specialized and often more junior. Companies always must be on the alert for shifts in the decision-making unit because these can create new opportunities and risks. Should one compete on price or make a more compelling value proposition to a senior decision maker?

Early in the product's life cycle, business-to-business companies usually address the needs of designers, developers and production personnel as well as purchasing. As these customers increase their familiarity with the use and performance of their suppliers' products and services, the title of the buyer often changes. Perhaps, a technical specialist introduced your type of products to his or her organization. Once the company gained familiarity with the product and its use, a generalist purchaser made subsequent purchases, the typical case for consumables and lower-priced capital goods. Firms dealing principally with or through purchasing agents will continue to experience pricing pressure because this has been the main "reason for being" of the generalist purchaser—to find ways to reduce the cost base of the company by reducing suppliers' prices. Unless your company is already the low-cost producer in your industry and intends to retain this position, the challenge is to build new and differentiated value into the purchasing relationship.

Category Differentiation

In most industries, products and services provided by different suppliers have features that are alike. It is hard for companies to find a meaningful basis for differentiation of product attributes in mature markets like alcoholic or carbonated beverages, automobiles, chemicals, grocery products, machine tools, and many other industrial and consumer goods categories. There are thus two alternative paths to pursue:

1. Create product and service differences.
2. Compete on scope, and differentiate the line of products and services provided to the customer.

Companies have adopted the first approach for some time, although the urgency of the marketplace has resulted in quicker decision making and less research. Companies innovate repeatedly, looking for good new ideas whenever they can find them to set their products apart. Product and service differences are researched or developed collaboratively with the firm's most important current customers or prospects. Customers are provided with designs, mock-ups, prototypes, samples or illustrations to avoid the trap of asking customers about new features, functionality or designs when they do not know the answer.

Brainstorming is used to come up with new product and service ideas. For example, a successful technology company wished to enter an entirely new line of business. Together with a five person team from the company, we followed the following process. We developed objectives for the process and then screening criteria. The team brainstormed 274 different concepts that would address the objectives, screened them against the criteria, evaluated 12 in overview, examined four in depth and identified a significant opportunity for which a detailed plan was developed. The plan examined the fit of the concept with the company's mandate and the feasibility of the initiative from a market, financial and operations perspective. The market assessment involved close collaboration with customers and examination of possible competitors in this new area.

However, it is not always possible to find fundamental points of product difference in the minds of individual consumers, especially when patterns of individual buyer behavior are entrenched. Some companies continue to try. One such example was RJR's smokeless cigarette, which did not result in market success. Many firms today seek to differentiate their offerings on the basis of brand and image.

While product and service differentiation is important if it can be achieved, it is equally important to differentiate the lines of business in which the company competes with targeted competitors. Differentiation of product and service categories means answering the question, "What scope of products and services are to be offered to specific customers, and how will this differ from what the targeted competitor offers?" A secondary decision is whether the company should produce the products or services itself or find other means to deliver it to the customer such as by private branding or outsourcing.

Increasingly, product companies are competing on scope by adding services to their lines of business, as IBM has done by using a customer help center to assist purchasers of the company's computers. Other companies offer benefits such as rapid delivery, assurance of delivery in the event of input shortages or disrupted production, consistent quality and inventory management services to provide a compelling lineup of products and services and continuing reasons to do business with the company.

In addition to developing a real basis for product and service differentiation, companies differentiate customers' perceptions compared to targeted competitors. We discuss this under Communications, Interaction and Positioning Differentiation, later in this chapter.

Capability Differentiation

As the future is uncertain, it is important that the company identify those capabilities that will give it strategic advantage over a targeted competitor. Capabilities by their very nature can accommodate different eventualities. Today, customers choose companies as much as companies select them, so the firm's capabilities—comprising its people, processes, technology and customer knowledge and insight—should set it apart from targeted competitors.

Differential capabilities may be defined as the ability of a company to outperform a targeted competitor and they derive from an understanding of the critical factors that enable success, which in turn may stem from the following:

- The objectives of a company. For example, a company focused on customer penetration might compete on scope, while one driven by product innovation may seek to grow by scale and declining costs from higher volumes. The former approach has the potential to bring a company closer to its customers, while the latter can enhance a firm's appeal to a mass market. In industries in which marketing to individuals creates new customer value, competing on scale may not be a winning strategy.
- Access to superior resources. Better resources—expertise, raw materials, labor and money—will have obvious benefit to the company that has such access and makes better use of it.
- Greater efficiency. This stems from:
  - *Scale or scope economies.* Scale economies come from size, while scope economies come from customers, such as reduced selling costs and more efficient ordering processes and logistics.
  - *Experience curve.* According to the experience curve, a company's costs decline as its production volumes increase, not just because overheads are spread across more units, but because the company gets better at what it does.
  - *Vertical or horizontal integration.* For example, a shoe retailer buys a shoe manufacturer (vertical) or a handbag retailer (horizontal).
  - *Financing cost structure.* For example, a company with no debts at a time of high interest rates may be better off than a highly levered competitor, while the latter may do better when interest rates are low.

- *Proximity to raw materials, labor, core customer and key suppliers.* Being close not only reduces costs such as transportation and communications, but has the potential to increase frequency of contact and improve the relationship.
- *Labor relationships and costs.* Companies with more peaceful labor conditions, more flexible relationships and lower costs are obviously better prepared to compete than a targeted competitor with relative deficiencies in any of these areas.

- Capital versus labor intensity includes a consideration of an appropriate level of automation. A very profitable company in the food industry makes ice cream cones in a labor-intensive process. It has less computerization in its plant and administration than most of its rivals. In this sector, at least, it seems to have demonstrated that it is not always profitable to replace labor with capital equipment.
- The sharing of resources between divisions or product lines enables improved cost effectiveness in areas such as marketing, the sales force, procurement, warehousing, transportation, distribution channels, manufacturing facilities, order processing, quality control and testing, maintenance, repair and overhaul, buyer financing, product or process technology, and research and development.
- Doing all the little things a little better—recognizing that, relative to competitors, a 1 percent improvement per year in all aspects of your operations and in customer satisfaction—will lead to an 11 percent advantage in a decade.

Cost, Profitability and Value Differentiation

A key role of the CRM company is to build customer profitability, primarily through creating new value with customers and then sharing this. Clearly, the company has two main options in creating value for business customers:

1. Make the customer more cost-competitive; or
2. Create new revenue opportunities for the customer such as through new product development and comarketing and sales initiatives.

The company that does this better than targeted competitors has an opportunity to increase share of customer. To do this, the company should know how its costs compare to that of the targeted competitor.

How does the mix of customer profitability in total and for specific customers compare to that of the target? How are customers to be managed to develop an increase in mutual and shared value relative to the value created with customers by the targeted competitor?

Contact-to-Cash Process Differentiation

The CRM company manages and controls the processes associated with contacts at the account by ensuring that cash is collected. Differentiating these processes compared to those used by a targeted competitor has the potential to deepen the customer relationship and shift share of customer from the competitor. The company should consider the company's processes from initial customer contact through product and service design and development, production, shipment and installation, information sharing, customer support to invoicing and cash generation. These should be compared with the targeted competitor to identify areas of opportunity. For example, when its most important customers are occasionally slow in remitting payment, how does the competitor respond? Does the competitor proactively propose solutions for the customer's upcoming procurements? Do they work collaboratively at the planning stage for product or service conceptualization?

Collaboration and Integration Differentiation

The CRM company is proactive in securing access to the key decision makers and support for joint learning, strategy sharing and other forms of strategic and operational collaboration leading to integration of some aspects of the customer's business with that of the supplier. The winner in key business-to-business purchasing situations would be expected to collaborate better than targeted competitors. The company would consider what it needs to do to engage executive management and other internal, customer-facing personnel and even its customers in a collaboration that ensures joint learning, strategy sharing and other forms of strategic and operational collaboration. How is management of these processes to differ from that of the targeted competitor? That is, how is the customer to be actively engaged in a collaborative manner that is competitively differentiated?

Customization Differentiation

The creation of new value for each customer means that the CRM company customizes aspects of the product and service development, production and/or delivery, and perhaps takes an expanded role in the management of the product or service throughout its lifetime. For example, computer companies are now providing "evergreen" programs for their customers, keeping up-to-date personal computers on the desks of the customer's staff serviced, clean, loaded with current software and fully functional rather than repeatedly making new sales of computers to the company. More generally, the CRM company considers how the customer is to be provided with a solution each considers to have unique relevance (not necessarily a unique product or service for each customer, just one that it considers to be a perfect fit for its requirement). How is the company to plan the creation of new value for the customer by customizing aspects of the product and service development, production and/or delivery, customized services and even pricing? How will this differ from that of targeted competitors?

Communications, Interaction and Positioning Differentiation

The CRM company engages the customer with real-time, interactive communications and not with "promotion" sent indiscriminately to the customer such as a broadcast television message or a mass-mailed brochure. The firm manages the positioning of the company with every customer. This includes understanding competitive activity in the account and ensuring that the company remains well positioned in respect of current and emerging developments in the customer's business relative to targeted competitors. Questions to be considered by the relationship marketer include how the customer is to be engaged with real-time, interactive, one-to-one and two-way communications. How is this to happen more effectively and efficiently compared to targeted competitors? How is differentiation to be conveyed to the customer? What communications channels are to be employed? More generally, how is the competitive positioning of the company in the minds of each customer to be managed?

Positioning is about occupying a place in the mind of the individual customer that is a preferred position to that of a targeted competitor. Positioning alternatives are established by each customer's needs. For example, if a teenager's most important need when buying sunglasses is to feel cool, companies such as Ray-Ban must know what "cool" is to this specific person and how to pursue it. Perhaps one customer will receive communications with a sports star endorsement, while another may see an ad with a rock music personality, according to the preferences of each.

Customers' needs are classified according to the Maslow[7] need hierarchy, shown in Figure 6-5. Most companies position themselves and their offering in the first tier, appealing to basic needs. Scroll through the Yellow Pages and you will find locksmiths who install locks for security and car dealers who sell dependable cars at fair prices.

Figure 6-5: Maslow's Need Hierarchy

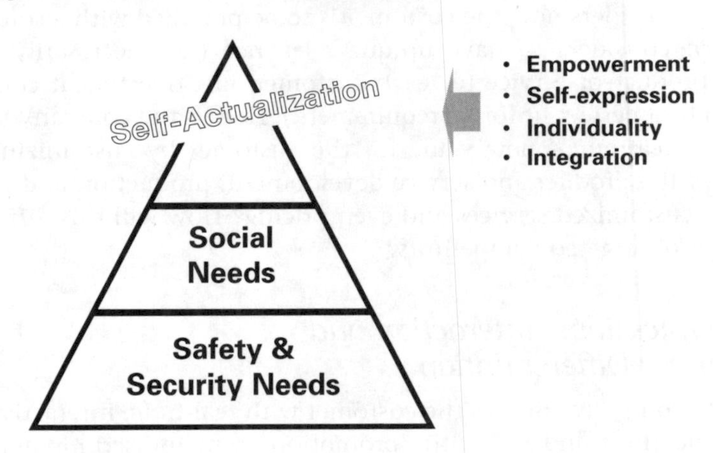

Some businesses such as beer companies, have migrated to the second level because they know that first-level needs have been satisfied. Here the basic idea is that an appeal to the peer group will influence the individual. Although apparently contradictory, they know from their research that individuals want to fit into a group and simultaneously stand out from it. For example, in a famous beer advertisement, Molson's featured their idea of an average Canadian beer drinker touting his reasons for being proudly Canadian, which is, not incidentally, also the name of their brand.

Some companies have approached the third level of the Maslow hierarchy. For example, in 1988, Reebok invited buyers to "UBU," essentially to live life as an individual in an integrated way, unfettered by social convention, presumably while wearing their shoes. One of the phrases in its advertisement was, "Insist on yourself, never imitate." Reebok's more recent Defy Convention campaign built on UBU

[7] Abraham Maslow (1908-1970) was a psychologist who identified a hierarchy of needs for each person, saying that more basic security needs are to be satisfied before social and then self-actualization needs.

by continuing to associate the brand with an attitude and personal confidence. Apple Computer has also communicated that its products enable users to achieve their individual intellectual and other potential, appealing to motives of power in addition to self-actualization. And other companies are seeking yet higher ground than this. For example, Benneton's famous graphic communications serve to position its brand in respect of a variety of societal issues.

Yet even so, few companies have fully and successfully addressed the high ground represented by the third-level needs of Maslow's hierarchy. This remains uncontested territory. There is potential for companies to find creative ways to differentiate themselves in the minds of individual consumers on the basis of empowerment, self-expression, individuality or integration (a way of saying that individuals balance the various forces and demands for time in their lives in a "well-rounded" manner). Give it consideration before your competitors do.

Customer Measurements Differentiation

Management has an old adage that you get what you measure. For differentiation to be achieved, the company should measure its performance relative to targeted competitors such as customer and market share. Measures such as these track historical performance. To know what the customer will do next, the company should assess the firm's performance in the customer's mind relative to the targeted competitor. This means each decision maker and influencer of the purchase decision-making unit should provide feedback independently to the company, rating and ranking its performance and that of the target. Track satisfaction and favorability, a measure of intent for the next purchase. See what your share will be in the future by examining the percentage of the customer's planned expenditures that your company stands to obtain compared to the competitor's.

Customer Care Differentiation

The relationship marketer sees customer purchase, use and repurchase as a cycle that never ends, but customers may not buy again if their experience has not been satisfactory. Think about customers not as purchasers, but as people or organizations with a reservoir of funds to be expended over their purchasing lifetime. They make purchases and enter into a period of inactivity before they buy again. The role of customer care differentiation is to ensure that in this period of inactivity, the customer continues to receive the information, guidance, support and advice they need (sometimes even before they realize they need it) to help ensure that they return again and again. The challenge here is to differentiate customer care from that offered by the targeted competitor to engage, interact with and satisfy customers. The relationship marketer could consider, for example, what processes and technologies are to be deployed for real-time information provision, training, feedback and restitution and any other relevant services required to increase the value of the product or service in use. How is the customer's Web contact to be integrated with the call center and direct mail? How can the ownership experience be made so wonderful that the customer wants to buy again? Many of us have had the reverse experience, dealing with customer service personnel who do not have the information they need, the listening skills or the power to sort out the problem. Generally, companies have invested in new technology for their customer contact centers and have trained their people to say the right words and type in what the caller says, but it is still hard to get issues resolved. Sometimes the call center person does not have the information. Sometimes they do not have the power to make decisions. And sometimes, they do their jobs in a rote manner and do not seem to care. Opportunities for differentiation abound.

Chain of Relationships Differentiation

Each company has a chain of relationships that starts with customers and extends backward through distribution channel intermediaries and partners; customer-facing employees; staff in support of those in the front line; and suppliers of goods, services and capital to the enterprise. The fully differentiated company will have a chain of relationships that is competitively superior. This requires that the company understand the key components of the chain of relationships and evaluates the differentiation of the firm compared with the targeted competitor. How can the chain be made stronger than that of the competitor? Can some of the competitor's employees be hired away? Can some among their suppliers be encouraged to enter into a *keiretsu* relationship with your company, using the Japanese term for a family-like structure of member firms that may exclude the competitor? What may be outsourced to others, and how might that change not only financial returns but ability to respond rapidly to customer requirements and strategic shifts in the market? What are the team-based processes for the development and management of the formal linkages in the company and with external stakeholders that enable the company to create the value end customers want, which is especially important in business-to-business marketplaces?

Clearly, differentiation of the relationship has a lot to do with differentiation of the company overall, embracing as it does many of the components that underlie differentiation more generally. As has been noted, there are many dimensions to the development of a competitively differentiated company, and the interrelationships among the various elements can be complex. The company should have a plan not only to target competitors and their customers, but also to manage the customer relationships of competitors in a manner that is competitively superior, which varies according to the context within which the company finds itself. This is discussed next.

Competing for Customers

As mentioned earlier in the chapter, strategies for competing for customers vary according to such things as the nature of customer relationships and the stage of development of competitive rivalry. For example, a comparison between the issues faced by companies in the mobile communications industry with those that produce bread shows differences in respect of barriers to entry, risks and rewards, industry evolution and opportunities to change the rules, to name a few. The response of companies to issues such as these has determined present levels of differentiation and the extent to which visions are differentiated and successfully implemented will decide the extent to which they are even more different in the future. The two main ways to develop differentiation come down to the management of the customer relationship and competitive rivalry.

Customer Relationships

The strength of customer relationships affects the share of customer that a company obtains; the reverse is true, too. The higher this share of customer, the stronger is the relationship or the potential to forge a relationship of enduring value. While share of customer may also be high for short-term reasons such as price reductions, companies that sustain a high share of customer over an extended period of time as a result of low prices are bonding with their customers by giving them the value they want. A relationship never was intended to avoid price competition but rather to be relevant to customers over their purchasing lifetimes.

Competitive Rivalry

The intensity of competitive rivalry for these core customers can be reviewed in many ways, including a consideration of factors such as:

- price reductions
- inability to increase prices commensurate with cost increases
- product and service proliferation and innovation
- company profitability
- industry capacity
- demand maturity
- the height of exit barriers

Importantly, from the perspective of customer share management, the most measurable evidence of competitive activity is that of a share shift and churn[8] within the base of a company's core customers. Of course, competition can be intense even without share shift or churn in an account or consumer. Companies may be able to protect their positions with an individual core customer whether by pricing or other action such as long-term contracts. But doing so can affect profits, which is magnified when multiplied across all core customers. More than this, when the cost of growing customer share reduces lifetime customer value, competition can be said to be intense indeed. And when customer share does actually change rapidly across an entire base of core customers, a company is in the battle of its life. Without core customers, there is no future.

Next we review the four strategic arenas within which companies compete, as suggested by Figure 6-6. They are: Compete on Scale and Innovation, Shift Customer Share, Compete on Scope, and Compete to Collaborate. In all of these situations, companies can collaborate with specific competitors that can complement their abilities or needs. We have called competitors of this type complementors and we discuss this in Chapter 8.

[8] Churn means customer turnover. Customers change suppliers repeatedly, sometimes returning to the company from which they recently switched. For example, this is a common challenge to companies in the mobile telecommunications industry in which customers are lured away by competitors' lower prices and may return for the same reason.

Figure 6-6: Competing for the Individual Customer

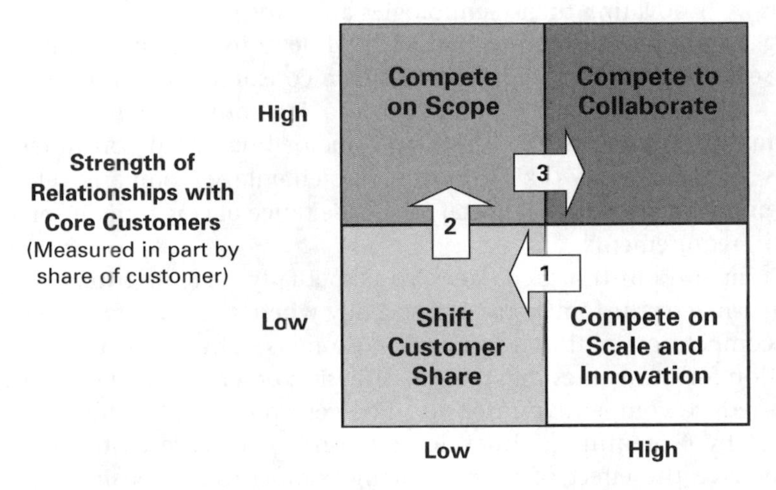

Compete on Scale and Innovation

In this arena, the relationships all companies have with your firm's core customers are not very strong—customer share is low here, yet competitive rivalry is intense for the available business. Here, companies usually produce products that are low involvement purchases such as consumables bought by businesses, institutions and consumers. Examples include companies that supply business forms and disposable cleaning products. Many companies today find themselves in this situation and wonder how to get out of it and into a more profitable, sustainable environment.

The central objective here is to reduce competitive intensity and rivalry. This might be accomplished by a wide variety of means from acquiring competitors focused on the same core customers to targeting competitors for their overall market share, and thereby also growing customer share within core accounts. In general, companies should seek to outperform competitors in terms of the factors core customers consider most important.

Increasing bonds with core customers can limit their interest and ability in switching to other suppliers, which has the effect of reducing competitive intensity for these specific customers, at least. For example, business-to-business companies can deepen customer bonds by innovating their technologies and processes such as facilitating on-line electronic procurement, while consumer companies may seek to build brand equity and create consumer bonds in new ways such as by using the Internet to provide consumers with the information they want. To illustrate, a major household consumer goods company is working with complementary companies to implement an information portal for a wide range of consumer information requirements.

Companies in this arena are also perpetually searching for new product-market-customer spaces to occupy where they will face limited competition within their core customers. Thus, the general direction for companies that face the situation described here should be to reduce competitive intensity. The very process of doing this such as by cementing and developing bonds with core customers, might have the effect of both reducing competitive intensity and increasing share of customer, which takes the company a long way from the problems it faces in this arena.

Companies typically need to reduce the fragmentation of their industry and competitive intensity if they are to develop their profitability still further. Otherwise firms will experience considerable competitive challenge when focusing on share of customer, with many companies wanting to develop similar relationships with the same customers. Companies should consider first building their scale relative to competitors in core customers, which can reduce the fragmented nature of competition and create more order, role definition and capacity management. As mentioned, this could have the effect of increasing share of customer but for reasons that have more to do with the management of supply than the management of the customer relationship.

Shift Customer Share

In this arena, core customers are not closely bonded to the companies that supply them, but the rivalry among existing participants is low. Here, no one company has a commanding share of customer for the relationships that are core to your company's business. This situation can occur early in an industry's evolution, particularly for low-involvement purchase decisions (such as for consumer nondurables) for which there are one or few suppliers and no company or brand preference has yet been established. This would have been the case for birdseed and dog food early in the industry's development and for many products made today by companies such as Rubbermaid and 3M.

The strategic challenge here is to grow share of customer by shifting customer share from competitors to your company. There are many ways to do this, and most deal with the concepts of relationship marketing, identifying how to be relevant to each customer and then providing, in a competitively superior manner, for their individual needs whether in communications, product, service, purchase experience or total solution. To succeed over time, a company needs to ensure that it is well positioned in respect of *future* customer spending. If the company has a greater share of future prospects than its share of present expenditures, its share of customer will grow. As we have said before, companies compete for the future because that is where the money is.

Compete on Scope

Companies in this arena have strong relationships as evidenced by high shares of core customers' expenditures but face relatively low levels of competitive rivalry. This is potentially a very profitable situation in which to be. There are two challenges here:

1. Defending against competitive encroachment, which can happen when the opportunity becomes large enough to be of interest to new entrants.
2. Succeeding against new competitors in other areas of the account or in the mind of the consumer.

In an arena such as this, Delrina dominated consumer preference for computer-based fax software with their Winfax product. When market demand grew large indeed, Microsoft noticed the opportunity and was about to increase the competitive intensity dramatically with their solution. Essentially a single-product company, Delrina elected to sell out to Symantec, giving the latter an ability to compete with a broader scope of product and helped Delrina avoid direct competition with Microsoft.

The challenge here is to broaden a company's base of products and services, which is what competing on scope is all about, and doing this while further solidifying its customer relationships to defend against any company wishing to penetrate the account and shift share of customer in their favor. Companies that succeed in competing on scope will become more relevant to their core customers and possibly even more dependent on them. Having developed a tight bond, though, they are now well positioned to win in the next arena in which competitors' customers and customer relationships are targeted for transfer.

Compete to Collaborate

Companies in this arena have strong customer relationships measured by high customer share and offer a broad scope of products and services. By the time companies are in this situation, they have already aligned with their core customers. By helping customers to succeed with their customers, a company can defend its high share of customer and their future relevance. The challenge is to compete with other companies to collaborate with customers so that new value can be created. After this has been done successfully, the winner can identify, penetrate and develop targeted competitors' customers that have some similarity to its most important ones. Many companies want to deal with challenges such as these rather than those mentioned for the other arenas. This ideal situation has been rarely attained. Therein lies the opportunity, precisely because it is hard to do and few have thought all the issues through enough to plan to achieve this preferred state.

CRM is very applicable in this arena. Here, the concepts of CRM will have been fully implemented, aligning the companies, customers, employees, suppliers and allies in a virtual chain of relationships. The focus now is on new and mutual value creation. Once companies plan with their customers and are sufficiently integrated that it is hard to tell where the customer ends and the company starts, the firm is well placed to go to the next stage and target competitors' customers.

Alignment of companies into a chain of relationships alters the competitive battlefield. Now it is not just competition between like companies. It is also between chains of relationships, with the better forged and aligned chains that comprise the strongest participants best able to succeed in capturing additional business from new customers.

Strategies for Winning

The approaches for winning depend on the competitive circumstances a company faces, as has just been discussed. What is evident here is that companies should diagnose the arena they are in and then use appropriate strategies for that situation. Doing otherwise could result in the failure of strategy to guide the business and continued dependence on tactics and technology over strategic focus, a situation faced by many companies today.

Companies should move progressively through strategies that take them through the different arenas—from competing on scale and innovation to shifting customer share to competing on scope and then to competing to collaborate. A company cannot readily move from the first-mentioned arena to the last without facing tremendous challenges in so many dimensions that the program definition and implementation would be fragmented, chaotic and ultimately unworkable. For those companies for which focus is hard to achieve, the root of the issue may stem from simultaneously pursuing initiatives not necessarily required (although possibly desirable) according to their specific situations. For example, companies not obtaining the full potential of their customer-focused investments might assess whether they might invest to secure competitive superiority to diminish competitive intensity.

You might read this and see your own company in more than one arena. This is quite possible since we are discussing individual core customers and the competitive intensity for the expenditures of those customers. Some core customers may face more competition for their business and others, less. More likely, though, if you see yourself in several places, you may be considering *marketplaces* for different products and services rather than *core customers* and their expenditures with your company.

Strategies for Competing on Scale and Innovation

There are several considerations to help a company improve its competitive position in this particular arena in which firms compete to become bigger with individual customers and to innovate with them. These include the following:

- Customer Considerations
- Managing Competitors
- Managing Customers that Compete with You
- Managing Regulators
- Lessening Competitive Intensity

Customer Considerations

In this situation, customers have considerable choice among products, services and vendors and are quite willing to exercise that choice by switching. Different companies and their products are seen by core customers to be substitutes for one another. Customers' preferences are transitory and mobile. Customers flit from one supplier to another, often more the result of modest provocation by their lead supplier than the result of a compelling value proposition from a competitor. This is an all-too-familiar situation for most companies, whereby many competitive strategies have been employed, yet relative competitive positions remain more or less similar, sometimes after considerable sums have been expended and time invested. In industries from software to computers and from cars to clothes, business-to-consumer and business-to-business firms find themselves in a similar challenge.

Companies have determined how best to make a high volume of consistently great products and provide excellent service. The problem is, so have their competitors. With too much capacity in the context of the available demand, companies compete ferociously using all the tools they can muster to defeat the enemy. Unfortunately, the enemy is rarely defeated using the traditional weapons because most competing managers learned the same options in business school. Now they compete from the same menu as though marching in lockstep. And all are governed by the same accountants and financial controllers asking what the initiative's near-term return will be. Attempts by any one competitor to increase share of customer can be very expensive as moves tend to be closely watched and matched by the enemy.

One area of opportunity to develop advantage in intensely competitive marketplaces is to build relationships with stakeholders other than customers such as with suppliers and channel intermediaries. Although noncustomer stakeholders may treat many competitors in a similar manner, this is not always the case, and some opportunities remain for developing competitive advantage. For example, companies in the household chemical industry are permitted to perform tasks for retailers that can include activities previously done by the intermediary, such as:

- handling consumer complaints on behalf of the retailers
- providing artwork for cooperative advertising and signage
- providing in-store informational literature
- training the retailer's sales personnel
- stocking shelves and managing the retailer's inventory
- "Ordering from themselves"—initiating the ordering process according to inventory levels and other parameters that have been agreed upon

Managing Competitors

Companies in these situations have not always established a systematic and multistakeholder approach to the formation of alliances and partnerships. While channel and supplier relationships will have been explored, these do not usually provide competitive superiority. In addition, few companies have examined the potential to create alliances with other organizations such as complementary competitors. In short, opportunities remain to align with a number of companies, including some competitors, for mutual advantage.

That is not to suggest predatory tactics or illegal collaboration such as in price fixing. Not only is this illegal, it is entirely inappropriate and unnecessary. What is being advocated for possible consideration is the potential to disaggregate the value chain and consider how different categories of participants and adversaries can realign to achieve their mutual ends. For example, in industries that are overcapacity, is there an opportunity for previously unaligned companies to spin off their manufacturing assets into a single company that will produce for each of the parent companies according to a predetermined pricing and other arrangements? This would turn the parent companies into marketing organizations.

Managing Customers that Compete with You

In cases in which customers are also sometimes competitors, companies have special challenges. What information should be disclosed to these customers? How can you ensure that they will not use what you tell them in competitive situations? Some suggestions for consideration are as follows:

- *Bond*—Rather than competing with customers or even thinking of customers as competitors, try bonding with them. Try to outsource their competitive activities and produce for them. Make them allies. Understand the value they are trying to create, and work with them to do it.
- *Customer Advisory Panel*—Make some of your customers into advisors. Meet once a quarter to review the key issues in your business when customer input is needed, and benefit from their direction. Having asked for their advice, use it or provide feedback as to why it was not used. Have a governance mechanism, and rotate customers on and off the panel to bring in new ideas continually.

- *Integrate planning*—By understanding what you are each trying to achieve, customers and competitors can manage their plans to minimize areas of overlap, which could lead, for example, to providing unique products through specific channels so that competition with the customer is either lessened or better defined.
- *Blur lines that separate*—You can keep your company at arm's length from customers, but that will not change much about how customers compete with you. It may be better to blur the lines that separate yourself from them. When your customers become more dependent on your company, they are more likely to collaborate than compete.
- *Share information*—Trust in your customers when they show early signs of warming to you. By sharing information, you have an opportunity to create understanding, leading to possible attitude and behavioral changes.
- *Give them a stake in your success*—Consider whether your most important customer should be given shares in your company or whether there are other approaches to help them want your company to succeed such as by promising them first rights to commercialize specific new technologies, etc.
- *Help them win their customers*—By helping your customer win with their customers, you may be able to convert an erstwhile competitor that transacts with your company into a closely bonded customer that wants a deeper relationship.

Managing Regulators

In this arena, companies try to obtain an advantageous position with those who set the rules for the industry such as regulators and others in positions of authority. It is precisely because so many firms try for these close relationships that few companies are allowed to develop this closeness, at least in most democratic countries. While some companies may be better managers of regulators and other rule makers (such as for the environment or health and safety) few succeed in establishing permanent long-term relationships, but it is significant that a few do succeed. Some companies—they shall remain nameless here—provide employment to bureaucrats and politicians wishing to leave public office. Most rule makers must know that an unfavorable ruling, a heavy-handed tactic or a license or favor denied could affect their future outside government, particularly when their actions are highly visible or traceable.

There are more strategic approaches for managing regulators. Have a vision for the industry that requires rule changes and which is best led by your company rather than an industry body such as an association. Then, by working with complementary competitors, a company can work closely with regulators without being seen to curry favor while gaining some advantage.

Actions that result in anticompetitive practices and that are geared to achieve marketplace monopolization often warrant examination by regulatory authorities whose job it is to preserve competitive markets. Having said this, there are at least three areas in which monopolization might be permissible:

1. *The mind of the customer*—Monopolization, if it is fairly achieved here, is probably quite acceptable to most regulators. If a customer wants a product or service and will not accept substitutes, who is going to say that purchases must be made from competitors in the interest of the individual?
2. *Structural bonding*—When companies align with customers so completely such as by integrating their technology, people and processes, it becomes difficult or impossible for rule makers to require that suppliers and customers uncouple. It is when companies use technology solutions to chain unsuspecting customers to them that the complaints can be loud and the backlash severe.
3. *Ownership ties*—When customers are owned in part by their suppliers or the reverse, transactions are no longer at arm's length, and customers may not be required to buy from competitors unless their core vendor fails to meet specific performance, pricing or other requirements.

Rule makers seem to pay particular attention to consumer marketplaces, perhaps because consumers are voters. Other situations that result in increased scrutiny include their perceptions of monopolization by successful companies, as evidenced by the notice regulators have taken at various times of companies such as AT&T, IBM and Microsoft. Smaller firms operating in fast-moving and accelerating environments may not be subject to similar levels of scrutiny, although they may also have secured monopolization of their particular product-market. Moreover, companies that have not invested heavily to develop favorable brand equity and which lack significant political presence may find that the rule makers operate to their disadvantage.

As mentioned at the outset and repeatedly, absolutely any action considered as a result of the observations noted here and elsewhere in this book merit examination by your company's lawyers before you even think of implementation.

Lessening Competitive Intensity

The overall strategic objective in this arena is to reduce competitive intensity. The main strategic opportunities include doing the following:

- Target specific competitors to lessen competition.
- Define or redefine "customers." Then create and nurture superior relationships with selected customers to outperform competitors in terms of factors affecting customers' forthcoming purchase decisions. Increasing bonds with core customers can limit their interest and ability to switch suppliers, which has the effect of reducing competitive intensity.
- Identify and commercialize new products, services or solutions for core customers, whereby competitive intensity will be limited.
- Manage various stakeholders for competitive advantage and to reduce competitive intensity.

What is suggested here is not simply a focus on CRM, although this may be desirable in some cases. Rather, the company wanting to succeed with CRM and realize a greater return on many of its investments should first consider developing an environment such as CRM that will support its customer positioning and investments.

Below we suggest selected examples of approaches to lessen competitive intensity. These are:

- Consolidate Industry Supply or Distribution Channels
- Develop Allies Who Will Work Together for Mutual Benefit
- Establish a Competitively Favorable Environment for Procurement
- Make Customers Out of Competitors
- Target Specific Competitors

Consolidate Industry Supply or Distribution Channels

Traditionally, this has been accomplished by companies acquiring competitors, retiring their capacity and erecting barriers to entry to lessen future competition. Some companies pursue strategies to do many of these things simultaneously. For example, Republic Industries, founded by Wayne Huizenga, well-known for founding franchises in the video and pizza businesses, competes on scale in the automotive retailing industry by both acquisition and business model innovation. Republic owns and has built a wide variety of retailing formats and has acquired rental car companies Alamo and National. With a combined fleet of over 300,000 cars, car rental companies provide a significant source of used cars to be retailed. Republic also operates used vehicle megastores under the name AutoNation USA, used vehicle retail outlets operating as Valu Stop or CarStop and two vehicle reconditioning centers. Republic's automotive retailing business includes 40 franchised automotive dealerships across a broad spectrum of automobile brands. While the potential exists for Republic to consolidate car retailing, it is not yet clear that this can be done without the investment of more funds than may be available to even well-capitalized ventures—and the willingness to be patient for a return on capital.

Develop Allies Who Will Work Together for Mutual Benefit

This strategy is followed by enterprise resource planning (ERP[9]) software companies such as SAP, Baan and PeopleSoft that collaborate with major accounting firms. Some of the accountants became more aligned with certain software companies partly because they did not want to learn too many systems, which would have the effect of reducing staff utilization, one of the measures accountants use to guide their profitability. Thus, the accountants developed vested interests in limiting competition to a handful of ERP vendors, which proved helpful to the pioneers and early incumbents, some of which rewarded the accounting firms with large implementation and so-called process reengineering[10] contracts.

Establish a Competitively Favorable Environment for Procurement

This would be the case of one or a group of complementary suppliers creating a cluster of customers that are favorably disposed to the suppliers, as can happen when e-marketplaces are established. For example, Commerce One's procurement portal, established with Covisint (with grants of warrants to a car company to help secure the opportunity), provides the automotive industry with an arena for exchanging goods and services and Commerce One with a potentially lucrative

[9] ERP software essentially runs a business, including financial management and control functions.

[10] Software implementation companies can promise that the reengineering will be done first, then applicable software selected in support of the reengineered business processes. More typically, processes are changed according to the requirements of the new ERP software.

contract, platform and experience—so much so that here, as in other industries, companies need to be sure that their initiatives will not invite government scrutiny for anticompetitive practice. The US Federal Trade Commission has reportedly shown some interest in examining Covisint, although not necessarily Commerce One's linkage to Covisint.[11]

Make Customers Out of Competitors

Some companies supply both original equipment manufacturers (OEMs) and customers in the marketplace. In addition to these categories of customers, firms may also supply competitors. In short, there may be opportunities for companies to consider customer profitability and strategic value. After taking into account all costs for sales, service and support, some companies may decide that competitors actually represent a better profit opportunity than selling to customers. Such an approach can make your company an ally of your former competitors while creating a new set of competitors.

Target Specific Competitors

Just as mass marketing is no longer affordable or achievable for many companies, so is mass competition an expensive and possibly unworkable proposition. Competitive intensity can be reduced by focusing on specific competitors for reasons previously presented such as to learn from them, to beat them or to collaborate with them. Obviously, this book deals with these issues in depth.

Strategies for Shifting Customer Share

There are a number of considerations to help a company improve its competitive position in this particular arena, whereby firms seek to build customer relationships at the expense of competitors. These include:

- Customer Considerations
- Managing Regulators
- Increasing Share of Core Customers
- Implications for Competitor Targeting

[11] "Battle to the Bitter End (-to-End)", *Business 2.0*, July 25, 2000, p. 144

Customer Considerations

In this arena, customers and suppliers do not have close relationships, yet competition for the available business is not particularly intense. When customers do switch suppliers, it is more the result of customer desire to change than the nature of the competitive rivalry that prompts the decision. The relationship between company and customer may be weak because the company's actions are not what the customer wants rather than the result of competitive choice. This occurs when the company's view of progress is not shared by the customer such as when a new model of a car does not have the desired styling. This can also happen when companies consolidate supply to a marketplace in an effort to build market share. Customers often resent their reduced options, as happened in Canada with the consolidation of the two major airlines.

In this arena, the following situations can occur:

- low involvement purchase decisions, whereby company or brand preference has not been established
- niche products and services, whereby the opportunity is not considered to merit investment by companies looking for larger opportunities (not many of these niches remain because companies in many industries are starting to compete on scope)
- products or industries in their early stages of evolution, whereby the relationship between customers and suppliers is weak because it has yet to be formed
- companies reaching a tacit understanding[12] with one another about their roles—such as which companies are the leaders or whether the pursuit of breakthrough competitive strategies is to be encouraged (some might wonder if a tacit understanding exists among companies in the oil industry to limit participation in other energy forms or the development of new forms of motive power)
- vendors cooperating selectively on major areas of new development such as formulation of product or service standards or investments in research and development
- situations where competitive positioning is very clear indeed, with limited overlap between competitors in the mind of a certain type of customer, which aids the purchase decision-making process and can result in stable shares of core customers

[12] Implicit understanding is more typical than explicit, for obvious reasons.

- low competitive intensity deriving from high barriers to entry, whereby companies that have secured strong patent protection for their innovations—as in the pharmaceutical industry or those companies that have made enormous investments in plant and equipment such as for aluminum smelting—can find themselves participating in industries in which the competitive intensity is low

With behaviors such as those mentioned, price competition would be rare or infrequent.

Relationships with Regulators

While relationships with customers may not be particularly close in this arena, those with regulators can be tight indeed. In fact, relationships with regulators and rule makers can be particularly important when industries are in the process of being deregulated or reregulated. Companies with an early indication as to the nature and direction of change have an ability to influence it in their interest. Large companies are often built by individuals with close relationships with regulators, as has happened in the telecommunications, financial services, oil and transportation industries, for example.

Relationships with other rule makers—such as individuals with roles in environmental agencies, health protection and safety—can also help companies operationally and strategically such as to understand pending changes.

Increasing Share of Core Customers

An important strategic challenge for companies in this arena is increasing share of core customer, principally by relationship development. Because relationships with core customers are not close, companies have many opportunities to build customer relevance and deepen the ties that bind.

Customer bonds were described earlier in this chapter and in Figure 6-1. A company should pay close attention to the bonds that core customers consider relevant and structure those in a way that these customers will appreciate. For example, Ford has worked to develop distinct identities and brand equities for its vehicles such as the Jaguar S-Class, Lincoln LS and Ford Thunderbird. Ford makes these cars using some of the same components, if substantially different shapes, for the external sheet metal. Consumers seem willing to pay a significant price premium for the Jaguar and Thunderbird, partly the result of emotional equity in these brands and other benefits such as perceptions of styles, uniqueness and peer group acceptance. On the other hand, Ford's uneven performance in respect of the management of customer relationships has so far placed some limits on equity that goes beyond strong brands, great products and excellent service. Amidst fanfare, Ford launched a loyalty program whereby users of a credit card secured points towards a new Ford product. The program was potentially lucrative, and many customers signed up, appreciating the investment Ford was making in the relationship and looking forward to a lifetime of association. Then Ford, together with the bank that issued the credit card, ended the program.

Some companies in this arena might not wish to focus on building customer relationships, preferring instead to replicate their successful product or service business model. This could prove to be a major error. If the intent of the company is to succeed by paying exclusive attention to product or service strategies, it will need to be in a position to defend against one or more competitors that could choose to develop relationships with the company's own core customers. Companies may find themselves ill-prepared to compete with adversaries that forge stronger relationships, no matter how good the product or service is, especially if customers see the differentiation to be modest. Nevertheless, when companies do decide to compete primarily or exclusively on product or service innovation, they will need to be able to commercialize new ideas that core customers consider relevant, continually and profitably.

A derivative challenge is a requirement that companies have a process for innovation. When the process has been institutionalized, new concepts are generated continually, flowing through a series of gates through which decisions are made to continue or end the specific initiative. This helps ensure that new concepts meet mandate/vision, financial, operational and marketing feasibility requirements while appealing to core customers. The company competing on innovation will need people who can conceive and research new and appealing concepts and it may need to have some tolerance for these people, as they are often stronger creatively than in terms of management. Usually creative people fit this profile, and the company will need to value the differences of these employees without requiring conformance to the usual culture and norms.

Of course, companies can maintain both a product/service strategy and a customer relationship focus simultaneously. This would appear to be the best way to ensure that competitive intensity remains modest, while the benefits of increased customer bonding are realized, as well. Some of these benefits are described in Figure 6-7.

Figure 6-7: Selected Benefits of Customer Bonding

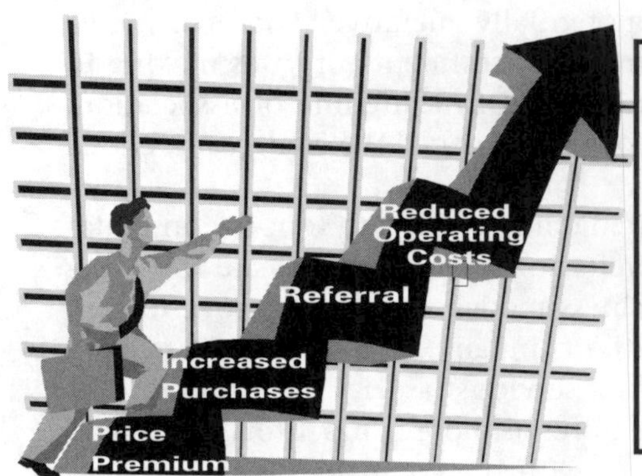

- Reduced head count
- New product concept development
- Beta test environment
- Forgiving climate for innovation
- Faster new product development
- Reduced contact to cash cycle
- Comarketing
- Share of customer
- Increased share of future spending
- Development of strategic capabilities that can be levered with other customer

Implications for Competitor Targeting

In this arena, selected competitors need to be monitored to ensure that there is little or no surprise departure from the status quo, such as:

- development of a new vision for their business which is substantially different from your company's and which would be very detrimental if achieved
- development of breakthrough product or service initiatives
- communications or behavior inconsistent with their historical role in the industry
- formulation or deployment of customer relationship initiatives
- independent deployment of Web-based or e-commerce initiatives, which would change the economics of the customer and your position in the industry

Companies can monitor several competitors to see if there is to be a major strategic departure, although they may choose to analyze but a few—those that represent the greatest threat or opportunity. In addition to monitoring for signs of a strategic change, companies can target specific competitors to determine how they can improve their value chain and financial performance. That is, companies can watch others, either direct competitors or firms that might be considered to be excellent in specific dimensions that are important to the customer—to learn and improve. The techniques of competitive intelligence are described in Chapter 5.

Strategies for Competing on Scope

For this arena, we discuss how companies can improve their competitive situation by bonding with customers and competing on scope by providing customers with the products and services they want from your company. These include:

- Customer Considerations
- Managing Relationships with Others
- Managing Regulators
- Implications for Competitor Targeting

Customer Considerations

Companies in this situation enjoy close customer relationships and limited competitive intensity. Their share of core customers is now high, and there is potential to lever these relationships in new ways, profitably. Customers are tightly bonded with their suppliers, so much so that in many cases, it is hard to tell where the customer ends and where the supplier begins. As suggested by Figure 6-8, blurring of the boundaries between company and customer could also be accomplished with others in the chain of relationships, including the customer's customers and the supplier's suppliers.

Figure 6-8: Blurring the Boundaries

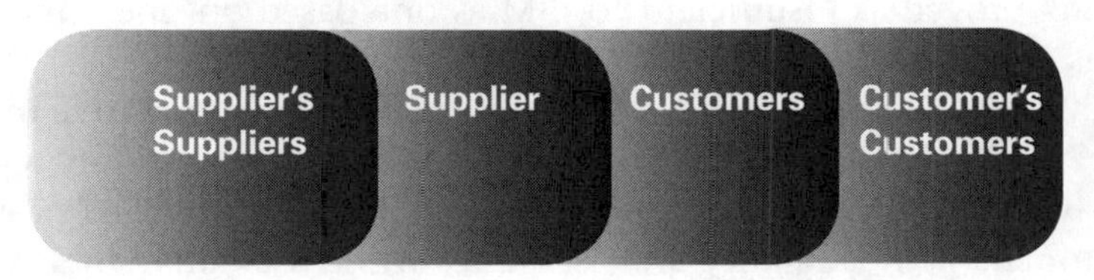

While there are not many examples of mature companies that have accomplished a blurring of boundaries with customers, there are some. Fastforms, a business forms and digital imaging company in Atlanta, Georgia and Guelph, Ontario is six times larger than it was before it began to compete on scope. Fastforms provides products, services and solutions to companies that go far beyond what a supplier normally does. It maintains its customers' warehouses, places orders to itself, manages logistics for the movement of small items on the customer's behalf, operates a call center for the customer and so on. It has essentially integrated with its customers where product competition is intense, resulting in Fastforms having limited competition for solutions customers consider valuable.

Some companies, having worked hard to provide a broad range of customer-centric solutions, have let much of the opportunity slip away. IBM has competed on scope since the 1960s. Then, as now, it would provide corporate customers with a complete solution and work with them, hand in glove, to provide customer-specific value in the implementation. Custom programming? No problem—just part of the service. Need more brains or hands? They were there. But, at a time when IBM derived its income from product sales or leasing, it focused more on shipment of "iron" (as they called computer sales) than on helping customers make money from the iron. More than this, IBM demonstrated a remarkable lack of vision for the industry they led and dominated.

First they opened the gates to the midsize computer marketplace, not fully appreciating the impact of Moore's Law of simultaneous increase in performance and declining price of semi-conductors. Through the entrance came companies like Digital Equipment (DEC). Then IBM watched while Apple continued to benefit from improving price performance and started to replicate the success of DEC for personal computers. Finally, IBM could stand it no more. It determinedly developed a personal computer that would maintain its preeminence in this product category. And in so doing, it opened the gates to, well, Gates. In effect, IBM created the enabling environment within which Microsoft could succeed. A vision based on "iron" proved as insufficient to IBM as one based on operating systems and software will be for Microsoft.

Other companies benefit from lower levels of competitive intensity and high share of customer by innovating, sometimes repetitively. For example, GM's OnStar satellite communications provide customers with assurance and assistance while they drive their vehicles. In at least one instance, a befuddled thief, who thought he had eluded police after racing off a dealer's lot in a new Cadillac Seville STS, was stopped by police after the men in blue were guided there by the OnStar operator who tracked the vehicle. If you were choosing between a Cadillac and competing brands, you might now pay more attention to the GM product.

Ten Square is pursuing similar innovation in the gas pump industry. It is also out in front, with solid relationships and exclusive contracts with gas companies such as BP Amoco, Chevron and Texaco and the manufacturers of the pumps, giving them sole or preferential access to the data on the pumps. With that, Ten Square has a considerable opportunity to build an information-based customer loyalty and value-creation business.

While Fastforms limits competition through process innovation and GM uses communications technology to create new customer value (and potentially a major new profit center) with OnStar, there are other ways companies can participate in this industry arena such as through brand equity development. Examples include Harley-Davidson, the icon American motorcycle, which once faced competition so severe it almost did not survive. Almost, but Harley's customers and dealers made sure this would not happen. The relationship of customers around the world, but especially in America, to the motorcycle is "directly akin to the way the cowboy of yesterday's West related to his horse...rugged independent souls moving to their own beat...Harley-Davidson seems to embody that spirit more than other machines."[13]

Harley avoided bankruptcy by bonding with its customers at all the levels that count, as follows:

- Functionally, it offered transportation, but so did competitors' bikes. Harley offered additional levels of bonding.
- Socially, it was an opportunity to belong to a peer group and be respected by it (and not just leather-jacketed biker gangs, but also leather-jacketed executives riding in formation), while simultaneously standing out from the group such as by having a new chromed or customized bike and being respected by the peer group for being able to fix the bike.
- Personally, individuals benefited from the unique feeling that comes from riding and, in the mind's eye, the potential to roam, unshackled and free.

Considering this, did Harley really have any competition? Even today, other companies have little resonance with Harley's core customers.

[13] Peter C. Reid, *Well Made in America: Lessons from Harley-Davidson on Being the Best.* New York: McGraw Hill, 1990.

Managing Relationships with Others

Companies in this arena have aligned with customers and have developed close relationships with other participants in the industry. To continue with the Harley-Davidson example, the firm views relationships with suppliers as central to its ability to deliver customer value. It sees the suppliers as members of the Harley family.[14] Companies with a family orientation to their business, whether or not they are actually family owned, are more likely to have stronger stakeholder relationships than others.[15] In respect to bonding with suppliers, Harley had to have close relationships if it was to drive inventory out of the production cycle because just-in-time production methods require close working relationships. More than this, Harley focused on building mutual profitability with its suppliers, which is the essence of a business relationship by, for example, entering into long-term contracts, smoothing production schedules and buying from a single supplier rather than spreading the business around.[16] A business-to-business company must experience some discomfort if an important customer fails. The reverse of this is equally true. If a supplier fails, a customer should also experience pain. No potential for pain means that no potential for a progressively deeper relationship and the resulting profits.

In addition to suppliers, companies have the potential and requirement to align with their distribution channel intermediaries. Some companies, seeing the opportunity afforded by the Internet to disintermediate their businesses and go directly to customers, have also lost some of the value created by middlemen. This utility can include on-the-ground knowledge, cooperative advertising, reputation with customers, personal guidance, integration of equipment and services with existing infrastructure and, in some cases, financing. Middlemen are required to deliver some of these benefits, although specific customers might prefer the direct business model, where the extras have little value. Thus, while Dell has made an effective business model by selling personal computers directly to consumers and businesses, there is potential for HP to not only sell some products directly, but to work with channel partners to give customers some of the value they cannot get by dealing directly with the vendor. This would include things such as providing a total solution of computers, software, servers, networks, computers, software and services on a subscription basis and so on.

---

[14] *Ibid*, p. 68.

[15] This view has been advanced by Professor L. Berry of Texas A&M University.

[16] *Ibid*. p. 184.

Part of the challenge in genuinely partnering with intermediaries is for the supplier and the intermediary to accept one another's culture and business models. Thus, the vendor needs to understand that the dealer or distributor might be guided by short-term profit, as is often the case with the entrepreneurs who often own and manage these businesses. Organizational cultures in short-term businesses are often very tactical and operational, reflecting the orientation of the owner. He who controls the cash usually frames the culture. The vendor that tries to exert its perspectives of vision, strategy and the long-term on the typically shorter-term horizon of its dealers is likely to be headed into a situation of conflict. I have seen this firsthand repeatedly and have often had to moderate these conflicts to help companies extricate themselves from the quagmire. I have learned that vendors that place demands on "their" intermediaries such as a requirement to add staff to focus on their products alone or to feed customer data to the company, suddenly find that they have more of a conflict than a relationship.[17] One car company experienced this when they decided they would reward dealers according to rules the dealers had already rejected. Although dealers seldom defect to competitors, they might skew their efforts to the supplier that they consider more responsive, especially in retail stores in which more than one product line is sold.[18] In this case, the car company paid a high price in lost dealer satisfaction.

On the other hand, intermediaries need to appreciate the strategic and operational drivers of their suppliers, particularly their most important suppliers. While companies frequently develop assessments of the lifetime profitability of their customers, middlemen can also consider the lifetime value of their suppliers and determine the value they derive and could derive from their suppliers. How profitable is the relationship? How valuable is it to the development of bonds with the intermediaries' core customers? What are the conformance and compliance costs associated with having this relationship (what does the supplier expect of your company that you find challenging or inappropriate)? What might the implications or response be from other suppliers that are not selected?

Having considered issues such as these, companies can adopt similar approaches to those employed for customer relationship management, including triaging the valued suppliers from those that

[17] Some say that to appreciate the meaning of any term, the obverse needs to be considered. Consider the meaning of customer and supplier *conflict*. Then you have a basis to expand the definition of a relationship in your business.

[18] This is called dualing in the industry.

are less so. Then the intermediaries can decide which among their suppliers best represents a strategic and tactical fit for their go-to-market strategy, including providing an ability to position the company well with its customers. This, in turn, can lead to closer alignment of strategy, structure and operations and even make culture and business models more common, allowing the intermediary to form a profitable and strategic chain of relationships with aligned suppliers and customers.

Managing Regulators

Regulators of companies in this arena pay close attention to the relative absence of competition. A near-monopoly, typically measured by regulators more in terms of market share rather than customer share, invites scrutiny and potential intervention by regulators. Companies can limit this likelihood in a number of ways, including doing the following:

- Position their offering or solution to regulators as the result of industry-wide collaboration among aligned companies—which it rightfully is, rather than the unique solution of their company alone.
- Ensure that customers have high levels of satisfaction and intend to buy again from the company, even in the event that competitors offer substitute products or services. More than this, communicate the data to regulators, as part of a focus on managing the regulatory environment to retain customer share.
- Involve regulators early in any decisions to acquire companies.
- Help regulators regulate by suggesting areas in which they might make positive contributions to customers and consumers, as would be the case in reshaping boundary conditions in an industry such as financial services and telecommunications.
- Position the company as having an intermediate share of market in the context of a larger industry. In Canada, banking is highly concentrated among a few financial institutions that often note that they are competing within the North American and global marketplace rather than in Canada alone. Additionally, when companies have high shares of core customers but modest shares of market, they have an opportunity to emphasize the competitive elements within the industry.

Implications for Competitor Targeting

In this arena, companies face new competitors within the account or the mind of the consumer as they begin to compete on scope, looking for alternative ways to create value with customers. Companies sell what the customer wants to buy, not necessarily what they make. This, again, is what competing on scope is about, and it brings the company a new set of competitors, some of which may also be trying to compete on scope. For example, a company selling a metal press may decide to also provide an automated feed unit for steel rolls as well as machinery to accelerate the exit of stamped units from the press. Together with the press, the input and exit units comprise a larger system for the customer and achieves a productivity benefit. The press company may buy the additional machinery from specialized vendors, branding it under their own name. However, in so doing, it may face new challenges. Perhaps some specialized producers of in-feed units are beginning to compete on scope too, and by providing presses under its name, it has become a new competitor in the process. This situation is occurring in many arenas, particularly the result of digital convergence, whereby companies broaden their product and service lines, often working with nontraditional companies to do so. Alternatively, a company may face traditional or new competitors as it seeks out new customers with profiles similar to its core customers.

Strategies for Competing to Collaborate

In this arena, we discuss strategies for companies to develop new relationships such as with targeted competitors' customers. These include the following:

- Customer Considerations
- Managing Relationships with Others
- Managing Regulators
- Implications for Competitor Targeting

Customer Considerations

By the time a company faces the strategic challenges of this arena, it will have succeeded in first reducing competitive intensity, building relationships with core customers and expanding the scope of the business within them. Now companies will compete in two ways:

1. *for the customers of their new core competitors*—those companies that supply a similar range of products, services and solutions to that of their companies.
2. *with customers*—working with those firms with which they have aligned to help them secure and develop their own customers and business opportunities in much the same way as their companies have succeeded to date.

Competing in this arena depends on companies and customers aligning into chains of relationships. Although few companies have yet attained complete customer alignment, there are instances in which this is occurring. For example, it is quite common now for companies to consolidate their suppliers, reducing them to a few or even just one and then work with them more intensively.

Companies also demonstrate preference, both in buying and selling from or to other companies, which has the effect of creating a chain of priority relationships, with competitors receiving secondary attention. Thus, a chip manufacturer might give a major purchaser such as IBM early access to its plans and even collaborate with it in the development of new chips, helping computer vendors to be first to market with the latest technology. The biggest companies usually also receive the lowest prices (since they buy in high volumes) in addition to other financial incentives and soft benefits such as collaboration, service, support and other advantages.

Consumers demand choice, looking for companies to treat them well, in a trustworthy manner and create new value with them. Their preference ladder is not highly prioritized in this competitive arena. When they do make their choices, it is from among alternative chains of relationships, comprising companies and their allies, although the consumer may not consider the chain but rather the lead vendor. For example, car buyers might think they are purchasing a Pontiac, but behind the brand there are many companies that are often highly aligned. The chain can comprise the assembler (GM), subassemblers, parts and components suppliers, the dealership, ad agency and market and customer research houses, to name a few. GM and its relationship partners compete with the chains represented by front-end companies such as Ford and DaimlerChrysler. At present, some companies are members of the chain of relationships of several auto manufacturers.

The question here is whether consumers want or need to deal with more than one car company, airline or hairdresser, if each of them really understands and helps consumers as they wish to be helped. Consider for a moment the reasons you want choice, and therein are the clues for companies to attain your loyalty and displace the competitors' chains of relationships from your purchase decision. For example, if you were a purchasing agent, would you want a second supplier in case the main one cannot deliver rush orders or in the event of labor disruption? Now, what might the primary supplier do to reassure the purchasing agent such as guaranteeing supply?

Managing Relationships with Others

As noted, by now, companies will have aligned with customers and other industry participants in a chain of relationships, in which the lines between any two organizations will be quite blurred. Companies will have worked with allies to secure advantage over other competitors, and now all the members in the chain of relationships will have been linked—in some cases inextricably. In addition to traditional supply relationships, some of the allies with which relationships will have been created include vendors of complementary products and services. Mutual dependence and value creation was the initial objective of customer relationship management, and by now, it will have been achieved.

Here, most of the members of the chain of relationships will be treating one another as partners in a common cause, with free and open information sharing, innovation, planning, technology implementation and communications. Now the chain of relationships is ready to engage other chains in a battle in which the stakes are much higher because failure of a chain has the potential to damage many firms.

Managing Regulators

In this situation, companies and other members in the chain of relationships seek relationships with regulators and other rule makers to advance both their common interests. When one member of the chain falters, the entire chain can be at risk, as happened when Firestone tires on some Ford Explorer sport utility vehicles failed. Then the lead vendor is in a quandary. Do they assume responsibility for one of their suppliers or do they cut the vendor loose to avoid damage to the chain as a whole? In this case, what will happen to the trust other suppliers have committed to their relationship? In a relationship based on trust, companies within the chain need a mechanism for managing discord in times of crisis or when things go wrong, as happens from time to time. From media stories on the

Ford/Firestone crisis, it seems that these companies did not have a mechanism in place to arbitrate and resolve their relationship differences in private.

The lead vendors among competing chains need to help regulators and other rule makers understand and manage change such as may occur with new technologies and new entrants. In fully aligned chains of relationships, the responsibilities for managing the political, regulatory and other rule makers should be clearly established and aligned as well.

Implications for Competitor Targeting

The main objective for the companies in this situation is to penetrate and develop customer relationships, winning selected customers away from competitors and their chains. Here, a company's chain of relationships is at war with the chain of one or more core competitors' chains.

Here, the company and its allies target the customers of competitors (and their allies) and develop a plan to secure the customers. The company may also seek to derail the competitors' chains by targeting their most important accounts and winning them over at almost any cost.

There are other means to disrupt competitors' chains, ranging from securing preference from mutual suppliers to identifying and securing or damaging the key assets on which competitors' chains of relationships depend. Typically, the key assets are intangibles such as customer preference and the competitor's relationships with employees, regulators, politicians and various other stakeholders.

Six of the implications and potential opportunities for companies that have aligned into chains of relationships with customers and suppliers are as follows:

1. Establish a council for competitor analysis and targeting, comprising representatives of companies in the chain of relationships.
2. Pool data already available to companies in the chain of relationships, including customer and competitor data.
3. Provide extranet or Internet access to the data, analysis and reports to all members of the chain.
4. Share expenditures on research required to understand customer preference, competitor performance and competitive intelligence.
5. Establish priorities jointly such as identifying core competitors and competitors' chains of relationships.

6. Assess targeted competitors and their chains of relationships together; then develop a joint plan to win key customer relationships from core competitors and their chains of relationships and to otherwise influence key rule makers, special interest groups and other stakeholders in the interests of your chain of relationships.

When business focuses on individual customers alone, they miss the important strategic challenge of beating specific competitors to win these and other customers of the targeted competitor. This chapter has provided a framework within which to consider the dynamic environment within which companies, allies and other participants wage business war and selected strategies for companies to consider as they target competitors. We discussed differentiation and other approaches to help the company to win. The next chapter discusses how to make a loser out of a targeted competitor, which, in some cases, might be another way to win.

CHAPTER 7

Turning Competitors into Losers

"To enjoy the things we ought and to hate the things we ought has the greatest bearing on excellence of character."[1]

—Aristotle

Customer satisfaction is not enough to succeed if competitors satisfy your customers even better. Having a wide range of innovative products is also insufficient if competitors' product lineups are wider and seen by customers to be more relevant. Offering lower prices than competitors do could lead to disaster if just one of them has a lower cost structure than you, will accept lower margins or has deeper pockets and the appetite to engage in a price war until you surrender. In short, there are times when working harder to succeed may not be enough. To win, you may need to make a loser out of a competitor you have targeted. In this chapter, we cannot discuss every competitive tactic there is that might align with your values, strategies and strategic competencies. But we can discuss a few ideas and approaches some companies have employed to win, tactically and in real time.

In the previous chapter, we discussed differentiation in terms of eleven Cs. Here we discuss a twelfth C: Competitor Differentiation.

---

[1] Aristotle, Richard McKein and Richard P. McKeon, *Basic Works of Artistotle.* New York: Random House, 1941.

Competitor Differentiation

All customers are not equal, and neither are all competitors. The term competitors does not distinguish the relative importance of these challengers. They are not an amorphous group with equal effect on your business. Competitors that covet your most important customers and are able to win them over are potentially more damaging. Rivals plotting to deploy new technologies or solutions that could appeal to the customers that are your crown jewels are also more important than those that act slowly or always seem to do the right things wrong. (Competitors that do the wrong things right tend to not last long.) The competitors you want to defeat are the ones that seek to secure the same customers you have chosen as the core of your business.

The word customer no longer means much because it is a single term that includes many individuals. The behaviors of each customer are quite unique and cannot be simply predicted by understanding and influencing the attitudes of a group of customers by knowing the individual's segment, demographics or psychographics. Just as the word customer is insufficient to describe individuals, so, too, is the term competitor inadequate to describe the very different threats or opportunities each one poses.

The first step in competitor differentiation is to determine from which company you are setting your firm apart. We have discussed some aspects of selecting a company to target. We noted that this can be done once you know which customers you want relationships with and understand the extent to which these customers consider a given company to be a substitute for your company. Seen another way, specific companies have a customer set that includes many of the companies you would like to capture and retain. You want to increase your share of the customer's expenditures relative to this defined competitor. You are already undertaking a number of initiatives to satisfy customers and advance your position with the best among them. Now you would like to make a targeted competitor a loser so that you can win. Undertaking many of the dimensions of strategic differentiation already mentioned will help considerably here as will tactical and real-time differentiation and targeting. But aspects of the question remain: How is a company to "create a loser" so that it can win over the long term?

Strategies for Making Competitors Lose

A close relationship has been demonstrated between market share and profitability.[2] It seems axiomatic that an increasingly high share of customers with those the company values most would also result in higher levels of profitability. But building share of customer means displacing competitors from the accounts and customers you want. This in turn implies that winning is not just about customer satisfaction but can also involve creating a loser out of a competitor.

Competing one-on-one with specific competitors is sometimes very easy indeed because they need no help in losing! Examples in military history include the use of red uniforms by the British during the early part of the Boer War, which made them easy targets for enemy snipers. Additionally, the British conducted the war according to the gentlemen's rules that they had previously used, such as the time of day when fighting could occur and when breaks should be taken for tea. The British did prevail in the Boer War, of course, but not before they used khaki uniforms and changed their rules for engaging the enemy.

There are similar examples in business in which a company's market position, capabilities, leadership and culture may cause it to fail. Even its very success may result in failure at another time or in another circumstance. For example, one software company began expanding by acquiring competitors. It stopped all in-house software development, conserving funds to be used to acquire yet more competitors as it consolidated capacity to supply. This was a great business model for a while, but then word of the company's approach to business spread, including the way it negotiated and dealt with people once it took over a firm. Soon few companies wanted to sell to the acquirer. The cost of buying rose. Customers left in droves because the company would not support them adequately and had no new software in development. The acquirer's stock dropped once investors became aware of the company's shortcomings, which were what had made it successful in the first place and not easily subject to change. Now the acquirer has become an acquisition candidate, although there is so little equity left in the remaining software and customer relationships that it is hard to fathom what a buyer would want in the company. All its competitors needed to do was wait while the company imploded. They did not need to make this company into a loser; it did fine all by itself.

---

[2] Robert D. Buzzell and Bradley T. Gale, *The PIMS Principles: Linking Strategy to Performance*. New York: The Free Press, 1987.

Generally, companies do not have the opportunity to win by simply watching competitors self-destruct. They need to intervene. Here we discuss selected approaches to strategic intervention. In this chapter, we do not focus on what your company could do to simply be better, but rather what it might do to cause a targeted competitor to lose a strategic battle and even the war such as by exiting the industry. The following twenty military analogies may be employed to aid in competitor targeting and make them into losers:

1. Change the Battlefield
2. Weaken Their Chain of Relationships
3. Help Them to Retreat
4. Cooperate with Their Enemies
5. Engage in "Co-opetition"
6. Lead, Follow or Leave
7. Conduct Reconnaissance
8. Avoid a Frontal Assault
9. Concentrate on Points of Weakness
10. Seek Out Uncontested Territory
11. Weaken the Enemy through Harassment
12. Operate Below Radar Range
13. Mask the Intention and Create a Diversion
14. Control Your Territory
15. Deploy Overwhelming Technology
16. Progressively Encircle the Enemy
17. Attack Yourself
18. Don't Let the Enemy Become Entrenched
19. Have Strong Allies
20. Learn Their Secrets

Change the Battlefield

We have noted that the customer's mind is the main battlefield on which your company will ultimately win or lose as the customer chooses to relate and transact with your company rather than a specific competitor. What if the customer thinks your competitor is really quite good in the ways that are important to him or her? How then is your company to make the competitor lose? One way is to change the battlefield. There are a number of ways to do this. For starters, you can try to change the relative importance of purchase criteria to customers. It can be difficult to alter the way customers prioritize their reasons for selecting, but choosing the right battlefield will make this more successful. Focus on one of the customer's selection criteria where the competitor is weaker, ideally a criterion that ranks among the most important. Emphasize this one and prove your superiority here. Accept the competitor's strengths in other areas, but choose an area where you can play on its weaknesses. For example, "Company X makes reliable cars, to be sure, but our cars are much safer according to recent crash test results. We look after you and your family."

You can identify another class of purchasing decision maker and relate to it. Perhaps your competitor is entrenched in the purchasing department, but opportunities remain to defeat it in the minds of operations, finance, development, information technology or senior executives, including the president. In consumer markets, perhaps the competitor is entrenched in the minds of the heads of households, but other members of the family could act as influencers in the decision to buy. If the influencer is a child or teen, perhaps the battleground is the pursuit of "cool," which is a very different competitive arena than that of parents who tend to be influenced more by rational economic arguments.

Reposition the competitor by communicating your areas of superiority in relation to their areas of weakness. By repositioning the competitor in dimensions in which your company is stronger, you have the potential to win. Politicians often do this, for example by emphasizing their opponent's poor, incomplete voting record in comparison with their own. This is also what Pepsi did so effectively with its "Pepsi Challenge," which invited Coca Cola drinkers to compare tastes. They knew that Pepsi's taste, at that time, was somewhat preferred by teens, a claim that Coke apparently could not refute.

It has been axiomatic in many businesses that it is unwise to compete on price, but some companies such as Compaq, have demonstrated that price reductions, when accompanied by similar declines in costs, can be very advantageous. A new entrant can also use price as a very significant weapon because their modest initial volumes do not handicap their profitability to the same extent as for the incumbent that must often lower its own prices for a much higher level of sales to remain competitive.

Another opportunity to shift the battlefield is to change success measurements. Some companies measure success by, for example, return on investment, revenues and profitability, shareholder value or balanced scorecard metrics. As has been mentioned, shareholder value is determined largely by the return on investment of the company and its growth prospects. Some companies emphasize one area over the other, most typically growth in revenues and profitability over return on investment. The balanced scorecard is a framework that, as the name suggests, measures achievement in several areas to balance the organization's performance and vision attainment. Four areas are measured: financial, customer, internal business processes, and learning and growth.[3]

If a company, in your judgment, is using the wrong metrics to measure success, it will reach no higher than the quantitative objectives it has set for itself. This can actually represent an opportunity to beat a targeted competitor. For example, by analyzing your competitor using a method similar to that summarized in Table 5-5 and described in Figure 7-1, you may determine that there is an opportunity to earn a better return on investment by focusing on an area where the competitor does not such as on inventory turns rather than product margins. This was the opportunity that Cosco seized when it opened its warehouse clubs and how Wal-Mart has triumphed over many of its competitors.

Figure 7-1: Financial Analysis[4]

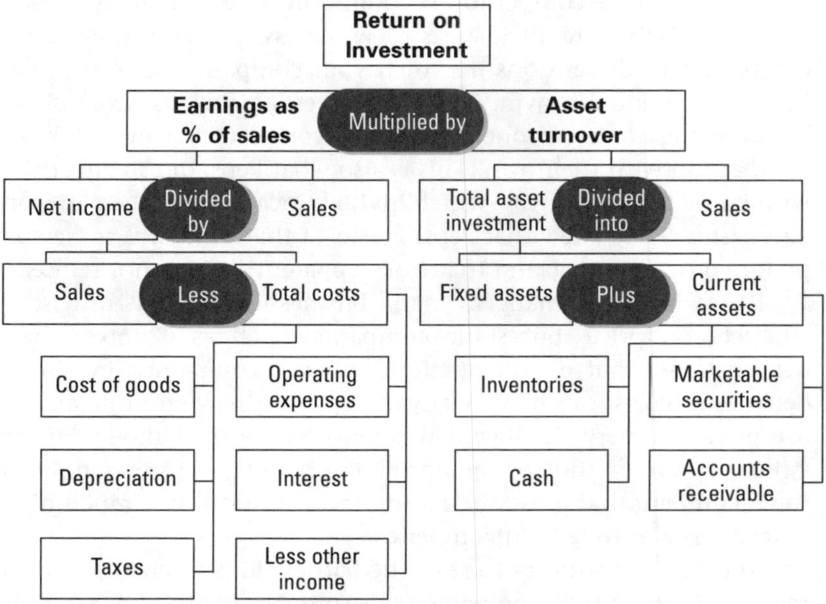

Return on Investment
Earnings as % of sales
Multiplied by
Asset turnover
Net income
Divided by
Sales
Total asset investment
Divided into
Sales
Sales
Less
Total costs
Fixed assets
Plus
Current assets
Cost of goods
Operating expenses
Inventories
Marketable securities
Depreciation
Interest
Cash
Accounts receivable
Taxes
Less other income

[3] Robert S. Kaplan and David Norton, "The Balanced Scorecard: Measures that Drive Performance." *Harvard Business Review*, January-February 1992, pp. 71-79.
[4] This method of analysis is sometimes called the DuPont Method, named after the company that made extensive use of this approach.

Compete on your own "high ground." A variant of the other considerations is to cause a competitor to compete on the territory *you* own, in which *you* have the high ground, on which *you* are entrenched and cannot be easily dislodged. Frequently, you do not have to do much to have this happen. For some reason, competitors, like moths to the flame, seem drawn to attack companies at their point of strength rather than building on their own position. For example, RCA may have had similar overall resources to IBM when they could have developed a communications computer, but instead, it attacked IBM head-on. (Northern Telecom—now called Nortel Networks—built the computer RCA did not and, in so doing, outflanked computer manufacturers and the much larger AT&T.) It almost seems as though IBM's success magnetized the minds of RCA's executives, causing their strategic pathfinders to point in the same direction rather than finding their own path to success.

Changing the battlefield offers one way to beat targeted competitors. While there are many approaches for so doing, the underlying idea is to get them to compete on your terms.

Weaken Their Chain of Relationships

Armies with vital lines of supply can be choked if they do not receive the replacement troops, equipment and armaments, fuel, ammunition, medical supplies, food and water needed to keep the military machine progressing. In business, companies are often dependent upon relationships with suppliers and other stakeholders that may operate at a physical, financial and emotional distance from their customers. This creates a point of vulnerability. What would happen to the manufacturers of IBM-compatible personal computers if they could not obtain chips to power their machines? What if IBM were to impact its lines of supply, perhaps resulting in late delivery, limited availability or increased costs of new chips to the compatibles?

Considering this more generally, there is a chain of relationships that comprises the formal linkages the company has with its stakeholders, including suppliers, employees, customers and others such as retailers and other members of the distribution channels, investors and the board of directors. (See Figure 7-2.) The relationship the company forms with end customers is only as strong as the weakest link in the chain. All are needed to maintain and deepen the relationship with the end customer. Therefore, the company wishing to weaken a competitor in the minds of valuable and desired customers can examine the chain of relationships to identify areas of opportunity.

Figure 7-2: The Targeted Competitor and Its Chain of Relationships

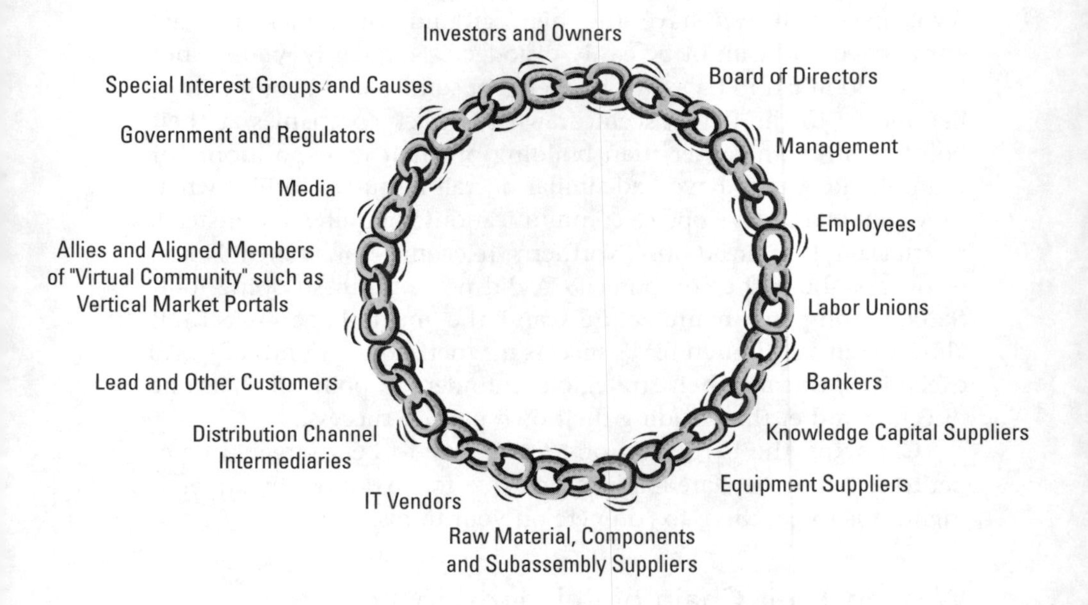

If the competitor has a constant stream of new products, who is conceiving and developing them? Can these people or team be hired away? If the innovations stem from suppliers, how can the company interrupt this relationship or strengthen its own ties to the source? If the competitor fields highly trained professionals to deal with customers, who is doing the recruitment and training of these professionals? Can these people be hired or lessons learned to improve your own performance? If the competitor's go-to-market effectiveness is highly dependent on a few distribution channel intermediaries or sales personnel, how is the company to deal with this observation?

In short:

- Chart the targeted competitor's chain of relationships.
- Focus on the relationships that are critical in the context of tomorrow's key success factors, including the internal relationships that represent enabling capabilities for the competitor such as conceive/design, develop, produce and so on.
- Identify options to weaken the relationships the targeted company has with selected members of its chain of relationships.

- Evaluate these options in a variety of dimensions, including financial and operational feasibility as well as risk management. Here, ask yourself what would happen if it became generally known what your strategy was? Again, as in virtually all the suggestions considered in this book, involve your lawyers long before implementing.
- Select among the options.
- Develop an implementation and communications plan before implementing.

Help Them to Retreat

Perhaps your competitor wants to leave the battlefield or abandon certain areas to your firm. This often happens in industries in which some of the product markets are unprofitable and will likely continue to be so. While you might be able to encourage your competitor to leave by, for example, signaling to its management and stakeholders, you also need to provide a benefit for leaving. Give it a door, show it the way, help it leave. For example, many companies will not leave a market when they have assets that have yet to be depreciated or customers that may be affected by the departure. Help the company to manage its write-downs, by, say, purchasing assets at or near book value, licensing their designs or arranging to produce and supply spare parts on an OEM[5] basis.

You might also force it to retreat by launching an intensive plan to weaken it, perhaps simultaneously targeting its most profitable customers while inquiring about its interest in being acquired. It happens.

Cooperate with Their Enemies

When you examine the strategic sets of competitors according to their positioning in the minds of customers, you may find that some companies are more naturally allies than competitors. It has been said that the enemy of my enemy is my friend. It may be in your mutual interest to cause a specific company to depart the industry or yield customer and market share to your combined interests. Opportunities may exist to align with one another and against a targeted competitor in order to defeat it. Some companies also work together to understand a mutual rival in a joint benchmarking exercise. This does occur

[5] Original equipment manufacturer—in this context, meaning that the company's name appears on the product.

in business. For example, a fast-growing European car manufacturer has recently been the target of a collaborative effort by at least two of its competitors, according to the marketing manager of one of them. The collaboration has apparently included sharing detailed competitive intelligence on the rival. Perhaps collaboration such as this seems audacious but it is increasingly common. Here, too, involve your lawyers before proceeding.

Engage in "Co-opetition"

Wars between countries are not usually fought on the same battleground between many enemies. More commonly, antagonists align themselves into a small number of camps, and then groups of forces from different locations attack one another. In business, too, few firms can afford to attack competitors on many fronts. Alliances are more common as companies seek to participate in a portfolio of high-risk/high-reward opportunities without underwriting the total investment, which can be immense. They are beginning to cooperate with their competitors to mutual benefit. That is, there may be opportunities to profit not only at the expense of a competitor but as an ally of the company. Simultaneously, cooperating and competing may be termed "co-opetition."

This happens routinely in industries such as aerospace, in which contracts involve the alignment of multiple companies in bid pursuits. On any given contract, companies might be competitors or allies. In other industries, companies have learned that it is in their mutual interests to collaborate to resolve certain areas of uncertainty such as technical standards, while competing to develop and market products that employ these standards. Cooperation can reduce risks in development of technologies in which there are many possible competing outcomes, none of them certain. In some cases, competitors may choose to invest in a number of other companies such as those engaged in the development of new technologies, so that they can both benefit if the technologies materialize as good substitutes. This is occurring in the search for replacements for conventional automobile engines powered by fossil fuels as car companies invest in developers of fuel cells, for example. DaimlerChrysler and Ford have invested in, and are working with, Ballard Power Systems Inc., a fuel cell technology company, to develop transportation fuel cell engines and electric drive trains.

Other areas of co-opetition include the development of vertical market portals and e-commerce capabilities for an entire industry, which has the potential to make electronic procurement much more efficient, benefiting all members of the industry. This is particularly apparent in the consumer durable and capital goods industries such as automobiles and airframes, in which competing vendors have aligned while competing in other dimensions at the same time.

Lead, Follow or Leave

Companies in an industry should know (or learn) their role. Without this understanding, they may engage in unusual short-term practices that can put the profitability of the industry at risk. Profitability for a whole industry is much harder to restore than it is for a single company, and that can be hard indeed. This is not to suggest that companies should work together to define their roles for this may be illegal, especially in areas such as pricing. But explore the possibilities of whether or not there are opportunities for you and targeted competitors to reach more tacit accommodation with regard to specific areas of leadership or dominance. For example, one company, a market share leader, has become well accepted as a responsible industry leader in a specific sector. Competitors tend to follow its actions, preserving prosperity for all of the firms. Before considering how best to signal to competitors your intent and preference, involve your lawyers at an early stage to determine whether, where and how this should be done.

When companies have similar market shares or if the industry is still rapidly changing, it may be premature to suggest role definition until later in the industry's life cycle. In some cases, market leaders may achieve highest profitability by having strategy at two levels: 1) a strategy to protect and develop industry profitability; and 2) a strategy to enhance the company's own performance within the industry such as at the expense of a targeted competitor. By working with a targeted competitor and others, the leader can protect the profitability and stability of all. For example, if industry capacity is unmanaged, it is possible that new construction or start-ups could result in more supply than needed. Too much capacity can seriously damage the profitability of all the companies in an industry. In some cases, market leaders, with the support of others, should acquire and retire capacity rather than let new competitors enter or have continuing price competition as all participants seek to fill up their plants.

Conduct Reconnaissance

Battles are usually won *before* they are fought. Using information about the scale, structure and deployment of the enemy's forces, a commander can plan the winning strategy. In the business context, information yields the insight from which business victory can be developed. That information is about things such as customers and their profitability, market size, growth rate, market shares, emerging and growing market segments, criteria for company selection and continuing use, product and service purchase, customers' perceptions of the competitors' products and the actions competitors are beginning to undertake to improve customers' perceptions and competitive positioning. These issues are discussed in detail in Chapter 5, in which competitive intelligence is reviewed.

Good information is not cheap. Senior executives may acknowledge this, yet they rarely commit the resources they need to make information their real strategic edge. Many prefer to invest in plant and equipment or other tangibles even though they may not know if this investment will make a material difference to their customers. Sustained tracking of customers' satisfaction with your performance and that of competitors and what can be done to improve your position is as vital to today's executive as a map was to Napoleon. Without this, a victory becomes a matter of chance, like two blind soldiers firing muskets at one another.

Avoid a Frontal Assault

Consider two enemies about to engage in hand-to-hand combat. One side has 1,000 warriors and the other, 500. When sent to fight, which side do you think will win? Unless your forces are qualitatively and quantitatively superior (people, technology, products, distribution, service) and have deeper pockets, it is foolish and perhaps suicidal to attack a competitor directly at their points of strength. Examine the graveyards in the computer industry for those that have tried to attack IBM head-on. Big companies made serious errors of judgment. They included RCA, GE, Xerox and Univac. Superior companies can gain by attacking weaker firms, but even they need to ensure that their strengths have the potential to overwhelm those of the entrenched defender at the point of attack.

Concentrate on Points of Weakness

Let's look back to our example of the two enemies fighting for control of a battlefield. If the side with 500 warriors attacks in a weakly defended area, perhaps on the enemy's flank, they can defeat a portion of the troops and then progressively repeat this until the enemy is defeated. This could best be accomplished when the enemy is overextended and trying to be too many things to too many customers. Opportunities for such an approach exist in virtually every industry in which overeager managers have extended the limited resources of their companies into too many regions, too many customers, too many product lines, and so on.

At one time, Apple Computer could have been such a candidate for attack when it was pursuing a wide range of technologies, ranging from the Newton to new operating systems and computers, but competitors' market participation never really challenged the company across a broad front. Employ the principle of divide and conquer to win over the customers you want most, perhaps starting with your competitor's least attached customers; then develop customer share. The least attached customers can be identified using research. In consumer markets, customers can be assessed using the Internet to contact them and Web sites to present the questions and receive the answers for your analysis.

Seek Out Uncontested Territory

Harder to find now than ever, uncontested territory still exists in many markets. For example, car companies using attitude and lifestyle segmentation rather than traditional methods have created new categories of vehicles that are in high demand such as the P/T Cruiser from DaimlerChrysler. "Company think" sometimes causes a "wisdom" to form in a competitor's camp that certain customers are not worth the effort, that technological advantage cannot be economically achieved, that mass customization is too costly and so on. Some years ago, the company think of the major North American automakers led them to conclude that it was not a good idea to produce small cars. After all, supposedly everyone knew that small cars were less profitable than large ones, and that American customers would not buy them anyhow. The Japanese automakers staked out their claim and expanded their bridgehead far beyond. This was to be anticipated. The Japanese did with cars what they had previously done with motorcycles. Their strategy could have been predicted had the Big Three been watching.

Weaken the Enemy through Harassment

Sometimes, executives deploy a guerrilla strategy, but such an approach can be more like an absence of strategy unless it is thoughtfully planned. Managers who advocate a series of apparently illogical actions to "keep the competitors off-balance" as their guerrilla strategy have not formed a basis for winning consistently. For example, some managers may suggest deliberately underbidding a contract to cause the competitor to reconsider its future bidding strategy (actually, this would be a decoy strategy). Actions such as this can serve to undermine the profitability of an entire industry. Rather, guerrilla action should seek to force the competitor to divert and/or waste resources to enable you to gain a foothold or expand your market position. Guerrilla approaches are invariably tactical, limited in scope and enable rapid withdrawal without much cost. Examples include the use of legal action, regardless of the foundation of the claim in law, to tie up the competitor's executives, waste their managerial time and talent and sometimes to buy time for a competitive response. A major razor blade company did this when a new entrant began to test a disposable razor and seek out acquisition candidates to market its product. A distributor of beer did this to protect the battleground in Alaska, where it was entrenched, when a European firm indicated it would build a brewery.

A more strategic use of guerrilla warfare is illustrated by companies that undermine a competitor's overall profitability by targeting the competitor's high-volume products with low-priced alternatives, which impacts the competitor's profits more than the company supplying only a modest volume at the low price. As we will discuss shortly, a marketer of vodka attempted to attack the industry leader in this way and lost only when the leader underbid the price of the upstart entrant with a low-priced flanker brand of its own.

Operate Below Radar Range

Your competitors are constantly scanning the environment looking for signals that your company is about to do something differently. Perhaps they have become used to dealing with the old you. They may be concerned about what you might become and are monitoring your company and the things you do for signs of change. (If you are watching them, you can be sure they are doing the same. Even as you read this book, a competitor is probably doing likewise!) If you are seeking to dethrone the incumbent, do not tell it in advance. Couch your moves in secrecy.

Make certain that all internal information is secure. You could classify the information you have. IBM has used four levels of information security: "for internal IBM use only," which applies to telephone directories; "IBM confidential," for maintenance manuals; and "restricted confidential," for product designs and business plans. The highest level is "registered confidential," which applies to the most sensitive material. Some years ago, when a Japanese company attempted to procure IBM plans covertly, these documents were labeled just "IBM confidential," yet that cost IBM's competitor around $300 million, so you can imagine the value the firm places on its even more sensitive information.

Operating below radar range suggests that stealth is required to achieve surprise and ensure that the competitor is caught unprepared. It will eventually respond, but the lag between your move and your competitor's gives you time to solidify your position.

Mask the Intention and Create a Diversion

Great battles are preceded by great subterfuge. In preparing for Operation Overlord, as the World War II Allies dubbed their D-Day action, many actions were taken to cause the Germans to believe that the invasion would occur at a different location. Aided by information gleaned from decoded German communications, the Allies formulated and communicated false landing plans through their secret agents.[6] The deception operation[7] was intended to fool the Germans into thinking the Allied landing would be in the Pas de Calais, France. The Germans were further deceived with the assembly of a diversionary invasion force. Although the Germans expected a landing, they did not know where it would occur. The German commander in chief thought Calais and Dieppe were the most likely locations for invasion because this was closest to England. Hitler and Rommel thought the Normandy area was possible. On June 6, 1944, when the Allies actually landed on the beaches of Normandy, the German Army still did not have its forces concentrated there.

In business as in war, the objective of a diversion is to lead the enemy astray. Make them think you will land your invasion forces somewhere else. Have them believe you will attack where you will not, perhaps by sending the generals, troops and selected armaments

[6] Including Juan Pujol Garcia, whose code name was Garbo. Michael Evans, "Double Dealing Aided the Allies." *Times* (London), 17 September 1999.

[7] The code name of the deception was Fortitude South. The First US Army Group was the fictitious invading force. It was assembled in Kent. Richard G. Ricklefs, "Fortitude South: D-Day Deception." *Military Intelligence* 22, no. 2 (Apr.-June. 1996): 48-50.

to the inoperative front. Develop an initial thrust in an area that will not be contested for a lengthy period just long enough to delay the enemy from focusing on your real intention. Principles such as these have long been used by the military. They apply equally in the business environment.

Companies could launch a product targeting a minor market segment to divert attention from their main thrust. Or they could concentrate their sales force to focus on a given region or type of customer in a blitz, planning to attack ground zero as soon as the competitor begins to realign its own forces. Or they could communicate specific intentions to their competitors through disinformation.

Thus, in addition to protecting unauthorized access to information or minimizing inadvertent leakage, ensure that what you do communicate to the market is managed. Develop an information plan and perhaps a disinformation plan, which would include a targeting of information recipients (such as financial analysts, customers, middlemen, suppliers and competitors), identifying the information (or disinformation) you wish to convey to them and describing who is authorized to conduct your communications. When you do indeed communicate with the competitor, seek to steer it away from the areas in which you intend to commit your resources.

Use communications to stake your claim to a specific position in the mind of targeted customers, while ceding other positions to competitors. In effect, this creates a situation analogous to the principle of hegemony previously discussed whereby countries tacitly divided the world into "spheres of influence" in which each would be the predominant, unchallenged power. Then, ensure that competitors appreciate that you will defend the territory you control at all costs. As warfare expert T.C. Schelling wrote: "the strategy of threat is not so much to inflict maximum damage on an adversary as to convince him that an attack will be costly."[8]

Control Your Territory

Wars are not easily waged on several fronts. It is almost impossible to fight when the home front is in turmoil. If your core customers are defecting to a competitor, you will not gain control easily of another market position. You absolutely must control what you already have. The strategies of doing this are many and will depend upon the specifics of the situation you face. Virtually all elegantly defensive

[8] T.C. Schelling, "Strategy, Tactics and Non-Zero-Sum Theory." In *Theory of Games: Techniques and Applications*, edited by A. Mensch. London: The Universities Press, 1966, p. 476.

approaches to entrenchment require that relationships be managed. The reason is simple. When your customers buy, your needs are satisfied. After all, you have supplied the product or service and have been paid for it. However, for your customers, the enjoyment (or nightmare) is about to begin. They will measure your performance over the entire period of consumption against their expectations at the time of purchase and thus will decide whether to buy from you again, refer others to your firm, approve you as a sole supplier and so on. Success therefore requires that the customer relationship be managed by the supplier throughout the course of product or service consumption.

Territory already governed should also be secured at the dealer, distributor or retailer level in addition to that of the customer. It may also ensure that a new vertical market portal or e-commerce strategy includes major industry participants but excludes others such as newcomers or noninvestors. If Company A gains share of shelf or additional support with specific middlemen, Company B can find access to its customers cut off or seriously eroded. This can be a powerful competitive strategy and particularly effective against offshore suppliers or smaller companies seeking to gain a customer presence or improve share of customer. It may force competitors to seek out alternative distribution that could be more costly and possibly less effective, although in the era of the Internet, it is harder to lock up distribution to competitors. The arrival of e-commerce creates a new dimension for competitive advantage, thoughtfully considered.

Deploy Overwhelming Technology

Armies with superior technology generally outperform the enemy laboring with inferior equipment. For example, the nineteenth-century Germans experienced much success on the battlefield thanks to their Krupp-made field artillery, which could lob heavier shells further than the enemy's could, thereby providing a protective shield for their soldiers. When nineteenth-century Afrikaners were attacked by Zulus with spears, they responded with rifles. To the surprise of no one other than their unfortunate attackers, the Afrikaners were victorious. World War II was won in the Far East when technology obviously triumphed as the atomic bomb. But overwhelming technology need not be the most advanced, it must simply be what is needed to win. For example, basic chemical and biological weapons provide some states with an advantage over others in their region and have been used callously but successfully by some regimes.

In the era of the Internet and mass customization of products, services and technology, technology offers important benefits to advance the company's competitive position, especially when the customer experience, over time, limits its interest in dealing with competitors. After all, if your design, research and development, purchasing and operations are integrated electronically with those of your suppliers, would you be prepared to invest the time and funds necessary to switch to a competitor if the service and value you otherwise received met your requirements? Well, your customers and those of your targeted competitors would likely feel the same way.

One area for consideration here is return on data. Companies are finding that their customer and competitor data have an experience curve effect, leading to better decisions made more economically (although the objective research in this area is thin). If your company and your competitor have little differentiation in most of the key dimensions of your offering, increasingly, your customer knowledge and predictive ability will set your firm apart. Technology plays a vital role here. If the technology seems expensive, consider the implications of not having the customer and competitor knowledge and insight you need. This seems a lot like going to war without a weapon.

Progressively Encircle the Enemy

Few firms have the resources to win in all their markets and for all their customers. IBM once came close in addressing virtually all customer needs in all market segments. But it, too, had gaps in its product line such as at the very high-end computers market segment in which Control Data (CDC) and then Cray Research were strong.[9] IBM wanted to lead this segment of the market as well, but even this large company was unable to do so and grew concerned about the success of CDC in accomplishing what it had not. Thomas Watson, IBM's CEO, contrasted CDC's small size yet major accomplishments compared to

[9] Seymour Cray was a pioneering visionary who wanted to make the fastest computers. His successes created the industry of supercomputing, starting with computer design at Univac, then Control Data Corporation (which he helped found in 1957) and Cray Research (started in 1972). In 1976, the Cray 1 computer succeeded where large companies had failed. This and subsequent models were the most powerful computers of their time. Cray insisted on simplicity, distilled problems to their essence and sometimes even redesigned computers to first make them simpler before making them better. Told that Apple Computer had bought a Cray to design their next Mac, he said he had bought a Mac to design the next Cray, according to Charles Breckingridge in 1996 who worked at Cray's last start-up, SRC. Cray left Cray Research in 1989. Cray Research was sold to Silicon Graphics in 1996 and then to Tera Computer Company in 2000. Now called Cray Inc., the firm remains a leader in supercomputers.

IBM's by saying, "I understand that in the [CDC] laboratory ... there are only 34 people, including the janitor...I fail to understand why we have lost our industry leadership position."[10] CDC and then Cray Research had an opportunity to extend what they had learned in high performance computing into other segments, but their ideas such as parallel processing, were commercialized for smaller machines by others. Had Cray been more commercial in his focus, he might have been able to repeat what he had done with supercomputing throughout IBM's product line and completely encircle IBM.

To successfully surround an enemy requires that you identify a source of the customer share you wish to transfer. Target a single competitor or a group that is sufficiently similar to be regarded as one. Engage it along a narrow front. Having achieved customer share transfer from the initial campaign, repeat the onslaught until the enemy is progressively excluded from the customers you want.

Kamikaze warriors lurk in almost every industry, waiting to unleash themselves against a rational economic adversary. A company may buy customer share, hoping that it can increase prices later as is common among accounting firms. Or it may act out of desperation, bravado, political imperatives or other reasons, as has been the case for some technology firms wanting to have well-known companies that they can mention as customers. Whatever the case, challenge such competitors, and encourage changed behaviors before they weaken your industry. Target their customers aggressively for share transfer to help get the message across. Ensure that they have enough problems to work on so that they will not easily focus on your customers in your markets. If you believe such companies exist in a foreign market and intend to target your country, consider entering their home market with the single-minded objective of undermining their domestic profitability to erode their ability to finance an offshore campaign.

Attack Yourself

In the battle for North Africa in World War II, both Montgomery and Rommel used men to monitor the campaigns and history of the enemy to predict what they would do. In business, by preparing to attack your own firm, you can identify your weaknesses better and deal with them. Such an approach can also help target the competitor by identifying the intelligence you need and by better preparing your company to anticipate its moves.

[10] As reported by Gordon Bell, a former vice president with Digital Equipment, now with Microsoft.

Taking the analogy further, you could also be your own most aggressive competitor by attacking yourself and giving your customers and potential customers choice. It seems unusual but some companies do compete with themselves by having more than one product line from which the customer can choose. Procter & Gamble does this with its multiple brands. Companies in the neon sign industry sometimes have more than one company with different sales forces competing with one another under different names. The signs are produced in a common facility. Approaches such as these may not be as "neat" as the ones you currently employ, but it is preferable for you to offer your customers choices than for your competitors to do so. When Ford introduced the Probe, it had intended it as a front-wheel drive replacement for the Mustang. Instead, it had the courage to let both compete side by side in the dealers' showrooms and let customers decide which they preferred. Both Mustang and Probe sold surprisingly well.

Don't Let the Enemy Become Entrenched

When an enemy attacks, its approach is often to establish a beachhead, consolidate and move out from the new encampment. The strategy of the defender must be to counterattack *before* the enemy becomes entrenched in a new beachhead. In business, companies that begin to supply new products to your customers (or potential customers) must be neutralized before they become a significant factor in the market. This includes small attackers, especially if they have radical innovation in product, service, delivery or positioning that could win them market share.

Counterattack can take many forms such as imitating and developing a superior offering of the type just introduced, repositioning the competition as suppliers of an inappropriate solution or even buying the upstart. Companies that have attacked and won have usually done so in full view of the competitor which stood by and watched, convincing itself that the new approach was wrong. This happened when American Airlines introduced the Sabre reservation system, when Ford announced that its vehicles would be shaped by the wind, when Chrysler put the PT Cruiser on display at car shows well in advance of its introduction and when Merrill Lynch developed the Cash Management Account. In all cases, there were losers that had to play catch-up once these spectacular innovations were already entrenched. But by then, it was too late. For example, General Motors, perhaps wanting to repeat the success of the PT

Cruiser, recruited the designer of this highly successful car, but not soon enough to win this particular battle.

The challenge here is to avoid being a foolish follower, a company that emulates a competitor simply because it did something first. This issue needs to be balanced with the risk of being too late to compete. Today, more than ever, time is money. As we have discussed, there are pioneers in marketplaces, companies that follow them quickly, and some firms that oppose the changes. Now, more frequently, to the first belong the spoils. In many markets, and for many customers, the second to enter has much less opportunity than the first.

Have Strong Allies

In addition to forming alliances with selected competitors in specific ways, the business strategist could seek alternative groupings of firms to disadvantage a specific competitor. The question here is whether true relationships can be created for mutual advantage in your industry, leading to your company being more completely integrated with your most valuable and desired customers, while a targeted competitor is progressively excluded from the customer set. Customers and suppliers operating according to the complete principles of relationship marketing would integrate their value chains—design, research, development and many aspects of operations—to achieve product and system superiority over similar attempts by a targeted competitor. For example, could a concrete company exclusively work with a construction firm to revolutionize building methods? Could a packaging firm aid a fast-food restaurant chain to keep its food warmer longer in biodegradable packaging? Could a plastics company work with a car assembler to produce orthopedically correct seating for an aging population? In situations such as these, the future success of both supplier and customer becomes common, and the commitment to one another increases to mutual advantage, leading to the development of a true relationship.

Learn Their Secrets

Wars depend on knowing the competitor extremely well. Intelligence is used to plan military initiatives. For example, in World War II's Ultra project, Allied intelligence monitored German and Japanese communications after the code for the German cipher machine Enigma was broken.[11] The radio signals allowed the Allies to anticipate strategic and tactical actions of the Germans and Japanese, helping to win the Battle of Britain, destroy German forces at Normandy, beat the Japanese in the battles of the Coral Sea and Midway and locate and shoot down the plane carrying the Japanese commander in the Pacific.

We have discussed competitive intelligence in Chapter 5 in the legitimate business equivalent of military intelligence. Using techniques such as those described, the direction and intent of competitors can be learned and their moves thwarted. Even their secrets can be determined from publicly available sources, ethically and fairly. In the movie *Wall Street*, the financier Gordon Gecko places a tail on a rival takeover specialist in an attempt to understand which companies he was after and to profit from this knowledge. There is no need to win this way. For example, it was an open "secret" for some time that Alcatel would make a bid for Lucent's business, which it did, albeit unsuccessfully, in 2001. Had competitors such as Nortel Networks been interested and watching, they could have made an earlier approach or planned with Alcatel for the subsequent purchase of selected assets, which might have helped the Alcatel bid succeed and, by consolidating and retiring excess capacity, the industry could have become more profitable.

Tactics for Making Competitors Lose

Tactics for beating the competition do not always require a complex strategy or a world-beating product. For example, a British firm aimed to succeed with a high technology mousetrap. It used infrared beams to track a mouse as it entered the trap. Computer controls transmitted a signal to a door that then closed on the unwary critters. A sound alert helped the owner know that the trap was occupied. This mousetrap was so good that it held a royal warrant from the Queen. Perhaps she was also the only person who could afford the price. An installation of twenty traps rented for around £1,000–£2,000 per year, plus servicing charges. The company that invented and sold the device said that it "expected the world to beat a path to their door" to buy its invention. Perhaps, but a cat, cheese and a spring-loaded trap or even a shoe might achieve a similar benefit at a lower price. No competitor needed to target this product, tactically or otherwise, as it had limited commercial appeal. After being installed in just a few sites in the UK and internationally, it was discontinued.

[11] The Japanese version of Enigma was called Purple.

Effective execution of tactics and real-time competition is absolutely vital if a company is to profit from the extensive investment in planning for competitor targeting and customer relationship management, strategic capabilities such as technology and databases and account planning, among much else. Tactically and in real time, it all comes down to doing what the plan calls for and what the capabilities enable. And sometimes it comes down to being a little smarter, a little more aggressive, a little more loving, having an ability to turn the competition against itself and having the wisdom to know when to do what.

Tactical competition can be planned and executed with the activities not necessarily occurring in real time. Companies used to be able to plan and execute their strategies and tactics in a fairly orderly manner, but the fast pace of change in many marketplaces now makes this difficult. The challenge now is to target competitors and win in real time. Here, we discuss selected approaches for doing this.

The main ways to improve share of customer and target competitors, once the necessary core strategic capabilities are in place, are by:

- Beating Competitors
- Collaborating with Competitors

In the following, we discuss beating competitors. This discussion is extended in Chapter 8, in which we review collaborating with competitors. Of course, companies can also acquire competitors, but since acquisition is such a large topic, we do not discuss it in this book because other texts deal with that topic at length.

Beating Competitors

There are several ways to beat competitors, which include the following:

- Targeting Them in Real Time
- Outperforming Competitors
- Blocking Competitors Out
- Shutting Competitors Down

Targeting Competitors in Real Time

Competing in real time means that companies develop the technology, processes and know-how needed to manage changing circumstances as it happens such as competitors reducing their prices or customers deciding not to buy from your company any longer.

While real-time competition can be tactical, the reverse may not be true—tactical competition may not be in real time. Here, we concentrate on competing in real time as well as reviewing selected tactics for targeting competitors. An example of real-time competition is a call to a customer service center eliciting the fact that the customer is considering switching to a competitor. The operator responds immediately to avert that possibility by identifying why the customer is considering a change of supplier and dealing with these issues on the spot or initiating a process to ensure that the customer can see that the issues are being dealt with. Bell Canada's Customer Contact Center functions in much this way, empowering their frontline staff to deal with customers' questions as they arise. The largest mobile phone company in Canada, Rogers, appears to operate in a similar manner and really swings into action when a customer announces a decision to switch. Then it tries especially hard to win the customer back, but it can be too late.

The same issue, but not in real time, would be the observation from customer research that all is not well in an account, leading to tactical account planning to avoid customers from switching. The difference between tactical and real-time competition is the use and role of technology, a critical enabler of tactical competition and the primary facilitator of real-time competition. We have discussed selected technology and other considerations that can give a competitive edge. Do you need to know the competitor's price for Product A in Customer X? Consult the files you have established for customers and competitors and the data that describes the intersection of customers and competitors. If your processes are keeping the data current, then you should have the intelligence you need and the ability to act on it, tactically and in real time. More generally, though, what are the principles for beating a targeted competitor in chosen accounts or in the minds of selected consumers? Figure 7-3 provides one way of considering approaches for competing tactically and in real time within chosen accounts.

Figure 7-3: Selected Considerations for Competing Tactically and in Real Time in Chosen Accounts

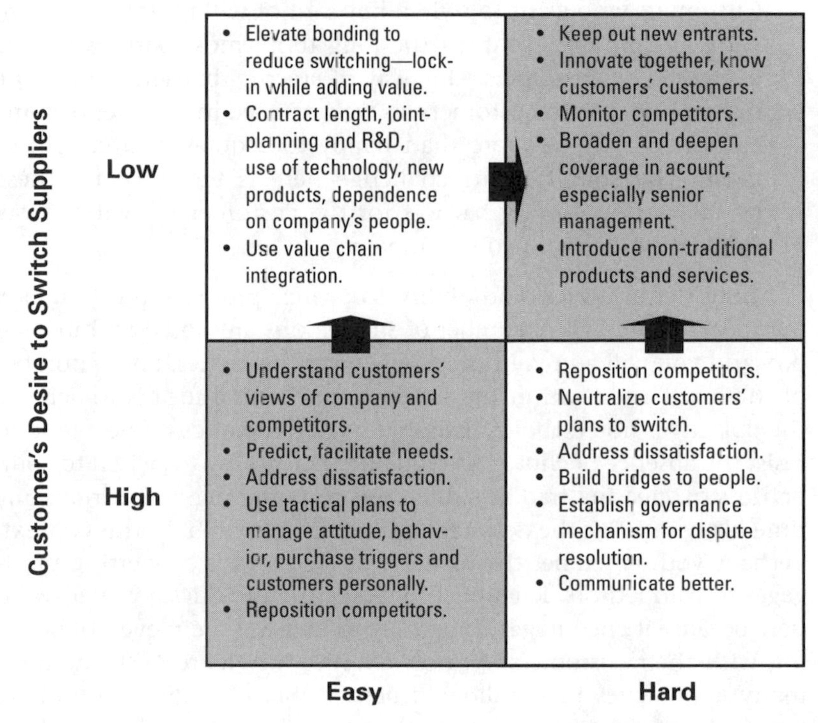

There are several ways to target competitors in real time. These include:

- Manage Switching
- Understand Competitors' Bonds
- Integrate Tactics with Strategies

Manage Switching

Customers will switch from one supplier to another according to their desire and ability to do so. The challenge for the company guided by the principles of relationship marketing and competitor targeting is to do the following:

- Reduce the desire of customers to switch from your company to competitors while simultaneously increasing their desire to switch away from competitors to your company.

- Reduce the ability of customers to switch to competitors by erecting barriers, particularly nontraditional barriers, to switching. Customers who want to switch but cannot will resent your company and in any event, in the long term, most barriers can be overcome by customers. One way of erecting barriers is to create tighter bonds with customers, as we discussed in Chapter 6. Some customers may be more than happy to acquiesce to certain of these. The simultaneous challenge here is to introduce these bonds while lowering barriers for the customer to switch away from competitors to your company.

Considering desire and ability to switch provides the four box matrix of Figure 7-3. A number of suggestions are noted within each box and you will add your own. Whatever the tactics, and a number of these are listed within the diagram, the central idea is to achieve the objectives noted above. It should be noted that customers tend to resist the absence of choice, so reducing their ability to switch to competitors by creating traditional barriers to switching will at the same time likely increase the desire for customers to switch. In this context, perhaps you remember the banks' exit charges for converting mortgages to competitors. Relationship marketing provides a way forward here because it encourages companies to increase their levels of bonding with their customers. As noted earlier (in Figure 6-1), there are many approaches to bonding: structural, brand equity, attitudinal, personal, information and control, value and zero option bonding. Few of these types of barriers involve penalties or costs on exit, and when they might such as displacement of one vendor's technology with another solution, the intent when implementing the technology is not to raise the customer's costs but to assist the customer to succeed. Bonding, like glue, represents an inhibitor to separation. Increasing levels of bonding raises barriers to changing vendors.

Understand Competitors' Bonds

Similarly, the company should understand the bonds enjoyed by the targeted competitor so that these can be reduced or eliminated. There are many ways of doing this tactically. Some could involve financial investment such as displacing the technology of a competitor with your own,[12] purchasing its inventory at the customer's

[12] This need not be the case for only business-to-business marketplaces. Trade-ins of automobiles is a long-standing practice, and similar opportunities exist for companies to clear the desktop, home office, and furniture inventories of their customers, replacing old with new. In some industries, it may be possible to extend this idea to evergreen programs, such as long-term agreements to keep new technologies on the desks on home offices.

cost (for subsequent liquidation on your account) or having your people do their work on the customer's premises, which can increase your share of customer by building deeper relationships and providing better intelligence. Because hurdles to switching can exist more in the minds of the customers than in reality, the opportunity also exists to reposition the competitor in the account or the mind of consumers while positioning your own company. If you really understand the competitor, you know the weak points of their products, services and the company as a whole. For example, if you are better capitalized than your competitor is in an industry in which the customer depends on supplier stability, you would know what to communicate to the chief financial officer of the customer to advance your position at the competitor's expense.

Integrate Tactics with Strategies

Approaches for tactical and real-time competition should integrate with strategies for competing. As noted earlier in this chapter, competing tactically and in real time requires prior implementation of strategic capabilities. Capabilities of particular note that can make a fundamental difference to the effectiveness of competing include framing rules for customer engagement, which allows a broader range of empowerment for frontline staff, thereby creating an ability to relate to the customer in real time and create competitive advantage in the interaction. Having established the rules for engagement, these need to be captured in technology and process, and front line personnel need to have appropriate training. What latitude do they have in respect of pricing and returns, for example? Some companies treat their customers as if they cannot be fully trusted and their policies reflect this, too, requiring front line staff to mindlessly repeat company policy to an increasingly exasperated customer. Just try complaining about some aspect of that new car you bought, and you will experience this frustration with several manufacturers. Even when companies give their employees leeway, they need to train them in using this newfound freedom. Some staff can be more miserly than most managers and owners.

I recently bought a used car from the dealership of a feline British nameplate. After signing some papers, I was handed the keys and papers and bid farewell. As I was leaving, the same salesperson gave the purchaser of a new car a leather bag adorned with the famous logo. I found my car for myself in the lot, while the salesman escorted the other customer to his vehicle. Perhaps you have to buy the dealership to get genuine attention.

Once the rules of engagement with customers have been framed, supporting technologies implemented (such as for the call center and sales force automation) and processes engineered, there may be an opportunity to automate aspects of the customer engagement, dialog, transaction and return processes, all with a view to making the experience a good one and competitively superior. With automation can come an opportunity to open the company up to its customers so they can interact in real time with the technologies, people and processes of the firm.

Outperforming Competitors

Outperforming competitors tactically and in real time means beating them in the minds of each chosen customer, according to the values of the customer. It used to be that winning was about securing the order at the expense of competitors. Now, winning means increasing bonding with the customer faster than competitors are able to, which gives the company the advantages that you would expect from a tighter bond. What are the tactics and approaches for real-time competition that can deepen the relationship?

If the typical buyer is to make himself or herself equally available to all companies wishing to broaden their base in the account, they will be deluged by calls for meetings. Most purchasers do not have the time or appetite for a large number of meetings, and most also want to limit the number of suppliers. Winning the battle for customer access provides an opportunity to extend the customer relationship and advance to the following stages:

- Connection
- Interaction
- Transaction
- Customization

Connection

The company that has preferential access to the customer can connect and interact with him or her to create the value each customer wants. The priority here is for the tactical and real-time winner to first establish preferred customer access if it is to outperform targeted competitors. We have previously discussed issues associated with accessing customers strategically, including people, process, technology and customer knowledge and insight. We noted the access edge that derives from integrating the customer with the company's information systems. Process integration and blurring the lines between where the company ends and the customer begins also helps to secure better customer access and sets the stage for a competitively superior connection. Bonding between people has always been important and always will be. More than this, how does a company secure competitively superior customer access tactically and in real time?

First, let us discuss how *not* to do it. Do not force access upon a customer. This is a little like the geek who keeps on calling the prom queen. Have you ever been called while having dinner by a telephone company or a newspaper eager for your business? Operating an outbound call center or direct mail initiative without customer sensitivity guarantees weak response and worse. Rather than succeeding in gaining customer access, it may be denied in future.

Instead of forcing customer access, position your company to each customer competitively and uniquely and *earn the access*. Customer-specific positioning is made possible by a deep understanding of customers and their context, their preferences, needs and behaviors. Your customer information files and other CRM capabilities should enable you to tailor positioning to individual customers. The challenge is to integrate competitive advantage into communications, both one-way and interactive. This is becoming quite feasible in several industries. In the pharmaceutical industry, for example, companies obtain data on the prescriptions of doctors so they can know, by doctor, who prescribes what and how often. That is, for every doctor and for every product, they should know their main competitor. They are then able to position the benefits of their products relative to the competitor's in tailored, one-on-one communications campaigns, comprising a combination of direct mail and visits by salespeople. The doctor approached with a combination of personally relevant information and competitive product comparisons is more likely to change prescription habits, especially when companies use research to measure what the doctor says he or she prescribes with what actually happens.

Try to encourage customers or prospects to call you for the meeting. Send them a note you know they will value. Clip articles from the press. Tell them about their competitors. Help them understand what other customers are doing. Make them feel important. Invite them to meet with your most important customers. Award them to recognize their individual importance. Celebrate them publicly such as at a dinner with your employees. Develop a plan to manage each customer connection such as a calendar of communications, comprising newsletters, calls, birthday cards, holiday greetings and so on. This can be enabled using available mass customized communications programs or done using manual methods, depending on the number of customers you have. Research their business and their customers. Have a plan to make more money for them (or address their other motivators). And so on.

Technology can make a big difference to the efficiency of mass customized communications. A number of companies use technology not only to manage each customer connection, but to increase the relevance of communications. A major hardware retailer reviews its customer database and sends highly tailored communications, including newsletters and coupons geared to motivate buyer behavior. A pharmaceutical company listens to doctors before it launches a new product so that it can send just those messages it knows will help the doctor and accelerate adoption of its product. A financial services and advisory organization also does one-on-one customer research, informs its brokers and equips them to manage the customer connection better than competing brokers. A dental products distributor knows what each dentist wants through its customer and competitor database; then it uses its telesales personnel to help dentists uniquely according to the motivators of each and the companies with which they now deal. Some dentists want to earn more money. Selected company programs and positioning are communicated. Other dentists want to improve preventative service and oral hygiene. Yet others want to build niche practices such as in cosmetic surgery, and the company communicates uniquely with each dentist to advance the required positioning relative to defined competitors and address the triggers of their behaviors, which vary according to the dentist, his or her customers and his or her present suppliers.

In addition to earning customer access, winning tactically and in real time means creating opportunities for the customer to connect with your company and doing this faster and better than targeted competitors. Taking everything to the extreme, companies will be open for business all the time from anywhere on earth, know everything about the customer history, make useful recommendations to the customer and integrate the company's people and technology, putting the capability into the hands of each customer. If that is the end state, why are you not there yet? Delay and you open a gate to the competitor.

Your firm should be available and open for business right now, whatever the time is. Customers should have access through whatever channel they want to the company such as via the firm's

Internet site as well as through links on multiple partner sites driving traffic to the company. New technologies mean new opportunities for connection such as cellular and emerging mobile platforms that provide much promise for customer access.

More traditionally, though, how accessible is your company for customers wanting to connect? How accessible are your targeted competitors? Perhaps your policies, processes, people or technology limit access to some customers more so than do those of the competition. Are you easier to do business with than they are? Some areas of accessibility to consider are presented in Table 7-1. In each case, the task is not just to improve, but to achieve higher levels of performance than those of targeted competitors. So benchmarks need to be established for the enemy as part of this assessment.

Table 7-1: Test Your Own Accessibility—Selected Considerations for Comparing Your Company with Competitors

- Is your company more accessible to your employees than your competitors are? If the company wants to be more accessible to customers, it should first really care about and be more accessible to employees.
  - For example, is your policies and procedures manual thinner than the competitor's and more understandable? Do the manuals really empower employees in the service of internal and external customers?
  - Can you call your director of human resources right now without reaching his or her voice mail? Is his or her after-hours number on the voice mail? Call your competitor's director of HR and compare accessibility.
  - Does each employee have a plan for personal development in terms that each person finds meaningful? Do competitor's have individually tailored personal growth plans?
  - Do employees' office environments encourage individuality, including children's drawings, personally chosen artwork and furniture and comfortable chairs?
  - Can people choose their hours of work and even the location in which they work?
  - Do working parents have opportunities to look after their children when they are ill or home for other reasons?
- Pretend you are your firm's best customer. How easy is it to enter the premises, visit the washroom, open the door, read the signs, twist the caps off your products, understand labels and contracts and use the products? Are manuals, documentation and user guides accessible for different types of customers and more so than competitors' in each of the cases mentioned? Try to access the company, imagining the following:

- You have a sight deficiency or are hard of hearing, aged, young or physically handicapped.
- You have a mother tongue other than English—consider hiring a company to call on your behalf, speaking in Spanish to an English-speaking operator, for example.
- You are not familiar with the operation of the product.
- You work when the company is open for business. What would you prefer in terms of hours of business, including evenings and Sunday openings?
- You are *not* computer literate. Is the Web site intuitive? Does it have the information you might need, not as a customer but as a person? Navigate the competitor's site and compare.
- You are computer literate. Can you take full advantage of the various benefits of the site, quickly?
- You are a business wishing to connect with your company. How might it establish how to interface with your technologies or engage in e-commerce?
- You are in need of help. Examine how many telephone numbers you have in the phone book. Are they arranged as your divisions are defined, or are they organized according to the needs of the caller? Is it obvious who to call, according to the reason for the call?
- You dislike the interactive voice response that meets most telephone callers. How quickly can you get to talk with a human, or do you have to dial many numbers? Call your competitors and compare.

• Review your invoices to see if they are accessible.
  - For companies selling multiple products and services to the same customer, in cases in which prices might vary by time of day and amount of consumption such as telephone companies or energy utilities, are your invoices comprehensible?
  - Do invoices recognize the buyers' importance and thank them for their business, or do they focus on payment terms, products bought and ask that all future references quote *your* file number? How do the invoices compare with those of your competitors'?

• Examine your strategies and tactics for customer access according to your relationship marketing plan.
  - Can you find it?
  - Do you have a relationship marketing plan?

If you are in business-to-business sales and marketing, you probably still depend upon creating new customers. As we saw, accessing those customers is hard if the incumbent companies are focused on blocking their competitors. The challenge in breaking through is to find a narrow point of entry and expand from the beachhead. It used to be that companies could use price as a point of entry, then develop more profitable business in the account. Accountants have done this for years, as have printers, advertising agencies and many other product and service providers. The problem is, if the company is willing to switch for price, will it remain with you when a competitor does likewise, or are your strategies for blocking competitors from the account so compelling that all rivals will remain locked out? Many companies have strategies for attracting customers. Fewer have strategies for keeping them. The founder of what was once one of North America's largest supermarket chains, Steinberg's,[13] Sam Steinberg, used price as a competitive weapon to create customers. When he had but one store, he would watch the loss leaders advertised by the competitors and then shop their stores to stock his own. He always had the lowest price in town but not necessarily enough product to supply every customer.[14]

Interaction

If you cannot connect with a customer, you will not have an opportunity to interact with each to form a competitively superior relationship and create value. If you cannot interact effectively with the customer, you will not have an opportunity to engage in a transaction and deepen the relationship. Outperforming competitors in terms of the customer interaction means winning the battle first to align core competencies such as the organization's technologies and processes. The battle then shifts to tactics to enter the minds of individual customers and manage their behaviors for mutual advantage. Winning the interaction in the minds of each customer means outperforming competitors in both hemispheres of each customer's brain: intellectual interaction and emotional interaction.

Intellectual Interaction

Customers must be presented with the information they need to make informed decisions. Without technology, this is a virtual impossibility for business-to-consumer companies. But by gathering customer data; developing customer knowledge, insight and a predictive understanding of buyer behavior; and then integrating this

[13] Steinbergs and Miracle Mart were one of the largest combined chains of supermarkets in Canada in the 1970s and 1980s. After Mr. Steinberg left the company to others and then died, the firm was without the leadership that had built it. Unable to retain its market position, it disappeared in this most competitive industry.

[14] According to Mr. Steinberg, as related to MBA students at McGill University, 1976.

with competitive comparisons, a company can manage the customer on an intellectual level. To illustrate, a car manufacturer's customer data show that a customer is likely more concerned about safety than performance and is sending "buy" signals when completing on-line profiles and visiting dealers and Web sites. Now you have an opportunity to offer the customer a special reason to buy a car soon, and position your vehicle to this buyer in terms of safety. By knowing brands he or she has owned in the past and watching other buyer behavior such as answers to questions asked at the dealerships and cookies in their computers, you can know what competitive cars the customer may be considering. You can now tailor your message with competitive product comparisons, interacting with the customer using the communications channels he or she prefers.

Emotional Interaction

While businesses are often persuaded in large measure by intellectual arguments in communications and presentations, consumers often exhibit a high degree of emotion in their purchases. And even business decision makers can have more emotion in their decisions than they communicate. Commercial loans can be made as much on the perceptions of the lender or the borrower as on the business proposition itself. Most companies appeal to the reason of customers by using intellectual content when positioning and differentiating their companies, products and brands, yet customer attitudes and behavior are managed best when the communications combine reason with emotion.

Goodyear Tire and Rubber has positioned its tires as having superior traction and other features, using advanced technology. Now they communicate "serious technology" and "freedom from worry," building some emotion into the brand in the last mention. Michelin appears to have focused more on emotion from the outset. Its personification of Michelin tires, dubbed Bibendum, is alternately a heroic, friendly or even seductive[15] rubber mascot compiled from a heap of Michelins, appealing to emotion differently in various countries. In much of its communications, Michelin presents a child sitting happily—and presumably safely—inside a Michelin tire, a powerful call to the emotion of the buyer.[16] Michelin has long had a competitive focus in their communications. When the company entered Britain, it understood it

[15] Bibendum was introduced in 1898. Bibendum was launched in Italy in 1907 with the image of a hero from a novel, "at once conqueror and seducer." Sources: Michelin Web sites.

[16] Recent advertisements also have the Michelin baby dancing a hula-hoop with a Michelin tire.

needed to beat Dunlop to succeed in that marketplace, and its communications at the time reflected this competitive context.

Creating emotion in one-to-one communications, together with messages that appeal to both reason and demonstrate competitive advantage, is not easy. Few companies do this well. Some provide competitive information mostly with reasoned comparisons on their Web sites. Some include emotion. Continuing with the tire industry, Firestone recalled millions of tires on sport utility and other vehicles, responding to much emotion in the aftermath of accidents and consumer warnings.[17] Goodyear's Web site discusses aspects of the Firestone tire recall and the fact that Goodyear is replacing some of the recalled tires, balancing emotion and competitive advantage well. If Bridgestone-Firestone had an evident strategy for CRM and competitor management and the benefit of a customer database, it would have been better positioned to manage the recall of its tires and restore faith, trust and other equity in the Firestone brand. Without this, competitors had the opportunity to target Firestone like shooting fish in a barrel.

Oracle is locked in battle with a number of competitors, including PeopleSoft. Its CEO has been quoted as saying that Oracle's Larry Ellison runs a "sociopathic company" addicted to "lying."[18] Although repositioning the competition does not have to be civil, balanced communications should have more impact. Ellison, for his part, reportedly has said of Bill Gates that Microsoft "distributes complexity" in the form of the Windows operating system, while IBM has "130,000 consultants to help you put (a multiple vendor solution) together."[19] Oracle, by contrast, communicates, among other benefits, that it lacks complexity and is a comprehensive, single vendor solution.

Table 7-2 presents some suggestions for possible interaction tactics in support of competitor targeting and CRM. Consider how customers interact with your company, and compare each point of contact with that of targeted competitors, to the extent this is possible and reasonable. More generally, consider each area of interaction that the customer has, or could have, with the company, as illustrated by example in Figure 7-4. For each area, consider the nature of the interaction between your company and your priority customers. Also think about how competitors approach this area of interaction and, to the extent possible, experience and measure their performance in much the same way that you do for your own. If competitors generate more

[17] From the National Highway Traffic Safety Administration (NHTSA).

[18] *eCompany*, November, 2000, p. 178.

[19] *eCompany*, November, 2000, p. 174.

awareness than you do—and customers will advise here—consider how to outperform them in that dimension. For example, if Goodyear has higher awareness than say, Continental, and the six airships operated by Goodyear are seen by customers to be a major contributor to that awareness, what might Continental do to increase awareness with its most important customers? Goodyear's competitors could develop an economical approach to create awareness directly with its most important customers and prospects once it knows who they are, by name and address. They might even find a way to turn Goodyear's strengths against itself. For example, Goodyear's first dirigible exploded and the crew was lost; a number of the later craft also crashed for reasons that are not clear.

Beating competitors by outperforming them in terms of every type of interaction is hard indeed, yet this is vital if the company is to win. It starts with understanding how competitors perform in each area of interaction with your best customers. If you do not now measure most of the areas of interaction described in Figure 7-4, you may want to consider metrics to add to your customer information files. If you do not know the measurements for your own firm, you likely do not have data to compare to the competitors you wish to target, so these data will also need to be established in a focused benchmarking initiative.

Table 7-2: Test Your Own Interaction—Selected Considerations for Comparing Your Company with Competitors

- Most importantly, does your company interact with customers to learn more about them and their issues and their experience with your company and the targeted competitor, building this database over time? Does your company then act on the information to develop knowledge and insight? Does your company ask customers the same question twice? Hopefully it never does.
- How does your company communicate with its customers? Pretend you are your company's best customer. Interact with the company through its various points of access. Do the same as though you are your firm's worst customer. This time, you are focused not so much on access but on the actual connection, including the nature and quality of the interaction. In each case, try to learn about your company and products, and then purchase and/or return them. Do the following:

- Try to reach a few people by name by calling the main line. Is this person in a meeting, or is your call answered by voice mail or by someone who does not know where this person is? If you speak with the person, is he or she well informed and able to help as required? Ask for technical, operating or price information about your products.
- Call your switchboard at precisely the times that your company says it is open for business such as 8:00 a.m. and at 5:00 p.m. Is your call answered by voice mail, security personnel, someone who happens to be passing the telephone or a professional receptionist who takes a message?
- Complain loudly and unreasonably (as your firm's worst customer) to the main reception and customer service personnel,[20] and see how the call is handled. Do customer service employees listen to even bad customers and care about them, hard though some customers may make such a disposition. Do they refer to policies and procedures as their reasons for denying the customer, or do they have cogent explanations. Do they follow the process for managing the customers your firm values least.
- Use a stopwatch to time any delays in having the call answered or receiving a response with which you agree. Track the number of people to whom you are referred, noting any wrong advice or cool reception.
- Try returning a product or finding information to repair it, and see how easy or hard it is. Most companies have inadequate "reverse channels of distribution" that allow customers to return products and receive credit.

• Query how your organization handles complaints.
  - Does it actively encourage consumers, or does it explain away pesky consumers and their complaints, dismissing them as unreasonable rather than blaming the company and its products or processes?
  - Does the company log complaints and consider them as a useful source of new ideas? Does it know which complainers have used competitors? And what were their complaints with regard to interacting with competitors?
  - Does it have a toll-free inbound calling number or does it ask consumers to pay long-distance charges when complaining?
  - Try complaining about an invoice, especially by querying a minute amount, and see how the call is handled.

• As for strategies for customer access, do you have strategies and tactics for customer interaction according to your CRM plan?

[20] Some people take it a little far. One manager called his company, a marketer of pet food, and complained that the high ash content in the pet food had killed his cat. He said he was speaking from the lobby of the building and had brought the newly departed cat with him for the company to inspect.

Figure 7-4: Winning the Customer Interaction

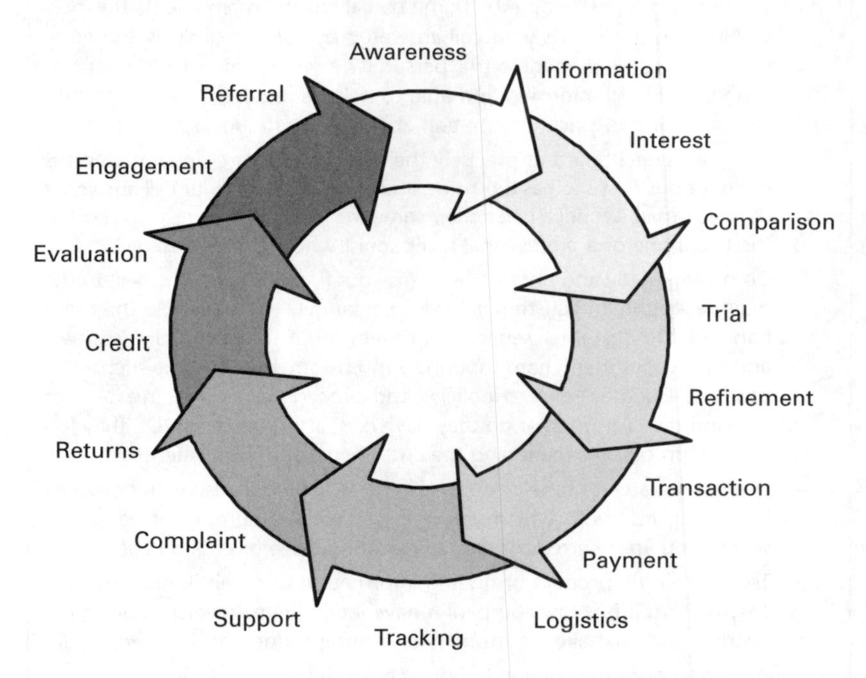

Transaction

Companies invest much time before they secure an opportunity to write a proposal or make a client or customer presentation. Then they make the presentation. Few vendors in business-to-business settings seem to have appreciated that their competitors sound just like them, with equally sophisticated presentations and similarly good reasons for buying from them. The customer sees a parade of suits and well-scrubbed people, some known, some anonymous. The challenge is to be known and to have won the transaction before ever presenting. It is hard for a company to outperform competitors at the transaction stage if it has not done likewise in the many areas of interaction that preceded the transaction such as those described in Figure 7-4.

In business-to-business competition, companies learn decision-making criteria and what they need to do to succeed. They assemble detailed proposals and make thorough presentations geared to winning the transaction. Yet, even in the most skilled companies, opportunities remain for improving the tactics of the transaction. In business-to-business companies, this can include training proposal writers and presenters, introducing competitive considerations, sowing doubt about the enemy, training customers in writing requests for proposals, making the vendor selection, and helping to write the actual terms of reference for the procurement. One professional services firm, after establishing the names of its competitors, lays land mines for them. Whenever possible, this firm presents first. It lays out the purchasing decision from the client's point of view, highlighting the kinds of issues to be aware of, that, not coincidentally, competitors may not be well placed to achieve. For example, knowing the competitor has recently been proposing the use of computer assisted telephone interviewing (CATI), you might say, "Our research approach calls for the use of personal interviews rather than telephone. We thought about the use of computer assisted telephone interviewing but dismissed this because it will not deliver the detail needed for this project, and it is an inappropriate way for your company to be interviewing senior executives." And when competitors present and tread into the arena prepared by you—bam!

In business-to-consumer companies, when it comes to the transaction, outperforming the competition includes making the company easier to do business with and creating more opportunities for nontraditional transactions. In retail, this can lead to improved store layouts and Web site designs that facilitate transactions. Home Depot moved its lumber department from the back of the store to the side, and cash registers were established for lumber purchases to make it easier for everyone to check out.[21] One retailer purportedly put its beer and diapers in proximity, ostensibly for the new father in a rush to purchase both. Amazon invented the "shopping basket" for its Web site, now widely copied on Internet e-tail sites. Some companies create new opportunities for transacting such as truck rentals and a wedding registry at Home Depot (yes, some people want to receive drills and saws as wedding gifts). The world is not short of ideas, and many of them can help a company outperform its competition when it is time for the customer to buy. But the company that manages only by idea will never take the series of linked steps needed to win.

And sometimes, the idea itself could benefit from a little more scrutiny. A hardware chain locked in battle with Home Depot aired a major media campaign inviting new customers to visit its stores with their Home Depot receipts to receive reduced prices on their purchases.

---

[21] Chris Roush, *Inside Home Depot: How One Company Revolutionized an Industry Through the Relentless Pursuit of Growth*. New York: McGraw Hill, 1999, p. 88.

The net effect was that customers bought at full price from Home Depot and then went to the competing chain to buy at a discounted price. This created temporary traffic and no guarantee that they would ever return. With competitors like this, Home Depot need not be praised too much for its performance.

However, some companies have succeeded in the face of the major chains such as Home Depot and Wal-Mart. What they have uniformly discovered is that they should not even try to compete with the majors as though they were the same size. Most customers expect smaller stores to charge more because they know that they have less scale economies. When customers shop at smaller stores, they expect better service and incentives for shopping there such as carrying their purchases to the car, friendly people, telephone ordering, on-time delivery and other services the big stores do not offer. Curry Hardware in Quincy, Massachusetts, competes directly and successfully with a nearby Home Depot. It is easy to do business with and visibly different from Home Depot, offering complimentary popcorn, for example. The Ace Hardware organization with which they are associated helps them keep prices within sight of the Atlanta-based giant, and Curry added staff to provide even better service rather than only trying to cut costs. With over 10,000 hardware products, it carries some specialty items its competitor does not. It caters to special orders. It knows its competitor well and has focused its business to compete. It understands it will not serve all customers for every transaction, yet its parking lot is mostly full.

The potential remains large indeed for companies to manage transactions using enterprise-wide e-business systems that allow internal and external customers to order over the Internet. Customers are never more satisfied than when they can serve themselves in about the same time as it takes to be served by others. After all, who do they blame for inaccuracy or if something they initiated does not work out? Self-service reduces costs for the company but, more importantly, helps it engage and keep satisfied customers. The company wishing to outperform competitors in this way need not be simply a large company with deep pockets.

For example, if the company uses certain computer applications such as the accounting and ERP systems, it can put relevant data on the Internet for customers to serve themselves with the information they need. These applications can often be linked to the main processes in the company, which also allows customers to monitor the status of orders, inventory and shipments, for example. They can also place their orders this way. Ask yourself, what would it take for customers to initiate their purchases on the Internet and for employees to use the Internet or intranet for most of their information and other needs such as scheduling training. Whenever you have people providing content, think about moving most of that to the Web. And when you have people facilitating a process such as order entry, ask why automation and the Internet have not eliminated some or all of the need for this type of employment. Now, if the company does not have many content providers and many process managers, this will be a different company indeed. The challenge is to get to that place before the competitors even understand that a destination such as this exists.

Customization

Customization is another key area in which to outperform targeted competitors. After achieving the transaction and even before, the company needs to create and keep individual customers economically with very specific and unique communications and solutions, including products and service. Doing this for all the customers the company wants is mass customization, which can be defined as the process of providing and supporting individually tailored goods and services, according to each customer's preferences with regard to form, time, place and price, and doing so in a profitable manner. Outperforming competitors in this arena means communicating with customers as individuals in a more relevant manner than competitors and then providing the customer with unique value before competitors do so, as well. Just as there is a cumulative effect that allows the company with more customer intelligence to be more relevant, the company that customizes first has an opportunity to prevail in the marketplace.

While mass customization is a key dimension of CRM,[22] it is an even more vital component of competitor targeting. Mass marketers have historically viewed mass customization as interesting in theory but too expensive to implement practically, particularly if a plant was to be radically overhauled. Until recently, this was the case for many companies. Now the words mass customization are no longer paradoxical. Mass customization is now practical as a result of declining costs of technology, and increasing flexibility of business processes. These create the potential to communicate individually and interactively with customers. Mass customization may have been an option to some

[22] An increasing number of books consider mass customization. The core concepts are presented in B. Joseph Pine, *Mass Customization: The New Frontier in Business Competition*. Boston: Harvard Business School Press, 1993. My earlier book, *Relationship Marketing*, also discussed this.

companies just a short time ago. Now, few companies can afford to cater to all customers equally. After all, this rewards the worst customers and penalizes the best, creating precisely the opposite impact of what the company wants.

Adoption of technology, company-wide and throughout the value chain, creates an opportunity for mass customization as never before. Now, all the marketing flows of the company can be engineered to create the unique value expected by individual consumers. Marketing flows include the flow of goods through distribution channels to the end customer as well as flows historically associated with the presales, during sale, and aftersale components of marketing:

- Presales consist of individualized communications, advertising and promotion to the end customer (consumer "pull") and initiatives with the intermediary to provide unique product and wrap the services around the product that customers want. The tactical and real-time opportunities here include development of a communications plan for each customer, blending a combination of print, telephone, e-mail and personal calls into a coherent campaign for every customer. This is quite feasible and is being done by a number of companies, from the financial services industry to hardware retailing and from pharmaceuticals to alcoholic beverages.
- During the sale include on-the-spot unexpected offers, financing, just-in-time training and computer-assisted customer management for up-selling, add-on selling, selling substitutes or cross-selling. This applies to the issue of outperforming competitors in the transaction, discussed above.
- Aftersales including warranty and service support, customer recognition, reverse-distribution channels (for any product that needs to be returned) and activities geared to building value as individual customers would expect.

While the concept of mass customization is not an option, the degree to which it is implemented is the stuff of which competitive advantage is made. The practical reality is that few firms can afford to implement mass customization in all dimensions for all customers. IBM cannot afford to custom-design every chip to the unique performance preferences of the customer. Buick might say, "Can we build one for you?" but if you asked for a car with more than "usual" uniqueness with, say, the front end of the LeSabre joined to the back end of a Regal, the company might not know whether to treat your comments as serious. Full compliance with mass customization would be absurdly expensive for most companies and would result in products being priced beyond the reach of customers. The alternative, as some companies might see it, is to think in terms of providing customers with an expanded array of choices they consider to have value without increasing inventory or otherwise adding costs for which customers do not wish to pay.

Mass customization need not mean unit-of-one production but modularity such as by sharing, reusing, swapping, sectioning or transforming specific components that make up the modules. Levis produces Personal Pair made-to-fit jeans that are assembled from stock clothing modules. Eyeglass maker Morrison International fits premolded lenses into snap-together frames that adjust to fit any face. By rotating the lenses to any of 180 positions in the frame, 26,000 prescriptions can be filled using a stock of just 152 lenses.[23] Catering to a segment of one means having the ability to mass customize, but to have the opportunity to mass customize, the company needs to achieve its mass customization potential before the competitors it wishes to beat does, and to better effect. Among other aspects of your intelligence effort, buy from the competitors to understand what they offer and whether or how they mass customize. As mentioned, mass customization is not an option in an era in which technology makes it possible and affordable, and consumers want what *they* want, not necessarily what you make today.

It is not easy for companies to mass customize when their history lies elsewhere. At its core, Ford has mass production, IBM has a sales culture and Procter and Gamble has market-segment-driven marketing and advertising. Before companies fully adopt mass customization, they will need to transcend aspects of their history. This will prove a challenging journey, as Ford found out when restructuring and aligning its dealer channel, possibly as part of its CRM strategy. The good news is that it is likely no easier for you to adopt mass customization as it is for the competitors you want to beat. The bad news is that they may already be ahead of you on this road.

Blocking Competitors Out

The company that is able to consistently outperform competitors should have the potential to go to the next stage and block them from an account or keep them out of the decision set in the mind of the individual customer. Whether or not your company is able to block competitors depends in large measure on relationships and customer

[23] Amy Borrus, "Eyeglasses for the Masses," *BusinessWeek*, November 20, 1995.

share. If your position with customers is strong and if your share is high—say twice the customer share of the next most important company—you have opportunities to further grow customer share tactically and in real time, leading to customer monopolies over time. You can erect barriers that will make it hard for competitors to stay in the account such as long-term contracts, outsourced operations, volume discounts, technology integration and joint ventures.

The following ways to block competitors out will be discussed next:

- Share of Customer Communications
- Listening
- Empathy
- Organizational Listening
- Blocking Access
- Blocking Their Strategic Requirements

Share of Customer Communications

Customer share affects share of customer communications because customers are more receptive to granting access to their most important suppliers. This access can increase the company's share of customer communications.[24] In turn, the increased share of communications, when combined with an ability to listen, can help the company to develop customer knowledge, understanding, insight and an ability to predict what the customer needs next and what the competitors will do to address this requirement. Using this information well for customization and to communicate and create new customer value can influence the customer and further develop trust-based relationships. The customer, in essence, has been rewarded for granting your company preferred access and communications, perhaps even telling you some things about the competitors that others might not. The customer bond deepens, and competitors are progressively marginalized. Helping the customer in this way can now lead to even more customer share in the cyclical process described in Figure 7-5.

[24] Share of customer communications is simply the volume of communications between your company and the customer's, divided by all communications between the customer and competing suppliers. This is somewhat analogous to "share of voice," which applied to mass communications, except that share of voice was measured using media spending while share of customer communications is determined more qualitatively, based on best assessments of customer "face time" (personal or nonpersonal—such as e-mail) and media impressions.

Figure 7-5: Share of Customer and Share of Customer Communications

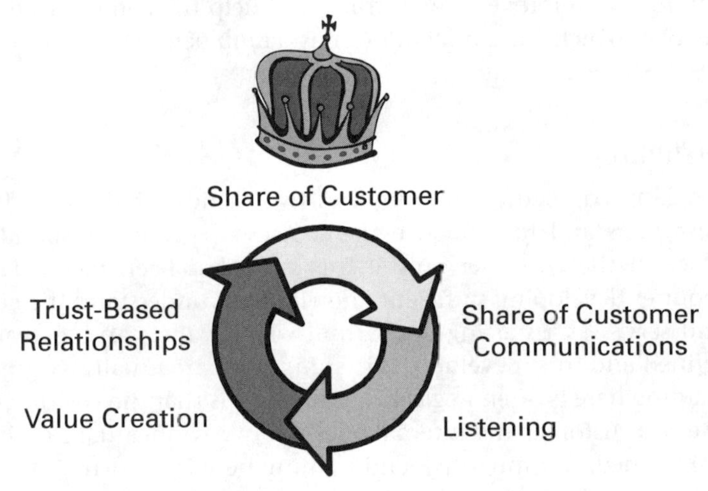

Consider whether your customer communications presently develops as much understanding as it might and whether any knowledge, once gained, remains in the minds of the listener or becomes accessible to all those in your company who need to know. One way for high customer share companies to block competitors from chosen customers is to give customers less reason to consider the other firm as a potential supplier. At every opportunity, learn about customers. Even more importantly, learn about your customers' customers. Position your company to win every important procurement that affects your customer's future. Winning these purchases will, over time, block out the competition.

The tactics for achieving this are many and varied, and they obviously differ significantly between business-to-business and business-to-consumer marketplaces. Early warning capabilities are important here. Some firms hire the employees of their customers and encourage some among their employees to join with preferred customers, in both cases leading to better communications and competitor insight. More generally, the company that is well bonded with its core customers, even if only with selected stakeholders, can be better informed than the competition, better able to intervene before competitors can address an opportunity. Whether the company is categorized as business-to-business or business-to-consumer, competitive intelligence systems can further improve early warning and help the company erect barriers over which the competition must climb before they can influence the customer.

Listening

Blocking competitors out requires two tactical abilities: to listen to customers and to influence them. A company can respond to the voice of the customer only if this voice has been heard. Listening requires developing sufficient knowledge to understand the customer and serves as a starting point from which value can be created and refined and trust developed. Listening skills are usually assumed, and training here is often neglected. The result is that the customer—both the end customer and internal ones—may go unheard. Listening skills are learned, not inherited, and training here is needed. Active listening plays a key role and involves paying very close attention to the spoken and implicit communications of the sender and understanding the history of the communications, the content of what is said and the context, both personal and corporate. Additionally, active listening requires an understanding of the range of decisions that customers are considering and how they view specific options. Opportunities for value creation should be identified and restated to confirm that you have received what was sent, to name just a few areas in which listening in new ways can be beneficial. Without active listening, customer knowledge and insight will not increase, new value will not be created to the extent it might and trust-based relationships will remain elusive. And without trust-based relationships, share of customer will not increase and may, in fact, deteriorate.

Empathy

Some personal attributes can be taught, others are innate and the wisdom of leaders when managing people is often in telling the two apart. While listening skills might be taught, the empathy on which active listening depends seems much deeper-seated. An executive with a major European car company talks derisively of his well-heeled but demanding customers. He says many of them, when bringing their car in for servicing, ask, “Do you know how much I paid for this car?” They all receive his sardonic reply, “As much as all our other customers.” And they also obtain service to match the comment. Do your customers feel well heard? Did someone say, “Pardon me?”

Organizational Listening

Customers want more than a salesperson who is a good listener. They want *organizations* that listen well. Of course, the listening company needs employees who are able to listen, effective technologies that interact and can learn, processes that engage customers uniquely and enough data to predict needs and behaviors. More than this, the listening organization also requires a supportive culture, senior managers who lead by example and compensation systems that reward aspects of listening such as competitive intelligence submitted from the field.

Blocking Access

It is hard or impossible to deny competitors any and all access to your cherished customers. There are so many media properties and channels to the minds of customers that complete denial of access is a virtual impossibility. This is not to say that a company cannot substantially influence or better manage the primary media channels or own the best properties such as the best shows on which to advertise, best placements of advertisements in print media, best banners on high traffic Web sites and best outdoor advertising locations. Blocking competitors from the best channels and properties raises their costs for customer access and reduces the effectiveness of their media buying. Review your media plans, and ask your agency for advice regarding blocking competitors so that you can relegate them to those bad places no one visits.

In any event, blocking competitors out completely may be less important than ensuring that your customers shut their mental doors to the competitors. This is done by repositioning them negatively but delicately in the minds of customers.

Blocking Their Strategic Requirements

Blocking competitors is not confined just to customers, important though this may be. In the video games marketplace, for example, content is king. The major games companies such as Sega, Sony and Nintendo, know this well, and some apparently strive to lock in the best content developers and block them from producing independently. Some firms have tried to ensure that software developers who produce for their systems are bound with licensing agreements that state that the game cartridge will be made by the hardware company. Independent software publishers cannot readily self-publish because some hardware companies have security features that defeat unauthorized software titles from running on their machines. The hardware companies are working hard to preserve their brands, focus on the performance of next generation hardware platforms and find the killer apps—games or characters like Donkey Kong, Sonic and Mario—they hope will cause a stampede for their products. Perhaps this focus on characters and technology has limited any interest in relationship marketing. Hardware companies do not know their consumers by name, do not understand what hardware and software titles they have and do not influence individuals to stay within the franchise rather than defect to that new system the competitor just launched. There seems to be an opportunity here for a company to beat a competitor by winning one customer at a time.

Shut Competitors Down

If a company has consistently outperformed the competitor in the minds of its most valued customers, and if the firm has also done all it can to block the competitor out of the account and mind of the customer, perhaps the competitor is ready for the *coup de grâce*—to be shut down. Some companies adopt a two-pronged strategy to snuff out a competitor. They pursue the competitor's most profitable customers and win them over, almost at any cost. Then, after they have inflicted pain, they offer to acquire the wounded competitor. Game over.

The market share leader has a particular responsibility when it comes to shutting competitors down. That leader is responsible for industry profitability and since that is closely connected with industry capacity, the share leader should acquire and retire capacity, especially in mature markets. This has been possible for many decades. Years ago, in 1985, Mitch Kapor demonstrated how this is done when his Lotus company acquired Visicalc and shut it down, overnight making Lotus 1-2-3 the standard in spreadsheets, at least for a while.[25]

The advent of the Internet, new entrants, the development of substitutes and the globalization of commerce makes capacity management challenging and, in some cases, prohibitively expensive and even futile. In some cases, but not all. Goodyear could have acquired and retired Firestone's assets when the latter was looking to exit the tire manufacturing business. Goodyear chose to not do so. Bridgestone, a Japanese company wanting to expand in the US, purchased Firestone's assets, starting with the LaVergne, Tennessee truck tire plant in 1983 and ending with the purchase of the entire company in 1988. Acquisition proved to be a less expensive way for

[25] Microsoft wanted to acquire Lotus in 1984, but instead developed Excel, which became the main spreadsheet program on personal computers. IBM's acquisition of Lotus did not aid Lotus 1-2-3 to regain its leadership position.

Bridgestone to produce for the North American market than building new capacity.[26] And with the acquisition, Bridgestone[27] also obtained the eighty-eight-year-old brand established by Harvey Firestone and customer relationships such as that with Ford that dated to 1906, when Ford first mass-produced cars.[28] By acquiring and consolidating Firestone, Goodyear had the opportunity to lessen competition and further deepen its relationships with key accounts such as Ford. By not doing so, Ford opened the door to a competitor. Goodyear may have found it less costly to buy Firestone than spending heavily to beat this newly capitalized company in the marketplace.

There are other approaches to shutting down a competitor than acquiring it with or without the wooing of its most profitable customers, as mentioned. The following are selected other ways that could lead to the competitor's demise:

- Manage Their Stakeholder Relationships
- Cut Their Supply Lines
- Manage Politicians and the Regulatory Process
- Establish a Flanker Brand or Company
- Turn the Competitors' Strengths Against Themselves
- Harass with Guerrilla Maneuvers

Manage Their Stakeholder Relationships

Like any organization, the competitor exists because stakeholders want it to. Which are their most influential stakeholders? On who do they most depend? Can these stakeholders be brought over to support your company preferentially? For example, in the auto industry, labor unions still wield considerable power. A company that is struck by labor will certainly face financial hardship. Labor unions tend to focus their attention on just one company at a time, using the gains there as a pattern for agreements with others. Generally, labor unions tend to choose one of the Big Three US nameplate companies as a target, but could they be encouraged to unionize elsewhere, for example? Could one of the Big Three direct intelligence to labor so they have complete information when they choose their next target? Could labor be guided to choose another among the Big Three as a target?

---

[26] Bridgestone had previously set up a sales subsidiary in California—in 1967. The company subsequently built tire plants, such as in Warren County, Tennessee, in 1990.

[27] Shojiro Ishibashi founded Bridgestone in 1921. Ishibashi translates into English as "stone bridge." He reversed the two words to make it sound more like Firestone.

[28] That relationship was cemented by marriages between Firestones and Fords. In 2001, the companies had a major and perhaps irreparable falling out over tires on Ford Explorers.

Venture capitalists and bankers who want to extricate themselves from their investments or loans can also represent areas of opportunity for the company wanting to manage stakeholders to advantage. Equity and financial instruments can be obtained in a manner that allows a company to enter and perhaps control the competitor through a back door.

Cut Their Supply Lines

Armies have been defeated because their vital lines of supply were choked off. They can be in serious trouble if they do not receive the replacement troops, equipment and armaments, fuel, ammunition, medical supplies, food and water needed to keep the military machine progressing. In the World War II, the D-Day invasion succeeded largely because Allied air forces destroyed bridges over the River Seine and the Loire, which affected supply lines and the ability of German reserves to join the battle quickly.

In business, companies are often dependent upon a few key suppliers, which may operate at a physical, financial and emotional distance from their customers. This creates a point of vulnerability. What would happen to the manufacturers of personal computers if they could not obtain the chips they need to power their machines? What if a major customer for chips such as IBM or Dell were to impact the company's lines of supply, perhaps resulting in late delivery, limited numbers or increased costs of new chips to the compatibles?

We conducted relationship research on behalf of a computer company wanting to develop even closer ties to the major chip and component manufacturers. Our research assessed the current state of relationships and explored opportunities for the client to deepen bonding that would lead to earlier and more complete involvement in new developments. Our client wanted to be in a position to be first to market and to obtain preferred access to strategic parts. This company understood that winning meant first gaining advantage upstream in the value chain.

Companies have an opportunity to leverage their supplier relationships in many areas—from intelligence on competitor's initiatives to preferred product access in times of shortage or strike to lower prices or better terms to joint new product development.

Manage Politicians and the Regulatory Process

In Chapter 6, we discussed managing politicians and regulators to help your company gain competitive advantage. We emphasize here that companies that manage regulators better than competitors have the potential to develop approved near-monopolies or be better prepared to compete when industries are reregulated or deregulated. Some of the world's great fortunes have been amassed by people close to power and best able to benefit from that knowledge. For example, a media tycoon who went to school with future politicians and statesmen was apparently able to use that relationship in later years to repeatedly advance the interests of his company. Some might say his entire firm was built on better management of the regulatory process than his competitors'. When regulators have the power to make decisions that may increase the costs of a company or an industry or when they can award licenses or grant other preferential treatment, the opportunity is there to treat the regulator as your most important ally and seek to manage the process more adeptly than competitors do, in your exclusive interest. In doing this well, the potential exists for an industry sector to defeat another and for a company to substantially weaken and even close competitors.

Establish a Flanker Brand or Company

Earlier in this chapter, we discussed how attacking yourself need not be detrimental but an approach to make the company better. It can also help to shut competitors down.

Vodka is vodka, I am told. It is produced in a similar manner and all apparently have much the same chemical properties. That consumers do not think all vodka is equal is high testimony to Madison Avenue. Some years ago, a new brand with a Russian-sounding name was introduced to consumers with an extensive advertising budget to compete directly against the premium vodka brand. The communications included reference to the limited difference between vodkas, threatening the leader's positioning and consumer trust. The new entrant was priced substantially below the premium brand. The leading company faced a dilemma. Should it reduce prices to match the new entrant? Should it introduce another product to counterattack? The leader chose the latter approach and launched its own new brand, a so-called flanker brand. It priced the product even below the new entrant. It also chose a Russian-sounding name. And it raised the price of its premium brand to accentuate perceived quality and other differences. Bracketed by a consumer perception of quality at one end and by a lower-priced competitor at the other, the new entrant folded.

Flanker brands and companies have opportunities to destabilize the competition because they can do things the core company cannot.

For example, if the premium brand discussed above reduced its price by 10 percent, then it would lose one-tenth of its revenues immediately if its volume remained the same. But the flanker brand, with a price even 20 percent below the leader, would not be foregoing the same amount of lost revenues. Firstly, the flanker brand had no revenues, so a low price did not discount a large volume base nor did it put the core brand's equity at risk by repositioning it. Secondly, volume for the flanker brand would come from a number of competitors with low prices, more so than the company's premium brand, which reduced cannibalization. Thirdly, by raising the price on the leading product, there was no erosion of company profitability. If there is a radical idea you think could weaken the competitor, but you do not wish to use your firm's equity in support of that idea, consider using a flanker brand or even another company.

Turn the Competitors' Strengths Against Themselves

The competitors' strengths can be used against themselves. Within greatness are also the seeds of destruction. For example, you could target a competitor in an area in which they are strong, and their very strength could be a problem for them. Most companies depend on profitable participation in some marketplaces or with specific customers to build their businesses elsewhere. If your company is able to weaken the competitor there, then they will be less a threat elsewhere. Fuji, an imaging and film company, is based in Japan, while its main competitor, Eastman Kodak, hails from Rochester, NY. When Fuji launched in the US and expanded its market position, Kodak grew concerned about the trends. Firstly, at the time, Fuji's films had higher levels of saturated colors. Although less lifelike, some consumers preferred this. Kodak offered a new range of film with more vibrant colors, but still Fuji increased its market presence, often with lower prices. For decades, the war between the two companies was fought in the US and in other countries. All the while, Fuji benefited from a dominant position in its home market. This was the source of Fuji's financial strength. If Kodak was to win globally, it had to win in Japan, so the company launched there. If Kodak should succeed in dominating the Japanese imaging marketplace, it may also succeed in crushing Fuji, but it does not actually need to dominate the Japanese market to win. It just needs to make the marketplace less profitable for Fuji, and that is much easier to do.

Whatever Kodak does, it had better hurry while there is a film market. Digital photography and companies such as Sony are now the real competition for Kodak. Even though Kodak was well placed to win in digital decades ago, it just could not bring itself to focus[29] on a competitive technology when it was so successful with standard imaging chemicals and films. This, then, was the strength that Kodak had that did not hold back competitors in the digital arena. Kodak would simply not move too far and too fast from its core. Before too long, its strength would be the source of its weakness.

What is the main strength of the competitors you must beat if you are to win with the customers you value most? If they are larger than you, are they also less flexible and more bureaucratic? If they are smaller than you, do they have the resources to do what they promise? Will they be there for the customer tomorrow? Will they protect the customer's investment? Or will buying a less expensive product or service from this competitor be the most expensive decision the customer ever made if they have to find a new supplier because this one was sold or went out of business?

Harass with Guerrilla Maneuvers

We discussed guerrilla strategies earlier in this chapter, but they are particularly relevant in blocking competitors out. Harassing the competitor might cause them sleepless nights and distract them from the more important war they are fighting. Harassment is a tactic that can weaken the enemy if actions are repeated and pursued vigorously such as in the courts regardless of the foundation of the claim in law. This harassment can tie up the competitor's executives and waste their managerial time and talent and sometimes buy time for a competitive response. One technology firm uses an internal legal counsel as a "pit bull" to bludgeon competitors. More generally, harassment should seek to force the competitor to divert and/or waste resources to enable you to gain a foothold or expand your market or customer position. Guerrilla approaches should be limited in scope and enable rapid withdrawal without much cost.

Beating a targeted competitor can be as much about making your company better as making the competitor worse. The key is to have each customer see that there is a difference between your company and the competitor you have targeted. As discussed in the preceding chapter, this can be accomplished strategically such as by ensuring

[29] No pun intended.

that the company wins in respect of the key success factors of tomorrow's industry. In this chapter, we have reviewed how this can also be achieved tactically and in real time such as by repositioning the competitor and weakening it to make it less of a threat overall and in specific accounts. In the following chapter, we provide another option for dealing with selected competitors. We review collaborating with competitors because there are some situations in which beating competitors or making them into losers may not accomplish your business objectives. Working effectively with selected complementary competitors—complementors—may be a preferred approach.

CHAPTER 8

Competition and Collaboration

"Trusting no man as his friend, he could not recognize his enemy when the latter actually appeared."[1]

—Nathaniel Hawthorne

Thus far, we have discussed how to focus on specific competitors while developing relationships with individual customers. We have considered key issues associated with competing strategically, tactically and in real time. The company that does these well has an opportunity to succeed with the customers it values most and increase its share of customer. But the company that wants the gains to endure will need to do more. It will need to develop a culture that is both oriented to individual customers and driven by specific competitors. It will need to define what a "competitor" is and consider whether all competitors are equal. It should evaluate whether it is better to collaborate with some competitors than to beat them, and when it should do so. Many books have paid attention to customer orientation. Here, we discuss aspects of collaboration in the context of competition in the further interests of building a company focused on individual customers and driven by specific competitors.

---

[1] Nathaniel Hawthorne, *The Scarlet Letter & Rappaccini's Daughter – The Leech and His Patient,* 1850.

From Conflict to Collaboration[2]

A zero-sum game is one in which a gain for one participant means a matching loss for the other. What one wins, another loses. Thus far, we have discussed beating a targeted competitor as a sort of zero-sum game and have described strategies and tactics for triumphing at their expense. But what if one could collaborate with competitors? One can still cooperate with competitors within a zero-sum game such as working together to displace another firm or firms. But, when collaboration is intended to create new customer value, one could increase the size of the pie and share the resulting rewards, thereby participating in what is called a non-zero-sum game. This would give mutual benefits to the collaborators and offers another perspective on competition: in some cases, collaboration may be preferable to beating selected competitors outright.

The essence of any relationship—business or personal, with customers and indeed with competitors—depends on collaboration. Collaboration might be thought of as the ability of more than one person or organization to continuously create new value for all participants in the relationship. Some companies need to overcome their propensity for conflict before building a collaborative environment and achieving the potential of relationship marketing and other business strategies.

Conflict and Competition

Before reviewing collaboration, we consider the opposite—conflict and competition—because issues are often illuminated when one looks at them in reverse. How, then, can conflict and competition shed light on collaboration? Why is it that people and organizations pursue or accept a path of collision? What is the state of mind or nature that drives this? Is it best to align, limit or focus conflict to gain advantage, or is collaboration better?

Intense conflict can arise when more than one entity wants a disproportionate share of scarce resources such as the most profit from the value chain, the best customers, smartest minds, more raw materials and extra capital. Pursuit of limited resources is one way to think about the company and how it competes to build its profit. In Chapter 2, we made reference to Michael Porter's Five Forces as a basis for understanding industry profitability and improving a company's

[2] This section draws upon an article I wrote, "Customer Relationship Management: Conflict to Collaboration," *Ivey Business Journal*, May/June 2001, pp. 9-11.

performance. Porter's approach served companies well in an era when marketing was a zero-sum game. Now, marketing is more concerned with the creation of new, customer-specific value rather than in just shifting market share to the company's advantage. In the era of relationship marketing and customer-centric business models, Porter's methods do not serve the company sufficiently because they do not talk to the issue of individual customer relationships and the resulting competitive advantage.

Rather than the macro view adopted by Porter, the relationship marketer focuses on a more micro perspective. Here, the pursuit of profit and competitive advantage starts with internal considerations that affect the company's ability to formulate a comprehensive and practical relationship marketing strategy. They include the following:

- *A company's identity and self-perceptions*—These perceptions form the core of its identity and have much to do with a company's ability to form enduring customer bonds.
- *The history of the company's evolution and its ability to recreate itself as it adapts to new challenges*—In essence, a company triumphs over behaviors learned in the past. A company that knows how to compete does not always know how to collaborate and relate. The reverse can also be true.
- *What companies think competitors, customers, and stakeholders are*—How do companies view the core identities of other firms and their direction and drivers? Some companies rationalize their approaches to winning on the basis of the nature of competition in the marketplace.
- *What companies want to become and why they need to change*—Vision is an often-used but important word for companies wanting to capture the potential of CRM and describe the role of collaboration in achieving the future state.

Identity

Strategic leaders have often asked, "What business are we in?" and "What are our core capabilities?" to clarify the company's identity. These are good questions, but identity runs deeper. Identity is how the company thinks of itself, how it communicates what it thinks and how it allows its competitors to position or reposition it. Identity is "mental labeling" or a self-perception of a company's position. When the label is stable, the company may not be able to change much if it cannot first shift its self-image. For example, relationship marketing strategically implies that companies compete on scope rather than on scale. This means companies provide what each customer wants rather than simply what companies make. If a firm's identity is fixed such as, "We are a developer of horizontal application software," then to become a "provider of integrated solutions" might be harder than it seems.

Change

The ability of a company to change depends on many things, but none more than its ability to triumph over the past. Companies, like people, retain memories of managing or coping with conflict as they achieved their success, and they tend to repeat these learned behaviors, which, for some, makes it difficult to adopt a collaborative business model. One company, rescued from bankruptcy some years ago, cannot overcome the anchor of its past. It remembers too well how to get out of bankruptcy such as how to fight its creditors—how to make others "take a haircut," as one board member is fond of saying. As a result, its organizational memory and past has become its future, and it cannot grow from operations.

Character helps overcome the past. Before elected as president in 1860, Abraham Lincoln's life included much failure. In 1832, he lost his job and was beaten in an election for the Illinois state legislature. His business failed a year later. He had a nervous breakdown in 1836. He was defeated for speaker in the state legislature, beaten in his nomination for congress and, although elected to congress in 1846, lost the renomination two years later. He was rejected for even low-level jobs, then again lost in his bids for the US Senate and to become vice president. Somehow, each time, he was able to shake off the past and focus on the future, determine what he needed to learn and change about himself, develop new plans and ensure that his successes overcame his setbacks. Character, discipline and integrity can help organizations triumph over the past and create an environment in which collaboration is possible. Without traits such as these in company leaders and the organizational culture, the company cannot easily escape the orbit into which its history has placed it.

Companies can compete by collaborating in this counterintuitive world, but this must flow from an altered perspective on the nature of the company and the role of the people in it. The first to see the reason of this counterintuition should be the CEO.

Perception of Others

A company's view of other organizations can be as important as its own self-image. Competition between companies arises when leaders perceive that they are in a business game which, if not zero-sum, is not far removed. For example, Ray Kroc, McDonalds' prime mover, reportedly (and rather unfortunately, given the industry) said, in reference to competitors, "This is rat eat rat, dog eat dog. I'll kill 'em, and I'm going to kill 'em before they kill me."[3] More generally, a company that focuses only on taking what another company has does not put itself in a position to create new value. For example, the thinking here goes, "Sales that go to the competitor will not come to us." Similarly, profits that our dealers, distributors and suppliers obtain in our value chain are profits that could have been ours." In much the same way, companies often seek to claim a disproportionate share of scarce raw materials, bright new recruits, patents, regulatory support, investor interest, customer engagement and so on without considering if there are collaborative means to achieve these ends better.

The leader who believes his or her company is one thing—and labels it in that way—and other companies are something else, has set the stage for combat. If you think another organization—whether competitor or stakeholder—is different from yours, collaboration will not come easy. Peer into Coca-Cola and Pepsi Cola, and you will find companies in which the perception of difference is deeply entrenched. Talk with some companies and their channel partners, franchisers and franchisees, and there are often similar perceptions of difference that precedes conflict. Companies often talk of their channel partners in terms such as "we" and "they," with the implication that "we" are right and "they" are not. Collaboration cannot easily flourish from this root.

Vision

A company must obviously have a view of the future and its position there. More than this, though, the firm should bring the future perspective into the present. That is, in addition to having a vision for the industry and the company's role in the future, there should be clear reasons to change. These reasons could include the rewards for vision attainment or threats if it is not achieved. If companies have not achieved the potential of CRM, perhaps they did not set their

[3] As reported by Jack Mingo, *How the Cadillac Got Its Fins and Other Tales From the Annals of Busines and Marketing*, New York, Harper Business, 1994, p.65.

organizations on the right path at the outset by describing a CRM vision and strategy and identifying the benefits of changing from the current state. CRM requires entirely new computing environments, production and other processes, success measures and cultures, among much else. As the amount of change is significant, CRM's benefits or the risks of not implementing should be generally perceived to be large, as well. Without this clear assessment, companies may commit themselves more timidly to the future state of CRM than their competitors, or they might invest more in CRM than prudence suggests.

Collaboration and Innovation

Now we return to the first-mentioned comment about competing for scarce resources. In previous eras, competition was about market share and winning the battle to sell what you make. In the era of CRM, competition is about customer share and winning the battle for each customer's mind and wallet. In this context, creating new, customer-specific value is more important than anything else. CRM requires innovation.

Innovation may change the nature of competition and stakeholder relationships entirely. Bill Lear, founder of the Learjet, and inventor extraordinaire,[4] had different stakeholders and eventually different competitors for each invention. A changing stakeholder and competitive landscape is characteristic of other first-to-market, multiple product companies such as Sony, Microsoft and Motorola. In companies like these, the focus has often been first on products and technology. Today's CRM firm innovates first by collaborating. This should also change how a company competes by doing the following:

- Unshackle the company from its past to address future opportunities. The company may need to change its accounting practices when these hinder change. For example, some firms require earnouts from historical investments or do not fully account for real rates of product or technology substitution and replacement.
- Develop a CRM vision and strategy that balances attention to the creation of strategic capabilities with the development of marketing strategy.
- Focus on process innovation for customer life cycle management, including collaboration throughout the value chain.

---

[4] Bill Lear was the inventor of the car radio, autopilot, eight-track tape player and held about 150 patents. This creativity was not confined to his inventions. He named his daughter Chanda.

- Pay attention to the strategies for competing on scope rather than scale.
- Provide the leadership to develop internal integrity, consistency and trust-based relationships with internal and external stakeholders alike.

Collaboration, like trust, underpins CRM, so it is also a precursor for the success of any business focused on relationships.

How to Choose Collaborators

All Competitors Are Not Equal

As has been noted, competitors, like customers, are not equally good or bad; they are individual entities and merit singular attention. Thus, a bad competitor has attributes that detract from creating new customer and shareholder value, but it need not be just another company that also seeks to serve the customers you value most. A bad competitor, seen more generally, could be anything or anyone that holds your company back from its future state. As Joseph Heller wrote, "The enemy... is anybody who's going to get you killed, no matter which side he's on."[5] Although their intentions are probably otherwise, you could get killed by suppliers, employees, leaders or customers. Watch out for the following:

- a supplier, supply chain or technology that limits your ability to cater to individual markets
- an employee unwilling to accommodate change
- a leader who bases decisions on what used to work
- a customer who accepts or insists upon the status quo

Important though they may be, these are barriers to competing well and not the subject of our focus in this chapter. We continue to see a competitor as a company that customers consider a substitute by winning the customers' scarce resources such as expenditures, time, access to its people, connection to its technology and the opportunity to plan with it.

Good Competitors

A good competitor is one that has the potential to help your company create and achieve its destiny and unlock value for shareholders. A

[5] Joseph Heller, *Catch-22*, 1962; republished New York: Scribner, 1996.

good competitor need not be accepting of the status quo or of its role in your industry, but through its insight, focus and aggression, might actually illuminate the future and incidentally jog your company. More typically and paradoxically, companies label a competitor bad if it is so good at what it does that it engenders fear. The temptation is to see the success of others as a threat to your own existence, and, as such, define the successful company as the target. This knee-jerk reaction is the historical way many companies see competitors, wanting to beat the most threatening among them. This may be appropriate, especially in the near term and for tactical reasons, but this view might be the very opposite of what your shareholders need in the longer term. In the success of others, there is not only an opportunity to learn and emulate or become even better, but also the potential to win them over and collaborate on the next opportunity. High-performing competitors provide more than a basis for learning and improvement. Good competitors, well managed, can provide shareholder value that your company may not be able to achieve independently.

Bad Competitors

It is becoming clearer that innovative companies are also collaborative ones so it is rare for the command-and-control management style of decades past to also result in competitive success. Today, competitors can be won over if they perceive their objectives will be better met by aligning with your company than with beating you. It thus may be better to define a bad competitor as one that not only destroys shareholder value in the present but also limits what is *potentially* achievable in the future. In this, a bad competitor is one without vision, without an ability to rise above itself, one that wants to control what it can. A bad competitor focuses more on yesterday and today than on tomorrow, more on selling than on creating. A bad competitor seeks no breakthroughs and resists change. A bad competitor operates from the inside out and is closed in terms of technology, process and listening. In short, a bad competitor is like many companies.

It seems obvious that bad competitors would eventually cease to exist by not adapting to the future. Yet many bad companies continue to prosper for now, rewarded by customers with low expectations, sustained by inertia and tolerated and not targeted by their competitors.

Competitors Can Create Shareholder Value

While all competitors inherently have the potential to detract from the shareholder value that is achievable by your company, some also have the ability to add shareholder value. For example, by collaborating in a vertical market portal—such as the Covisint example noted earlier in the book—your company and selected other competitors might be able to reduce supply chain costs and increase customer orders, with potential benefits to all. Some competitors—by their culture, technology, market or customer position or their leadership—will not wish to collaborate with your company, perhaps remaining as targets for you to destroy. On the other hand, when competitors offer your company a new or complementary way to achieve its vision and deliver the value shareholders expect, they could merit consideration as candidates for collaboration. Some competitors distinguish themselves as collaborators by being focused on primary demand development and increasing the size of the pie, whether by customer or by market.

Figure 8-1: Competitors as Targets or Collaborators

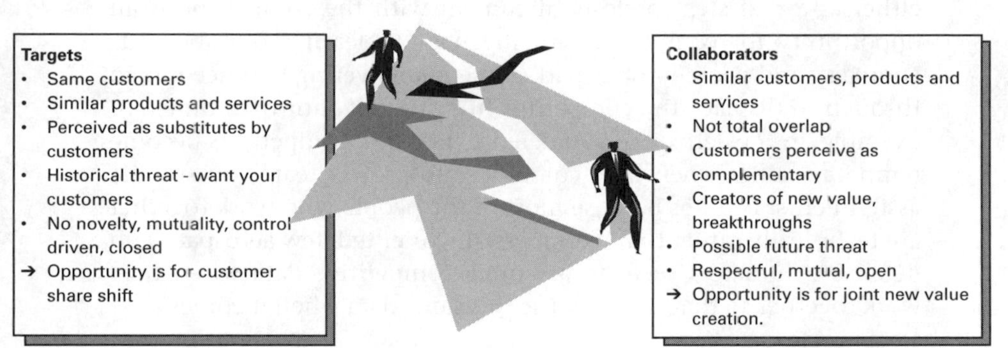

Choosing Collaborators

Which competitors merit collaboration, and which should remain pariahs until you defeat them? Four suggestions will help you to discriminate among competitors and find those with which to collaborate:

1. Your Customer Tells You
2. Your Strategy Dictates
3. Technology Makes It Possible
4. Collaborating Builds Customer Share

Your Customer Tells You

If your customer invites you to cooperate with selected competitors take this as a requirement rather than a suggestion. The customer is telling you that he or she sees reasons for you to work together. Reject the suggestion only if you believe there are important strategic or tactical reasons that outweigh the preference of your customer. Reasons to decline might include a rational fear that transferring knowledge or know-how to the competitor will cause damage in other accounts or situations.

You need to understand who the customer sees as the primary vendor with the main responsibilities such as design and system integration, which would help you work more effectively together. And you need to reorient rapidly from thinking about the other company as an enemy to considering what will help you advance your position in the account. Ensure that there are processes in place for governance of the initiative in the event that matters deteriorate from friendly rivalry. What happens if the competitor and your company start to feud again? How will these issues be resolved?

Thinking strategically, you may want to view this collaboration either as a first step to closer alignment with the competitor as an opportunity for competitive intelligence—to learn more about its company and people—or as part of the maneuvering you need to go through to displace the competitor from the account over time. For example, in the aerospace and defense industry, competitors become temporary allies when they combine into project teams on specific assignments. Perhaps because most of the people who work together are technically rather than commercially oriented, few aerospace and defense contractors seem to assemble competitive data when they work together so that they can use this same data when it comes time to compete.

Your Strategy Dictates

Perhaps your company is weak in areas in which specific competitors are strong and they can help you address these weaknesses in a number of ways. For example, if you wish to compete on scope, is your product or service line broad enough to allow you to be a credible vendor in a number of different areas? Some competitors may wish to make products or even provide services for you on an OEM basis. You might want to do the same for them in another area, especially if your customer base does not have much overlap with theirs. For example, in the airline industry, companies form alliances to fly one another's passengers.

If you want to broaden distribution, can a competitor help you to achieve this, again, perhaps on a reciprocal basis? If technology requires too much investment, perhaps it makes sense to share the risks and costs for research and development in exchange for also sharing some of the rewards? There are numerous examples of competitors collaborating in R&D partnerships such as USCAR,[6] a collaborative effort of the Big Three auto manufacturers in research and development on emissions control technologies.

If your company does not have weaknesses of the type described above, perhaps there are still opportunities to work together with selected competitors for mutual advantage. For example, can your company and selected competitors combine certain components of your value chains in a third enterprise—such as a distribution and logistics company, a sales and marketing firm or a research and development organization—that can be jointly owned by all parties?

Perhaps your company and a competitor with which there is limited overlap bring a more complete solution to both your customers. For example, can your company and chosen competitors establish a data-sharing mechanism to help you all to better manage your businesses? Some companies do not see data as competitive advantage in itself, believing that the way it is used is more important than who owns it. But if we accept that in this era, winning depends more on strategic capabilities than on strategy per se, then data is the ultimate capability from which advantage flows. Bearing this in mind, data sharing must therefore be approached with care or not at all.

General Motors and Toyota together established the New United Motor Manufacturing Inc. (NUMMI) joint venture in Fremont, California, in 1984. Although NUMMI helped Toyota transplant its production methods to America, perhaps the company also benefited by watching GM up close. There is an old saying, "keep your friends close and your enemies closer," so Toyota must hug General Motors very tightly indeed if it is to succeed in its goal to become the world's largest car company. While Toyota was observing GM, GM was doing the same thing to Toyota. At the time, terms such as *kaizen*,[7] *kanban*,[8] just-in-time and standardized work methods were being heralded as important reasons for Toyota's ability to build high-quality small cars. GM may have wanted to learn from Toyota

[6] United States Council for Automotive Research.

[7] *Kaizen* means continuous process improvement in a collaborative workplace.

[8] *Kanban* is specifically a signboard, card or placard used to communicate the need for replacement parts in a production process. It has become more generally known as a just-in-time system of production.

to advance its own quality and reduce costs to produce small cars while also improving other processes such as for training, advising and collaborating with suppliers, areas in which Toyota excelled. When GM established its Saturn division, the management team studied the NUMMI assembly plant.[9]

It is common for companies to establish formal joint ventures to achieve their mutual ends. Companies have done this for years but increasingly, the joint ventures include competitors such as the case for NUMMI, described above. In another example, when chemical companies E.I. DuPont de Nemours and Dow Chemical wanted to expand their elastomers businesses, they established an equally owned joint venture subsidiary called DuPont Dow Elastomers to provide a marketing and sales capability for both firms. Since 1996, DuPont Dow Elastomers has been marketing specialized synthetic elastomers used by industries such as general rubber, chemical processing, automotive and wire and cable. Founded in 1996, within five years, the firm's sales were over $1 billion.

Collaboration is occurring not only between a few chosen companies, as in the DuPont Dow example mentioned above, but it can also involve most of the firms in an industry. For instance, together with companies such as Bayer, PolyOne and Zeon, DuPont Dow is an investor in an e-marketplace—ElastomerSolutions.com. This collaboration may go beyond traditional e-marketplace functions such as procurement to include a linkage between the back-office operations of its members, setting the stage for further collaboration as well as benefiting customers and suppliers.

At a higher level yet, e-marketplaces are collaborating with one another. To extend the previous example, ElastomerSolutions.com has aligned with Elemica, an e-marketplace sponsored by chemical companies such as BASF, Celanese, Degussa and Rohm and Haas, as well DuPont and Dow. It is quite likely that there will be many more alliances among e-marketplaces as it becomes clearer that a broader base for the e-marketplace can benefit all participants.

Car companies are assemblers of subassemblies rather than manufacturers of the entire vehicle. Volkswagen (VW) appears to have asked itself whether being in the car business requires any assembly at all. The company owns a plant northwest of Rio de Janeiro at

[9] In addition to NUMMI, Saturn's management team also examined a number of other leading manufacturers, both competitors and noncompetitors, including Hewlett-Packard, IBM, Kawasaki, Saab, Volkswagen and Volvo, as well as many GM plants, such as the famous Corvette plant in Bowling Green, Kentucky. Jack O'Toole, *Forming the Future: Lessons from the Saturn Corporation*. Cambridge, MA: Blackwell Publishers, 1996, pp. 12, 13.

Resende at which suppliers such as Rockwell, Cummins, Delga Automotiva, Remon, Iochpe-Maxion and MWM assemble trucks and buses, but no Volkswagen employees perform any assembly. For example, Iochpe-Maxion assembles the chassis, Rockwell incorporates axles and suspensions, Cummins adds motive power, and Bridgestone/Firestone provides tires. In this environment, the customer and suppliers have blurred the lines between where one ends and the other begins. Suppliers order from themselves, ship to themselves and work with other suppliers to complete the vehicle. They get paid only when Volkswagen approves the final product. This approach to vehicle assembly has the potential to affect more than manufacturing. In this example, Volkswagen owns the processes for car and truck manufacturing and it owns the responsibility for the customer, dealer and supplier relationships. And it obviously retains the brand equity of Volkswagen. It may not need to own much more. By not tying up capital in equipment, companies such as VW can turn their assets more often, leading to higher returns on investment. Firms in other industries are also shedding assets to improve their asset turns and the VW strategy shows how at the same time, supply chains can be integrated, customers served with mass-customized product and shareholders provided with improved financial performance, while the company becomes progressively more virtual.

Technology Makes It Possible

Technology enables new go-to-market strategies, can take time out of most processes, introduces intelligence into customer interaction and vendor production and gives buyers the information to choose and makes it easier to shift their allegiance. Technology is pervasive and powerful, but this alone is insufficient reason for collaboration. There are several other reasons to deploy technology for collaboration, such as:

- New Customer Value
- Marketplaces
- Business Models

New Customer Value

Sophisticated customers—which today means *all* customers—know the opportunities to use technology to reduce their costs, improve quality, mass customize, obtain specific information, facilitate choice and expedite procurement, among many other benefits. Customers understand at least as much as their vendors about how technology can create customer value, and, increasingly, they are insisting that their vendors collaborate using process or technology innovation to deliver this value. For example, John Deere expected efficiency gains from its two lawn mower blade suppliers. One vendor achieved the gains Deere wanted, while the other was slower and lost the account as Deere consolidated suppliers.[10] In this instance, Deere appears to have set suppliers against one another, but there are occasions where customers would benefit from supplier collaboration.

We know from a year-long study of auto industry customer relationships that car buyers, informed by the Internet, know more about the car they want than most car salespeople when they walk into the dealership. Car companies have not yet collaborated[11] on a significant scale in aggregating and presenting comparative product and pricing information to customers. This is unfortunate for the car companies. Customers buy from whom they trust and they are inclined to trust sources of knowledge. These sources used to be car salespeople but today customers learn from infomediaries, such as Auto-By-Tel. There seems to be an opportunity for collaboration here, but the cultures of some car companies make this difficult.

Auto companies may never have fully recovered from cultures forged in the era of mass production and Frederick Winslow Taylor's principles of so-called scientific management. Attitudes established then have been somewhat resistant to collaboration, especially downstream in the interests of the customer. Now, car companies are focused on e-business and customer satisfaction, recognize the customer as integral to the supply chain and are moving rapidly to serve individual customers. As previously mentioned, Covisint is a collaborative on-line exchange which is the launching pad from which major car companies plan to advance their supply chain, build-to-order and mass customize.

Marketplaces

More generally than Covisint, business-to-business (B2B) vertical market portals give customers an array of suppliers from which to buy while also providing additional services such as career, product and

[10] R. David Nelson, vice president for worldwide supply management at Deere & Co., as reported by Jennifer Reingold and Marcia Stepanek, with Diane Brady in "Why the Productivity Revolution Will Spread," *BusinessWeek*, February 14, 2000.

[11] GM and some among its dealers may provide comparison information in a company and dealer owned site but the credibility of information would be increased if customers were assured all companies would be treated equally and if one company did not own the site. "GM and Its Dealers Propose Auto Web Site," *Information Week*, August 21, 2000.

other information. These exchanges, in which buyers and sellers "meet" to engage in a sale, are sometimes called marketplaces or market communities.[12] Companies have long transacted business electronically, but now, e-marketplaces have moved beyond simply facilitating transactions to changing the way goods and services are purchased. In essence, a portal takes an information system and adds on-line procurement to make it into an e-marketplace.

Earlier in the evolution of the Internet, predictions were made that "friction," the markup taken by each member of the distribution channel, would be reduced by the increased efficiency of on-line transactions. Most people thought that margins would decline most significantly for lower-priced consumer goods. However, the area most dramatically affected has proven to be B2B exchanges. In this space, businesses not only buy and sell products that are uniform and relatively easy to describe such as chemicals, seeds and fertilizers but, increasingly, services and high-value items that are dissimilar one from another such as bulldozers and logging machinery. The categories of e-marketplaces are:

- open exchanges such as VerticalNet, mySAP.com, Oracle-exchange.com, Commerce One, Ariba, Ventro and FreeMarkets
- industry-specific exchanges such as Altra, BuilderSupplyNet.com, CandyCommerce.com, ChipCenter, FastParts Inc., Instill, Inventory Locator Service, MetalSite, NECX, Paper-Exchange.com, PlasticsNet.com, RailNet-USA.com and XS Inc.
- company-specific exchanges such as GE Information Services (GEIS) Trading Partner Network Register discussed below

VerticalNet, for example, operates 57 vertical marketplaces in areas such as communications, energy, environment and utilities, financial services, food and packaging, foodservice and hospitality, healthcare, high technology, discrete manufacturing, process manufacturing, public sector, science and services. Customers know they can go to sites such as these. Companies may find that if they are not there, they may be losing sales from opportunities that were never visible to them according to the old, more personal rules for customer engagement.

SAP and Oracle have a large installed base of software implementations running the businesses of many large companies. Using e-marketplace capabilities of firms such as these, companies can engage in exchanges with others using similar software. As mentioned earlier,

[12] Selected data are sourced from Morgan Stanley Dean Witter, April, 2000.

companies such as Ariba and Commerce One are developing exchanges such as Exostar and Covisint for networks of companies.

Some of the exchanges are company-specific. As mentioned, at GEIS, a system called Trading Partner Network Register allows employees to order office supplies from prequalified vendors over the Internet. GEIS benefits from significantly reduced transaction costs, and the cooperating competitors also save money on their customer management processes with on-line ordering. Vendors able to participate with companies such as GEIS early in the design and testing of similar systems have the opportunity to derive additional benefits from system implementation and become even more entrenched within the account, together with selected other, hopefully complementary, vendors.

For a long time, General Electric did not get it, but now it appreciates the benefits of the Internet and has moved quickly to transform divisions into e-businesses. For example, GE Power Systems is establishing the GEPS Supplier Center, a B2B portal to collaborate with suppliers in its global supply chain, with applications serving areas such as purchasing, accounts payable, engineering, production support and logistics.

E-marketplaces have two important impacts on CRM and competition: commoditization and reintermediation. E-marketplaces facilitate comparison of like products and services. This makes it possible for buyers to focus on price, which has the effect of reducing differentiation and making commodities of most goods and services. This commoditization can undercut CRM investments. When customers define procurement requirements on the e-marketplace, they make it harder for a supplier to work with them in a collaborative process, as would be expected from firms employing CRM principles.

An e-marketplace that is not operated by a single buyer reintermediates the supply chain by adding another level between supplier and customer. This distances the company from its customers and creates a new series of processes and communications that are channeled through the e-marketplace. When an e-marketplace is operated by customers, a CRM initiative must recognize, address and integrate e-marketplaces into CRM. If not, the CRM initiative will increasingly create relationships with customers who do not do the buying. Worse yet (from the perspective of the suppliers), some of these customers will not give as much time to their vendors because customers will expect that contact and collaboration will be through the e-marketplace.

What, then, is the company to do about advancing its competitive position if its customers are using e-marketplaces? First, it should think about what is missing from the e-marketplace and how targeted competitors are changing their marketing practices. E-marketplaces can be efficient but may lack the information that fully describes the context within which the customer does business such as:

- the customer's business vision, mission, objectives and strategies
- the personnel who comprise the purchase decision-making unit
- product, service and company selection criteria, especially the informal criteria comprising likes and dislikes that are not posted on the e-marketplace
- the process by which the terms of reference for the product or service were determined
- the process by which the vendor will be selected and the timing for this decision
- the positioning of existing and potential suppliers in respect of key criteria
- the willingness of the customer to entertain a primary or second-source bid from an untested supplier and the extent to which the decision varies for a new buy, modified rebuy or straight rebuy decision
- opportunities for the vendor to go beyond the terms of reference or to innovate

If considerations such as these are missing from an e-marketplace, the company has to decide whether to transact business only through the e-marketplace or to also pursue CRM, perhaps in a modified form. Companies that choose to do business only through the e-marketplace may win some initial contracts and reduce some of their costs, but these gains could come at the expense of longer-term competitiveness, especially if targeted competitors continue to develop customer relationships. Early on, the loss rate on bids may also be high if the company does not have lines of communications to provide it with the intelligence it needs to prepare winning bids.

By complying with the customers' preferences to do business exclusively or largely using the e-marketplace, the potential exists for vendors to become little more than reactive producers and pricers. Innovation will be customer-led and customer-defined. The company will have abdicated its strategies to its customers and will have very few levers left to innovate and differentiate.

By the time opportunities appear on the e-marketplace, the CRM company should know about them, which would give it an obvious advantage over a competitor that did not. The company that becomes aware of opportunities from the e-marketplace has no meaningful relationship with its customers. Further, the company that has not been shaping the initiative from the outset is also not sufficiently close to its customers and at an immediate competitive disadvantage.

In most industries, the opportunity exists for only a few companies to get close enough to customers to:

- know how the product or service will help the customer achieve its objectives
- help customers to specify the product or service or to help shape the specifications
- understand the unsaid purchase criteria and vendor positioning
- understand the customer's perceptions of the strengths and weaknesses of competitors
- know what it will take to differentiate the winning bid from competitors

The opportunity to get close to customers is not available to every supplier and, with e-marketplaces, it is possible that fewer suppliers will obtain widespread customer access and less opportunity to plan and innovate together. The customer's door is slowly closing on suppliers that are either efficient or less than effective. These companies are being steered to the e-marketplace to do business. If a company is to gain competitive advantage, it will need to keep customers' doors open and evolve its CRM initiative to incorporate the role of the e-marketplace.

Business Models

Technology creates entirely new business models, as some of the above examples demonstrate. Sometimes, the marketplace and buyer behavior changes wrought by technology can be so significant that companies not adapting can fail. As noted in Chapter 1, Egghead Software had a chain of retail stores that were having a hard enough time competing with major chains. The advent of the Internet and on-line retailers sealed the fate of Egghead's retail operations, which were closed. Emerging phoenix-like from the ashes is the on-line e-tailer, Egghead.com, which only sells on the Internet.

In its infancy, the Internet provided companies with a way to reduce the cost with the same business model they had previously employed in the physical world. So, most retailers, for example, entered cyberspace as a way to broaden their audience using another channel. The Internet then helped companies to manage communications costs with stakeholders such as customers and suppliers, reducing the cost of interaction, if not always the effectiveness of the communications. More recently, the Internet and other technologies are providing a vehicle for managing the customer relationship. All of the foregoing could be accomplished by individual enterprises—operating in their individual interests and those of their chosen customers.

Now technology is creating opportunities for customers and suppliers alike that cannot easily be achieved independently. The marketplace exchanges mentioned earlier can have a profound impact not just on commoditization, customer-supplier communications and mass customization, important though these are. The exchanges can drive entirely new business models. Envera is an example of collaboration across the petroleum and chemical industries, in which chemical companies[13] are collaborating to not only facilitate exchange of their products, but to develop a fully integrated supply chain and with it, a new, more automated, more virtual business.

Increasingly, competition is not only between individual firms but between collaborative networks of competitors. For example, Envera's network of collaborating chemical companies is competing with Elemica, another supply chain integration and connectivity hub backed by even larger chemical companies.[14] Technology alliance partners may be the critical weapons in the outcome of the battles between marketplaces. Envera is partnered with companies such as IBM, Oracle, webMethods, Whitlokebs, and XML Solutions, while Elemica's partners include Commerce One and SAP.

Perhaps customers will want to deal with both Envera and Elemica, but over time, there will probably not be room for both networks. One set of collaborators will be in a position to set the rules for admission by the others. And, while networks of collaborators position themselves to integrate supply chains with customers, some third-party business-to-business marketplaces that operate independently of

---

[13] Envera's strategic partners include Albemarle, Borden Chemical, Equistar Chemical, Ethyl Corporation, Lubrizol, Lyondell Chemical, Mays Chemical, Occidental Chemical, Phenolchemie and Solutia Inc.

[14] Elemica's strategic partners are companies such as Air Products, Atofina, BASF, Bayer, BP, Celanese, Chemcentral, Ciba, Degussa, Dow, DSM, DuPont, Millennium, Mitsubishi, Mitsui, Rhodia, Rohm & Haas, Shell, Solvay.

financial backing from industry participants look set to take a terrible beating. Starved of suppliers on their exchanges and, in some cases, denied venture capital, it is quite likely collaborative networks will first succeed against the independent marketplaces before focusing their attention on one another.

As business-to-business competition moves from a contest between individual companies to a challenge among collaborative networks of companies, the basis for competition is also changing. Formerly, competition was discrete in that it involved individual products and services and was based on relative value at a point in time. Many consumer marketplaces, whether technology enabled or not, remain in this mode. But for business-to-business marketplaces, the battleground is shifting from discrete, point-in-time engagement to continuous interaction. As it does, the basis for winning shifts from product, service and price advantage into newer territories associated with strategic capabilities, business models and trust-based relationships. The question customers will increasingly ask is not which product or service best meets their needs, but with which companies they should associate or integrate to provide the solutions they need over an extended period. In answering these questions, the vendor-selection decision will be more senior and one in which the selection criteria will include evaluations of issues such as the supplier's:

- business models
- potential contribution to the company's business model
- strategic capabilities, including the strength, nature and plans for information technology
- customer-integration processes
- processes for innovation, including customer involvement in the processes
- willingness to participate with customers in capturing, serving and integrating with end customers
- ability to forge enduring, trust-based relationships, including the trust engendered by their leaders, senior management team and organizational culture
- relationship governance mechanism (customers using a dispute-resolution mechanism to ensure that one negative instance does not destroy the relationship more generally)

In the building design and construction industry, Buzzsaw.com provides an on-line environment in which professionals can collaborate throughout the building construction process. It connects building owners, architects, engineers, contractors, suppliers and manufacturers in a secure environment in which, for example, drawings and documents can be shared, bids managed, materials purchased and issues resolved during the construction process. Drawings and specifications for commercial building projects are stored on the Buzzsaw.com site. Architects and engineers can create and analyze drawings using CAD tools and communicate in real time using on-line multimedia capabilities. In short, this is a different, collaborative business model for participants in the industry, in which complementary and competitive service providers alike work collaboratively on projects. And it is proving to be a well-used business model—over 20,000 projects have been hosted by the site.

When customers want new value, as discussed earlier, they sometimes want to collaborate with one or more of their suppliers. About 400 retailers are collaborating with Merrill Lynch in the launch of a new portal, a one-stop shop with financial services as well as other offerings to differentiate itself from Merrill's main competitor, Charles Schwab.[15] Retailers such as Barnes and Noble apparently think they are better off collaborating with Merrill Lynch to reach financially aware consumers than attempting to access these customers directly, on their own. In situations such as this, the first companies signing up for a consortium or collaboration sometimes demand and receive exclusivity, which provides an additional incentive for collaboration: locking out the company's direct competitors. In the above instance, Barnes and Noble is obviously complementary to Merrill Lynch, but there are many instances in which competitors collaborate in their mutual interests, often because they cannot achieve the ends each wants independently. In addition to the examples provided previously for marketplaces, instances in which competitors collaborate include the need to move markets, codevelop technology and change customer purchase behavior.

There are also occasions when competitors perceive an external threat—such as a substitute technology—to be so significant that they work together to fend off the challenge. Some may also feel that if they do not collaborate, they might be excluded from a much larger opportunity, if it works. Companies collaborate to spread costs and risks, especially in the area in which research and development can lead to a major breakthrough. An example that includes many of these dimensions is the California Fuel Cell Partnership, a

[15] Leah Nathans Spiro, "Merrill's E-Battle," *BusinessWeek*, Nov. 15, 1999.

collaboration of several companies and government entities working together as independent participants. As you might expect from real collaboration, this is not a formal joint venture, legal partnership or incorporated entity.

The partnership provides an opportunity to assess and demonstrate the feasibility of fuel cell-powered electric vehicles under California conditions and the feasibility of an energy infrastructure such as hydrogen and methanol, among other objectives. Partners comprise car companies DaimlerChrysler, Ford, General Motors, Honda, Hyundai, Nissan, Toyota and Volkswagen; oil companies BP, Texaco and Shell; and fuel cell developers Xcellsis,[16] Ballard Power Systems Inc. and International Fuel Cells. State and federal government departments are also participants in the partnership. If it is successful, the internal combustion engines that today propel virtually all cars will be displaced to some extent by motive power that comes from hydrogen, which, when combined with oxygen, produces electricity.[17]

The stakes are huge, but the costs of developing the engines and infrastructure and then shifting the market are too large and risky for a single company. The risks of not participating might be even larger if one company is able to achieve a breakthrough, so many companies have seen it to be more in their interests to collaborate than to bet so much on an immature technology.

Collaborating to Build Customer Share

Companies also collaborate with competitors to build customer share and develop primary demand to benefit from this growth together with customers and chosen competitors. Customer share and primary demand can be created in many ways according to the focus of the innovation, as described in Figure 8-2.[18] In this business-to-business model, existing or new products, services, processes or solutions are provided to customers for their existing purchase requirements or for new purchase needs.

---

[16] Xcellsis is itself one model of collaboration, a joint venture of DaimlerChrysler, Ford and Ballard Power Systems Inc. to develop fuel cell technology.

[17] Have you ever held a match to a small amount of hydrogen? My ears could still be ringing from a high school science experiment when a teacher lit hydrogen to demonstrate the formation of a little water—and, not incidentally, a lot of energy. A huge blast blew out a window in the classroom and stunned us all. I assume fuel-cell vehicles will not shatter all the city's glass each time they crank up.

[18] This makes the Ansoff Matrix, which discussed products and markets, customer-specific. The Ansoff Matrix was described in 1957! H.I. Ansoff, "Strategies for Diversification," *Harvard Business Review*, Sept.-Oct. 1957, pp. 113-124.

Figure 8-2: Building Customer Share and Primary Demand for Specific Customers

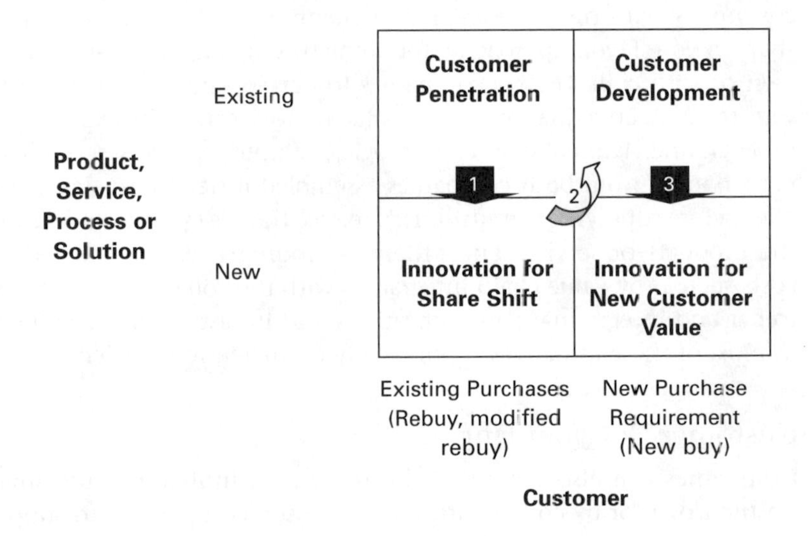

This results in four strategic alternatives for building revenues with individual customers. These are:

1. Customer Penetration
2. Innovation for Share Shift
3. Customer Development
4. Innovation for New Customer Value

Customer Penetration

Customer penetration seeks to increase share of customer by displacing targeted competitors from the account. There may be opportunities to align with some competitors to displace others. Some of the ways of doing this include working with collaborative competitors to market new uses or applications for products or services; grouping your products and services with theirs, perhaps into tiers or bundles; finding additional departments, divisions or country operations that you and collaborative companies can supply; and repositioning competitors and exploitation of their weaknesses. Pricing is often used as an initial approach to shift customer share and is an option here but should be followed by the development of more durable customer benefits as may flow from CRM bonding.

Innovation for Share Shift

Entirely new products, services, processes and solutions supplied for a customer's existing purchase requirements can also shift customer share in your favor. Approaches for doing this include working on your own or with collaborative companies to develop new product or service features and quality levels. Collaborators can help expand the broader line, launch new technologies, simplify processes (such as parts bought from both companies assembled instead into subassemblies before supplying the customer), reduce the life cycle costs of using the products or services and otherwise finding new ways to reduce costs such as by value chain integration with the collaborator and customer and integrating communications and infrastructure. The focus in most of these initiatives is principally on increasing efficiency.

Customer Development

Companies can also grow their business with individual customers on their own or by collaborating with chosen competitors to supply existing products or services for new requirements and purchase situations. Examples here include integrating with the customer to plan, design and develop initiatives together, process innovation, cross-vendor collaboration and, more generally, aligning to help customers create new business value.

Innovation for New Customer Value

The strategic focus here is on effectiveness to help the customer create new opportunities by developing new products, services, processes, solutions and technologies to help customers achieve their strategic objectives such as primary demand creation. Companies can collaborate with competitors to do what they cannot or should not do themselves such as when they need to benefit from the specialized expertise or customer relationships that competitors possess or other reasons that are discussed in the next section.

Many companies have already developed strategies for customer penetration and innovation for share shift, suggested by arrow one in Figure 8-2. Most are now in the process of innovating processes for customer engagement and interaction such as by using the Internet and electronic data interchange between individual companies. Many firms are now undertaking strategic changes as indicated by arrow number two. Suppliers, competitors and customers are innovating together to create marketplaces and other processes, often technology enabled, to create new business value.

Supply chain management is an example of technology adoption and process innovation that aligns suppliers with customers' production and goods replenishment requirements. Some companies are now transitioning their strategies as described by arrow number three. They are beginning to develop new products, services, processes, solutions and technologies collaboratively with customers rather than simply to penetrate customers. Increasingly, the focus is on assisting customers to increase their share of customer with their own chosen customers and to build primary demand in a manner similar to that which you are trying to develop with them.

Complementors

Competitors that are complementary to your company can be called complementors. We discuss this special type of competitor below.

Ten Types of Complementors

Complementors can be categorized into a number of types, according to the role they might play in collaborating with your company. The ten types are:

1. Product Complementors
2. Embedded Complementors
3. Service Complementors
4. System Complementors
5. Value Chain Complementors
6. Aggregator Complementors
7. Customer Mover Complementors
8. Market Mover Complementors
9. Relationship Leverer Complementors
10. Accelerator Complementors

Product Complementors

Product complementors are companies that market products that your company does not, so they can assist you in rounding out your line of products, helping you to compete on scope in the minds of consumers or in specific businesses. For example, Reebok, well known for its sports gear, marketed a watch branded with the Reebok name. Reebok did not make the watch itself, but rather a product complementor produced this new product for Reebok to that firm's specifications. When companies such as Xerox and Staples market paper for use in photocopiers and printers, these firms have the products produced for them under an OEM branding arrangement.[19]

Sometimes, complementors start to view one another as more direct competitors when there is substantial overlap of their product sets or benefit delivery. For many years, most of the enterprise resource planning software implementations of SAP used Oracle databases. Then, Oracle positioned itself as more than a database company by providing an expanded capability, looking much more like an end-to-end solutions company. SAP is now implementing databases from a firm it has acquired: Adabas D.

Embedded Complementors

Embedded complementors collaborate with vendors to round out the capability of OEM's products or services with strategic subassemblies or components that are integrated into the vendors' offerings, in the process broadening the capabilities of the products and expanding the product lines. This is different from product complementors. Whereas product complementors provide discrete products, embedded complementors provide parts or assemblies that become part of the company's products. For example, some car companies supply engines to lower volume, specialized car manufacturers that do not make their own engines, and some major car and truck companies use the specialized engines built by others. For example, DaimlerChrysler uses Cummins diesel engines in some of its pickups. In another example, NETsilicon, Inc. develops and markets technology that connects electronic devices such as printers, scanners, fax machines and copiers with the Internet and intranets. NETsilicon simultaneously collaborates with competing manufacturers such as Minolta, NEC, Ricoh, Sharp and Xerox.

Service Complementors

Service complementors provide an expanded customer benefit by rounding out gaps in the delivery of the solution to the customer.

[19] For example, paper is made for Xerox in countries such as USA, Canada and Sweden by companies such as Domtar.

Manufacturers of white goods such as refrigerators, ranges and dishwashers use independent contractors to service their appliances under warranty, operating as though they are the manufacturer themselves. Similarly, natural gas companies contract to have independent operators service home furnaces, gas fireplaces, barbecues and the like. Home Depot and Sears provide home services and equipment installation through independent contractors, and some accounting and consulting firms use specialists to provide a broader range of benefits to their clients. The challenge in all of these situations is for the company with the primary customer relationship to ensure that complementors do consistently good work.

System Complementors

System complementors are companies that supply products that integrate with those of the manufacturer to provide an extended solution to the customer. For example, Canon produces peripherals for a number of brand-name manufacturers, helping them to position themselves as suppliers of a broader line than computers alone. Similarly, Sony manufactures many of the better computer monitors, again with the names of the prominent manufacturers on them. System complementors are different from embedded complementors in that they provide fully functional products that operate together with those of the manufacturer, extending the capability or positioning of the manufacturer's products. Products provided by embedded complementors are not fully functional in their own right. Thus, Cummins diesel engines in a DaimlerChrysler vehicle or GE or Pratt & Whitney turbofan engines in a Boeing aircraft are products provided by system complementors in that they enable vehicle or airframe companies to position themselves as providers of the total solution—in this case, transportation.

Value Chain Complementors

As companies review their value chain, they may decide that specialists are better able to perform specific functions than they can themselves. They might consider that they are better able to design, develop, produce and service than to sell and install, for example, choosing to have other companies perform the latter tasks. Or they may conclude that some of their infrastructure should be outsourced to third parties, making these companies value chain complementors. For example, Xerox provides outsourcing for the in-house printing, mail room, distribution center, data center and basic administration operations of many major companies, while companies such as Andersen Consulting and CGI have major technology outsourcing agreements with companies such as Canada Post and Bell Canada. Some companies may be in a position to use technology to make their value chain alignment more open.

Aggregator Complementors

Aggregators are another category of complementary companies. They assemble the products, services and solutions of a number of companies to deliver value to the end customer. Examples include systems integrators and vertical market software and solution companies. One such company is Compugen, which provides a wide range of technology solutions to businesses. Another example is the electronic catalog aggregators that obtain, standardize and compare data about different products or services from multiple vendors, making it easy for customers to compare alternatives and simplifying the task faced by suppliers wanting to keep their comparison data current. In the used car industry, well-known providers of current prices for used vehicles in the US include Edmunds Used Vehicle Pricing Guide (edmunds.com) and Kelley Blue Book Pricing (kbb.com).

Customer Mover Complementors

There are occasions when one company cannot change the behaviors of a customer in the interests of all companies, but an assembly of complementary suppliers might be able to accomplish this. For example, when vendors establish an electronic marketplace, they naturally need customers to use the forum. A single company might face resistance to the use of its own e-business capability but, when combined with other companies in an electronic marketplace, customers might be more prepared to purchase or interact on-line. A number of examples of e-marketplaces were cited earlier in this chapter.

Market Mover Complementors

Moving a customer can be hard enough, but moving an entire market can be extremely challenging for all but the largest companies. Microsoft can encourage users to upgrade their operating systems and purchase new versions of its software, and customers may be persuaded to lease new Xerox machines en masse, but smaller companies in both industries may face more challenges in lifting and shifting customers unless they are associated with a market mover, work together or have a truly revolutionary and beneficial product or service. Sometimes, the purchasing power of specific companies can be so large that they can move an industry. Ford's AutoXchange may be one such example, in which Ford procures a wide range of products and services such as subassemblies, components, capital goods and office consumables. In effect, companies will belong to the Ford family or someone else's. DaimlerChrysler's FastCar provides another forum for the alignment of its suppliers, while facilitating design and engineering collaboration, supply chain management, inventory management and logistics.

Relationship Leverer Complementors

Relationship leverers help companies to market their products and services to the complementors' customers. Many technology companies approach accounting firms to lever their strong customer relationships. One such example occurred when SAP, the German enterprise software company, wanted to enter North America and lacked two things: knowledge workers and relationships. It found both in the major accounting firms, while the accountants were eager to take pressure off their declining accounting revenues and find low risk, standardized ways to benefit from the IT explosion. ERP companies have been able to lever the relationships of accounting firms to gain high-level entry into major organizations while retaining the strategic core of the business: software development.

Accelerator Complementors

Companies that accelerate time to implement any aspect of the value chain are accelerator complementors. A company can speed implementation by benefiting from a leading force in the industry. For example, Xerox's e-community sends printing jobs to graphic arts customers. Service providers are organized around a Web site, from which they can gain access to graphic arts courses, job opportunities, business strategies, work-flow tools and applications and an opportunity to route and share print production work. Graphic arts companies using the community have the potential to interact with one another in a more seamless and lower cost manner than if they attempted to do this themselves. More importantly, they can be up and running much more quickly than if they attempted something similar on their own.

Choosing the Right Complementor

Clearly, there are very different types of complementors. Select the type of complementor most suited to your business challenge, and establish relationship objectives before you identify those that most suit your requirement and before you engage in discussion with any among them. Relationship objectives can be established according to the unique issues in each customer, for groups of customers or for the marketplace as a whole. Generally, companies have paid attention to the issue of complementors for the marketplace as a whole. The opportunity for many companies is now to consider how to collaborate within individual customers.

When choosing a competitor with which to collaborate, consider how the complementor will: 1) create unique customer value; 2) create shareholder value for your company; and 3) do the same for itself. If the complementor can enable these three components of value creation and especially if it can facilitate the entire spectrum of customer engagement—from connection to customization—then your company may have identified a winning opportunity to collaborate. But even if it cannot add value in all respects, by considering in which areas it might complement your company within specific accounts, you can provide your customer with more value and advance your own customer relationships.

As with any relationship, you will need to work together with the complementors on engagement and interaction processes and on methods to govern the relationship. Retain a clear customer and competitor imperative as you proceed through the discussions, and weigh adoption of new technologies carefully if they have limited impact on your ability to outperform competitors in the minds of your chosen customers.

Bonding With Competitors

Knowing the Risks

As we have seen, collaborating with competition is not always the same as sleeping with the enemy, but it can be. Collaboration offers distinct advantages such as those mentioned, but also a number of risks. Downsides can include the loss of proprietary information, loss of key employees to the competitor that knows them as a result of the collaboration and the competitor using your relationships for its advantage. If a competitor is targeting your company, it may view collaboration as a guise to advance its competitive position, something that is difficult to tell at the outset. The potential for this needs to be guarded against such as by assessing whether or not its leaders are trustworthy. While one might adopt a more open stance with customers, competitors should earn your trust one step at a time before you start to relate to them as you would to a stakeholder in your business.

Bonding Hierarchy

As with the customers you have chosen, establish a bonding hierarchy and objectives to be met for each step in the progression. A bonding hierarchy with customers is a progression of steps by which the customer demonstrates its affinity for your organization. An analogous continuum can be established for competitors, as presented in Figure 8-3 on page 357. We discuss bonding with individual customers first, then with complementors.

Customer Bonding

Customers can be grouped according to their demonstrated behaviors such as the share of business your company receives from each customer. Share of business refers to your proportion of the customer's total expenditures on goods and services for which you might be eligible. Share of mind means the extent to which your company enjoys favorable repeat purchase intentions and a perception that momentum favors your firm in your industry. Customers' purchasing and other behaviors link to the share of mind your firm enjoys.

A bonding continuum grades the intensity with which customers bond with your company, from being prospects to becoming the company's advocate with others. Customers advance from being prospects, testers, shoppers, accounts, patrons and, finally, advocates. Each of the six categories of buyer is discussed below, according to the nature of the bonding of the customer with the company. Bonding is examined from the lowest to the highest levels.

Prospects

Prospects are those customers drawn from the general population whose profiles match that of your desired audience. If you consider the recency of customers purchases, the frequency of those purchases and the expenditure value of current customers with your firm and the costs of serving them, you can identify similar customers that appear to offer interesting potential and fit with the focus, capabilities and products and services of your firm. These are the firm's prospects.

Testers

Testers are prospects who have become aware of your company and have begun to explore the extent to which you are relevant to them, perhaps with initial trial purchases. Based on their satisfaction with this experience, they will wish to gauge the potential to establish a more significant flow of business to your company.

Shoppers

Shoppers are testers who are satisfied with their initial experience and have begun to do business with your firm but not as a matter of course. They likely continue to do business with their current supplier but are interested enough in your offer that they consider your firm a second source or alternative for all their business in the event that their main vendor fails to satisfy them in some dimension.

Accounts

Satisfied with the period during which your company has been catering to their needs, the shoppers standardize key aspects of their procurement and purchasing processes to include your firm as a major supplier for their needs. As a result, these types of customers become what are termed accounts. By this stage, you have earned the accounts' business, but not yet their full trust. As a result, they retain alternative sources to the business they direct to you. Accounts can still switch to your competitors or slide back in the bonding continuum to shoppers or even stop buying from your firm entirely. And they do not feel a need to give reasons for the change. You remain in a state of being constantly under evaluation and trial. Even small missteps can create the dissatisfaction that can erode the trust relationship.

Patrons

Patrons are longer-term accounts whose trust you now have and who have adopted your processes and values as their own. They will seek to integrate your company not only in their procurement/purchasing processes, but also in other key strategic components of the business. For the business-to-business sector, this could include design and development, for example. In so doing, the business-to-business customers do more than give your firm a progressively higher share of their business. The high share of mind you enjoy leads to a higher share of their future business. As your future and theirs become interlinked, your mutual commitment will grow and lead to the next step in the continuum. In the consumer market, patrons will consider buying from your firm as a matter of course, with little or no consideration of competitors, expecting that each time the result will be the same happy outcome it has been previously.

Advocates

With advocates, your company enjoys patrons who are so committed to your firm that only a major violation of trust would erode this goodwill. You have virtually their entire attention in this product or service category. Advocates will stand up for your firm and tell others of your wonders. They will make business referrals. They will be "good complainers," inviting you to get better without being negative in their guidance. The Saturn division of General Motors has succeeded in bonding with customers at this level. The company hosted an event to invite owners to come to the factory at which their cars were built, and thousands enjoyed a rain-soaked weekend in a muddy Kentucky field, without complaint. When a Saturn owner's T-shirt invited people to ask her about her happy ownership experience, Saturn could claim customer bonding that transcends the relationship most people have with many other car firms.

Progress along the bonding continuum can occur in either direction. Trust, like antipathy, is cumulative, but it is more difficult to build and easier to erode. Thus, it is harder to progress up the hierarchy than it is to fall down. The main reason most retrogression occurs is as a result of ineffective communications processes and style between the organization and its customers. An appropriately sensitive company—with scripted responses and processes that effectively manage key areas of potential discord—will more likely preserve gains on the bonding continuum and even accelerate progress. Unhappy customers whose complaints are recognized and remedied, for example, tend to be happier than others at the same level of bonding, and they communicate their happiness, shifting them toward the advocate.

Advancement along the continuum must be won one step at a time. As in any courtship, it is unlikely that the heart of the intended can be earned forever in a single encounter. (If it were, it would be one amazing encounter!) While heroic efforts help, it is more important to know at which level each customer is in your bonding continuum and to have objectives for customers at each level.

The purchase process and the end state of the customer category are closely linked. Prospects who have limited awareness of the firm and its relevance are unlikely to become shoppers until awareness increases. Thus, elevating levels of company or product-service awareness may be an important issue for shifting customers from prospects to shoppers but may play no role in moving the customer from patron to advocate. Complementors can help a company address customer-specific issues, and they can be selected according to the value they bring to each customer and in helping your company advance customers along the bonding continuum. If a company is to do this well, it will also need to develop progressively deeper bonds with complementors because customer relationships cannot be strong or durable if there are weak links underlying them.

Complementor Bonding

As mentioned, complementary competitors may be termed complementors, a type of competitor that benefits your company. As you seek to advance customer bonds in association with complementors, your complementor relationships advance from benign competition until they work closely with your company in your mutual interests. We have excluded aggressive competitors from the following bonding consideration as they are not complementors until they are turned from a benign into a more supportive company. This can be done only with considerable intervention such as financial investment.

The five different levels of bonding a company can have with complementors can be described as follows:

1. Benign Competitor
2. Colleague
3. Supporter
4. Ally
5. Partner

Each category differs from the next according to the observed and measurable behaviors of the complementor.

We have termed the highest level of close cooperation with a complementor as a partner. The term partner is sometimes associated with financial ownership or investments, but there is no such implication here. By considering complementors according to the value they add in specific accounts to advance customer bonding, you can select those competitors that will create most customer value in each specific situation and plan to deepen bonds with them. When it becomes apparent that the same complementor can be helpful for many customers, the company can enter into a broader accord with it. Complementors, as a special form of competitor, must be managed if the firm is to benefit fully from any association. In the following, we discuss the different levels of bonding with complementors to serve as a basis for considering how to advance bonds with these companies while doing likewise with individual customers.

Figure 8-3: Bonding with Complementary Competitors

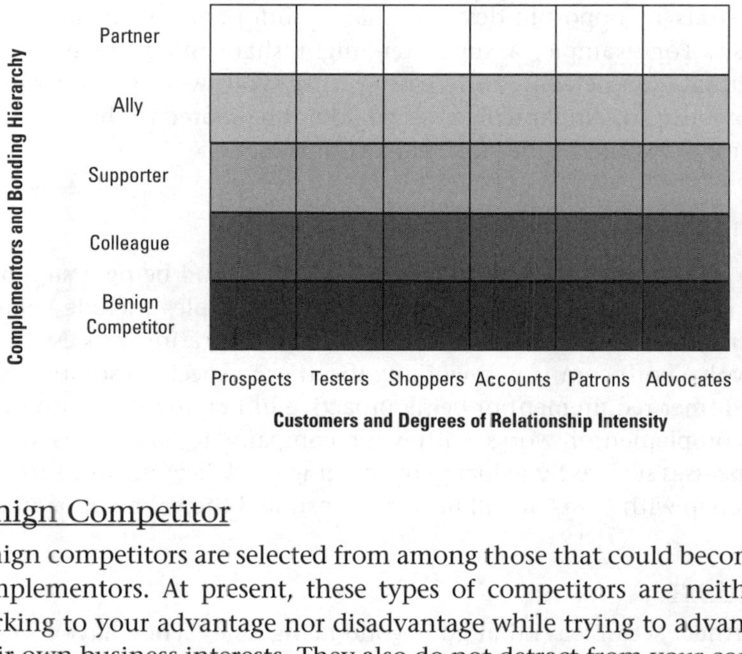

Benign Competitor

Benign competitors are selected from among those that could become complementors. At present, these types of competitors are neither working to your advantage nor disadvantage while trying to advance their own business interests. They also do not detract from your company. For example, they do not malign your company with customers. If they have complementary interests in the account, they may occasionally communicate something of interest to you such as an initiative the customer is about to launch.

Colleague

A colleague with a customer is one that demonstrates behaviors that are of a collegial and friendly nature, as may be evident at events hosted by the customer in a business-to-business customer situation. A distinction needs to be made between the person who behaves as a colleague and the organization itself. If a person operates somewhat in your interests, he or she may want to join your company or perhaps want to keep doors open. While of some possible interest to you, the focus here is on creating bonds between organizations. Any initial bonding between individuals now has to be taken to the next level—to create bonds between companies.

Supporter

A supporter is a complementor who demonstrates some alignment with your company in the account such as by making occasional referrals of opportunities and sharing information on an ad hoc basis. For example, a supporter might share intelligence about a mutual competitor, anticipating that you would do likewise. Obviously, pricing intelligence would not be shared in this way since doing so would be illegal in most countries.

Ally

An ally is a complementor that has gone beyond being a supporter to actively aligning with your company. Examples include collaborating to serve the customer such as by integrating processes that involve both companies, working together to specify a solution for a customer requirement or being proactive in helping the customer. If a complementor works with your company to take costs out of processes such as by reducing by merging stock-keeping units to limit overlap with yours, it will have demonstrated the behavior of an ally.

Partner

Partners act in ways that go beyond being allies. They have a vested interest in your success as you do in theirs, and they work with you in support of many customers and selected strategic capabilities. For example, if competitors work with your company to help you begin to assemble components from both of you into subassemblies for customers, these complementors depend on the success of the outcome and have demonstrated a willingness to collaborate that goes well beyond being allies. The more the bonds between companies are of a structural nature, including processes and technologies, the more likely that these complementors will become partners.

Examples of structural integration include more efficient communications between organizations as a result of back-office financial and operating systems and more effective support of customers by integrating call center databases. Partners are visible supporters of the organization, featuring your company on their Web site, for instance. In so doing, they invest in your brand equity. Partners collaborate with companies in the service of many or most companies and have integrated processes to the point that they aid any needed customization and personalization of communications, products and services. In short, partners always conduct themselves in your mutual interests, seeking to benefit from an association with your company while creating shareholder value for you, as well.

Building Deeper Relationships With Competitors

Earlier in this chapter, we discussed choosing a complementor. We noted that complementors should be selected from among all competitors according to criteria such as the value they can create with you for specific customers. Having considered the value you need from a competitor to complement the value you want to create for your most valuable customers, and once you have assessed each competitor for its ability to deliver and sustain the provision of that value, you are in a position to select complementors. These firms will have a level of bonding with your company that you will wish to improve. Advance the relationship through the bonding continuum in a planned manner, one step at a time.

By now you would have a plan to manage each targeted competitor. Include your approach to move complementors through the bonding continuum in your plan. Establish objectives for each stage of relationship development—from benign competitor to partner. Ask yourself what behaviors your company and the complementor's would need to exhibit to achieve each level of bonding, and establish the strategies and tactics to accomplish this.

As your trust in them develops, complementors move through the bonding continuum toward becoming full partners, in which case they have earned the right to more openness and mutual access to plans, people, technology and customer knowledge and insight that can help the joint initiative succeed. The word *mutual* should be emphasized here. Competitors should similarly demonstrate their commitment to creating value with you as you do with them. A one-sided relationship with a competitor is much worse than a similar situation with customers. While customers may not do business with you, a competitor may create negative value for shareholders based on what you have helped them to know.

There is potential for antitrust examination of any collaboration among competitors or legal action, especially when the government or other competitors consider that any information exchange or other collaboration may lessen competition. The advance of technology will likely create yet more opportunities for companies to work together to achieve mutual ends, and the antitrust regulators could be looking over your shoulders to satisfy themselves that collaboration does not diminish competition. In particular, they could want assurance that collaboration improves efficiency without increasing the market power of specific companies or groups of companies. Unfortunately, the latter is probably what most companies want. Therefore, prior to collaborating with competitors, whatever the venue or context, the reader should consult with legal counsel and review the relevant legislation and guidelines for collaboration.[20]

In this chapter, we reviewed opportunities for working with competitors to create new customer value such as by collaborating to reduce costs, identify new product or customer opportunities for customers or by collaborating to displace other competitors to increase customer share. As you would plan your relationships with customers, do likewise with competitors, paying special attention to advancing relationships with those complementors that can help you create the value your most important customers want.

[20] Such as "Guidelines for Collaborations Among Competitors" *United States Department of Justice and Federal Trade Commission*, April 7, 2000.

CHAPTER 9

Competing for Tomorrow's Customers

"Check your road and the nature of your battle. The world you desired can be won."[1]

—Ayn Rand

As noted at the outset of this book, our purpose has been to describe how to target competitors to win selected, valued customers and make your firm more competitive. We have considered many issues associated with competitors such as choosing specific competitors that represent a business threat or opportunity to your company, collaborating with some of them, learning about them, increasing share of key customers, and developing competitively superior approaches to win in the marketplace strategically, tactically, and in real time. We have reviewed opportunities to make industry structure and competitive rivalry more favorable by targeting competitors. We discussed a wide variety of ideas, including how to outperform competitors, block them out from key accounts and even how to shut them down. In short, we have noted the importance of looking two ways to win: at individual customers and specific competitors. Here, we bring the book to a close by reviewing aspects of competitively superior customer relationships and then competition in this context.

---

[1] Ayn Rand, *Atlas Shrugged*. New York: Penguin Books, 1957, p. 983.

Competitively Superior Customer Relationships[2]

New Rules, New Challenges

Since the 1960s, informed marketing executives have been guided by the marketing concept of making a profit by identifying and satisfying customers' needs. From the mid-1990s, however, relationship marketing has focused many executives on the creation and sharing of new value with individual customers. Even as they segment their markets into the ultimate market segment—the single customer—they face a number of challenges such as the following:

- *Intensifying competition:* Marketing has the potential to create profits but competition constrains and limits opportunities. Segments of one provide no respite from competition as many firms, including new entrants and nontraditional competitors, go down this road.
- *Returns on investments for customer marketing:* Companies are having difficulty securing returns on their heavy investments for customer marketing such as technology for CRM and data warehouses.
- *Internal hurdles:* Marketers are facing more internal pressure than ever to deliver short-term financial results, which makes it difficult to secure internal consensus to pursue strategies that will take a while to pay out.
- *Changing rules of the game:* As marketers focus on the individual customer, many find that the nature of marketing has changed. The old rules exemplified by the 4 Ps no longer apply, and the approaches enabled by new technologies are not sufficiently comprehensive to make their firms more competitive.

Many companies are competing for customers by trying to develop better relationships than their competitors. They use the principles of CRM promoted so well in books such as *The One to One Future,*[3] but the promise of CRM remains largely elusive. Companies have made significant investments in new technologies and changed processes, yet customers continue to flit from vendor to vendor. There are a number of reasons for this, from the perspective of both the customer and the vendor.[4] Foremost among these is the fact that the customer

---

[2] Based on Ian Gordon, "CRM is a Strategy, not a Tactic," *Ivey Business Journal*, September-October, 2001, p. 6-8.

[3] Don Peppers and Martha Rogers, *The One to One Future: Building Relationships One Customer at a Time*. New York: Currency Doubleday, 1993.

[4] Susan Fournier, Susan Dobscha and David Glen Mick, "Preventing the Premature Death of Relationship Marketing." *Harvard Business Review*, January-February, 1998, p.42.

is being asked to enter into too many relationships, which can complicate rather than simplify their lives.

Most consumers can identify with the abundance of competitors simply by checking the many plastic loyalty cards in their bulging wallets. On the other hand, some vendors may not always see the customer relationship either as mutual or as meriting a reward, and even fewer see relationship development to be a competitive strategy. It seems that some companies use the word relationship as a sort of code for avoiding competing on price.

Current State of CRM

CRM has come a long way from the early days. Today, most managers believe that CRM is fundamentally important to the future of their business and are investing heavily in technologies to understand and touch the customer, so much so that many think that CRM is actually the implementation of technology. Yet technology investment is often fragmented among numerous initiatives, often without the strategic integration and alignment needed to deliver superior customer value. As a result, the investment rarely has competitive context. Furthermore, most companies are not yet obtaining a good return on their CRM investment, and many customers report that they have yet to benefit from a meaningful relationship with their suppliers. Perhaps because of the tight linkage between CRM and technology, few companies have strategic plans for CRM.

The lack of a strategic plan is the single most important reason why companies have yet to achieve the potential of CRM. If your company is dissatisfied with the performance of its CRM investments, perhaps it is because those programs are independently justified in business cases without strategic integration. This seems to be one of the main reasons why companies have yet to secure sufficient yield from CRM. Lack of integration has yielded a patchwork of programs that individually, seem to be reasonable, but together, fail to add up to real vision. If there are differences of opinion as to whether the company's CRM initiative is creating new, mutual, enduring, and competitively superior customer value, then it is quite possible that the implementation has been tactical rather than strategic. It is not surprising that this has occurred. After all, strategic planning for CRM is uncharted territory for many companies. What is surprising is that so few executives have moved to develop and implement a CRM strategic plan.

CRM Strategy

We have noted that CRM is the ongoing process of identifying and creating new value with individual customers and then sharing the benefits of this over a lifetime association. It involves the understanding and managing of ongoing collaboration between suppliers and selected customers for mutual value creation. We can use this definition as a basis for providing some direction for CRM strategy before considering selected changes that consider competitors. The definition of CRM suggests that companies should do the following things:

Identify the Best and Worst Customers

A business relationship, as in a personal one, requires that we identify good customers who want a relationship with us, and collaborate with them to create new value from which we can both benefit over the long term.

Then we have to decide which customers we need to form a meaningful relationship with. Do we want just the biggest or the most profitable customers today, or the ones that will be most profitable tomorrow? Perhaps we prefer those that are most amenable to a relationship with us? Or perhaps we even want other customers. Choosing customers on which to focus on and which to ignore, is the first and most important strategic decision.

Distribute Customer Value Differently to Different Customers

The company should determine which are its best, average and worst customers and ensure that each receives appropriate value. As we have said, absurd though it sounds, most companies reward the worst customers and penalize the best by giving both average value. Sometimes this is the result of not fully allocating all customer costs, including those that occur after gross margin, such as inventory carrying costs, late payments, customer communications, and merchandise returns.

Compete on Scope

One way of discriminating among customers is to become more relevant to each one. For many companies, this means broadening the range of products, services or solutions they sell, whether or not the company makes them. Firms can collaborate with third parties to ensure that the customer receives the value each wants rather than insisting that the customer buy what the company makes. This is a major strategic departure from the old belief that simply growing larger would give the company the economies it needed to succeed. In a world of individual customers, unique value is created for each one, and being larger may not offer the opportunity to be more relevant. Frequently, the opposite is true. Larger companies often are less able to cater to individual needs, especially where their technologies and processes have been engineered for efficiency rather than effectiveness.

Focus on Strategic Capabilities

Managers sometimes do not want to plan because they fear their plan will become rapidly outdated (it will) or that some of the strategies will be wrong (quite likely). Rather, in the era of CRM, strategies should be framed in terms of strategic capabilities rather than strategies per se. Base a plan on the range of capabilities a company should have including process, technology, people and knowledge/insight.

CRM initiatives can experience difficulty when the focus has been on technology and insufficient attention has been paid to people and their organizations. Stakeholders, such as suppliers, employees, and channel intermediaries, form a chain of relationships, and the end-customer relationship is only as strong as the weakest link. Plan to create durable, aligned bonds with these stakeholders, too. For example, when considering employees, pay attention to the link between relationship management and performance reviews, recruitment, training and compensation.

Win Through Customer-Specific Innovation

Creating new and mutual customer value, the core of CRM, means that companies need to have a process for customer inclusion and collaborative innovation. Most firms continue to innovate in the old style, comprising off-line research and product definition, rather than customer involvement throughout the process. More than this, as innovation is customer-specific, the challenge is to involve customers as the company works with each to define and create new value.

Integrate the customer's technology, people and business processes with your company's. If you can tell where your firm ends and the customer's starts, you probably have not yet fully implemented relationship marketing. If you can tell when the sale starts and when it ends, there may be additional opportunities to improve integration with customers, make design and development collaborative and the purchase process continuous.

Measure Customer Performance

Focus on customer profitability with the goal of improving it rather than the traditional approach of measuring only product, product line and divisional profitability, customer costs and customer value perceptions. It is quite in order to sell some products at a loss if the whole relationship is profitable and/or strategic.

Unlearn and Relearn

Companies should unlearn the principles of mass everything to achieve the benefits of CRM. This means that mass communications must become customer-specific and mass production should become build to order and mass customized. Relationships with employees and other stakeholders in the chain of relationships should be focused on the individual, as well. For example, employees should have their own development plans that create the value each wants in his or her career such as financial reward, recognition and respect. Unlearning is really needed if a company is to shed what made it successful in the past, but which now threatens its ability to adapt and rise to new heights. And unlearning is hard to do. It means changing entrenched attitudes throughout the chain of relationships that results in a delighted end customer.

Inside most companies, there is tension between those who get CRM and those who do not. If CRM is to take root and move the company into new territory, the group that doesn't get CRM will need to learn (or relearn) what it is and the potential it has. In particular, the CFO should be involved in the visioning exercise; his or her commitment is most important if the plan is to work.

Redefine What Focus Means

Many leaders encourage their firms to "focus," by which they often mean focus on products or services. The CRM company should instead see focus in terms of customers, not products or services, and should welcome the very significant changes that this redefinition of focus will cause. In particular, the CRM company will face significant change in its processes as it begins to supply what customers want rather than just what the company makes. This disruption of processes can undermine the initiative in the early going unless the changes are anticipated and presold to internal managers.

New Rules for Competing

As we have said, the old rules of marketing are mostly broken and ineffective, providing a poor basis for making the company a winner. After all, there are only so many good customers to go round, and all competitors want them. The 4 Ps of marketing made little or no provision for this reality, nor did they create an opportunity for adjusting each aspect of product, price, promotion and distribution according to the unique preferences of the customer. Today, customers target companies rather than the other way around. The 4 Ps do not address this new reality.

In Chapter 6, we reviewed the 11 Cs of relationship marketing differentiation so that a company can improve its competitive position. These provide an important opportunity for companies to set themselves apart from competitors in the minds of individual customers. As such, the 11 Cs provide a new way for companies to consider differentiating their firms and winning against targeted competitors. The new rules of marketing include the targeting of competitors, as we have discussed.

What Companies Compete For

In this era of relationship marketing and intense competition, companies compete for eight things:

1. *Preferred access*—to the best customers and other stakeholders such as suppliers and channel partners and the media
2. *Share of customer*—by creating preference through customer-specific differentiation from exceptional performance and targeted competitors
3. *New customers*—which can be obtained from specific competitors
4. *Opportunities to collaborate with customers*—to develop new opportunities, integrate people and processes and to plan and work together
5. *Efficiency*—to develop the know-how and capabilities needed to become the "lowest-time" producer, which will take up as little as possible of the customer's most precious resource
6. *The right new employees*—especially to secure those who get CRM, whatever their functional job titles
7. *Alignments*—to collaborate with a selected group of companies, both competitors and non-competitors

8. *Customer data, knowledge and insight*—to develop more of this than competitors and to doing this faster to make the company more relevant to its customers, such as positioning the firm favorably where and when customers are most likely to buy

Importantly, companies compete for the future, for tomorrow's customers and their expenditures and for the capabilities companies need to win. These include things such as sufficient financial resources and good people.

The Competitive Company

Most companies treat competing as an informal consideration and something that should be regarded as part of everyone's job. With the responsibility applicable to everyone in a company, few people pay sufficient attention. As a result, the company as a whole may not be well prepared to compete, although it is probably working very hard to become better. This may not be enough to win because the company that seeks to improve usually compares itself with what it is, not what it could be or what competitors will be. Many leaders want their companies to become more competitive, and some work to change their firms' cultures to make competing a state of everyone's mind. This can be helpful, but competing is much more than a state of mind. The salesperson who thinks and acts like a lion may be no more successful than a lamb if, for example, the company's strategies, structure, processes, products, services and relationships are not in alignment with customer requirements and better than competitors'.

This book has described how companies can go from competing informally to developing a more planned, formalized approach. As we noted in Chapter 6, the competitive company develops a differentiated vision and a differentiated execution of the vision for the company as a whole, for its products, services, and solutions, as well as for customer relationships and bonds.

In the competitive company, leaders will appreciate that winning requires a clear understanding of the following things:

- tomorrow's industry landscape and the main criteria for succeeding there
- priority customers and key competitors in the future
- how the company is to win and keep individual customers and increase the satisfaction and profitability of each one

- how the firm is to manage specific competitors to contribute to shareholder value such as by being beaten, acquired or complementing the company

A number of observations stem from these considerations:

The Future

Companies need to see the future with even greater clarity than they see the present. Whether companies succeed or fail today is largely a consequence of yesterday's vision, strategies and tactics. The future will be won by those companies better able to conceive it, interpret the opportunities and plan and implement the right initiatives. The two key areas of initiative for which most companies need plans and which they do not have today are those that deal with customer relationships and competitor targeting.

Operations

Operations must be in alignment with strategic direction or leaders will find they are trying to steer a ship with multiple bows, an obviously impossible task. When operations are focused exclusively on quality and efficiency, it should be clarified whether this is what customers want most. Sometimes, competing is not just about operating efficiently—efficient companies can go out of business when their customers want additional value, as some Internet service providers have found out to their dismay.

Customers

Competing also means being different and relevant to the customers that will be the core of the company's future business. The company should integrate its various approaches to creating customer value—from innovation to CRM technology to customer collaboration processes—to ensure that bonds with key customers will be deepened and that various investments are aligned to this end.

Other Stakeholders

Customers merit individual attention, but they are not the only such stakeholders. The company should seek to deepen specific relationships with priority employees, channel intermediaries, suppliers and others such as investors. This means that all stakeholders, just like all customers, are not equally important to the company's future. Those stakeholders that matter most should receive individualized attention in much the same way that some companies have identified their most important customers and are seeking to differentiate their relationships with these buyers. Ideally, all stakeholders would receive individualized attention and to the extent that this can be done, it would obviously be very desirable.

Innovation

Competing means focusing on new value: how to identify this value and how to create it better than competitors'. It is particularly important for the company to create this new value with priority customers, but the firm should also do this with other key stakeholders. Innovation is specific to each stakeholder. Without innovation, relationships rely solely on goodwill and wither over time. The competitive company will increasingly use technology, process improvements and training to enable relationships with all stakeholders. Leaders will think about what it will take to innovate throughout the chain of relationships.

Competitive Positioning

Competing requires knowing what a competitor is, as seen by core customers, understanding individuals' perceptions of the company and its competitors and improving the company's competitive position such as by targeting and managing competitors. Companies that want to compete will generally need to utilize some of the budget they may have cut from market research, and invest it in customer research. Also, research should be conducted with individual stakeholders in addition to customers and the data used to develop specific plans.

Learning

In the Darwinian world of competition, slow learners lose. Competing means being the fastest to learn about what the future will look like, how the current state is changing, what matters most to core customers and other stakeholders, what competitors are doing, how to deliver competitively superior value to stakeholders and how to beat or collaborate with competitors to increase shareholder value. And winning means acting on this knowledge quicker than competitors. It has never been truer than today—time really *is* money.

Plan to Win

To put insight into action, companies need plans. While most organizations can point to their financial, marketing and strategic plans, few have developed plans for customer relationship management or competitor targeting and even fewer have integrated these into their other business plans. No one said that winning the battle for the customers was easy, but this much we know: wars are not won without planning, and the competitive war is no different.

Without a plan, your company relies on two factors to win:

1. *The past*—deriving benefits from what you have done in the past including the relationships you have established, the employees you have hired and the capabilities you have put in place
2. *Statistical chance*—for example, benefiting from the growth of customers with whom you have strong relationships, the misadventures of competitors and new investments turning out well.

That is, without plans, companies benefit from what they once did and from luck. Companies have financial plans because they view money as vital for their survival and growth. It is curious that companies do not always have the plans that determine how much money is made: plans that deal with individual customer relationships (and the associated implications for the company) and plans that focus on competitors to increase shareholder value. Without such plans, how is a company to create deeper and more profitable stakeholder relationships and competitive superiority?

Planning for competitor targeting was described in detail in Chapter 4.

Concluding Comments

We have described approaches for companies to achieve the benefits of competitor targeting and reviewed how targeted competitors can contribute to your firm's profitability. You should now be in a better position to develop winning plans that can help accomplish the following main objectives for competitor targeting:

- learn from targeted competitors so that you can improve
- develop a differentiated position with the competitor's most important customers

- develop a differentiated position with the competitor's customers you have selected, causing these customers to buy from you instead
- gain advantage relative to targeted competitors in order to strengthen your business directly at their expense, especially with respect to the limited resources you both need
- achieve competitively superior results for shareholders
- identify competitors that are relatively benign and/or who represent potential partners in specific situations, perhaps in battle with other competitors
- establish how and where the company can best collaborate with competitors
- identify whether or not to acquire a competitor
- win specific bids or contracts

We have stressed the view that focusing on customers is not enough to build businesses. Marketers should manage both individual customers and specific competitors to win the war of the marketplace, and it is also necessary to understand the direction of your industry and create your destiny. Build a preference for your company over its competitors by identifying and collaboratively creating the new value that individual customers and other stakeholders want. Learn faster than rival companies and target some competitors to help achieve your business objectives.

Index